Imagery of Love in the Old Testament

Biblical Hermeneutics Rediscovered

The Series as the name suggests will focus on Biblical Hermeneutics, i.e., literary works concerned with methods of interpreting the Old and New Testaments of Bible via different stream of topics like Literature & Poetry, Indigenous Philosophizing, Ethical response towards Ecology, Health & Healing, Science & Technology, Feminist Theology, Sociological approach towards Human Rights, Law & Politics, Arts, History of Ideas, Ancient Civilizations, Cultural Contiguity, Religious Cosmologies & Mysticism, Appraisal of various Theologians, World Peace & Harmony, Global Capitalism, Network Marketing, Cybertheology, Population & Demographics, Epigraphic Studies, Contextualized Education, and many others. We welcome a Mss. on any topic/s mentioned, whether they are original works, scholarly monographs, collections of conference papers, revised dissertations, or translations of historical documents. Through the Series we, the Publishers, are striving to put forward published works that may help Institutions, Academic Bodies, Researchers, Scholars and the World at large in furthering their respective knowledge and understanding on the concerned subject. We welcome your comments on our efforts and further suggestions on how we can enshrine new ray of analysing & explaining the written Texts through our upcoming books.

Biblical Hermeneutics Rediscoverd - 23

Imagery of Love in the Old Testament

A Socio-Rhetorical Reading of the Book of Hosea

N. Subramani

CWI

Christian World Imprints

First Published in 2020 by

Christian World Imprints
Christian Publishing & Books from India
C-3, Shop No. 14, Ground Floor
Wazirpur Industrial Area, **Delhi-110052**
cwidelhi2017@gmail.com
www.ChristianWorldImprints.com
Phone: +91 11 41526079

ISBN: 978-93-5148-370-0 (HB)
ISBN: 978-93-5148-464-6 (PB)

Printed in India.

Dedication

This book is dedicated to honour
my father, guardian, wife, children,
family members and friends.

Contents

FOREWORD

It is indeed a great privilege for me to write a Foreword to the book IMAGERY OF LOVE IN THE OLD TESTAMENT authored by Rev. Dr. N. Subramani. The book is originally his doctoral dissertation submitted to the Serampore University based on which he was awarded the Doctor of Theology degree by the University at the Convocation held in Serampore in 2018. The book is a true depiction of dedication and commitment to Biblical scholarship of a person who experienced the Love of God as he faced challenges and hardships in life. It is a journey from the known to the unknown. I congratulate the author for his achievements in life thus far and wish him all the very best in his continuing task of making the Love of God known to all through Bible Translation endorsed by the Bible Society of India.

God's steadfast love in the face of Israel's rejection is the constant theme of the whole book of Hosea. In it, three human relationships - marital, parental and healing are used to bring out many important aspects of God's steadfast love. The metaphorical language of these relationships is used to depict the covenantal relationship between Yahweh and Israel. The problem according to the researcher is that other researchers have used only the marital image to define the themes of judgment and the Yahweh-Israel covenantal relationship. The author stresses the significance of all the three relationships in depicting the covenantal relationship between God and Israel.

Among the eighth-century BCE prophets, Hosea was the first to develop the concept of covenantal relationship between God and Israel by finding a parallel in human love. This research goes further and focuses on the purpose behind Yahweh's concern for Israel, which is to use Hosea to restore Israel back to God so that they will become 'a light to the nations.'

The researcher has also discovered that in the book of Hosea, Yahweh reveals a different face. Instead of the traditional stern and often angry judge God is generally presented in the Old Testament, in the book of Hosea God is pictured as revealing a compassionate, loving and caring attitude in the midst of total rejection by Israel of the Sinaitic covenant relationship. The researcher argues that the book of Hosea describes a crucial point in the Yahweh Israel relationship not just a breach of covenant by Israel, but Yahweh's efforts and willingness to draw her back into that covenant relationship. It is the researcher's contention that this action by Yahweh demonstrates the underlying theme of the book steadfast love which can overlook hurt and still hold out welcoming arms to the offending party.

The researcher has examined the personal love imagery in the text to demonstrate how Hosea defines Yahweh's love for God's people and how Hosea regards the covenant in establishing that relationship.

I commend this book to a wider readership with the hope that the God of the Bible, particularly as depicted in the book of Hosea is understood for God is, i.e. **God as God of Love** embracing the entire humankind, in fact the entire creation of God paving the way for all to experience life in all its fullness.

Rev. Dr. M. Mani Chacko, Ph.D. (London)
General Secretary
The Bible Society of India
Bangalore

Acknowledgement

"God is faithful in his calling, how far I am faithful to Him

that YOU have brought me thus far?"

At this juncture, I would like to thank…

- Rev. Dr. M. Mani Chacko who is my mentor and General Secretary for his constant encouragement and support in the midst of his tireless work. Rev. Dr. Jonadob Nathaniel, Director Translations for his constant support and help in my study program. Rev. Prasad for his help in hard times and finding suitable people for proof reading and editing my thesis. The entire Bible Society of India staff for their continual prayer support officially and personally.
- Dr. Lee Soo Ann for his tireless financial support throughout my study program for four years in the seminary.
- My thesis supervisor Rev. Dr. Eliya Mohol, for his meticulous constructive comments and advice that kept me focussed and provided the necessary momentum for the research to proceed smoothly; also for trusting me by letting me traverse the path of approaching an Old Testament text Socio-Rhetorically, which has been attempted only by few scholars.
- The Library Staff of Union Biblical Seminary, faculty; the United Theological College, Bangalore; Dharmaram Vidya Kshetram, Bangalore; Orthodox Theological Seminary and Marthoma Theological Seminary, Kottayam for their cooperation, friendly and helpful attitude.
- Special thanks to my friends Mrs. Lesliewood, Mrs. Elsie, Mrs. Vasthi, Mrs. Veda, Mrs. Julie Olson, Mrs. Lima Eugene, Mr. Manoj and Ms. Shakina Mohol for their help during different stages of the work and who offered me their support many times through many difficult situations. Mr. Sandey Dennis, Mr. Jebastin Chelladurai for helping in final page layout.
- My wife Ruby and daughters Esther Joanna and Eva Judith for their immense support throughout my years of study. My wife...God's best choice for me; for her unceasing prayers, love, motivation, and for her innumerable sacrifices without which I could not have accomplished my study.
- Last but not the least, thanks to my daughters, whose cheerful smiles always instilled hope and induced in me the impetus to bring the work to fruition.

Abbreviations

AB	Anchor Bible
ABD	Anchor Bible Dictionary, Edited by D. N. Freedman. 6 vols. New York, 1992.
ANET	Ancient Near Eastern Texts Relating to the Old Testament. Edited by J.B. Pritchard. 3rd ed., Princeton, 1969.
BASOR	Bulletin of the American Schools of Oriental Research
BDB	Brown, F., S. R. Driver, and C. A. Briggs. A Hebrew and English Lexicon of the Old Testament, Oxford, 1907.
BHS	Biblia Hebraica Stuttgartensia. Edited by K. Elliger and W. Rudolph, Stuttgart, 1983.
BTB	Biblical Theology Bulletin
CBQ	Catholic Biblical Quarterly
GKC	Gesenius Hebrew Grammar. Edited by E. Kautzsch. Translated by A. E. Cowley, 2nd Ed. Oxford, 1910.
HALOT	The Hebrew and Aramaic Lexicon of the Old Testament. L. Koehlerand W. Baumgartner. Translated by M. E. J. Richardson. 5 vols. Leiden, 1994.
ICC	International Critical Commentary
IDB	The Interpreter's Dictionary of the Bible. Edited by G. A. Buttrick. Vols. 4, Nashville, 1962.
JBL	Journal of Biblical Literature
JNSL	Journal of Northwest Semitic Languages
JSOT	Journal for the Study of the Old Testament
JSOT Sup	Journal for the Study of the Old Testament: Supplement Series
JSS	Journal of Semitic Studies
KAT	Kommentar zum Alten Testament
LXX	Septuagint

MT	Masoretic Text
NAC	New American Commentary
NCBC	New Century Bible Commentary
NICOT	New International Commentary on the Old Testament
NIDOTTE	New International Dictionary of Old Testament Theology and Exegesis, edited by W. A. Van Gemeren. 5 vols. Grand Rapids, 1997.
NRSV	New Revised Standard Version
OTL	Old Testament Library
OtSt	Oudtestamentische Studiën
SBL	Society of Biblical Literature
SBLDS	Society of Biblical Literature Dissertation Series
SBLWAW	Society of Biblical Literature Writings from the Ancient World
TDOT	Theological Dictionary of the Old Testament. Edited by G. J. Botter weck and H. Ringgren. Translated by J. T. Willis, G. W. Bromiley and D. E. Green, 8 vols. Grand Rapids, 1974.
TLOT	Theological Lexicon of the Old Testament
TOTC	Tyndale Old Testament Commentaries
TWOT	Theological Workbook of the Old Testament
VT	Vetus Testamentum
VTSup	Supplements to Vetus Testamentum
WBC	Word Biblical Commentary
ZAW	Zeitschrift für die alttestamentliche Wissenschaft

List of Tables

Chapter 1

Imagery of Love as a Paradigm for Covenantal Relationship in the Book of Hosea: A Socio-Rhetorical Reading

Introduction

God's steadfast love in the face of Israel's rejection is the constant theme of the book of Hosea as a whole. The book of Hosea takes "God's word" as Love, not just love on its own, but rather as "steadfast love." One that endures despite Israel turning its back on what God offers. The prophet Hosea ministered God's word to the people of Israel with a sense of commitment. He used his dramatic preaching style to demonstrate this steadfast love. For Hosea, love marked the covenant of mutuality between God and Israel, a covenant that God expected Israel to keep. When Israel failed to keep the covenant, God then called Hosea to take His message to the people. Hosea adopted three sets of metaphors and symbols in human terms that were familiar to the people of Israel and he used these symbols to re-enforce this message to describe the God-Israel relationship in a way that people could easily understand and relate to. He spoke to them of the love between a husband and wife, the love of a father for his son, and the love of a doctor/healer for his patient. Firstly, Hosea referred to adultery, a familiar human concept to portray Israel's covenantal breach, in a marriage. Secondly, Hosea used the imagery of a father who loves his son but is nevertheless angered by the son's failure to obey and therefore is prone to punish this disobedience. God is likewise angry with Israel's breach of the covenant. Thirdly, Hosea used the image of the healer-patient relationship to describe how the healer can appear to be cruel when applying treatment which would nevertheless save the patient.

In the book of Hosea, marital, parental and healing relationships are used to bring out many important aspects of his message. These relationships are used in various chapters and verses often in different terms such as אהב, חסד, דעת אלהים and ברית. The terms used are linked through interpersonal events or associations that constitute a set of meanings that establish and confirm the relationship between God and Israel. These structural connections are important, and this study brings out their significance as used in Hosea by highlighting the different terms and their combinations.

There are already several literary and theological approaches to אהב, חסד, דעת אלהים and ברית in Hosea. However, there is a gap in understanding these terms with regard to the marital, parental and healing metaphors in the light of the interrelationships between them and also when viewed against the background of other Old Testament writings. This research therefore focuses on the relationship between the three metaphors and their use in depicting the covenantal relationship between God and Israel. The research examines inter-textual relationship and the use of rhetorical imagery to bring out the several meanings implicit in the text. It also shows how this three faced relationship imagery is designed to emphasise God's covenantal love for his people namely Israel, a covenantal love which is consistent and steadfast despite Israel's rejection of it.

1.1. Basic Framework

Hosea's emphasis on the concept of love is distinct by comparison to the other prophets of the eighth century BCE. Many scholars[1] have considered the imagery of love, acknowledging its relationship to the covenant tradition.[2] A number of studies

---

[1] Scholars such as Derek Kidner, William J. Doorly, John T. Willis, Kakkanattu, Kyung Hee Park, Anderson and Freedman, J. Mauchline, Christopher Wright, and John Oswalt have talked about the concept of love in the book of Hosea in different ways. David Hubbard points out that the prophets' phrasings, figures of speech, and emphases were their own, and their personalities, cultural background, and talents all operated in the revelatory process. Wolff finds in Hosea a fully allegorized metaphor of Yahweh as the loving yet rejected husband of Israel. Other scholars who adhere to the same view are Douglas Stuart, and James L. Mays.

[2] H.W. Wolff, *Hosea* (G. Stansell, Trans.), Philadelphia: Fortress Press, 1974; Mays, J.L. Hosea, Philadelphia: Westminster Press, 1969; Ward, James M., *"Hosea:" A Theological Commentary,* New York: Harper and Row, 1966; the author's explanation about the historical and covenantal relationship between God, his people and the prophets is very good. Walter Brueggemann, *Tradition of Crisis: A Study in Hosea,* Richmond, John Knox Press, 1969; M. Buss seems to be using form critical method of Claus Westermann, *Basic forms of Prophetic Speech,* translated by H.C. White, Philadelphia, Fortress Press, 1967; Derek Kidner, *Love to the Loveless: The Message of Hosea,* Downers Grove: Inter–Varsity Press, 1982, 142; The Hebrew has the simple imperative, 'love' carrying no suggestion that love was already there, merely awaiting an outlet. William J. Doorley, *Prophet of Love: Understanding the Book of Hosea,* New York, NJ: Paulist Press, 1991; S. Ackerman, *"The Personal is Political: Covenantal and Affectionate Love* (אהב, אהבה) *in the Hebrew Bible,"* VT 52, 2002, 437-458; Kyung Hee Park, *Divine Love in Hosea 11,* Southern Baptist Theological Seminary 2004; Kakkanattu, Joy Philip, *God's Enduring Love in the Book of Hosea:* A Synchronic and Diachronic analysis of Hosea 11:1-11 (FAT, 2. Reihe, 14: Tubingen: Mohr Siebeck, 2006; R Abma, *Bonds of Love Methodic Studies of Prophetic Texts with Marriage Imagery (Isaiah 50: 1-3 and 54: 1- 10, Hosea 1-3, Jeremiah 2-3)* Studia Semitica Neerlandica, Van Gorcum, 1999, McCarthy in Treaty and Covenant affirms the kinship aspect in the covenantal relationship. Unlike the suzerainty treaty, Israel belongs to the family of Yahweh and therefore the conditions relating to the covenant can be described as aspects concerning continuation in the family, McCarthy, D.J., *Treaty and Covenant,* Rome, Biblical Institute Press, 1963, 133-143. The book of Hosea emphasises the relationship between God and Israel, explained through emotions ranging from wrath to love. For this, the prophet uses several metaphors to illustrate for them the message of hope and salvation. Hosea's warning to the people is that they deserted Yahweh by following other gods. The warnings were given through judgment, and Hosea speaks comprehensively about theocracy in his writings. The book has several key expressions, the important ones being אהב, חסד, דעת אלהים and ברית which play an important role in understanding God's love for His people. The terms bring out the relationship between God and Israel through the prophet's use of imagery. The marital, fatherly and healing metaphors bring out the faithfulness and the knowledge of God and the possibility of forgiveness, return and restoration of salvation for the people. Several scholars have notice that this metaphor/simile is not used in connection with the divine love theme. Still, the theme belongs to periphery of the immediate

on Hosea have focused primarily on the concept of judgment. However, these studies have always placed the emphasis on the relationship between God and Israel, rather than on human love. But this presentation re-emphasises the fact that Hosea appears to be the first to speak of the steadfast love of God. Therefore, this research aims to explore the relationship between human love and covenantal love in the text[3] and to do so concentrate on three particular aspects of God's love towards Israel, shown through the marital, parental and healing imageries.

These three images used by Hosea are described using five different textures, the Inner texture,[4] Inter-texture, Social and Cultural texture, Ideological texture and Theological texture. The research pursues the exploration of the rhetorical imagery through these textures and evaluates Hosea's distinctive contribution to the understanding of God's unique and covenantal relationship with the people of Israel by drawing a parallel between this relationship and the human love imagery.

1.2. An Elaboration

Imagery plays a vital and distinctive role in expressing the concept of love in the book of Hosea. The imagery of love is often expressed through covenant based metaphors. Though the use of imagery is common in prophetic literature, it is specifically mentioned in Hosea chapters 1-3, 11 and 14 in parallel themes depicting both divine and human love.

Despite being a dominant idea, the imagery of love varies in importance according to the type of love under discussion. The different kinds of imagery and their specific uses are briefly discussed in the following section.

1.2.1. Marital Love

The first metaphor used by Hosea occurs in chapters 2 and 3 and it concerns marital love. James Ward perceives the marital imagery as the "most effective in denoting both the enduring responsibility and the passion that characterizes the God-man relationship."[5] Hosea adopts this picture of marital love as a parallel to God's gracious covenant in order to emphasise His unconditional love for Israel.

---

context of the metaphor/simile is very identical with the context of the divine love. Divine love is used here as metaphor/simile that is compared with human-love. The emotional aspects of God's love are stressed by the prophet by use of several emotive metaphors/similes. The metaphors/similes are marital, parental, physician-patient healing simile objects God's love. The sub-theme of divine election is also emphasised in Hosea and Deuteronomy. Another major idea is seen is that Israel's physical and spiritual restoration to God's loving kindness. Hosea uses, marital, parental and healing metaphors within the field of vision of the divine love theme.

[3] The research examines Hosea's understanding of the covenant based upon the concept of love, אהב, חסד, רחם, נכם, אמת and דעת אלהים concluding that Hosea perceived the covenant as endorsing a relationship of steadfast love. This relationship originates from the incomprehensible love of God and is central to Hosea's whole message. Thus, the researcher aims to bring out some applications of the imagery of Hosea to the contemporary present context.

[4] The definition of texture is the physical feel of something smooth, rough or something in between. Inner texture consists of the familiar elements of literary and rhetorical closed reading. Inner texture focuses on words as a communication tool, a technique that seeks to determine first of all the "meaning" of the words and then the "real interpretation of the text." Socio-rhetorical criticism basically looks only upon the text and analyses deeply into the text.

[5] J. Ward, *"Hosea: A Theological Commentary,"* New York, Harper and Row, 1966, 390.

Marital imagery serves as "a powerful polemic against Baal worship"[6] and hence Jerome and Calvin are of the opinion that Hosea's marriage is a parable to explain the violation of law and the sins of Israel.[7] Both view marital faithfulness as a metaphor for the necessity for God's chosen nation to remain faithful to the covenant relationship.

William Moran (1963) and McCarthy (1978) argue that marriage was a covenant in ancient times.[8] According to them, covenant is the basic theme that runs through the book of Hosea, with marriage being used as a symbol to bring out the meaning of mutual commitment and being legally bound involved in any marital relationship. According to Moran, this understanding of the covenant is implicit in Hosea's marriage, and this theme is carried over into other books in the Old Testament. Hosea also uses the language of love to emphasise genuine obedience and the portrayal of covenant loyalty. Edward Schillenbeechex, (1965) comments that the marriage imagery is "the prism through which the prophets saw the saving covenant of God with His people and enabled the people to comprehend the covenant."[9] Wolff (1974) writes: "The marriage imagery in Hosea and later in Jeremiah and Ezekiel describes Yahweh's relationship with Israel as an expression of the historically and legally oriented covenant relationship."[10] In Eichrodt's (1997) opinion, "the ancient Israelites believed in a covenant God who chose them from amongst all nations and entered into an agreement with them."[11] The concept of all people and all nations being included in the covenant brings out the inclusive idea and the hope that they will all enjoy the blessings of the covenantal relationship with God in the future. This emphasises that the people of the covenant become people of God.

This study argues that the emphasis in all these authors is only on the covenantal relationship between God and His people; while the parallel image of the Hosea-Gomer relationship of love and marriage has not been given adequate importance. Hence this research argues for the emphasis on the covenantal aspect of human marriage. This image once again not only emphasises the covenantal relationship in marriage (human) but also its parallel the covenantal/marital relationship between God and Israel in terms of fidelity and love.

1.2.2. Parental love (נער)

Parental love is the second metaphor that Hosea uses. It expresses the concept of dependency. The imagery of parental love is expressed through Hosea's use of the terms "child" (נער) and "son" (בן). He uses "נער" to express Israel's total dependence upon Yahweh. God loves the way Israel refers to itself as God's "son" (Hos. 11:1)

---

6 Gibson. J.C.L, *Language and Images in the Old Testament,* Peabody, Hendrickson Publishers, 1998, 15.

7 John James. Given, *Hosea*, Grand Rapids, Eerdmans, 1950, 18.

8 Moran W.L, The Ancient Near Eastern Background of the Love of God in Deuteronomy," *Catholic Biblical Quarterly,* Vol. 25, (72-87) 1963, 79; D.J. McCarthy, *Treaty and Covenant: A Study in form in the ancient oriental documents and in the Old Testament,* Rome, Biblical Institute Press, 1978.

9 Schillenbeechex, E., *Marriage: Human Reality and Saving Mystery,* New York: Sheed and Ward, 1965, 31.

10 Wolff, H.W., *A Commentary on the Book of the Prophet Hosea,* Philadelphia: Fortress Press, 1974, 16.

11 W. Eichrodt, "The Holy One in Your Midst: The Theology of Hosea," *Interpretation* 15, 1961, 258-273.

Kyung Hee Park (2004) explores the meaning of a parent (father) as the God of Hosea is characterized as *"Yahweh, the Loving Parent" and as "Yahweh, the Holy One among Humans,"* as a logical understanding of divine love in Hosea 11. He interprets the parental metaphor as depicting the *"Holy One in your midst."*[12] Joy Philip Kakkanattu (2006) uses the synchronic and diachronic method to interpret Hosea 11 as an expression of Yahweh's parental love and care towards Israel. According to him, it is this parental love in which *"Hosea finds a reason for Israel's survival."*[13] N. Lohfink (1963) also focuses on love that is related to the covenantal relationship between Israel and Yahweh.[14] This covenantal love discloses the inner struggle of God, who is depicted in the image of a father grieving over his wayward son (Hos. 11:1-3) and ends with an outburst of pain (11:8-11). Hosea thus reveals God's aggrieved, but still loving, heart towards Israel in a father-son image.

Ackerman (2002) explores the connection between the texts describing Yahweh's covenantal love for Israel and those concerning the interpersonal loving relationships of a man and a woman in marriage, and between a parent and a child. The covenantal love, then, is seen to be a parallel for interpersonal relationships and familial love in the Old Testament.[15]

Despite the emphasis on the God-Israel parental relationship, the authors mentioned above relate the relationship to the covenant and pay little or no attention to human parental relationships which run parallel to the covenant connection. This research argues that these human relationships are highly significant as emphasising God's attempt to make Israel understand the relationship between Himself and Israel as His favoured nation. This research considers that if the humans can understand the (human) parent-child relationship as a form of covenant, then they can surely understand the God-Israel relationship as also being a covenant having an effect on human relationships.

1.2.3. Physician-Patient

Healing plays an important role in Hosea. The Hebrew term used for healing (רפא) appears 67 times in verb conjugations in the book, with the meaning of "repair," "mend," "make wholesome," "heal," and "restore."

The primary purpose for adopting this physician-patient imagery is to focus on therapeutic treatment. T. W. Walker (1997) explores the use of the healing metaphor attributed to Yahweh in Hosea chapters 4 to 14. Walker cites the metaphor of healing as evidence of Hosea's message for Israel's restoration.[16] The idea is that healing is a process and the sick individual appeals to Yahweh for healing. This process includes repentance leading to restoration. To convey this idea, Hosea employs the Hebrew word רפא to imply restoration of Israel (Hos. 5:8; 6:2-7, 11:1-11; 14:2-9.)

[12] Kyung Hee Park, *Divine Love in Hosea 11,* Louisville, Southern Baptist Theological Seminary, 2004.

[13] Kakkanattu, Joy Philip, *God's Enduring Love in the Book of Hosea: A Synchronic and Diachronic analysis of Hosea* 11:1-11, FAT, 2. Reihe, 14: Tubingen, Mohr Siebeck, 2006.

[14] Lohfink. N, "Hate and Love in Hosea 9:15," *Catholic Biblical Quarterly,* vol. 25, 1963, 417.

[15] S. Ackerman, *"The Personal is Political: Covenantal and Affectionate Love* (אהב, אהבה) *in the Hebrew Bible,"* VT 52, 2002, 437-458.

[16] T.W. Walker, *The Metaphor of Healing and the Theology of the book of Hosea,* Ph.D. Dissertation, Princeton Theological Seminary, 1997.

This process moves from an emphasis on Yahweh's desire for repentance to achieving gracious healing. According to Seong-Hyuk (2006), Hosea 14 explicitly or implicitly opens the door to fresh insights into health, healing and illness. Seong-Hyuk applies the metaphor theory and the comparative study between ancient Israel and Korea's contemporary context.[17] Brad Kelle (2010) applies the synchronic, literary and theological methods of reading to Hosea 14 to bring out the traditional meanings, which remain unexplored till now.[18] Kelle applies synchronic and literary studies in Hosea to bring out poetic analysis, semiotic and deconstructionist treatments and final form of readings of the Persian period and canonical interpretation. However, Sharon Moughtin-Mumby (2008) interprets Hosea 14 in a different way. She encourages readers to read the diverse metaphors and similes, which have the potential to make a vivid impression, within the distinctive literary context and depicts just how powerful the texts really are.[19]

The authors concentrate on the covenant aspect highlighted by the God-Israel imagery, ignoring the human doctor-patient symbolism, which is equally important if Israel is to be brought to an understanding of the importance of the covenant relationship.

1.2.4. Love imagery and the Covenant

The varied meanings of the imagery of marriage, parent and physician or healer shows a glimpse of God's relationship with Israel. The continual use of metaphorical language helps Hosea to develop his theological framework centred on the imagery of love, both human and divine. In Kruger's view, this use of the imagery of love offers the possibility of exploring its varied meanings using the rhetorical devices in the text.[20] This research suggests that the imagery of love, especially human love, is used to emphasise and clarify the covenant relationship. By using the images of human love, with which the Israelites were familiar, God clearly hoped that they could be brought more easily to understand their covenant relationship with Him.

Other scholars have previously done a considerable amount of research into the book of Hosea, but they have concentrated mainly on the themes of sin, wrath, and judgment. Similarly, the theme of love has also been discussed widely in Old Testament scholarship. However, the concept of human love and covenantal love, and the imagery used to link them, has not been explored thoroughly in the existing literature. Therefore, the current study explores the relationship between human love and covenantal love using the three types of human love already mentioned as examples.

---

[17] Seong-Hyuk Hong, *The Metaphor of Illness and Healing in Hosea and Its Significance in the Socio-economic Context of Eighth-century Israel and Judah,* New York, Peter Lang Publishing, 2006.

[18] Brad E. Kelle, *Hosea 4-14 in Twentieth-Century Scholarship,* Currents in Biblical Research, San Diego, Point Loma Nazarene University, 2010.

[19] Sharon Moughtin-Mumby, *Sexual and Marital metaphors in Hosea, Jeremiah, Isaiah and Ezekiel,* Oxford Scholarship, 2008.

[20] P. A. Kruger, *"Prophetic Imagery: On Metaphors and Similes in the Book of Hosea,"* Journal of Northwest Semitic Languages 14, 1988, 140-144. The author explains the relationship between God and Israel by different metaphors and similes in the book of Hosea to show how the author is different from others in his work. Example "*Prophetic Imagery*," 143-151, the Marriage Metaphor in Hosea 2:4-17. The work is compared with Ancient Near Eastern Background, *Old Testament Essays*, 1992, 7-25.

1.3. Significance of the Subject

The eighth century BCE prophets generally dwell on the themes of judgment and hope. Interestingly, Hosea appears to be the first to speak of the love of God. Cole thus writes, "Any discussion of love in the Old Testament must begin with the prophet Hosea, who married a harlot. All the developments in early Hebrew are in some sense preparatory to and gathered up in the career and the message of this wronged husband."[21] Hosea's prophecies are thus an attempt to use the old themes and develop them from a love perspective. This is especially true with his treatment of the covenant.

The book of Hosea is referred to as the "the hymn of divine love"[22] due to the way it parallels the covenantal Yahweh-Israel relationship with the three human love relationships. Yet despite intense study over the years of the Hosea text, none of the authors have seriously considered the concept of love as an important part of the Hosea message. From Cole, writing in 1954, to Wolff, in 2010, authors have not considered the love imagery in depth, and it was Morris, writing in 1981, who was prompted to comment that the "subject of divine love appears to have been neglected." This research therefore argues that the covenantal/human love relationships and parallels have not yet been studied in detail, as the following authors make clear.

This work lays emphasis on the examination of the Jacob tradition. Neef uses the insights of Rudolph.[23] According to Leon Morris, the subject of divine love appears to have been neglected by those who studied the Old Testament:

> It cannot be said that the idea of love really grips the leading writers [Davidson, von Rad, Eichrodt, and Vrizen] on the Old Testament… On examination, it is clear that they interweave references to the love of God with their discussion of other topics. Many scholars have written much about the Old Testament with so little formal recognition of the love in it. They do not put it in a place of major importance to suggest that it is a leading theme…[24]

Many works published after Morris also confirm this. G. I. Emmerson, employing redaction criticism, argues that Hosea deals with salvation sayings (2:16-17, 18-25 [14-15, 16-23]; 11:8-11; 14:5-9 [4-8]), Davidic monarchy, (12:3[2]; 5:5, 10-14; 6:4, 11; 8:14; 12:1 [11-12]) and Judah's corrupted cultic worship practices in Judea.[25] Vollmer and Willi-Plein, in order to help him, examine the tradition.[26] Willi-Plien considers that the eight redactors were from different periods and they are not more than theological interpretations to create the final composition.

So also G.A. Yee concentrates on the composition and transmission of the text in four growth stages. Redaction criticism helps Yee to pick up the composition from

---

[21] W. G., Cole, *Sex and Love in the Bible,* New York, Association Press, 1954/1959, 15-16.

[22] H. Bussche, "La ballade de l'amourmeconnu, *Commentary on Hosea,*" BVC 41, 1961, 18.

[23] Rudolph, W. Hosea, *KAT.* XIII/1. Gütersloh: Gütersloher Verlagshaus Gerd Mohn.1966.

[24] Morris, L., *Testaments of Love,* Grand Rapids, Eerdmans, 1981, 4-5.

[25] Emmerson, G.I., *Hosea: An Israelite Prophet in Judean Perspective,* JSOTSup 28, Sheffield, JSOT Press, 1984.

[26] Willi-Plein, *Vorformen der Schriftexegese innerhalb des Alten Testaments,* BZAW 123: Berlin, De Gruyter, 1971, cited in Gale A. Yee, *Composition and Tradition in the Book of Hosea: A Redaction Critical Investigation,* SBLDS, 102; Atlanta: Scholars Press, 1987, 18-21

Deuteronomistic Judean orientation and to use it to investigate the tradition of Hosea.[27] The works of Stuart emphasise the concept of covenant found in the Old Testament, and he looks at the book of Hosea as a restoration of the blessings and a warning of the curses in the Pentateuch.[28] According to Dempsey among the eighth century BCE prophets, Hosea was the first to develop the concept of covenantal relationship between God and Israel by finding a parallel in human love.[29] Weems, in her book "*Battered Love*," supports the view that Hosea was the first prophet in the Hebrew Bible to develop the idea of the metaphor of the covenant relating to the marriage bond between Israel and Yahweh.[30] Her research deals with a textual analysis and engages with this metaphor from a womanist perspective, using traditional readings of the text, such as historical and social-scientific methods. She also includes newer approaches, such as gender criticism, literary studies, and ideological analyses. She explains how metaphors are specific to their socio-historical contexts and how the marriage metaphor fit in the Hebrew prophets' patriarchal context. She tries to build her textual analysis by interpreting these metaphors within this patriarchal context and explains how hypothetical audiences heard and understood the metaphors used in this book.

Bernard Oestreich has worked on the study of the pictorial language in Hosea.[31] Oestreich (1998) describes God's love through healing, using the analogy of dew and tree.[32] However, he concentrates more on the Israelite culture and language traditions, in which these metaphors are deeply rooted. He also expands his interests in an eschatological hope, working on Hosea 14:2-9. The commentary on Hosea by Dearman explicates the verses exegetically.[33] Dearman (2010) in his commentary on Hosea, deals with the historical context of the prophetic figures and historical roots in the covenant traditions of ancient Israel. He identifies the important aspects of Hosea's poetic language and metaphorical message and emphasises the difficulties in translation and how to read the text with textual aids. Dearman used the early pattern of interpretation, earlier than the Ugaritic texts, by using extra biblical texts. According to Wolff, the prophet used the word 'love' אהב as a technical term to interpret the election of God's people. It is also noted that Hosea employed the term along with the metaphor of marriage and family.[34] It is clear the above authors did not see the love imagery in Hosea as being of any real importance; this research sets out to show that the imagery was of vital importance and why Hosea used it.

[27] Yee, G.A., *Composition and Tradition in the Book of Hosea: A Redactional Critical Investigation,* SBLDS 102, Atlanta, Scholars Press, 1987.

[28] Stuart, D. *Hosea-Jonah, Word Biblical Commentary* 31, Waco, Texas: Word Books, 1987.

[29] Carol J. Dempsey, *The Prophets: A Liberation-Critical Reading,* Minneapolis, Fortress Press, 2000, 154

[30] Renita J. Weems, *Battered Love: Marriage, Sex, and Violence in the Hebrew Prophets,* Minneapolis, Fortress Press, 1995, 27-28.

[31] Bernhard Oestreich: *Metaphors and Similes for Yahweh in Hosea* 14:2-9 (1-8): *A Study of Hoseanic Pictorial Language,* Friedensauer Schriftenreihe, Reihe A, Theologie, 1, Peter Lang, 1998.

[32] Bernhard Oestreich: *Metaphors and Similes for Yahweh in Hosea* 14:2-9 (1-8): *A Study of Hoseanic Pictorial Language,* Friedensauer Schriftenreihe, Reihe A, Theologie, 1, Peter Lang, 1998.

[33] Dearman, J.A., *The Book of Hosea,*" NICOT, Grand Rapids, Wm. B. Eerdmans Publishing Company, 2010.

[34] Wolff, *Hosea*, 197; cf. Dearman. J.A, *The Book of Hosea,*" NICOT, Grand Rapids, Wm. B. Eerdmans Publishing Company, 2010, 358.

These authors are primarily looking at Hosea through the image of the covenant as defining the relationship between God and Israel. In pursuance of this idea, this research starts by seeking to comprehend the meaning and the development of covenant thought in the Old Testament through a socio-rhetorical reading. To do this it examines Hosea's understanding of the covenant based upon the concept of love אהב, חסד, רחם, נכם, אמת and דעת אלהים and concludes that Hosea perceived the covenant as endorsing a relationship of steadfast love. This relationship originates from the incomprehensible love of God and is central to Hosea's whole message. This study goes on to bring out some applications of the imagery of Hosea relevant to the present-day Indian Christian marriage culture, in the wider context of Indian Christianity. The situation exists that traditional definitions of what constitutes a family, as well as marriage, are being challenged within the growing urbanized culture in Indian cities. The Diaspora culture that is developing due to globalization also raises new questions about the loving relationships depicted in Hosea's marital and parental imagery. The comparison can be made between Hosea's marriage imagery and modern Indian marriages many of which are becoming a mere formula and moving towards a secular, costly, glittering ceremony rather than one with a religious meaning. This is something to be considered in a later chapter.

1.4. Definition of the Terms

1.4.1. Love

The concept of love plays an important role in the book of Hosea. For this, the prophet uses different terms to describe God's love for the people of Israel.

1.4.1.1. אהב

This Hebrew word "אהב" is the most generic term for love. Wilson defines אהב in the following way: "human love for another, affection for family, human love for or to God."[35] To Wolff, this is an onomatopoeic word which means "to breathe after," and "to pant."[36] The word signifies emotion and strong desire. אהב refers to the love between husband and wife and parent and child, but also, in a broader sense, the love of people towards God and the love of God towards people. In Hosea, where אהב occurs 18 times, it is used in various ways but basically to convey physical and emotional love in one form or another human or divine.

1.4.1.2. חסד

The most important word that is used in Hosea's vocabulary of love is חסד. The word refers to God's love or kindness towards people and people's mercy or kindness towards others.[37] The term is translated as "covenantal love" or "loyal love," "steadfast love" and "loving kindness" and is defined as faithfulness, steadfastness or loyalty to a covenant relationship. This word combines two ideas strength and love.

---

[35] The *NAS Old Testament Hebrew Lexicon,*" Brown Driver, Briggs and Gesenius, "Hebrew Lexicon entry for אהב.

[36] Wolff, H.W., *A Commentary on the Book of the Prophet Hosea,* Philadelphia, Fortress Press, 1974, 35.

[37] C. Lalmuankima, Challenges from the Book of Hosea in Understanding the Kindness of God, *Bangalore Theological Forum,* Vol. XL, No. 1, June 2008, 149 (149-160).

Norman contrasts the covenantal love that commits its loyalty to God with the ritual love that offers sacrifices and things to God.[38]

1.4.1.3. חשק

The term חשק has certain emotional dimensions, as in a man deeply attached to a woman, and who wants to marry her. חשק is sometimes used for human love (Gen. 34:8, Deut. 21:11).[39] It is generally translated into English as "be united," "adhere to," "have pleasure," "love someone" and "lying with or lust."[40] However, the basic meaning of the verb is "be united to" or "adhere to" and is best considered as being used to convey human love and affection.

1.4.1.4. רחם

The next word found in Hosea's list of words for love is רחם, which, in its verb form, can mean "warm and tender love" and, in its noun form, "pity," which can be extended to mean "womb," and is then defined as the feeling of a mother towards her child in her womb.

1.4.1.5. נחם

נחם is a close parallel to חסד. The word נחם means "comfort" or "compassion." The word "compassion" is translated as "to love" or "pity" by Hosea to describe God's love: "The Lord says that He will not have mercy upon the house of Israel." The phrase "I will not have pity," is used as a prophetic message. The naming of the second child לא־רחמה is changed from a negative meaning to a positive connotation in "I will have pity," "I will show them compassion." This magnifies the impact of God's announcement that He is not breaking away from the covenant relationship but is reminding Israel of His love and commitment.

Hosea insists more on God's love for people (3:1) and emphasises the call "to share the love of God and be true to that love" (11:1.) The message of the book also stresses the need for the people of Israel to be reconciled to God by turning away from sin and it strongly encourages them to turn to God, reflecting and executing love in action (14:1ff.). God's compassion is waiting for them.

1.4.1.6. The other meanings of love

The terms of אהב, חסד, חשק, רחם and נחם used in Hosea show the varied meanings of "love" utilised in the text. That is, as human love for another, affection for family, human love for or to God; kindness; human love; love with compassion; and comfort and compassion. The use can be seen in Hosea 14:1-8 (MT 2-9), where it brings out the theme of steadfast love that God shows Israel even though they have broken the covenant.

1.4.2. Covenantal Relationship

For Hosea covenantal relationship is an important concept in all the prophetic messages he delivered. As shown above, love is the most significant theme in the

[38] Norman D. Snaith, *Mercy and Sacrifice: A Study of the Book of Hosea,* London: SCM Press, 1953, 39-40.

[39] G. Wallis, חשק, *TDOT,* vol. 5, 261, cf. David Talley חשק, *NIDOTTE,* Vol. 5, 318.

[40] David Talley חשק, *NIDOTTE,* vol. 5, 318.

book. This is emphasised by its use to establish the covenantal relationship which God wishes to keep alive, despite its rejection by the Israelites. The relationship dates back to Moses and is the essential bond between God and His chosen people. Therefore Hosea uses the covenant as a means to remind Israel of the relationship between Yahweh and themselves.

1.4.2.1. ברית

The Hebrew word for covenant is "ברית." According to Mendenhall and Herion, "a covenant is an agreement enacted between two parties in which one or both make promises under oath to perform or refrain from certain actions stipulated in advance."[41] Most contracts have an end date, but a covenant is a permanent arrangement. The word can also mean "promise, a compact, contract, an agreement" which is also parallel with "oath": to express a solemn pledge. Wenham prefers to translate covenant as "to confirm," contending "whereas 'to cut' describes the point of entry into a covenant, 'to confirm' is used of ratifying pre-existing 'covenants.'"[42] According to Wenham, the covenant demands God's fatherly compassion towards Israel, his children. The covenant also conveys a sense of loyalty within a family, between children and parents. The Sinatic covenant at the heart of the Yahweh/Israel relationship is an agreement or bond made between God and the Israelites at Mt. Sinai in which God promises to love Israel but requires certain duties in return from them. The covenant thus binds the two with specific responsibilities.

1.4.2.2. דעת אלהים

The term דעת אלהים is translated as "knowledge of God." The word is related to intellectual, emotional and spiritual knowledge.[43] The Hebrew word brings out the idea of relationship with a person, which can be extended to caring about or having sexual intimacy with someone. In the Hebraic view, it means having a life in relationship with Yahweh. In Hosea, knowledge of God is seen as intimacy with God as a son would know his father. Heschel points out that the prophet is the one who coined this expression: דעת אלהים (Hos. 6:6).[44] ברית and דעת אלהים in Hosea describe the covenant relationship by paralleling this with the covenant of marriage. The above section is discussed in more detail in a subsequent chapter.

1.4.2.3. Imagery

According to Webster's Dictionary, "imagery is a language which causes people to imagine, such as pictures of people or things in a work of art or in the mind. It can also mean a figurative language." The Oxford Dictionary defines it as "language using similes and metaphors that produce images in the mind."[45] A. Strawn cites a

---

[41] Mendenhall, G. E, and Gary A. Herion, *The Anchor Yale Bible Dictionary,* David Noel Freedman, New York, Yale University, 2008.

[42] Gordon J. Wenham, *Genesis 1-15, Word Biblical Commentary,* Vol. 1, Waco, Texas, Word, 1987, 145-147.

[43] Ucheawaji G. Josiah, *"Hosea's Perspective on the Knowledge of God and its Relevance to Rivers State, Nigeria,"* Vol. 11, No. 1, March, 2014, 9.

[44] Heschel, *The Prophets,* New York, Harper and Row, 1962, 103-139.

[45] Catherine (ed), *Paperback Oxford English Dictionary,* New Delhi, Oxford University Press, 2006, 375.

working definition of imagery given by Ryken, and others as *"any word that names a concrete thing (such as tree or house) or action (such as running or threshing)."*[46] In this sense, any object or action that can be pictured is an image.

For the purpose of this study, imagery is defined as a way of creating a visual representation in the mind of the reader by using figures of speech such as simile, metaphor, personification, symbolism and assonance in order to derive a meaning. Using the imagination to understand the characters in Hosea helps convey the meaning and overtone of the text.

1.4.2.4. Metaphor

The term metaphor means "to carry over" and generally points to the transference of a word or meaning from one element to another. Abma (1999) says that metaphor is a "literary device in which terms from two different areas of life are brought together in order to achieve a special meaning which goes beyond the ordinary meaning of words or concepts."[47] However, the full meaning of a metaphor must be reconstructed from the historical context, rhetorical purpose, and speaker's intentions.[48]

1.4.3. Socio-Rhetorical Reading

Socio-rhetorical interpretation is a multi-dimensional approach to texts[49] guided by a multi-dimensional hermeneutic.[50] Rather than being one more method for interpreting texts, socio-rhetorical interpretation is an interpretive analytic an approach that evaluates and reorients its strategies as it engages in multi-faceted dialogue with the texts and other phenomena that come within its purview.[51] The approach uses a trans-modern philosophical position of relationism to interrelate ancient, modern and post-modern systems of thought with one another.[52] Both sociological and rhetorical

---

[46] B. A. Strawn, "Imagery," *Dictionary of the Old Testament: Wisdom, Poetry and Writings:* Ed. by Tremper Longman, Peter Enns, England, Inter Varsity Press, 2008, 306-7.

[47] Abma, Bonds, 7. Cf. Yee, *Hosea,* 209 and J. Galambush, *Jerusalem in the Book of Ezekiel: The City as Yahweh's Wife,* SBLDS 130, Atlanta, Scholars Press, 1992, 6.

[48] T. Cohen, "Figurative Speech and Figurative Acts," in *Philosophical Perspectives on Metaphor* ed. M. Johnson; Minneapolis, University of Minnesota Press, 1981, 184-185.

[49] V. K. Robbins, *The Tapestry of Early Christian Discourse: Rhetoric, Society and Ideology,* London, Routledge, 1996, 108-18 and idem, *Exploring the Texture of Texts: A Guide to Socio-Rhetorical Interpretation,* Valley Forge, Trinity Press International, 1996, 58-63. For a programmatic description of the goals, idem, 'The Present and Future of Rhetorical Analysis', *The Rhetorical Analysis of Scripture: Essays from the 1995 London Conference* (ed. S. E. Porter and T. H. Olbricht; *JSNTSup* 146; Sheffield: Sheffield Academic Press, 1997, 24-52; 'The Rhetorical Full-Turn in Biblical Interpretation: Reconfiguring Rhetorical-Political Analysis,' *Rhetorical Criticism and the Bible* (ed. S. E. Porter and T. H. Olbricht; *JSNTSup* 195; Sheffield: Sheffield Academic Press, 2002, 48-60; idem, 'Where is Wuellner's Anti-Hermeneutical Hermeneutic Taking Us? From Scheiermacher to Thistleton and Beyond,' *Rhetorics and Hermeneutics: Wilhelm Wuellner and His Influence,* ed. J. D. Hester and D. Hester; Edinburgh: T. and T. Clark, 2004.

[50] V. K. Robbins, 'Socio-Rhetorical Hermeneutics and Commentary,' *EPI TO AYTO, Essays in honour of Petr Pokorny on his sixty-fifth birthday,* ed. J. Mrazek, S. Brodsky, and R. Dvorakova; Praha-Trebenice: Mlyn Publishers, 1998, 284-97;

[51] Robbins, *The Tapestry of Early Christian Discourse: Rhetoric, Society and Ideology,* London, Routledge, 1996, 11-13; idem, 'The Present and Future,' 25-33.

[52] V. K. Robbins, 'The Rhetorical Full-Turn in Biblical Interpretation and Its Relevance for Feminist Hermeneutics', *Her Master's* Tools? ed., C. Vander Stichele and T. Penner; *Global Perspectives on Biblical Scholarship Series;* Atlanta, GA: SBL and Leiden: Brill, 2004.

analyses are helpful in studying the Bible. Both methods (sociological and rhetorical) help to demonstrate that the Bible is 'both inspired by God and the result of human participation.'

Sociological analysis helps to show how Scripture is part of an intricate social matrix that must be taken into consideration to achieve a holistic interpretation. Rhetorical analysis helps to show how the authors (in this case, Hosea) logically crafted their arguments in order to present intellectually stimulating and appealing presentation of the message of their faith. Both the social factors involved in understanding the text, and the rhetoric of the text itself, prove to provide very stimulating studies of Hosea.

Studying the Socio-rhetorical interpretation of the selected texts in Hosea provides an understanding of the words, the world and the context of the chosen passage, thus revealing the meaning of the texts.[53] This study also brings new insights into the Old Testament texts where Yahweh is portrayed in different images and forms which are used to depict God's love for His people. Also, it conveys the distinctive nature of the socio-rhetorical methodology. Each of the textures of Socio-rhetorical interpretation has sub-textures. In this research the socio-rhetorical approach is used to bring out the sociological aspect of the imagery of love and also assist the analysis of the socio-cultural context and the sources from which the prophet in his book formulated his concept of love.

1.4.3.1. Sociological Criticism

The sociological approach is the method of interpretation in which the social scientific method is utilized to understand the social world. It provides us with ways of trying to understand the world.[54] It seeks to understand typical patterns of human relations in their structure and function, both at a given time in history and in their courses of change over a specified time span.[55] The synchronic approach is the method applied to Biblical studies giving importance to the text or being text centred. Here, all the non-historical aspects are taken together to explain or analyse the text. The diachronic approach evaluates the text in the light of its historical development by means of examining the issues of authorship and the historical setting of the text. This approach is applied to advocate that "within the social science paradigm, there is a broad concurrence that the Biblical writings were rooted in interacting groups of people organized in social structures that controlled the chief aspects of public life."[56] The sociological reading of the text thus takes into consideration every aspect of the social dimension of the text, including its transmission and interpretation.[57]

---

[53] Vernon Robbins, *The Tapestry of Early Christian Discourse: Rhetoric, Society and Ideology,* London, Routledge, 1996, 14.

[54] E.C. Cuff, W.W. Sharrock and D.W. Francis, *Perspectives in Sociology,* London, Routledge, 1992, 1-2.

[55] Norman, Richard N. Soulen and R. Kendall Soulen, *Sociological Interpretation: Handbook of Biblical Criticism,* Louisville, Westminster, John Knox Press, 2011, 197-198.

[56] Norman K. Gottwald, *The Hebrew Bible: A Socio-Literary Reading,* Philadelphia, Fortress Press, 1985, 26.

[57] Daniel Jones Muthunayagam, "Contemporary Approaches to Old Testament Interpretation," in Interweaving Methodology and Praxis: Exploring Disciplinary Options in Today's World, eds. Indukuri John Mohan Razu Bangalore, BTESSC/SATHRI, 2007, 183.

1.4.3.2. Rhetorical Criticism

Foss defines Rhetorical criticism as the process of systematically investigating and explaining symbolic acts and artifacts for the purpose of understanding rhetorical processes.[58] This method can be applied to the Bible in a number of different ways in research studies, both in the Old Testament as well as the New Testament. The study helps to bring out "the art of effective communication." Rhetorical criticism is an author-centered interpretative approach.

1.4.3.3. Socio-Rhetorical Approach

Hosea is all about persuasive speeches interpreted according to their rhetoric. Hosea's prophecy is written in poetic form. This study takes up the notion of the author as a 'poet,' and focuses on word play in the text and on the lyrical plot of the book; it is in fact a lengthy poem of unlimited power. The prophet is a master literary craftsmanship. His prophetic style is emphasised in the book and it is difficult to distinguish where his poetry ends and prose begins. According to Andersen and Freedman, the first three chapters are basically written in narrative prose, while the rest of the chapters, 4 to 14, are typical poetry.[59] Although it is believed Hosea 1-3 have the characteristics of prose, it is noticed that the genres, types of instructional accounts and the intensity of speech, literary richness, urgency of the tone and the message all characterize poetry.[60] The first three chapters are distinctly more narrative in style, and the oracles embedded in them are brought as a tight cluster within the narrative. The narratives in the book are arranged in chiastic structure through the metaphors. Hosea's prophecies display a rich variety of images and literary features, including metaphors and similes (e.g., 3:1-5, 11:8, 14:9), which he uses to portray God as a husband, a parent and a healing physician. To understand Hosea's use of metaphors and similes it is important to study both the sociological and rhetorical aspects of his time. For this, the socio-rhetorical approach helps us to understand the book better.

A socio-rhetorical approach focuses on values, convictions and beliefs in literary texts. It views texts as performances of language in particular historical and cultural situations. Robbins presupposes that a text is a tapestry of interwoven textures, including inner texture, intertexture, social and cultural texture, ideological texture and sacred texture.[61] They are in dialogue with each other and reveal the social systems from which they come and even information on the interpreter.[62]

1.5. Methodology Adopted

The socio-rhetorical interpretation methodology has been applied predominately to New Testament passages because of its use of first century rhetorical categories.

---

[58] Foss, Sonja K. *Rhetorical Criticism: Exploration and Practice,* Illinois, Waveland Press, 2008.

[59] Andersen and Freedman, *Hosea, Anchor Bible,* Garden City, Doubleday, 1980, 60-66.

[60] Richard D. Patterson, "Old Testament Prophecy," in *A Complete Literary Guide to the Bible,* eds. Leland Ryken and Tremper Longman III, Grand Rapids, Zondervan, 1993, 305-306.

[61] Vernon K. Robbins, *Exploring the Texture of Texts,* Valley Forge, PA: Trinity International, 1996 and Vernon K. Robbins, *The Tapestry of Early Christianity: Rhetoric, Society and Ideology,* London and New York: Routledge, 1996.

[62] Duane F. Watson, "Why we need Socio Rhetorical Commentary and what it might look like?," *Rhetorical Criticism and the Bible,* Stanley E. Porter and Dennis L. Stamps, *JSNTSup* 195, Sheffield: Academic Press, 2002, 140.

So far, the Old Testament texts have not received any major attention from socio-rhetorical analysis. However, it can be successfully applied to Old Testament books via the two or three interpretive devices which Robbins calls textures."[63] Scholars such as Gina Hens-Piazza, in Of Methods, Monarchs, and Meanings: *A Socio-rhetorical Approach to Exegesis,* surveys rhetorical criticism and social science criticism by defining the point of contact between these two methods of biblical interpretation, using three exegetical passages: 1Samuel 14:36-46, 2Samuel 14:1-22, and 1Kings 3:16-28.[64] Martin Oosthuizen has successfully applied the socio-rhetorical methodology in *interpreting Deuteronomy* 15:1-18, which results in bringing new insights into the text.[65] Others have applied the textures of the socio-rhetorical method to the text itself. S. S. Ndoga and H Viviers,[66] has also written a book, *Is the woman in the Song of Songs really that free? A Socio-Rhetorical Reading of Song of Songs 1:2-4.* Mmapula Diana Kebaneilwe[67] in This Courageous Woman: *A Socio-rhetorical Womanist Reading of Proverbs 31:10-31,* studies Proverbs 31:10-31, entitled, אשת־חיל 'a woman of courage,' in Kebaneilwe thesis, beginning with the premise that social, cultural, historical, ideological and anthropological data are represented rhetorically in the text.

Using the socio-rhetorical method to study Hosea, this research analyses the function of the imagery of love within the covenantal relationship in its literary and socio-cultural contexts and interprets the texts using sociological and rhetorical approaches.

This study analyses the passages section by section (Hosea 2:16-3:5; 11:1-11; 14:2-9) rather than verse by verse. Using this methodology, this research examines the structural features of a text, to determine the main themes and ideas of passages and the levels of textures. The order of texture is carefully designed by Robbins to lead to the discovery of new and original ideas. It is a gradual analysis that separates the researcher from his/her biases and lets the text reveal its richness. The main purpose of inner texture is to focus on words as a communication tool, a technique that seeks to determine first of all the "meaning" of the words and then the "real interpretation of the text."[68] This technique enables the researcher to acquire "an intimate knowledge of words, word patterns, voices, structure, devices and modes in the text," which complement and supplement other understandings of the text.[69]

---

[63] Vernon. K. Robbins, *Exploring the Texture of Texts,* Valley Forge, Trinity International, 1996.

[64] Gina Hens-Piazza, *Of Methods, Monarchs, and Meanings: A Socio-Rhetorical Approach to Exegesis,* 1996

[65] Martin J. Oosthuizen, "Deuteronomy 15:1-18 in Socio-rhetorical perspective," in *Zeitschrift fur Altorientalische und Biblische Rechtsgeschichte,* eds. Eckart Otto, and Klaus Baltzer, Wiesbaden: Harrassowitzz Verlag, 1997, 64-91.

[66] S. S. Ndoga and H Viviers, Is the woman in the Song of Songs really that free? A Socio-Rhetorical Reading of Song of Songs 1:2-4, *HTS* 56 (4), 2000.

[67] Mmapula Diana Kebaneilwe, *This Courageous Woman: A Socio-rhetorical Womanist Reading of Proverbs 31:10-31,* 2012.

[68] Robbins, *The Tapestry of Early Christian Discourse: Rhetoric, Society and Ideology,* London, Routledge, 1996, 30.

[69] Robbins, V.K, *Exploring the Texture of Texts: A guide to Socio-Rhetorical Interpretation,* Pennsylvania, Trinity Press International, 1996, 8.

1.6. Scope and Limitation

The Old Testament prophets constantly speak of God's love in terms of justice, compassion, judgment, etc. Yet in Hosea the theme of personal love husband-wife, father-son, physician-patient (healing love) appears to be emphasised when God speaks of His relationship with His people through the Sinai covenant. While many authors have studied Hosea, none of them have studied the use of the theme of personal love in examining the character of God as shown in the book and, through that character, the relationship between God and the Israelites through the Sinai covenant. This research has chosen the nature of this relationship for its investigation since there are various possibilities to be examined. These include the type of covenant, legal or non-legal, and the motivation which drives Yahweh. The text might give a hint about motivation; God may have wanted Israel to honour the covenant so He could send a message to other nations. The research examines these theories in a later chapter through the use of rhetorical imagery. By probing these questions, the investigation can assess Hosea's special contribution to the understanding that Israel had of its unique covenantal relationship to Yahweh and its role in reaching out to the other nations.

The book is considered to be a single unit, as it displays a consistency of language, symbols, theological insights and uses of literary style. The basic form of the text was written in a situation where particular people were in conflict with Yahweh. The prophet used rhetorical devices, and three sets of imagery to bring out the idea of Yahweh's steadfast love in the book. Hosea uses this imagery to demonstrate Yahweh's love and to strengthen Israel's faith and adherence to Yahweh. The focus of this research is to emphasise the use of the imagery of love through applying the socio-rhetorical method. The comprehensive analysis of love in the book lies within the scope of this dissertation.

The research focuses on the imagery of love אהב, חסד, רחם and ידע, in the texts of Hosea 2:16-3:5; 11:1-11 and 14:2-9. The study first reviews a general understanding of love among the prophets, especially of divine love in the eighth century BCE prophets, and in ancient Western Asia. It then considers a fuller and more comprehensive reading of love in Hosea against that background. Both biblical and extra-biblical sources are also used to unravel the socio-political and socio-cultural sources that influenced Hosea's concept of love and his expression of it.

The above three passages have been selected and are examined exegetically; the significance of the concepts of "love," "covenant" and "repentance" and their theological relevance and sociological importance for today's ministry are brought out. A study of the analogy of metaphors used in the book is also considered to find out in which ways they are helpful in expressing the love of God in the context of Israel's breach of the covenant.[70] In doing so, the different facets of God's love emphasised through these analogies are made clear. The study also shows how the Hosea text differs from the other eighth century BCE prophets in emphasizing these particular facets of God's love.

[70] Watson, W.G.E., *Classical Hebrew Poetry,* A Guide to its Techniques, JSOT 26, Sheffield, 1984, 251.

This research is limited to the basic theme of the book, which is "steadfast love." This love plays an important role in the life of Hosea and in his message to the people of Israel. The texts selected for this study best represent this theme: 1. Hosea 2:16-3:5, (God has suffered because of the unfaithfulness of Israel); 2. Hosea 11:1-11 (unconditional love of God in the face of people's rejection); 3. Hosea 14:2-9 (God will continue to love Israel despite her behaviour towards Him).

1.7. Survey of the Previous Research

The research done on the book is quite extensive, and the books published on it are numerous. However, all the earlier works have concentrated on judgment and on love, except a few that speak of the covenantal relationship between Yahweh and Israel. This research, while subscribing to and strengthening the aspect of God's love towards his people, attempts to delineate the significance of the imagery of love "אהב" in the context of person to person relationships.

In previous studies, several scholars have drawn attention to Hosea's use of language and metaphors. According to Eichrodt, the theology of Hosea is based on his message of God's love, which is the essence behind the action God took for Israel.[71] Robinson deals with Hosea's marriage and contends that it is his struggles within his marriage that brings him to understand the love of God. Further, he argues that it is the context of societal wickedness that provides the background for the prophet's message of God's love.[72] Gerhard von Rad, in his book, deals with particular chapter on Hosea and confirms the oracles uttered by the prophet.[73] Robertson in his work deals with Yahweh as loving husband, loving father and healing physician analogies from Ancient West Asia, and Israelite background.[74] Eichhorn comments that Hosea's use of literary style is to bring out the richness and imagery of the prophet's own life.[75] A. Scholz moves one step beyond Eichhorn and says that the prophet Hosea's organization of images shows great skill. He continues that the images not only decorate but also bring out the important themes and purpose of the book (sin, punishment, and salvation).[76] W. R. Harper, in his commentary, acknowledges that images are part of Hosea's writing style.[77] Ziegler concentrates more on the first division of the book of Hosea and focuses on the metaphors.[78] For example, in Hosea 1-3, the author chose to focus on the metaphor of the relationship between a husband and wife, while in chapter 11 he used the metaphor of a parent and child.

---

[71] Walter Eichrodt, "'The Holy One in Your Midst,' *The Theology of Hosea," Interpretation: A Journal of Bible and Theology,* XV 3, July, 1961, 263.

[72] H. Wheeler Robinson, *The Two Hebrew Prophets: Studies in Hosea and Ezekiel,* London, Lutterworth Press, 1948, 11-48.

[73] Gerhard von Rad, *The Message of the Prophets,* New York, Harper and Row Publishers, 1967, 110-111.

[74] N.J. Robertson, *A Study of the Analogies used for the Love of God in the book of Hosea,"* Senate of Serampore, 1991.

[75] Eichhorn, *Einleitung in das Alte Testament,* Gottingen, 1824, 286.

[76] Scholz, *Kommentar Zum Buche des Propheten Hosea,* Wurzburg, 1882, xxvii-xxviii.

[77] W. R. Harper, *A Critical and Exegetical Commentary on Amos and Hosea,* New York, 1915.

[78] J. Ziegler, *Die Liebe Gottesbei den Propheten. Ein Beitragzur alttestamentlichen Theologie,* ATA 11.3, Munster, 1930.

H.S. Nyberg's interest was to analyse and develop the textual-critical problems in the book of Hosea.[79] He concentrated more on the "positive philological and religious historical section of the work."

There seemed to be a focus on the study of Hosea during the 1960s and 1970s by scholars such as Wolff,[80] Mays,[81] Ward,[82] Brueggemann,[83] and Buss.[84] However, in the past few decades, there have not been many works on it. It is noticeable that the analogy that links the love of God for Israel, as in Hosea, to the human (husband-wife) situation has not received attention in any of these studies.

1.7.1. Themes of Study

1.7.1.1. Divine love

The thesis by F. Buck was probably the first monographic study to deal specifically with the theme of divine love in the book of Hosea.[85] Buck investigates the depiction of God's love for Israel through the metaphors of marital love, parental love and the love of physician and healer.

The monograph of H.D. Neef[86] on the book of Hosea deals with the historical traditions of Israel and brings out the consistency and continuity of God's love in changing traditions, which help the people to come back to the covenantal relationship.

Schaeffer in *"JHWH, Hosea und die drei Frauen im Hoseabuch"* (Yahweh, Hosea and the three women in the Book of Hosea) portrays a vulnerable God through the life of the prophet Hosea.[87] In this work, Hosea stands as a symbolic picture of the God of Israel whose love for Israel is completely steadfast.

Ackerman explores the connection between texts describing Yahweh's covenantal love for Israel, the interpersonal loving relationships of men and women, and parents and children.[88] *Divine Love in Hosea 11,* by Kyung H. Park, has as its focal point the theological understanding of divine love.[89] He interprets the parental metaphor to express God's love. Park also examines the general meaning and usage of divine love אהב and חסד in the book of Hosea and the main metaphors that express divine love.

---

[79] H. S. Nyberg, *Studienzu Hoseabuch: Zugleichein Beitragzur Klarung des Problems der alttestamentlichen Textkritik,* Uppsala, 1935, iii. Nyberg was the proponent of the traditional interpretation used in the book of Hosea. His interest was on the composition and transmission of Hosea.

[80] H. W. Wolff, *Hosea* (G. Stansell, Trans.), Philadelphia, Fortress Press, 1974.

[81] Mays, J. L. *Hosea*, Philadelphia, Westminster Press, 1969.

[82] Ward, James M, "Hosea": *A Theological Commentary,* New York, Harper and Row, 1966.

[83] Walter Brueggemann, *Tradition of Crisis: A Study in Hosea,* Richmond, John Knox Press, 1969.

[84] Buss, *The Prophetic Word of Hosea,* Berlin, Verlag Alfred, Topelmann, 1969.

[85] F. Buck, "*Die Liebe Gottesbeim Propheten Osee*" (unpublished doctoral dissertation at the Pontifical Biblical Institute), Rome, 1953.

[86] Neef, H.D., *Die Heilstraditionen Israels in der Verkündigung des Propheten Hosea,* BZAW 169, 1987.

[87] Christa Schaeffer, *EVT* 55, 1995, 114–140.

[88] S. Ackerman, *"The Personal is Political: Covenantal and Affectionate Love* (אהבה, אהב) in the Hebrew Bible," VT 52, 2002, 437-458.

[89] Kyung Hee Park, *Divine Love in Hosea 11,* Southern Baptist Theological Seminary, 2004.

Kakkanattu conducts a detailed study of Yahweh's love for Israel as found in Hosea 11:1-11.[90] He deals with God's enduring love using synchronic and diachronic analysis. For Kakkanattu, though Hosea 11 understands God to be a father (not mother, contrary to some feminist scholars), 11:4 assigns some traditionally feminine roles to Yahweh.

Derek Kidner also talks about the 'loveless' people and the constancy of the love of God toward such people, as he looks at Hosea through the perspective of the love of God.[91] He places Hosea in the place of God, who extends this kind of love to the people of Israel.

These authors concentrate on divine love as the main concept in the book of Hosea, rather than linking this with human love to show the similarities. This study argues that the mere concentration on God's love, rather than giving importance to both forms of love, (divine and human), obscures the balance of the idea of what God is trying to convey to the Israelites through Hosea and his failed marriage.

1.7.1.2. Use of the marriage metaphor to show the concept of Love

The theme of divine love in Hosea is connected with the marriage metaphor. God loves Israel who runs after other lovers. On the use of אהב, Praveen Paul discusses the concept of love from the post-colonial perspective.[92] The use of the word אהב is distinctive in Hosea. To express love, Hosea uses metaphors which are significant. Praveen Paul finds the marriage metaphor to be an appropriate example for divine love. He recounts that in Hosea, אהב has political and colonial connotations. Moreover, the use of the word אהב is somewhat distinctive in Hosea because of its use for explaining love. Owens' concentration is on the motif of parenting, with God as a mother figure.[93] He has devoted a full chapter, in his book, to bring out a new relationship within the marital relationship. Here, he highlights the love of God in the role of a tender mother. In the marriage metaphor that Hosea uses God still loves the adulterous woman. God still loves her and the aspect of merit is emphasised through the symbolic act of redeeming her. The prophet shows that divine love means an active emotive act in order to gain her back through payment.

In her book Renita Weems questions and critiques the use of sexual imagery as a figure of speech, in prophetic literature in particular, and in the Hebrew Bible. She studies the portrayal of God's divine love, compassion, and commitment between partners. She suggests that the use of trope, a figurative or metaphorical use of a word or expression used to this extent, should not be dismissed as a literary device. The prophet's use of rhetoric such as parables, metaphors, contrasts, and parallelisms flourishes in the male dominated ancient society. Marriage plays an important part in the life of the community. She says Hosea uses the powerful marriage metaphor of the adulterous wife and, in this way, engages his audience and wins them over to

[90] Kakkanattu, Joy Philip, *God's Enduring Love in the Book of Hosea: A Synchronic and Diachronic analysis of Hosea 11:1-11,* FAT, 2. Reihe, 14: Tubingen, Mohr Siebeck, 2006.

[91] Derek Kidner, *Love to the Loveless: The Message of Hosea,* Downers Grove, Inter Varsity, 1982, 142.

[92] Paul Praveen, *Power and Love in the book of Hosea: A Postcolonial Reading,* Living Insight Translators and Publishers Pvt. Ltd, Delhi, 2015.

[93] Owens. J.J, 'Exegetical Study of Hosea,' *RevExp* 54, 522-543, 1957.

his view.[94] R. Abma seeks to bring out the idea of the imagery related to marriage in Isaiah, Hosea and Jeremiah.[95] These books illustrate the dynamic relationship between Yahweh and Israel.[96] In Hosea, R. Abma looks at the marriage imagery from a feminist perspective, while designating the texts in Hosea and Jeremiah as sexual imagery. The purpose of this study is to offer a fresh interpretation of various prophetic texts that present the covenant relationship as only a marital relationship. This is not a comparative text study. The focus by many authors is marriage imagery, ignoring the other metaphors of father-son and healing. The goal of this study is better understanding of the three metaphors and their relationship to the Yahweh-Israelite covenant.

This metaphor is significant because it sheds light on the character of Yahweh and his relationship to Israel. Abma's purpose is to read these texts as separate voices that share a certain amount of vocabulary and imagery. Bringing them together gives the reader a fuller picture of an intriguing model of divine and human partnership. On "Methodology," she discusses the synchronic approach used in her study, prophecy as poetry or speech, the different audiences these texts were directed to, and Abma's model of interpretation. According to Chris Wright, Hosea's use of the marital imagery reminds one of God calling Israel back to faithfulness in a husband-wife relationship.[97] For him, the focus throughout is on the imagery of marriage in Hosea.

However this research puts forward the argument that in concentrating on the marriage theme, the authors have again created a lack of balance in their studies. It can be argued it is more useful to study the three human aspects of love, their importance and relevance to the context as well as their parallels to the covenant relationship between God and Israel, rather than considering only the marriage aspect.

1.7.1.3. Use of Metaphors in Hosea

In recent years, several studies have been done on the concept of metaphor in Hosea, with scholars studying his metaphorical language. L.J. Braaten uses the parent-child imagery in Hosea.[98] He uses two father-child metaphors to bring out the relationship between Yahweh and Israel. First is the image used in chapters 1 and 2 where he talks about Israel being God's offspring of the land, and second, the image of adoption or election, in which the author brings out the fact that Israel had been rescued from the land of Egypt because of God's love.

The study of metaphors in the book of Hosea was popular during 1980's. The feminist scholars turned the focus on marital and sexual metaphors concerning God, Hosea and Gomer in Hosea 1-3. The feminist approach was developed by Stetel[99]

---

[94] Renita J. Weems, *Battered Love: Marriage, Sex, and Violence in the Hebrew Prophets,* Minneapolis, Fortress Press, 1995.

[95] R. Abma, *Bonds of Love Methodic Studies of Prophetic Texts with Marriage Imagery (Isaiah 50: 1-3 and 54: 1- 10, Hosea 1-3, Jeremiah 23),* SSN 31, 1999.

[96] Marvin A. Sweeney, *The Prophetic Literature: Interpreting Biblical Texts Series,* Nashville, Abingdon Press, 2005, 145.

[97] C.J.H. Wright, *Living as the People of God,* Leicester, IVP, 1983, 21.

[98] Braaten Laurie, *Parent and Child Imagery in Hosea,* Boston University, 1987.

[99] T. D. Setel, "Prophets and Pornography: Female Sexuality and Imagery in Hosea," in L. M. Russell (ed.), *Feminist Interpretation of the Bible,* Philadelphia, Westminster, 1985.

and further developed by Weems.[100] This paved the way for metaphorical study looking at imageries found in the entire book during 1990's. The major contribution of work was by Eidevall and Moughtin-Mumby. G. Eidevall applies the metaphor theory and forms in linguistics to Hosea 4-14 and tries to develop a new exegetical approach, namely metaphorical criticism.[101] In his work, he tries to bring out models, patterns, and themes from different metaphors. Various authors studied all kinds of imagery, focusing mainly on marital and sexual metaphors. B. Seifert's work is based on how metaphors are used in the texts in Hosea and how they relate to the prophetic proclamation.[102] For E.O. Nwaoru, the metaphors in Hosea are used as a literary device.[103] Here Nwaoru compares the ancient Near Eastern influence on his use of metaphors and similes.

According to Kelle, Hosea 2 is full of metaphors and rhetoric dealing with the issues of the immoral lives of the Israelites during Hosea's lifetime.[104] Kelle argues that the rhetorical situations demand a study of the basic forms of Hosea 2. For William Sanford, the marriage of Hosea and the naming of the three children bring out the idea of the metaphor here. The names of two of the children play an important role: לא-רחמה (not loved); לא-עמי (not my people).[105] The latter name highlights the reversal of the formula of the covenantal relationship.

To sum up, in Hosea, there are two expressions used, חסד and אהבה. These belong to the terminology of the covenant (cf. Deut. 5:10; Jer. 31:3). It would seem that using these words expressly connotes the covenant, with Hosea employing the theme of the covenant to explain the spousal and parental and healer images as being metaphors for the relationship between Yahweh and Israel. Hosea thus brings out the idea of Yahweh as the husband of Israel in his attempt to portray God's covenant election of Israel in a marital analogy. Besides this, there are other images that describe the relationship between Yahweh and Israel in terms of the relationship between father and child, and with respect to healing in chapter 14, as Yahweh is the healer of the people from their apostasy.

Hosea was the first to employ the metaphor figure of speech in a significant way. The research argues from this that the pursuit of the use of metaphor by various authors obscures the essential message of Hosea the relationship between God and Israel depicted through the human love images used to bring Israel to a realization of Yahweh's love for them. This study argues that metaphors can be very effective

---

[100] R. J. Weems, "Gomer: Victim of Violence or Victim of Metaphor?" *Semeia* 47: 87-104. She deals with a textual analysis and engages with this metaphor from a womanist perspective, using traditional readings of the text, such as historical and social-scientific methods, includes newer approaches, such as gender criticism, literary studies, and ideological analyses. She explains how metaphors are specific to their socio-historical contexts and how the marriage metaphor fit in the Hebrew prophets' patriarchal context. She tries to build her textual analysis by interpreting these metaphors within this patriarchal context and explaining how hypothetical audiences heard and understood these metaphors in this book.

[101] G. Eidevall, *"Grapes in the desert: Metaphors, Models, and Themes in Hosea 4-14,"* ConBOT 43, Stockholm, 1996.

[102] B. Seifert, *"Metaphorische Reden von Gottim Hoseabuch,"* FRLANT 166, Gottingen, 1996.

[103] E.O. Nwaoru, *"Imagery in the Prophecy of Hosea,"* AAT 41, Wiesbaden, 1999.

[104] Kelle, Brad E., *Hosea 2: Metaphor and Rhetoric in Historical Perspective,* SBL Academia, Atlanta, SBL, Leiden, Brill, 2005.

[105] William Sanford, *Old Testament Survey: The Message Form, and Background of the Old Testament,* Grand Rapids, Wm. B. Eerdmans Publishing Company, 1982, 337.

if used carefully, but they can be overdone and can blind the reader to the core message. While metaphors and similes are extensively used by Hosea, they are used as rhetorical devices.

1.7.1.4. Theological Themes

Theological interpreters use Hosea to bring out the concept of the personality of God and the nature of the divine-human relationship. Hosea's central theological proclamation is the personal and enduring love of Yahweh, shown through Yahweh's deep affection for Israel and willingness to accept the pain of unfaithful people in order to save them. Stuart gives more attention to the Hebrew text by analysing a combination of both the prophetic composition and the characters.[106] He writes that Hosea's good news is that the eschatological Israel would again benefit as Israel was in the original Sinai covenant cf. Leviticus 26:45, including "ownership" by Yahweh *("I will be their God").* Djik-Hemmes looks at Hosea from a feminist perspective. For her, the book of Hosea is a distorted fragment of Gomer's love - poetic love songs were analogous to women's parts in Song of Songs.[107] Francis Landy also looks at the book from a feminist viewpoint and writes a commentary from the perspective of sexual harassment.[108] He studies the book to show how the Old Testament is relevant to contemporary situations in terms of the socio-political context of the prophet. He interprets the book from a viewpoint of liberation theology.

The articles written by E. Baumann,[109] W. Reiss,[110] and J.L. McKenzie[111] concentrate more on the concept of "knowledge of God," which is very significant for the theology of Hosea. For this, these scholars have selected the word ידע to bring out the nuances in relation to Yahweh and the people.

D. Hubbard's[112] commentary deals with the historical, cultural and theological dimensions of the book to reveal the significance of God's love for the people through the story of the adulterous woman who betrayed her husband as he seeks to restore the intimacy. Hubbard, with a limited textual commentary, focuses more on the Christological significance of God's love.

A social analysis was done by Premnath on eighth century prophets through his method of systemic analysis.[113] Victor H. Matthews, in his *Social World of the Hebrew Prophets,* examines the prophets chronologically, placing them and their messages in the historical context and explores the pertinent aspects of historical geography, economic conditions, and social forces that influenced a prophet's life and message and explains why the prophets served as an integral part and purpose in the

---

[106] Stuart, D, *Hosea-Jonah,* Waco, TX: Word, 1987.

[107] Evan Dijk-Hemmes, "The Imagination of Power and the Power of Imagination: An Intertextual Analysis of Two Biblical Love Songs," *JSOT* 44, 1989, 75-88.

[108] Francis Landy, *Hosea,* Sheffield, Sheffield Press, 1995.

[109] E. Baụmann, ידע und seine Derivative," *ZAW* 28, 1908, 22-41.

[110] W. Reiss, "Gotttnicht Kennen' im Alten Testament," *ZAW* 58, 1941, 7-98.

[111] J.L. McKenzie, "Knowledge of God in Hosea," *JBL* 74, 1955, 22-27.

[112] Hubbard, D.A., *Hosea: An Introduction and Commentary,* Tyndale OT Commentaries, Leicester, Inter Varsity Press, 1989.

[113] Premnath, D. N, *Eighth Century Prophets: A Social Analysis,* St. Louis, Chalice Press, 2003.

development of the ancient Israelite religion.[114] He also explores how the prophets addressed their audience and how they employed rhetorical methods, images, and metaphors to communicate effectively.

This research puts forward the argument that these authors, although they draw out interesting and challenging themes, overlook the essential elements of Hosea the three human love situations which God uses to parallel His covenantal love for Israel. The research examines these situations closely in chapters 2:14-3:5, 11:1-11 and 14:2-9, and analyses how God's love is portrayed through the three groups of metaphors and its inter-linkages with the concept of restoration and reconciliation.

1.7.1.5. Methodologies Used by other Authors

Apart from the above, there have been several other researches into the book of Hosea from different angles, using different methodologies.

H.W. Wolff is convinced that what is offered in Hosea "is indeed a new covenant." The author also discusses the nature of the covenant relationship between Yahweh and Israel as shown through the metaphors in Hosea 2:19-23, using the methodology of form criticism.[115]

Laurie Braaten has studied parent-child imagery in Hosea from an anthropological perspective, leaving out sociology.[116] Socio-rhetorical research into the book of Hosea is available except for the work of D. N. Premnath which is based on the social-science method.[117] Chubamongba Ao, in recent socio-rhetorical thesis deals with 'the work of your hands' and is unique and widely used in the book of Deuteronomy. The 'work of your hand' is an intentional usage to bring out the theology of work in Deuteronomy and the scribes advocate for the interest of the people at the margin. Following on from that this study argues that God is the center of life and obedience to the covenantal law is the scale to measure the quality of one's work. It concludes by bringing this implication into the Indian context involving *Tribal/Dalits/Adivasis,* and women.

The author continues to demonstrate that the recurrent phrase 'in all the work of your hands' in Deuteronomy is a rhetorical topos - a rhetorical topic of argument. Its primary rhetorical purpose is to persuade the audience to express a right attitude of work. The topos 'work of hands' is derived from a concoction of three Hebrew phrases: בכל מעשׂה ידך ('in all the work of your hands'); בכל משלח ידך ('in everything you put your hand'); and פעל ידיו ('work of his hands'). The repetition is too frequent to be accidental; therefore, the research regards the communicative end of this repetition as corresponding to the high rhetorical nature of the book and considers how it fits into the rhetorical purpose of the book. The concept of blessing occurs consistently in the discourse where the topos appears; therefore the study examines the relationship between blessing and the work of hands. Major theological themes

---

[114] Victor H. Matthews, *The Hebrew Prophets and Their Social World,* Grand Rapids, Baker Academic, 2012.

[115] Gary W. Light, *The New Covenant in the book of Hosea,* Review Expositor, 90:2, Spring, 1993, 220

[116] Laurie Braaten, *Parent and Child Imagery in Hosea,* Boston University, 1987, 73.

[117] D.N. Premnath, *Eighth Century Prophets: A Social Analysis.* St Louis, Chalice, 2003.

such as law, obedience, worship and social care appear prominently and it is necessary to ascertain how work of hands is associated with such themes in the book.

Though there are several methods are applied to the book, this research applies socio-rhetorical interpretation and demonstrates the function of the phrase in various facets or textures of the text: inner texture, social and cultural texture, inter-texture, ideological texture and theological texture. Socio-rhetorical interpretation considers the text as a fabric or a tapestry made out of different textures and therefore it uses various readings such as literary, rhetorical, historical, sociological, anthropological, ideological and theological interpretations. Very few attempts have been made however, to analyse the book of Hosea from the socio-rhetorical point of view. So there is a need for more research in this area. The biblical texts originated in a variety of contexts and have various forms, themes and objectives. The study explains the metaphorical usage of ministry the relationship between husband and wife, father and son, and physician and patient. This concept of love, prophesied by Hosea, is interpreted as a concept for use in ministry.

For this study, the researcher uses a thorough exegesis of the text in order to bring out the theological significance of love. Most scholars understand love in the book of Hosea as a consequence of God's love based on the divine-human covenantal relationship. In these works, the aspect of God's love is brought out in a subtle but obscure manner. The book insists more on God's love for people (Hosea 3:1) and emphasises the call 'to share the love of God and be truthful to that love' Hosea 11:1. The message of the book sets out reconciliation between the sinful people of Israel and God, thus reflecting and executing love in action (Hosea 14:1.) Thus, the predominant concept that revolves around the theme of the book is 'love.' Hosea's mission is to bring Israel back to God so that they will be model to other nations. This implication paves the way for others to research on the book from a missional aspect.

The following chapters examine the love imagery in the text to demonstrate how Hosea defines God's love for his people and how Hosea regards the covenant establishing that relationship. This is an aspect of the book of Hosea which has never been studied in depth before the parallels between the attitude of God, family relationships and the Yahweh/Israelite covenant. By examining this in depth it is possible to ascertain the basis on which God's love is founded not an emotional basis but a covenantal one. It is clear the covenant has been broken, but God appears to be willing to use Hosea to try to bring the Israelites back into a renewed relationship.

The Chapter details are: this first chapter has discussed the statement of the problem, its elaboration and importance, definition of the terms, methodology adopted for this research study, details of other methodologies that have been employed, a brief survey of socio-rhetorical criticism and a review of previous literature to place the research in its wider context. In the second chapter, the methodology to be used social scientific analysis, rhetorical analysis, and socio-rhetorical approach is set out in detail.

In chapters three, four, and five, the primary focus is on study of selected texts. The exegesis work is based on the historical-sociological contexts of Hosea. Exegesis of selected passages are analysed in detail under the following topics; exploration, demarcation, establishment and analysis of the text; the inner texture and sub-texture of inner texture; the repetitive, progressive, narrative, sensory-aesthetic, argumentative, and opening-middle-closing textures, and inter-textuality; the literary, social and cultural textures; ideological, theological textures, and a summary of the section.

In chapter six, the concept of covenant is examined: what it is, the different covenants referred to in the book, the terms associated with it, its importance and uniqueness. For this, there are various terms used to convey the meaning and imageries that are employed to bring out the meaning of love in the book.

Chapter seven deals with the present Indian context, how this imagery of love would be applied. It also contains the conclusions drawn from the study.

Conclusion

The dominant theme of the book of Hosea is God's steadfast love even in the face of Israel's rejection. Imagery through the use of metaphors plays a significant role in expressing the concept of love as it is described throughout the book. This study concentrates on describing God's love towards Israel through Hosea's use of three particular human relationships, namely marital, parental and healing imagery. The focus of the study is to examine the use of these images in depicting the covenantal relationship between God and Israel, the rhetorical devices employed, and their intertextual relationships. This is designed to bring out the many layered meanings implicit within the text to show the steadfastness of God's covenantal love, despite Israel's rejection of it. This chapter deals with the definition of the term "love" and the many meanings the term can take.

It is clear from the literature review that researchers in the past have concentrated on the relationship between God and Israel, their covenantal relationship and the consequences of Israel breaking the covenant. However, the grammatical and literary devices with which Yahweh conveys his love for Israel in the book have been overlooked. Yahweh portrays himself as a husband, father, and a physician. The love which he expresses through these terms can be argued to be Yahweh's attempt to express love in familiar human terms so as to help Israel understand His love for them. An examination of these terms brings out Hosea's usage of the love imagery in metaphors which are designed to help Israel understand the depths of Yahweh's love for her and also act as a parallel for the covenantal relationship between God and Israel. The imagery also provides strong theological impetus within the text. This has not been previously explored in depth but following chapters deal with it.

The next chapter deals with the detailed exploration of the methodology socio-rhetorical analysis and its implications for the exegetical study of the selected passages. It examines the various elements of the selected methodology and shows how they are used to define and interpret the passages.

Chapter 2

A Detailed Introduction to the Methodology

Introduction

This chapter deals with the methodology used to examine the way in which Hosea conveys Yahweh's message, with particular emphasis on the interpretation of the three love themes. The book combines oral and written imagery to convey Yahweh's message and takes place against specific cultural, historical, and ideological backgrounds. These complex correlations between the text and its contexts need to be examined using a socio-rhetorical analysis. This analysis is the combination of two methods wherein both sociological and rhetorical analyses are combined into one critical method. This chapter delineates how the socio-rhetorical interpretation introduces major components of this methodology and why it is an effective tool in interpreting the text. Firstly, the sociological analysis will be discussed, secondly, the rhetorical analysis, and thirdly, how the socio-rhetorical approach has been combined into one critical method. Sociology and rhetorical studies will be examined to help to understand the way in which Hosea conveys Yahweh's message, with particular emphasis on the interpretation of the three love themes. The socio-rhetorical interpretation and methodology contains five textures: the inner texture (getting inside the text), the theological texture (seeking the divine in the text), the inter-texture (entering the interactive world of the text), the social and cultural texture (living with the text in the world), and the ideological texture (sharing interest in commentary and text). This study seeks to employ the inner texture of socio-rhetorical analysis from among the available five textures to study the words, forms and textual complexities in Hosea.

2.1. Sociological Analysis

The term "sociological analysis" is often used interchangeably with socio-scientific criticism within the context of biblical analysis and it focuses on the social environment of the text in question. Within its scope, it covers the following areas: Firstly, the practice of social-scientific criticism of the Bible. This employs methods, data, and theories from the social sciences (anthropology, economics, political science, and sociology) to clarify the relationship between biblical literature and ancient society.

Secondly, the study of the social organization of ancient Israel, in its larger or smaller units, either at a given moment in the cross-section (synchronic) or over the course of time, which may expand into a full-scale social history (diachronic). Thirdly, the identification of patterns of social life within the Bible is to determine if it is prescriptive or exemplary in some way for contemporary religious or secular life.[118]

As the current study looks at the social system from the social and cultural dimensions of the text and its environmental context through the utilization of these perspectives, the theory, models, and research of the social sciences are discussed in terms of socio-scientific criticism.[119] As mentioned earlier, these two terms "sociological" and "socio-scientific" are used interchangeably in this study.

Social-scientific criticism investigates biblical texts as meaningful configurations of language intended to communicate between the author and the audience or readers. In this process, social-scientific criticism firstly highlights the social aspects of the form and the content of the texts. Secondly, it looks into the correlation of the text's linguistic, literary, theological, and social dimensions. And thirdly, it sees the textual communication as a reflection of and a response to a specific social and cultural context.

Social-scientific criticism is thus concerned not only with the original meanings of the biblical documents but also with the aggregations of the meanings down through the centuries. It asks how and under what conditions the Bible continues to be relevant to modern times. According to N. K. Gottwald, the guiding question of the social-scientific approach is: "how social structures and social processes are explicit or implicit in the biblical literature, in the scattered socio-economic data it contains, in the political history it recounts and in the religious belief and practices it attests?"[120]

The sociological method was first adopted by George E. Mendenhall and then further developed by Norman K. Gottwald.[121] Conroy was one of the early proponents of this sociological methodology for Biblical studies. He reflects on the exegetical task and adopts this method to view the exegetical task in a comprehensive way. This would be approached through two phases of work: the first phase is a description and interpretation of the text as it stands; the second phase is a study of the process by which the material reached this final form. That is, the study starts with what is most accessible and examines that as thoroughly as possible, then moves to other parts that are accessible.[122]

---

[118] N.K. Gottwald, "Sociology of the Old Testament," *Anchor Bible Dictionary,* New York, Doubleday, 1992.

[119] John H. Elliot, *What is Social-Scientific Criticism,* Minneapolis, Augsburg, 1993, 7.

[120] N.K. Gottwald, *The Hebrew Bible, A Socio-Literary Introduction,* Philadelphia, Fortress Press, 1985, 607.

[121] G. E. Mendenhall, "Covenant," *The Interpreters' Dictionary of the Bible* Vol.1, edited by George Arthur Buttrick, Nashville, Abingdon Press, 1962; Norman K. Gottwald, *The Hebrew Bible: A Socio-Literary Reading,* Philadelphia, Fortress Press, 1985.

[122] C. Conroy, *"Reflections on the Exegetical Task:* Apropos of Recent Studies on 2Kings 22-23" in C. Brekelmans and J. Lust (eds.), Pentateuchal and Deuteronomistic Studies. Papers read at the XIIIth IOSOT Congress Leuven 1989, *BETL* 94; Leuven: Leuven University Press, 1990, 258.

Mendenhall (1962) presents a sociological approach through the peasant revolt model for understanding Israel's establishment.[123] He reconstructs the history of Israel's establishment in Palestine within an economic, sociological, and political framework and tries to step away from the more scientific historical approach. Mendenhall's contribution to sociological reading is the assertion that "religion" (i.e., ethical values) shapes society. Secondly, Mendenhall tends to contrast his "religious ethics" nexus with a "political power" nexus, thereby drawing a sharp distinction between ethical values (religion) and social control interests.[124] For N.K. Gottwald, sociological study aims to grasp the typical pattern of human relations in their structure and function, both at a given moment or stage (synchronic) and their trajectories of change over specified time spans (diachronic). The sociological method further includes all methods of inquiry proper to social sciences (e.g., anthropology, sociology, political science, and economics).[125] Derek Tidball argues that "sociology is certainly an attempt to understand society and societal relations within the society in a disciplined way."[126] Therefore, adopting a sociological method to study biblical texts is an attempt to explain group "behaviour, societal structure, functions and social processes of the biblical communities." In general, the sociological approach broadens the exegetical enterprise and brings to it many positive aspects.[127] For Herbert F. Hahn, the sociological approach is the study of religion, social origin, and its relation to the group rather than to the individual.[128]

Historical-critical methods have given us a fresh understanding of the Bible in its proper context. However, the tools of analysis used in these methods have failed to take into consideration the social aspects of the texts. This gap is filled by the introduction of the sociological analysis, which complements the values of historical and literary methods of biblical criticism. In this context, Gottwald has noted that the Hebrew Bible gives us theological reflections embedded in historically changing social situations which are articulated in concrete literary genre, besides presenting a consistent religious idea. No message of the Hebrew Bible can thus be lifted out of its social context and literary forms without altering its meaning.[129]

The social sciences play an important role in the study of Hebrew literature in the work of Herman Gunkel too, whose form of critical approach was influenced by 19th century folk studies. Gunkel argues that every literary genre in the Old Testament had an original setting in Israel's national life. The Hebrew literature therefore has to be studied in isolation, restricted to a specific social matrix. Sigmund Mowinckel

---

[123] Danna Nolan Fewell, (ed), *The Oxford Handbook of Biblical Narrative,* Oxford University Press, Oxford, 2016, 519. G. E. Mendenhall, "Covenant," *The Interpreters' Dictionary of the Bible* Vol.1, edited by George Arthur Buttrick, Nashville, Abingdon Press, 1962.

[124] Gary E. Herion, "The Impact of Modern and Social Science Assumptions on the reconstruction of Israelite History" in *JSOT* 34, 1984.

[125] Norman K. Gottwald "Sociological Method in the Study of Ancient Israel," in *The Bible and Liberation: Political and Social Hermeneutic,* Maryknoll, Orbis Books, 1993, 27.

[126] D. Tidball, *An Introduction to the Sociology of the New Testament,* Exeter, The Paternoster Press, 1983, 12.

[127] Lalfazuala, *Human Rights in Deuteronomy: A Sociological Approach,* Delhi: ISPCK, 2004, xviii.

[128] H. F. Hahn, *Old Testament in Modern Research,* Philadelphia, Muhlenberg Press, 1954, 158.

[129] N.K. Gottwald., *The Hebrew Bible: A Socio-Literary Introduction*, Philadelphia, Fortress Press, 1985, 607.

developed Gunkel's findings and stressed the importance of an oral tradition in the formation of Hebrew literature. Modern practitioners of the sociological approach have balanced social theory with a thorough examination of the textual evidence to arrive at a comprehensive understanding and interpretation of the text in question. Following this approach, Abraham Malamat, Paul Hanson,[130] Mannheim[131] and Troeltsch[132] amplified the picture of the social-religious conflicts that led to the emergence of the Israelite apocalypse.

Social-scientific criticism finds its place under the umbrella of a new literary criticism. The text is given importance, and the meaning of the text is derived from the social structures existing at the time of writing and then applied to the social structure of the reader. A new meaning evolves as the text is interpreted by studying the social structures. There are several works by various scholars who use this method: Philips R. Davies sees the approach as "giving the most promise for advances in the study of the Hebrew Bible." This approach examines not only the literature and social setting of "Israel" but also "the social forces underlying the production of literature." As Davies puts it, one must distinguish between the "society *behind* the text and the society *within* the text."

Lately, the social context of various books of the Old Testament is being studied, though not in detail. Recently, in his work *Prophecy and Society in Ancient Israel,* Robert R. Wilson examines the prophetic movement associated with Israel and suggests that the anthropological theory of "intermediaries" has a close resemblance to biblical "prophecy."[133] Wilson used anthropological studies to show that prophets are intermediaries between the human and the divine and his main thesis is that, "intermediaries do not operate in a vacuum. They are integral parts of their societies and cannot exist without social guidance and support." He further says that any prophet of Israel is a product of the society, so he should not be approached as an individual sharing the conviction he expresses.

Thomas Overholt and Burke Long compare the Israelite prophetic movement with ethnographic parallels, especially with that of Native American *shamanism.*[134] They suggest that, as with the shaman, the prophetic authority does not reside in the word uttered alone but in the society to which the prophet belongs. To them, prophecy is not just a message from God alone but is shaped by the community to whom the prophet speaks.

This study approaches the text socio-rhetorically. Therefore, since the biblical texts originated in a variety of contexts and have various forms, themes and objectives, an exegetical analysis of the selected texts is necessary to determine their meaning and importance. The three passages selected for the exegetical study are Hosea 2:16-3:5;

---

[130] Paul D. Hanson, *Isaiah 40-60, Interpretation A Bible Commentary for Teaching and Preaching,* Louisville, Westminster: John Knox Press, 1995.

[131] Karl Mannheim has done extensive study on social-scientific theory using sociological theory.

[132] Ernst Troeltsch has focused on the relation to apocalyptic and division of the postexilic society, *Semia,* 21.

[133] Robert R. Wilson, *Prophecy and Society in Ancient Israel,* Philadelphia, Fortress Press, 1980.

[134] Thomas Overholt, "Prophecy: The Problem of Cross-Cultural Comparison" *Semia* 21, 1982, 55-78. Burke O. Long, "Prophetic Authority as Social reality" in *Canon and Authority,* ed. G.W. Coats and B.O. Long, Philadelphia, Fortress Press, 1977, 3-20.

11:1-11; and 14:2-9. The study explains the metaphorical usage of ministry the relationship between husband and wife, father and son, and physician and patient.[135] This concept of love, prophesied by Hosea, is interpreted as a concept for use in ministry. Very few attempts have been made however, to analyse Hosea from the socio-rhetorical point of view. So there is a need for more research in this area.

2.2. Rhetorical Analysis

Rhetorical analysis is important because it is one of several tools used in interpreting the Bible. But, in its wider sense, the term "rhetoric" has a diversified role and meaning in literature. The word "rhetoric" means the art of using words impressively or impressive language. Lloyd Bitzer defines rhetorical criticism as an interaction between the persons and their circumstances.[136] Rhetoric is considered to be an art of persuasion.

The use of the term "rhetoric" is significant in writing as well as in oral materials. Rhetoric is not so concerned with what a text communicates as much as how effectively it communicates. In other words, rhetorical analysis realizes the power of language - the language that constructs, for example, a new sociology. Majercik defines "rhetoric as here the art of composition by which a language is made more descriptive, interpretive or persuasive." He adds that it is also associated with "the art of effective public speaking."[137]

Rhetorical analysis stresses how the author or speaker affects the reader or hearer. It is not concerned with beauty but with effect and the persuasive nature of words. The key term suggested here is "audience," the reader or hearer. Rhetorical criticism focuses on the audience. It stresses the effect on the audience more and *"sitz-im-laben* less." The persuasive nature (effect) of rhetoric is traditionally not confined to the words or the idea or to the combination of the two; but it relies on the union with the character of the orator and the emotions of his/her audience.[138]

According to Richard N. Soulen, rhetorical criticism is a term adopted in 1968 by the late Old Testament scholar Muilenberg to denote a methodological approach to Scripture designed to supplement form criticism.[139] Today, the main focus of rhetoric is on describing how the text can be used to persuade and be effective in the present day context. The focus here is not so much on the relationship between ancient authors and ancient audiences, but rather on the relationship between the text and its present day interpreters and audiences. Phyllis Trible defines the goals of rhetoric as: the emotional goal of appealing to emotions and the aesthetic goal of pleasing so as to hold attention.[140]

---

[135] Kyung Hee Park, *Divine Love in Hosea 11,* Southern Baptist Theological Seminary 2004, and Bernhard Oestreich, *Metaphors and Similes for Yahweh in Hosea 14:2-9 (1-8): A Study of Hoseanic Pictorial Language,* Friedensauer Schriftenreihe, Reihe A, Theologie, Frankfurt, Peter Lang, 1998.

[136] Quoted from Brad E. Kelle, *Rhetoric;* L. Bitzer, "Functional Communication: A Situational Perspective," in *Rhetoric in Transition: Studies in the Nature and Views of Rhetoric,* ed. E. White, University Park, Penn State University Press, 1980, 21-38.

[137] Ruth Majercik, "Rhetorical Criticism," in *Anchor Bible Dictionary* 5: ed., D.N. Freedman, New York, Doubleday, 1992, 710.

[138] G.F. Drury, "Rhetoric," *New Catholic Encyclopaedia,* vol. xii, ed. McGraw, 458.

[139] Richard N. Soulen, *Hand Book of Biblical Criticism,* London, Lutterworth Press, 1977, 145.

[140] Phyllis. T, *Rhetorical Criticism: Context, Method and the Book of Jonah,* Minneapolis, Fortress Press, 1994, 27.

This method thus facilitates one's understanding of how one should generally treat the text, rather than dissecting it into numerous hypothetical sources and interpolations. Its focus is on the text, not on the history of Israelite religious beliefs, or the use of literary genres, nor on the redaction of history. Rather, it continually points to the text to ask what it says and how it goes about saying it. It also considers what it is trying to do and how it attempts to do it. It evaluates the text as it is without any bias towards any value system prevailing in society.

2.3. Socio-Rhetorical Approach

One of the greatest contributions of socio-rhetorical criticism is that literary, social-scientific, rhetorical, postmodern and theological criticisms together form an integrated approach to interpretation.[141] This approach allows the exploration of issues concerning language, text, society, culture, ideology, and theology.

This method is both new and old. According to de Silva, this method deals with exegesis. It helps to reveal the meaning of the text within the social systems out of which the text and the interpreter come.[142]

The work of D.N. Premnath (2003) is based on the social-science method.[143] In recent socio-rhetorical work Chuba (2017) deals with the phrase 'the work of your hands' is unique and widely used in the book of Deuteronomy. The 'work of your hand' is an intentional usage to bring out the theology of work in Deuteronomy and the scribes advocate for the interest of the people at the margin. This research demonstrates that the recurrent phrase 'in all the work of your hands' in Deuteronomy is a rhetorical topos - a rhetorical topic of argument. Its primary rhetorical purpose is to persuade the audience to express a right attitude of work. The topos 'work of hands' is derived from a concoction of three Hebrew phrases: בכל מעשׂה ידך ('in all the work of your hands'); בכל משלח ידך ('in everything you put your hand'); and פעל ידיו ('work of his hands'). This research applies socio-rhetorical interpretation and demonstrates the function of the phrase in various facets or textures of the text: inner texture, social and cultural texture, intertexture, ideological texture and theological texture. Socio-rhetorical interpretation considers the text as a fabric or a tapestry made out of different textures and therefore it uses various readings such as literary, rhetorical, historical, sociological, anthropological, ideological and theological interpretations.[144]

Not much socio-rhetorical research is available on the book of Hosea. In an effort to understand the texts of Hosea chapters 2, 3, 11, and 14, this study adopts a methodology that has not formerly been applied to the book of Hosea. Socio-rhetorical analysis however, is a relatively new paradigm applied mainly to

[141] Robbins, *Exploring the Texture of Texts: A Guide to Socio-Rhetorical Interpretation,* Valley Forge, Trinity Press International, 1996, 1-2.

[142] Duane F. Watson, "Why we need Socio Rhetorical commentary and what it might look like?," *Rhetorical Criticism and the Bible,* Stanley E. Porter and Dennis L. Stamps, *JSNTSup* 195, Sheffield, Academic Press, 2002, 140.

[143] D.N. Premnath, *Eighth Century Prophets: A Social Analysis,* St Louis, Chalice, 2003.

[144] Chubamongba Ao, *'In all the Work of Your Hands' in Deuteronomy: An Inquiry on Rhetoric of Work,* D.Th Dissertation, SATHRI/UBS, Pune, 2017.

New Testament studies. The advantages of this approach can be observed in the works of Ben Witherington III and Kayle de Waal.[145]

V.K. Robbins, on the other hand, has proposed "a socio-rhetorical analysis in studying the New Testament." While rhetorical interpretation deals with the style of the language in a text for communication, socio-rhetorical interpretation uses the presented thought and arguments for the integration of literary, rhetorical, postmodern, and theological criticism. In addition, social class and systems, personal and community status, people on the margins, and the people in power are all given serious attention.

The approach invites a detailed attention to the text itself. In addition, it moves into the world of the people who wrote the texts and into our present times. The socio-rhetorical interpretation and methodology contains five textures, as described by V.K. Robbins (1996) in his book *Exploring the Texture of Texts: A Guide to socio-rhetorical interpretation:* the inner texture (getting inside the text), the sacred or theological texture (seeking the divine in the text), the inter-texture (entering the interactive world of the text), the social and cultural texture (living with the text in the world), and the ideological texture (sharing interest in commentary and text).[146] These five textures that Robbins proposed are further discussed in the following sections.

Though there are various images in Hosea, it is the images used in the three selected passages which are of primary importance in defining the Yahweh-Israel relationship. The socio-rhetorical reading of the metaphors in Hosea has merged recently. The methodology deals with metaphors in the time of Hosea, social, political, economic and religious relationships. There are various methodological perspectives available to study Hosea 1-3. This kind of study combines metaphorical study with feminist, anthropological, materialist and rhetorical perspectives.

2.4. Methodology of Inner Texture

Inner texture explores the multiple textures within a text. The main purpose of the inner texture is to focus on words as a communication tool, a technique that seeks to determine first of all the "meaning" of the words and then the "real interpretation of the text." It refers to the way in which a language or text communicates between people. This technique enables the researcher to acquire "an intimate knowledge of words, word patterns, voices, structure, devices and modes in the text," which complements and supplements other understanding of the text. Inner texture is getting "inside a text" for purposes of interpretation. Historically this texture has been called "exegesis."[147]

Robbins promotes his own unique set of six ways to explore the inner texture in a text: "(a) repetitive (b) progressive (c) narration (d) opening-middle-closing

---

[145] David A. DeSilva, *Perseverance in Gratitude: A Socio-Rhetorical Commentary on the Epistle "To the Hebrews"* Grand Rapids, Eerdmans, 2009. Vernon K. Robbins, *Jesus the Teacher: A Socio-Rhetorical Interpretation of Mark,* Minneapolis, Fortress Press, 2009.

[146] V.K., Robbins, *Exploring the Texture of Texts: A Guide to Socio-Rhetorical Interpretation,* Valley Forge, Trinity Press International, 1996, 3.

[147] V.K., *Robbins, The Tapestry of Christian Discourse: Rhetoric, Society and Ideology,* London, Routledge, 1996, 30.

(e) argumentative and (f) sensory-aesthetic texture." He recommends that the researcher choose two or three of these strategies of analysis and apply them to interpret a particular passage.

2.4.1. Repetitive

This texture identifies any word that occurs at least twice in a text. Also, multiple occurrences of different types of grammatical, syntactical, verbal, or subjective phenomena emphasise a recurring text.

2.4.2. Progressive

This is a sequence of words and phrases alternating with one another but capable of being arranged in a systematic diagram. Progressive textuality emerges out of the repetition of words and phrases in the text unit. It identifies the sequence of words and phrases throughout the text. It helps the researcher identify the progress of forward movement and a sequence of sub-units in the texts that function as stepping stones to the rest of the other characteristics of the text.

2.4.3. Narration

Narration is the speaking voices or the words of the characters in the text. Narration can be established by identifying direct speech. Robbins explains that the narrative texture shows a "pattern that moves the discourse programmatically forward." The opening word in the text automatically assumes a narrator is speaking the words.

2.4.4. Opening-Middle-Closing

The opening-middle-closing of a pericope is usually created by repetition, progression, and narration. Opening-middle-closing texture is applied at the beginning, in the body and at the conclusion of a section of discourse. It analyses what is complex in the exegesis and helps refine and improve the analysis.

2.4.5. Argumentative

Argumentative texture throws light on and examines many kinds of internal reasoning, either logical or illogical. It looks at the presence of opposites, contraries, counter arguments and the quality of images that portray truth and reality in the minds of listeners or readers in a persuasive manner. It investigates various types of internal arguments in the discourse. The main argumentative device here is the citation of ancient written testimony.

2.4.6. Sensory-Aesthetic

Sensory-aesthetic texture in a text can be identified by grouping the references to bodily senses and actions, such as thought, action, feeling, sight, sound, touch and smell. Such sensory-aesthetic texture helps us discover reasoning, imagination, and humour within the text. Here the interaction is mostly in metaphorical language.

2.4.7. "Textures" of Socio-Rhetorical Interpretation

In order to understand the imagery of love in Hosea socio-rhetorically, the text is analysed using the different textures described under "inner texture." This provides an understanding of its intended meaning. The use of multiple textures is to bring out the modes and the functions of the people who lived within the context. As mentioned earlier, this study employs a section by section analysis rather than a verse by verse analysis.

While socio-rhetorical interpretation has been applied predominately to New Testament passages because of its use of first century rhetorical categories, it can still be successfully applied to Old Testament books, via the textures which Robbins has described. The methodology also examines the structural features which help the scholar determine the main themes and ideas of passages.

2.5. Theological Texture

As a result of integrating the six layers of the inner texture, the theological texture can then be clarified. Sacred texture brings out the deeper meaning and the role of divinity in the text. It deals with how the text brings out the divine, religious life, and the relationship between man and the divine.[148] Robbins suggests that human ethics are motivated by one's commitment to the divine when perceived in the context of religious commitment.

Biblical scholars generally have not given consideration to socio-rhetorical interpretation in Hosea. The research related to the phrases, words, the wider cultural background of the times and the particular life situation of the prophet and his community are found in the interpretations of chapters 2-3, 11 and 14. This work brings out the theology related to the imagery of love. This is the main goal of this work.

The theological texture is also called sacral textuality. This exists in texts relating to the divine-human relationship.[149] In Biblical texts, sacred textuality can be seen in passages that deal with any communication concerning the gods, holy persons, spirit beings, divine history, human redemption, human commitment, religious community, and ethics.

2.6. Inter-texture

Inter-textuality talks about the relationships between the texts and external/other texts. According to Robbins, inter-textuality is more about entering into the interactive world of the text.[150] In inter-textuality, the text is integrated and contains complex patterns and images. For Venter, the text is a meeting place of different texts.[151] This texture uses oral or written literature for comparing the text and becomes the foundation of the predecessor texts.[152]

The aim of intertexture is to begin with the context of the text itself. This concept helps to identify literary references or inspirations. Inter texture deals with the experiences of the prophet and communicates his ideas with/to his audience/s in

---

148 Watson, *"Why we need Socio Rhetorical commentary and what it might look like?"*..., 149.

149 Watson, *"Why we need Socio Rhetorical commentary and what it might look like?"*..., 149.

150 V.K., Robbins, *Exploring the Texture of Texts: A Guide to Socio-Rhetorical Interpretation,* Valley Forge, Trinity Press International, 1996, 40, 70.

151 Venter, 1997, 328-329.

152 Wesley Hiram Wachob, *The Voice of Jesus in the Social Rhetoric of James,* Society for New Testament Studies, vol. 106, Cambridge, Cambridge University Press, 2000, 114.

a simple way. In intertexture, the text can be a "practiced, re-contextualization, form, shape or elaboration" of other textures, their meaning and their themes.[153]

2.7. Social and Cultural Texture

Social and cultural textuality looks at the social and cultural elements of the text. It refers to the ability of the text to bring about social reform, bring about support or the withdrawal of opposition and change cultural perceptions of domination, subordination, indifference or exclusion, and retaliation.

2.8. Ideological Texture

The ideological texture deals with an integrated system within the belief system. The text brings out the ideas of the author and helps the readers to achieve a certain goal. John H. Elliot asserts that "an ideology is an integrated system of beliefs, assumptions and values, not necessarily true or false."[154] The ideological texture looks at the system of beliefs, assumptions and values that reflect the particular needs and interests of a group of people at a particular period in history.[155] One of the major concerns regarding the ideological texture is that of power within the society and how that society influences people's response to the power structure.[156] Ideological texture differs from social and cultural texture, as the latter refer to the behaviour, location, and progress of a certain group of people; whereas the ideological texture deals with the individual places ideologically of both the writers of the text and the readers of the text. Ideological texture analyses the power relationships in a particular text for study as well as the elements which are emphasised or ignored in interpreting the text.

Ideological texture helps to identify modes of intellectual discourse in Hosea. Here, the ideological texture helps bring out the idea of love that is portrayed through metaphors. Ideological texture helps to identify the goal of the author and also helps to consider how his own agenda may have influenced his interpretation.[157]

2.9. The Challenge of the Socio-Rhetorical Approach

The socio-rhetorical approach therefore poses a challenge to exegesis of a text and examination in a systematic and comprehensive way. Underlying the method is the assumption that words work in complex ways to convey meanings and those we only understand them partially. Therefore, the socio-rhetorical interpretation helps in finding meanings and how they relate to other meanings. Discourse analysis and social science models are used within the inner texture area of research.

---

[153] Robbins, *Exploring the Texture of Texts: A Guide to Socio-Rhetorical Interpretation,* Valley Forge, Trinity Press International, 1996, 52.

[154] John H. Elliot, *A Home for the Homeless: A Sociological Exegesis of 1Peter, Its Situation and Strategy,* Philadelphia, Fortress Press, 1981, 268.

[155] Robbins, *The Tapestry of Christian Discourse: Rhetoric, Society and Ideology,* London, Routledge, 1996, 192-193.

[156] De Waal, *A Socio-Rhetorical Interpretation of the Seven Trumpets of Revelation,* Lewiston, Edwin Mellen Press, 2012, 52-53.

[157] DeSilva, *An Introduction to the New Testament: Contexts Methods and Ministry Formation,* Illinois, Inter Varsity Press, 2004, 24-25.

This combination of methods has been adopted as being more fruitful than the traditional approaches to the text.

This shifts the focus to divine history that shows how the divine powers have been placed in the history of the world to achieve a particular outcome. In this section, the study discusses what the text is saying and how to relate it to the theological ideas. This helps to understand the author's theological purpose, the relationship between the people and the divine, and the theological theme of love embedded in the text.

Another focus of this study is the human commitment and its role in revealing the ways of God to other people. The category of ethics, which is concerned with how the people are committed to God and what their actions are, is also explored.[158]

This thesis investigates the pericopes of 2:16-3:5, 11:1-11 and 14:2-9, using the principles of socio-rhetorical criticism. These pericopes occur at the centre of a chiastic structure of Hosea that is identified in the exegesis.

For this study, the research explores the context of Hosea in the eighth century using a model of Vernon K. Robbins' approaches, which include the examination of the layers of the texture, using discourse analysis as part of the inner texture approach and social science models as part of the social cultural texture. Since it is an integrative method, it helps in the analysis of each texture separately, section by section rather than verse by verse. Hence the imagery of love is taken as a single section in this passage and is analysed for a particular purpose.

This socio-rhetorical approach to the book of Hosea represents a new contribution to the study of Hosea. Since socio-rhetorical analysis was introduced in 1996, only a limited number of scholars have used this approach in Old Testament studies. S. S. Ndoga and H Viviers[159] have written a book, *Is the woman in the Song of Songs really that free? - A Socio-Rhetorical Reading of Song of Songs 1:2-4,* and Mmapula Diana Kebaneilwe[160] wrote *This Courageous Woman: A Socio-rhetorical Womanist Reading of Proverbs 31:10-31.* Very few scholars have applied the socio-rhetorical method in their writings. According to Chuba, the rhetorical topos 'in all the work of your hands' in Deuteronomy is a rhetorical topic of argument which occurs more than 20 times with minor differences which have a human subject, that is the work of the Israelites. The author continues to investigate whether the phrase has coherency, emphasis, and rhetorical effect in achieving a persuasive end, as he felt the need of addressing the questions neglected by previous scholars such as: its literary, rhetorical, historical, socio-cultural, ideological, and theological context.

Inner texture in the whole book of Deuteronomy is used to identify the role of the topos 'work of your hands' in the discourses. The analysis of the social and the cultural in Deuteronomy permeates specific laws which motivate care for the people at the margin through one's work. This research concludes by bringing an implication for the Indian context: *Tribal, Dalits, Adivasis,* and women in India.[161]

---

[158] Robbins, *Exploring the Texture of Texts: A Guide to Socio-Rhetorical Interpretation,* ..., 131.

[159] S. S. Ndoga and H Viviers, Is the woman in the Song of Songs really that free? A Socio-Rhetorical Reading of Song of Songs 1:2-4, *HTS 56 (4),* 2000.

[160] Mmapula Diana Kebaneilwe, *This Courageous Woman: A Socio-rhetorical Womanist Reading of Proverbs 31:10-31,* 2012.

[161] Chubamongba Ao, *'In all the Work of Your Hands' in Deuteronomy: An Inquiry on Rhetoric of Work,* D.Th Dissertation, SATHRI/UBS, Pune, 2017.

Socio-rhetorical analysis enables the interpreter to approach the texts from an inner texture. The combined method (sociological and rhetorical criticism) is very useful in many ways. First, it helps to provide fresh ways of conceptualizing the relations among the social phenomena. This helps to understand the society better, its social organization and institutions. The comparative method leads one to understand ancient societies comprehensively. Second, the information sheds light on social function and its character. This is employed more in terms of existing data. Third, the literary and the fragment bring out the picture of the lost. The comparative approach aids in understanding the models for interpreting and reconstructing past cultures.[162] The result of the combined method gives orientation to systematic sociology to explore and reconstruct the socio-rhetorical dynamics of eighth century Israel and to interpret the text of selected passages from Hosea. The result of applying the socio-rhetorical approach is incorporated into the metaphorical perspective.

Conclusion

In this chapter, the study has defined socio-rhetorical analysis and why it has been selected as the method of examining the selected texts in Hosea. Socio-rhetorical analysis draws temporary boundaries around the text for the purpose of a close examination from one point of view, followed by the intentional integration of several approaches to exploring the text through inner texture, inter-texture, social-cultural texture, ideological texture and theological texture. Sociological analysis is used to show how the book is part of an intricate social and cultural environment which can be taken into consideration for a more holistic interpretation. Similarly, Rhetorical analysis would be helpful to ascertain how Hosea logically crafted his arguments. Applying the theories of sociology and rhetoric analysis in the study helps to bring out more ideas and theories for a better understanding of the text.

Hosea used the most basic of human emotions, represented by husband, father and physician to explain Yahweh's love for His wayward people. He did this out of the necessity to translate Yahweh's message into terms that Israel would easily understand. In the following chapters the three key chosen passages related to the imagery of love are studied using socio-rhetorical analysis. As shown in this chapter, this method is effective in establishing the imagery of love as a paradigm for covenantal relationship. The methodology is used to detail and highlight the meanings and implications in the three passages, starting in the next chapter with the husband/wife marital situation which is at the heart of Hosea, and which is used to demonstrate to Israel the depth of Yahweh's "steadfast love" which is the foundation of His entire effort to get Israel to return to Him.

---

[162] McNutt, Paula, *Reconstructing the Society of Ancient Israel*, Louisville, Westminster John Knox Press, 1999: 29, 30.

Chapter 3

Hosea 2:16-3:5: Love Between Husband and Wife as a Metaphor for Covenant Relationship Between God and Humans

Introduction

In the Bible, the most important theme is "Love" and is oft-repeated. The emphasis is always placed on Yahweh's love for Israel, directly through metaphors and similes. In Hosea the focus is on the covenantal relationship between Yahweh and Israel. It achieves this by dividing the book into three sections, each of which deals with a particular human love relationship which parallels the Yahweh and human love relationship. First, in chapters 1-3, Hosea uses the husband-wife marital relationship; second, in chapter 11, Yahweh is portrayed as a loving and caring parent dealing with a rebellious son. Third, in chapter 14, Yahweh is portrayed as a physician and Israel as a patient. Having established the appropriate methodology to be utilised in this research, it is now in order to move to a detailed examination of these three passages. This chapter will undertake an exegetical study of the first section (2:14-3:5), the husband-wife marital relationship and its parallel to the Yahweh-Israel relationship.

By applying the socio-rhetorical method to the texts, the study emphasises the manner in which Yahweh manifests his love for Israel and restores the relationship between Himself and his people. The socio-rhetorical analysis is employed to uncover the meaning of the text. To present the message of God's redemptive love, Hosea uses the marriage metaphor to describe the covenantal concept, made between Yahweh and Israel at Mount Sinai. In this chapter, the manner in which the marriage metaphor is presented and how it is linked with the covenant relationship will be studied to determine why marriage is a good symbol for the covenant relationship, and why Yahweh uses it to teach Israelites about His attitude to the covenant relationship? The context, the poetical structure that defines the text, and an exegesis of Hosea 2 and 3 are studied to better understand the marriage metaphor. Additionally, the socio-rhetorical study follows each unit of the text to bring out the imagery of love as a paradigm for covenantal relationship.

3.1. Marital relationship

The marital relationship is considered to be one of the strongest of the three love themes in Hosea. In Hosea 2 to 3, there is a picture of a wife whose marital unfaithfulness is mirrored in the prophet's personal experience and paralleled with the Yahweh-Israel relationship.[163] Mays states that Hosea is commanded to renew his relationship with Gomer, a "woman of harlotry," whom he had married in obedience to God's earlier command (Hosea 1:2); she had then abandoned him for a promiscuous lifestyle (Hosea 2:2-7).[164] De Silva says that Hosea 3 is probably one of the separate cycles of judgment and restoration in narrative form (2:2-23). This is best interpreted using the socio-rhetorical method discussed in chapter 2. Hosea chapters 1 to 3 are considered to be actual prophecies in the Old Testament.

From the earliest days of scholarship to the present diversity of critical approaches, the interpretation of Hosea has concentrated upon the marriage metaphor in Hosea 1-3 at the expense of serious engagement with other aspects of the book. Scholars are in general agreement concerning the twofold division of the book; chapters 1-3 and chapters 4-14. These two sections within the book culminate in the prophecies of salvation establishing commonality with the other prophetic books of the Old Testament. According to Ehud Ben Zvi, the themes in the book show that the actions of the prophet are symbolic. Moreover, he also highlights the legitimized ideologies concerning gender and the family roles to illustrate the sociological condition of Hosea with his wife and children through marital relations in parallel to the relation between Yahweh and Israel.[165] According to Matthews, for Hosea, obedience to the law is the key to a vital and vibrant fellowship, which could be the truthfulness demanded in a covenantal relationship.[166] For him, "knowledge of God" is more important than other themes that are found in the book.

3.1.1. Historical background to the book

Hosea's preaching is a strong attack against the Northern Kingdom because it had been unfaithful to its covenant relationship with the Lord, as demonstrated in its widespread corruption in moral life, both publicly and privately.[167] Thus, the message of Hosea is against a particular nation, and it is concerned with sacred matters. The general thought of Hosea's message is summed up briefly in a few propositions: (a) Israel is wicked through and through, and her moral fabric is rotten. (b) Israel is politically doomed, the last stages of decay having now been reached. (c) Yahweh is Israel's Father, with all of a father's love and interest; he is Israel's husband, with all of a husband's love and devotion. (d) Israel does not know Yahweh and fails to comprehend Him. (e) Israel deceives herself in her acts of repentance; it consists of

---

163 Samuel J. Schulz, *The Old Testament Speaks,* New York, Harper and Brothers Publishers, 1960, 389.

164 Mays, James Luther., *Hosea: A Commentary,* OTL, Philadelphia, Westminster, 1969, 58.

165 Ehud Ben Zvi, *Hosea:* FOTL, Vol. XXIA/1, Grand Rapids, Wm. B. Eerdmans Publishing Company, 2005, 35ff.

166 Victor. H. Matthews, *Social World of the Hebrew Prophets,* Peabody, Massachusetts, Hendrickson Publishers, 2001, 78.

167 Gale A. Yee, *Composition and Tradition in the Book of Hosea: A Redactional Critical Investigation,* SBLDA 102, Atlanta, Scholars Press, 1987, 124-125.

turning back to Yahweh. (f) Israel's present attitude toward Yahweh's love in the end leads her towards total destruction.[168]

Gale A. Yee considers chapters 1-3, 4-11, and 12-14 to be in canonical order of some kind.[169] B. S. Childs seeks to do justice to the logic of the material in its canonical context. His focus was on how Hosea's words were preserved and shaped to serve as Scripture.[170] Hosea's words and speeches are collections uttered involve a critical activity of selecting, shaping and ordering of the material. She thinks chapters 2-13 are directed against the political alliances of the Northern Kingdom to which exilic and post-exilic glosses were later added.[171] She dates chapters 2, 4, 6, 8 and 9 during the time of Josianic reformation. The words דבר־יהוה אשר היה אל־הושע בן־בארי in the superscription, serve as an index to authenticate the prophetic speeches of Hosea. This suggests that the book was probably written in Judah after the fall of the northern kingdom capital Samaria (722-721 BCE).[172] The references to Judah throughout the book (1:7, 11, 4:15, 5:5. 10:13, 6:4, 11) support this. This leads us to believe that prophecies once directed towards Israel were later redirected toward Judah.[173] The Judean editor can be readily recognized because the four Judean kings were named first and Jeroboam afterwards. It would seem then that the final compilation of Hosea was done during the time of exile when the compiler appended chapters 3, 11, and 14.[174] However, the whole message was transmitted to Judah soon after the fall of Samaria in 722/721 BCE.

3.1.2. Socio-rhetorical approach to Structure of book

Scholars until now have applied form critical reading, redaction, rhetorical and post-colonial readings to interpret Hosea. However, the socio-rhetorical approach is one that can help to analyse the various textures inherent in the text while viewing the work as a whole. The larger structure of the book unfolds in a rhythmical way forming a macro-chiasmus. Therefore most scholars divide the book into two sections: Chapters 1 to 3 and chapters 4-14. Chapters 1-3 introduces the marriage metaphor (Yahweh-Hosea and Israel-Gomer) through narrative and poetic elements. Chapters 4 to 14 contain fewer prose sections and poetic constructions, dealing with oracles of judgment, punishment and salvation. While chapters 1-3 comprise some of the major themes of love connected to the covenantal relationship with Yahweh, chapters 4-10 develop in the form of oracles of judgment. Thereafter, the narrator sustains the theme of love from chapters 11-14, and this is convincingly brought

---

[168] William Rainey Harper, *The International Critical Commentary on Amos and Hosea,* Edinburgh, T and T Clark, 1905, cxlvii.

[169] Gale A. Yee, *Composition and Tradition in the Book of Hosea: A Redactional Critical Investigation,* SBLDA 102, Atlanta, Scholars Press, 1987, 126.

[170] B. S. Childs, *Introduction to the Old Testament as Scripture,* Philadelphia, Fortress Press, 1979, 377.

[171] A. A. Macintosh, *A Critical and Exegetical Commentary on Hosea,* Edinburgh, T and T Clark, 1997, lxxiii.

[172] Wolff, H.W., *A Commentary on the Book of the Prophet Hosea,* Philadelphia, Fortress Press, 1974, xxi.

[173] L. J. Wood, Hosea, *The Expositor's Bible Commentary,* ed., Frank E. Gaebelein, Grand Rapids, Zondervan Publishing, 1985, 162; see also C.L. Seow, The Book of Hosea, *Anchor Bible Dictionary,* ed., D.N. Freedman, New York, Doubleday, 1997, 291.

[174] James D. Newsome, *Columbia Theological Seminary,* Georgia, Decatur, 1984, 303-45.

out in chapter 11. In chapters 11-14, the narrator maintains a specific format. First, chapter 11 talks about the covenantal love relationship; second, chapters 12-13 discuss the lawsuit aspects against the people of Israel; and third, chapter 14 delineates the aspect of healing in the form of true repentance.[175] Thus, the narrator forms a chiastic structure. The aspects of judgment upon the nation of Israel are inserted between the covenantal love aspects at the beginning and at the end of the book. By placing both the aspects (i.e., love and judgment) in a strategic and rhetorical way, the narrator captures the attention of the reader:

A **Love** (chaps. 1-3)

B **Judgment** (chaps. 4-10)

A' **Love** (chaps. 11-14)

W. Brueggemann divides this unit into 2:2-13 accusations and sentence, vv. 14-15 invitation, vv. 16-20 renewed covenant and vv. 21-23 restored creation.[176] The narrative brings out God's continuing love as a model of His future relationship with Israel through the life of Hosea. This narrative section progresses from disobedience to rehabilitation. The text (2:2-23) is concerned with Yahweh's rejection and not His creation. Brueggemann affirms that Israel is changed from being cursed to being abundantly blessed. Walter Kaiser argues that Yahweh moves with passion to charm her and to renew Israel back to a relationship.[177] The text uses God's work in creation to explain more about his covenant. God uses Hosea's continuing love as a model of His future relationship with Israel. This passage, then, reminds the prophet to look forward to God's eventual and complete renewal of His relationship with Israel (3:5). Brueggemann and Kaiser divide the book mainly based on the metaphor of marriage. They opine that the dominant reading of the book is influenced by theological themes, particularly that of the covenant.[178]

Various other biblical scholars, however, base the structure of the book on the context of the writing.[179] According to them, the book can be divided based on the literary and ideological characteristics.[180] However, the book can also be divided based on the redactional method where the divisions are made according to either the redactional work or the development of a series of stages of the book by looking for important catchwords and common themes.

The *form-critical method* focuses on the basic forms of prophetic speech that are further divided into three or four parts. However, all authors agree on the critical

[175] Steven L. McKenzie, *The Old Testament, its background, Growth and Content,* Nashville, Abingdon Press, 2007, 225-226.

[176] W. Brueggemann, *Theology of the Old Testament,* Minneapolis, Fortress Press, 1997, 222-223.

[177] Walter Kaiser, *Toward an Old Testament Theology,* Grand Rapids, Zondervan Publishing House, 1978, 198.

[178] Alice A. Keefe, *Woman's Body and the Social Body in Hosea 1-2,* London, Sheffield Academic Press, 2001, 34.

[179] James Mays, *"Hosea"* The Old Testament Library, Philadelphia, Westminster Press, 1969, 9 and Andersen and Freedman, *Hosea, Anchor Bible,* Garden City, Doubleday, 1980, 44.

[180] Atchemeier, 8; Andersen and Freedman *Hosea, Anchor Bible,* Garden City, Doubleday, 1980, 44, 61; Goran Eidevall, *Grapes in the Desert: Metaphors, Models and Themes in Hosea 4-11,* Stockholm, Almqvist and Wiksell International, 1996, 5.

methods used in the book: messenger formula, prophetic call and prayer of repentance for their sins. Such an analysis of the structure of Hosea helps to understand the units within the book and their relationship with the surrounding units. There have been various efforts to subdivide the book by Mays and Wolff.[181] Wolff further divides chapters 4 to 14 into the following sections:

4: 1-5:7	The cult of the last years of Jeroboam II
5: 8-9:10	The time of the Syro-Ephraimite War and shortly thereafter
9: 11-12:15	The silent period before and after Shalmaneser V's accession in 727 BCE
13: 1-14:1	The capture of the prophet Hosea
14: 2-9	Shortly before the fall of Samaria

Hubbard[182] divides the book on the basis of the following topics:

4: 1-5:7	Emphasis on infidelity; it dates from the last years of Jeroboam II
5: 8-7:17 (5: 8-7:16)	Political upheavals during the Syro-Ephraimite War
8: 1-9:6 (8: 1-9:9)	Cult and kingdom during the Assyrian domination
9: 10-11: 9 (9: 10-11: 11)	About historical events

The third main part:

11: 12-12: 1 (12: 1-2)	Ephraim and Judah now
12: 2-14 (12: 3-15)	Jacob then and now
13: 1-16 (13: 1-14: 1)	Ephraim then and now
14: 1-8 (14: 2-9)	Repentance and restoration
14: 9 (14:10)	Final reminder

Vosloo[183] systematizes the similarities in these various attempts to create the fifth part:

The transgression of Israel (1: 2-3:5)	
1: 2-9	The disintegration of Hosea's marriage
2: 1-3	God's restoration is portrayed in figurative language
2: 4-17	The recapture of the woman

[181] Wolff, *A Commentary on the Book of the Prophet Hosea,* Philadelphia, Fortress Press, 1965, XI-XII.

[182] Hubbard, *Hosea: An Introduction and Commentary, Tyndale OT Commentaries,* Leicester, Inter Varsity Press, 1989, 33-34.

[183] Vosloo, 1992, 246-251.

2: 18-25	The new relationship begins with the betrothal
3: 1-5	The restoration of Hosea's marriage
The "knowledge" of Yahweh is missing (4:1-9:9)	
4: 1-5: 7	Three lawsuits
5: 8-7: 16	The Syro-Ephraimite war and after
8: 1-9: 9	Cult, festivals and exile
The lost innocence of the past (12:1-14:1)	
9: 10-17	Grapes in the desert / young palm tree
10: 1-8	Lush vine
10: 9-15	The prophecy of judgment
11: 1-11	A child saved from slavery
The present in the light of the past (12:1-14:1)	
12: 1-15	The history of rebellion
13: 1-14:1	The great changes
Yahweh is faithful (14:2-9)	
12: 1-15	Confession by a fine song
14: 5-9	Forgiveness through a love song

Due to the agreement on the unity of chapters 1 to 3 on the one hand and controversial divisions of 4 to 14, various other authors have followed their own methods of dividing the chapters.

3.1.3. The Present Division:

The previous studies have generally divided the book into two main sections: 1. Chapters 1-3 and 2. Chapters 4-14.[184] This division is supported by Carol Dempsey, the author continues that 1-3 and 4-14 speak about Hosea's use of imagery and figurative language.[185] However, this research argues that unlike the arguments of other authors it suggests the book can be divided into three sections; this makes it easier to discuss the varied imagery used to bring out its meaning to the reader. Using this threefold division the first section (Hosea 1-3) focuses largely on the relationship between Hosea and Gomer, and their three children. In this regard, the metaphor in Hosea 1-3 refers simply to marriage (husband-wife). The second section 4-11 consists of a collection of oracles addressing predominantly the political, religious, and social issues. This section primarily highlights the parent-child metaphor that characterizes Israel's violation of the law in religion, and politics.

The final section, 12-14, deals with the divine accusation of wrongdoing by betraying Yahweh (cf. 12:2-14). It refers to a historical reference with a contemporary critique and ends the section with a final plea for repentance and a picture of restoration (cf. 14:1-8). The entire book insists on Israel returning to Yahweh their God.

---

[184] J.L. Mays, *Hosea,* OTL, 1969, 15-16.

[185] Carol J. Dempsey, *The Prophets: A Liberation-Critical Reading,* Minneapolis, Fortress Press, 2000, 153.

It is important to note that the imagery of love is repeated many times in the book, especially in Hosea 2-3, 11 and 14. The book is divided based on the thematic and structural connections in the larger sections (that is 1-3; 4-11 and 12-14) to better understand the imagery of love in the smaller units. The following structure has been made based on the survey of previously drawn structures for the book and in keeping with the socio-cultural, political, and thematic background of the text.

I. Unfaithful Israel and Faithful Yahweh 1:1-2:13
II. Unbroken love from a broken heart 2:14-3:5
   Hosea's symbolic marriage and ensuing reconciliation 3:1-5
   - Prophecies against Israel and Yahweh's lamentations 4:1-10:11
III. Yahweh's unconditional love 10:12-11:12
   a. Yahweh's love and compassion for Israel illustrated by a father's love 11:1-11
IV. Retelling Israel's redemptive history 12:1-14:9
   a. Yahweh's call for continual love 12:1-14
   b. Affirmation of Yahweh's zeal 13:1-16
   - Yahweh's assurance of Israel's loyalty, and love triumphs 14:1 - 8
   - Concluding remarks 14:9

For this study, chapters 2 and 3 are combined for the purpose of weaving the images together. In line with the overall thematic structure of the book, in this passage, Hosea begins with renewal and restoration and ends with God's love for the people of Israel.

Andersen and Freedman divide this unit as follows:

- Hos. 2:16-20 as renewal and restoration between husband and wife ("you" and "her")
- Hos. 2:18 deals with covenant peace made between them and animals
- Hos. 2:21-22 talks about betrothal culminating in a remarriage (in v. 20)
- Hos. 2:23-24 is about antiphonal liturgy observing the restoration of harmony
- Hos. 2:25-26 is about the reunion of parents and children; 3:1-5 is about Israel's repentance and restoration through God's love.[186]

This structure unifying Hosea 2-3 is about redemption of both mother and her children (Yahweh-Israel). In this structure, Israel (mother), who is experiencing the tender love of God, is then reunited to him in an eternal covenant. At the same time, children experience the security of God for the future and their accursed names turned into names of blessing. This division shows the repetition of the overall structure of the book within the pericope. Throughout these sub-units, the word "love" plays a critical role. אהב is repeated many times, and so it is necessary to clarify the meaning before proceeding. The repeated use of אהב in 3:1 emphasises the importance of love in the relationship between Yahweh and Israel. It also serves as a motivation for Yahweh's dealings with Israel. The word אהב with the connotation "to fall in love,"

[186] Andersen and Freedman, *Hosea, Anchor Bible,* Garden City, Doubleday, 1980, 264-265.

is not a euphemism for "sexual intercourse."[187] The word אהב means "spontaneous help/assistance" (11:1) and "healing" (14:4) which is the opposite of anger and hatred (9:15). Where אהב is the father bringing up a child in 11:1, and the physician's healing of disease in 14:4, in 3:1, it has to do with a husband receiving back his errant wife.[188] "Another meaning of the word אהב is "lustful desire," which shows itself as fornication;[189] אהב has thus the overtone of being naturally inclined to behave in a particular way."

This chapter deals with the background and analysis of the first section of Hosea; which is 2:16-3:5. This is followed by the exegesis of the same section based on the inner texture model in chapter four. The other two sections Hosea 11 and 14 are dealt with in chapters four and five of this thesis.

3.2. Context of Hosea 2:16-3:5

The context of Hosea 2:16-3:5 deals with Hosea's own personal experience and ends with the restoration. The relationship between Hosea and his wife is intended to explain the relationship between Yahweh and Israel. This section may be labelled as 'salvation' because the previous section Hos.2:1-13 talks about judgment.[190] Ben Zvi points out however, that Hosea 3 is a didactic work, and this is the overarching context of the passage. A prophetic reading of the text is reported as symbolic acts, but significance does not lie in the acts themselves. It is clear in the passage that:

> The meaning of these acts provides hope for the future of the intended and primary readerships and supplies them with an explanation for the fall of the monarchies' polities and for their present situation.[191]

It is also through these acts that we understand the importance of the socio-political religious context of post monarchic Israel. Hosea 3 is considered as a human monologue, but it is presented as being as authoritative as the preceding divine monologue. The human monologue is in itself embedded in Yahweh's word and in turn it explicitly embeds Yahweh's words as authoritatively reported by the speaker in the book in Hosea 3:1. There is a clear distinction between Yahweh's words and the human monologue.

Hosea 3 not only helps to identify the relationship between husband/Yahweh but also gives an idea of the actual situation of the woman, Israel. Hosea 3 represents Israel collectively, as the symmetry of address in 3:3-4. Hosea 3:3 gives an insight into the working of the man's reported speech. At some point, the text branches in different directions to show the link within the chapter itself: the link is explained in

---

[187] Cf. Wolff, H.W., *A Commentary on the Book of the Prophet Hosea,* Philadelphia, Fortress Press, 1974, 60; Quell, 1952, 23.

[188] H. I. Ginsberg, 'Hosea,' *EncJud* 8, cols. 1971, (1010-1024) 1012, weaken the power of the word to indicate that at 3:1 only the meaning to "befriend." cf. Wolff, 1978, 60; Van Leeuwen, *Hosea,* PredOT, Nijkerk,1968, 84-85; Anderson and Freedman, *Hosea, Anchor Bible,* Garden City, Doubleday, 1980, 295-296.

[189] Cf. Wolff, H.W., *A Commentary on the Book of the Prophet Hosea,* Philadelphia, Fortress Press, 1978, 60.

[190] Renita J. Weems, *Battered Love: Marriage, Sex, and Violence in the Hebrew Prophets,* Minneapolis, Fortress Press, 1995, 12.

[191] Ben Zvi, E. *Hosea,* Grand Rapids, Eerdmans, 2005, 78.

the following way: the multiple links of 3:3-4 is also in 3:5 as well; the dependent character of the clause that begins in v. 4 and; the absolute lack of any textually inscribed marker pointing at the end of his address to her is in v. 3.

Here the context . can be analysed through the differences between chapters 1 and 3. "In chapter 1 the emphasis falls more on the children of the marriage, where as in chapter 3 it falls upon the nature of the marriage itself."[192] In this passage, Hosea speaks directly to Gomer (v. 3) for the first time in this book (earlier, in 2: 2-3 he speaks to her through the children). These verses show how Yahweh's love works through humans in a pessimistic situation *"to love again the prostitute"* (3:1). This action shows the steadfast love of God which demands a deliberate return and obedience to him.

To interpret these sections of chapter 2 and 3 properly, it is necessary to give close attention to the various types of interpretation which can be brought to bear on the sections in order to clarify the rich meaning lying in and behind the words. To do this, the examination is divided into several parts (1) The structure of 2.16-3.5, (2) Exploration of the text, (3) Texture and pattern (4) Sensory-aesthetic texture, (5) Inter-textuality, (6) Definitions of certain words, (7) Summary and conclusion.

3.2.1. Poetic Structure: Hosea 2:16-3:5

Table 1: Poetic Structure: Hosea 2:16-3:5

Stanza	Strophe	Strings		Translation	Parallelism
I	A	[16]לכן הנה אנכי מפתיה	16aA	Therefore, behold, I will allure her;	Synonymous parallel phrases
		והלכתיה המדבר	16aB	and bring her into the wilderness	
		ודברתי על־לבה׃	16b	and I will speak to her heart.	
		[17]ונתתי לה את־כרמיה משם	17aA	Then I will give to her her vineyards from there	
		ואת־עמק עכור לפתח תקוה	17aB	from there and the valley of Achor for a door of hope	
		וענתה שמה כימי נעוריה	17bA	and she shall sing there as in the days of her youth,	Synonymous parallelism
		וכיום עלתה מארץ־מצרים׃	17bB	so as the day when she came out of the land of Egypt.	
		[18]והיה ביום־ההוא	18aA	and it shall be on that day,	
		נאם־יהוה		says the Lord	

[192] H. Mowvley, op.cit, 111.

		תקראי אישי	18aB	you shall be called "my husband"	Antithetic parallel phrases
		לי עוד בעלי:	18b	and you shall call me no more "my Baal" (master).	
		והסרתי את־שמות הבעלים מפיה	19a	for I will take away the names of Baalim from her mouth	
		ולא־יזכרו עוד בשמם:	19b	and they shall not be remembered again by their name.	
		[20]וכרתי להם ברית ביום ההוא	20aA	and on that day I will make a covenant with them	
		עם־חית השדה	20aB	with the beasts of the field,	
		ועם־עוף השמים		and with the birds of the heaven	
		ורמש האדמה		and with the creeping things of the ground,	
		וקשת	20bA	and the bow	
		וחרב		and the sword	
		ומלחמה אשבור מן־הארץ		and the battle out of the land, I will break	
		והשכבתים לבטח:	20bB	and will make them to lie down in safety.	
		[21]וארשתיך לי לעולם	21a	and I will betroth you for myself forever	
		וארשתיך לי בצדק ובמשפט	21b	and I will betroth you for myself in righteousness and in judgment	Synonymous parallelism
		ובחסד וברחמים:		and in steadfast love and in mercies.	
		[22]וארשתיך לי באמונה	22a	and I will even betroth you for myself in faithfulness	
		וידעת את־יהוה:	22b	and then you shall know Yahweh.	
	B	[23]והיה ביום ההוא	23aA	and it shall come to pass in that day,	
		אענה נאם־יהוה		I will answer says Yahweh,	

		אענה את־השמים	23aB	I will answer the heavens	Progressive parallelism
		והם יענו את־הארץ:	23b	and they shall hear the earth.	
		[24]והארץ תענה את־הדגן	24a	and the earth shall hear the grain,	
		ואת־התירוש ואת־היצהר		and the wine, and the oil;	
		והם יענו את־יזרעאל:	24b	and they shall answer Yizrael.	
	C	[25]וזרעתיה לי בארץ	25aA	and I will sow her for myself in the earth	
		ורחמתי את־לא רחמה	25aB	and I will have mercy on her that had not obtained mercy;	
		ואמרתי ללא־עמי	25aC	and I will say "not my people.	Synonymous parallelism
		עמי־אתה		and he will say, You are not my people;	
		והוא יאמר	25b	and they shall say	
		אלהי:		(you are) My God.	

Hosea 3:1-5					
II	D	[1]ויאמר יהוה אלי עוד	1aA	Then Yahweh said to me once again	The Oracle / God speak
		לך אהב־אשה אהבת רע	1bA	go love a woman beloved by another	Synonymous parallelism
		ומנאפת		an adulterous	
		כאהבת יהוה את־בני ישראל	1bB	Yahweh loved Israel as the children	
		והם פנים אל־אלהים אחרים	1cA	while they turn to other gods	
		ואהבי אשישי ענבים		and love cakes of raisins	
	E	[2]ואכרה לי בחמשה עשר כסף	2aA	So I bought her for myself for fifteen pieces of silver	

		וחמר שערים ולתך שערים		and half barley of homer	
	F	[3]ואמר אליה		then I said to her	
		ימים רבים תשבי לי	3aA	you shall wait for me many days,	Chiastic structure
		לא תזני	3aB	you shall not be promiscuous	
		לא תהיי לאיש	3bA	you shall not have a man,	
		וגם־אני אליך	3bB	and I will be yours	
	G	[4]כי ימים רבים ישבו בני ישראל	4aA	yes the children of Israel a long time to wait	
		אין מלך ואין שר		and without king or prince;	Synonymous parallel phrases
		ואין זבח ואין מצבה		without sacrifice, and without an image (statue)	
		ואין אפוד ותרפים		without ephod and teraphim	
	H	[5]אחר ישבו בני ישראל	5aA	Then shall the sons of Israel will return	Progressive parallelism
		ובקשו את־יהוה אלהיהם	5aB	and they shall seek Yahweh their God	
		ואת דוד מלכם		and David their king;	
		ופחדו אל־יהוה ואל־טובו	5aC	and then they will tremble at the Lord and His goodness	
		באחרית הימים	5bA	in the last days.	

3.2.2. Chiastic Structure of Hosea 2:16-3:5

A look at the way the language is used in Hosea 2:16-3:5 reveals the intentional use of the chiasm, a common oral literary device in ancient Hebrew literature. In the Old Testament world, the text was either read or recited aloud in gatherings. Since the people heard or witnessed what had happened in their community, they passed on their memorable stories and repeated chiastic patterns, which served both pedagogical and liturgical purposes.[193] The chiastic literary model assists in understanding the chiastic

[193] James L. Bailey and Lyle D. Van der Broek, *Literary Forms in the New Testament: A Handbook*, Westminster, John Knox Press, 1992, 182.

parallelisms, which enable the interpreter to better understand the author's use of the terms in the text.

The centre of the chiasm focuses on the climax of this study's literary analysis. The chiastic structure is as follows:

A' (2:12-15) 2:12 so now I will lay bare her shame before the eyes of her lovers (2:12)

A (2:16-19) 2:18 on that day, says the LORD, She shall call me "My husband," and never again "My Baal." (2:18)

B (2:20-22) 2:22 I will espouse you in fidelity, and you shall know the Lord. (2:22)

A' (2:23-25) 2:25 I will sow him for myself in the land, and I will have pity on לא רחמה. I will say to לא עמי, "You are my people," and he shall say, "My God!" (2:25)

a. And Yahweh said to me, "Go once again, love a woman who is loved by a friend, and committing adultery, as Yahweh loves the children of Israel, although they turn to other gods and loves cakes of raisins. (3:1)
b. So I bought her for myself for fifteen shekels of silver and a homer of barley. (3:2)
c. Then I said to her, "you shall dwell with me for many days. You shall not commit adultery, nor shall have a man (3:3a).
d. so I will be also toward you." (3:3b).

c'. for the sons of Israel will remain for many days without king or prince, without sacrifice or sacred pillar, and without ephod or teraphim (3:4).

b' afterward the sons of Israel will return and intensely seek the Lord their God and David their king. (3:5a).

and they will come with trembling to the Yahweh and to His goodness in the last days. (3:5b)

The chiastic structures in Hosea give insights into the dynamics of the Hosean community while the chiastic centre focuses its climax on the people who went away from Yahweh. Hosea 3:1-5 describes the Israelite community; here chiasm is apparently used by the author as a means of organizing a set of antithetical statements[194] for his readers or listeners, which are raised and examined as a self-contained literary unit.

3.2.3. Discussion on the Structure of Hosea 2:16-3:5

Hosea 2:16-3:5 indicates the major complaint of Yahweh against His people, as they have chosen to worship the Baals, so they are not recognized by Him as His people (v. 15 says that they have forgotten Him). Hosea 2:12-13 talks about the relationship that will come to an end, but the term "love" plays an important role here. It is "God's love" that enables them to escape the impending judgment and to return to Yahweh.[195] There is an antithesis in verses 11-14 and 16-17. Consequently, they experience a new exodus (v. 17b).

---

[194] Cf. Hos. 6:1-2; 9:12; 11:8 and 14:2-9.

[195] Macintosh, A.A., *A Critical and Exegetical Commentary on Hosea,* Edinburgh, T and T Clark, 1997, 70.

The people's return to Yahweh will bring restoration of the Promised Land and the benefits they would have enjoyed. It reminds them of their sojourn in bondage and their wilderness experiences, which are called a "new exodus."[196] Here, it is important to note that Hosea 2:9-10 talks about the love between husband and wife (Yahweh and Israel), which connects with Hosea 2:18-19 which talks about the love between Baal and Israel. Therefore, the restoring back of His lover in verse 20 is an antithesis to the love between Baal and Israel.

The broken relationship stands for the sinfulness of Israel (2:25). Hosea 2:4-25 begins with a lawsuit that leads to pronouncement of judgment on this sinfulness. The complaint is זנה, which is adultery. Hosea 2:4-25 can be seen as a thematic unit, having Israel heading towards adultery and then a new marriage through restoration of the covenantal relationship.[197]

Andersen and Freedman find that the key term in the pericope is אהב, which appears four times and repeats itself in 3:1 to lay emphasis on the relationship between Yahweh and Israel.[198] The repetition of the word "love" is effectively used in this verse to bring out the contrast between the selfless love of the Lord towards His people of Israel and the love of Israel for Baal, which is a self-centred love.[199] The sign of Yahweh's אהב is worked out in 3:2, 5. The pericope is written in prose, but contains poetic phrases.[200] The parallelism gives enrichment and meaning. There is a synonymous parallelism in v. 1b with 1c אהב־אשה אהבת רע ("go love a woman beloved by another:"[201] MT uses a passive form) parallel to כאהבת יהוה את־בני ישראל ("just as Yahweh loved the children of Israel") and ומנאפת ("and adulterous") in parallel to 1bA והם פנים אל־אלהים אחרים ("while they turn to other gods") in 1cA.[202] Yahweh's love is so similar to the love of the beloved woman while the adultery is described as turning to other gods. Turning to other gods is synonymous with ואהבי אשישי ענבים ("be fond of raisins") in 1cA.

A chiasm follows in v. 3a-b where ימים רבים תשבי לי ("you must dwell as mine for many days")[203] is parallel to וגם־אני אליך ("and then I will be yours"). Next, לא תזני ("you will not go back to promiscuous") is parallel to לא תהיי לאיש ("you will not be without man"). The idea is developed here that Yahweh and Israel will have a mutual relationship for a long time.

---

[196] Dearman, J.A., *The Book of Hosea,*" NICOT, Grand Rapids, Wm. B. Eerdmans Publishing co, 2010, 122; Stanley Jones, *"Exodus Motif in the Book of Hosea and its relevance to the Socio-religious Context of India,"* Faith Theological Review, Vol. 16, No. 1, March 2015, 36.

[197] Brueggemann, 1968, 110-118; Jeremias, *Der Prophet Hosea,* Gottingen, Vandenhoeck and Ruprecht, 1983, 38, 46-48; Van Leeuwen, *Hosea,* 3e aangevuldedruk, Nijkerk, Callebach, 1984, 52, 65.

[198] Andersen, F.I and Freedman, D.N., Hosea: *A New Translation with Introduction and Commentary,* New York, Doubleday, 1980, 295-296.

[199] Hubbard, *Hosea: An Introduction and commentary,* Tyndale OT Commentaries, Leicester, Inter Varsity Press, 1989, 91-92.

[200] Cf. Wolff, H.W, *A Commentary on the Book of the Prophet Hosea,* Philadelphia, Fortress Press, 1978, 58.

[201] W.R. Harper, *A Critical and Exegetical Commentary on Amos and Hosea,* Edinburgh, T and T Clark, 1956, 218.

[202] W. Brueggemann, *Theology of the Old Testament,* Minneapolis, Fortress Press, 1997, 415. Cf. W.R. Harper, *A Critical and Exegetical Commentary on Amos and Hosea,* Edinburgh, T and T Clark, 1956, 217.

[203] Mays, James Luther., *Hosea: A Commentary,* OTL, Philadelphia, Westminster, 1969, 58.

The word "without" appears five times in this section, especially in v. 4a: ואין שר אין מלך (without sacrifice and without prince) to ואין זבח ואין מצבה (without sacrifice, and without pillar[204]) and ואין אפוד ותרפים (without ephod and teraphim).[205] The emphasis is used to make the point that the Israelites must forsake the Canaanite gods (live without making offerings to those gods), then "return and seek the Lord." It indicates that God expects true repentance from the people תשבי.[206] Hosea 3:5 contains a progressive parallelism: אחרי שׁבו בני ישׂראל (then the children of Israel's life will change) is parallel to ובקשו את־יהוה אלהיהם ואת דוד מלכם (and they will take Yahweh as their God, and David as their king) and ופחדו אל־יהוה ואל־טובו (and then they will receive goodness and mercy from Yahweh when they turn to Him with a respectful approach). The argument developed here is to persuade repentance (change the direction of your life), to seek and return to Yahweh, with reverence and honour.[207] The discussion of the structure helps to understand the chiasm and structure in the text.

3.2.4. Exploring the Text of Hosea 2:16-3:5

Hosea 2:16-3:5 explore marriage as a symbol. The lawsuit and rejection is symbolised through the broken marriage, but there is a message of hope to Israel through the renewal of covenantal relationship and promise of restoration to Israel.[208] Macintosh says that Israel forsakes Yahweh and his loving kindness for the worship of Baals.[209] Stanley Jose says that Hosea 2:18-25 is referred to as a new exodus offered to her.[210] According to Hubbard, Israel's response in 3.1.5 closes this salvation speech, as Israel's answer in the wilderness began it. This reversal of the judgment, accompanied by a change of the children's names, thus expands the prophetic hope of 2:1-3 and shapes the intimate unity of chapter 2 with chapter 1.[211] This view is supported by Charles Dyer and Eugene Merrill to show that the change of names emphasises God's new blessing to them through crops and products of the land.[212] Stanley Jose identifies that 2:18 (ביום־ההוא), 2:20 (ביום־ההוא) and 2:23 (ביום־ההוא) takes the וכיום of 2:17 so that 2:18-25 gives us an overall view of a closer explanation of the "new exodus" offer.[213] The theme of Hosea 1-2 does not move along a straight line to a

---

[204] In Hebrew, sacred stones are used, the word means a "pillar" that is thin and a tall stone placed in the ground. During the time of Hosea these pillars were used for worshipping the idols.

[205] Dearman, J.A., *The Book of Hosea,*" NICOT, Grand Rapids, Wm. B. Eerdmans Publishing co, 2010, 136-137.

[206] Dearman, J.A., *The Book of Hosea,*" NICOT, Grand Rapids, Wm. B. Eerdmans Publishing co, 2010, 137.

[207] Sandhya Shency, "A Call to Return to the Lord (Hos. 6:1-6)," Vol. XXXX, No. 3, September 2014, *Bible Bhashyam,* 146-147 (146-156).

[208] Renita J. Weems, *Battered Love: Marriage, Sex, and Violence in the Hebrew Prophets,* Minneapolis, Fortress Press, 1995, 92.

[209] Macintosh, A.A, *A Critical and Exegetical Commentary on Hosea,* Edinburgh, T and T Clark, 1997, 65-66.

[210] Stanley Jones, *"Exodus Motif in the Book of Hosea and its relevance to the Socio-religious Context of India," Faith Theological Review,* Vol. 16, No. 1, March 2015, 36.

[211] Hubbard David Allan, *With Bands of Love* (Hosea), Grand Rapids, W.B. Eerdmans publishing co, 1968, 86-87.

[212] Charles Dyer and Eugene Merrill, *Nelson's Old Testament Survey,* Nashville, Thomas Nelson Publishers, 2001, 728.

[213] Stanley Jones, *"Exodus Motif in the Book of Hosea and its relevance to the Socio-religious Context of India,"* Faith Theological Review, Vol. 16, No. 1, March 2015, 36.

single climax. The problem and its situation are brought into focus again so that there are many climaxes. In particular, 2:16-25 sums up the resolution with courtship, betrothal, covenant making, exchange of vows, and the giving of the new names. Each of these moments has a key expression that strikes a note of finality "the door of hope," "my husband, I will make them lie down in safety," "you will know Yahweh," "(you are) my God." According to Patrick Miller, Hosea's reference to knowing Yahweh is to do with Israel's fickleness and betrayal of her creator. But now the prophet comes with the message of hope, saying when they return with faith and abandon Baal, that action will bring newness and life.[214] The attribute of marriage reveals the heart of God. Knowing Yahweh brings new life and hope for the future of the people.

For Harrison, Hosea 3:1-5 is a recalling of 1:2-3:5[215] and is the unit of a story within the book (3:1-3). It offers an autobiography of the prophet, representing his symbolic actions.[216] The imagery used by the prophet here is to explain the inexplicable.[217] 3:4-5 is a prophetic judgment on Israel.[218] Hosea 3:4-5 connects directly to vv. 1-3 by the accentuated words כי ימים רבים ישבו in v. 4, which express the meaning ואין in v. 3. The negative לא in v. 4 takes the negative judgments in v. 3. This combination of an event with the interpretation belongs to the genre of the particular memorabile. The subject of *memorabile* is the prophet's symbolic handling.[219] A *memorabile* endeavours to set apart something unique from a common occurrence, which as a whole signifies the meaning of this occurrence.[220] The creation of such an image by the prophet has its own definite purpose and its application to the point. As the prophet's personal experience plays a strong role in establishing the imagery, his skill in connecting to social life is to be appreciated.[221]

Hosea sees through the culture of his time and tradition of his people, exposing Gomer, who was found to have committed adultery. This is the texture of the rhetorical purpose that connects his society with his writings.

Hosea is required to do something to honour Gomer by paying a ransom which is called as challenge-response (vv. 3 and 4.) In chapter 3, the challenge is stated clearly: Israel will be without a king for many days.[222] The desired "response" here is spelled out in v. 5 as שוב. The principle of reciprocity in the patron-client relationship

[214] Walter Brueggemann, Patrick D. Miller, ed., *Old Testament Theology Essays on Structure, Theme and Text,* Minneapolis, Fortress Press, 1992, 290.

[215] Andersen, F.I and Freedman, D.N., *Hosea: A New Translation with Introduction and Commentary,* New York, Doubleday, 1980, 295.

[216] R.K. Harrison, *Introduction to the Old Testament,* London, The Tyndale Press, 1969, 861.

[217] Hempel, J., "Prophet and Poet," *The Journal of Theological Studies,* XL, April, 1939, 113-32, "Jahwegleichnisse," 75-77.

[218] cf. Wolff, 1974, 57; Mays, James Luther., *Hosea: A Commentary,* OTL, Philadelphia, Westminster, 1969, 54-55. Cf. Andersen, F.I and Freedman, D.N., *Hosea: A New Translation with Introduction and Commentary,* New York, Doubleday, 1980, 291-294

[219] Wolff, H.W, *A Commentary on the Book of the Prophet Hosea,* Philadelphia, Fortress Press, 1974, 58.

[220] Andre Jolles, *'Einfache Formen,'* Leipzig, 1930: Darmstadt, 1969 reprint of the unrevised fourth edition quoted in Wolff, H.W., *A Commentary on the Book of the Prophet Hosea,* Philadelphia, Fortress, 1974, 57.

[221] Robinson, "Hosea," in *Die Zwölf kleinen Propheten,* HAT 1/14, Tübingen, 1964, 3.

[222] Daniel Patte, Jose Severino Croatto, Teresa Okure, *Global Bible Commentary,* Nashville, Abingdon Press, 2004, 268.

between Yahweh and Israel will come to the fore in rebuilding the broken "marital relationship" (v. 1).

Writers use imagery in literary studies to create a picture in the minds of the people. The three main elements of the symbolic act in this case are Yahweh's command (v. 1), the report of the implementation (vv. 2f) and the interpretation (vv. 4f). The keyword in the pericope is אהב, found four times in v. 1, and the signs of Yahweh's אהב worked out in vv. 2 and 5. The pericope is in prose.[223] The other significant terms are בקש, שוב and פחד (v. 5). These words show that the covenantal relationship is reflected in the language of love and reconciliation between Yahweh and Israel.

3.2.5. Demarcation of the Unit of Hosea 2:16-3:5

It is interesting to note that while Hosea 1 and 2 talk about marriage, and chapter 4 contains Yahweh's angry speech about the Israelites turning away from him, Chapter 3 stands alone. Not only that, but it reverts to the first person with Hosea speaking. This could be construed as a pause in the action, in which parallels are drawn between the renewed marriage, in which Gomer is told no longer to act as the prostitute ("you must not be a prostitute or be intimate with any man") and the necessary behaviour of the Israelites ("they will live for many days without…") to show their repentance. Both characters, Gomer and the Israelites, "must not" revert to their old behaviour. Bearing chapter 4 in mind, the reader could almost imagine the Israelites sitting in the shadows, heads bowed, in fear and trembling at the fury of Yahweh's remarks in that chapter.

Chapter 3 is a description in the first person, as against the third person and first person description predictions in the previous chapters.[224] It is quite different from the אהב, the prophetic formula, in chapter 4 (4:1). The spacing at v. 2 (ואכרה) and v. 3 (ואמר) is due to the first person's view of the third person in vv. 1, 4 and 5. On further investigation, אהב is found four times in vv. 1, 2 and 5, indicating that 3:1-5 is a separate unit.

According to Beeby, this first pericope, 2:4-25, is thematic and it deals with the themes of adultery and a new marriage.[225] The unit 2: 4-25 on the whole is a beautiful poetic structure. Here, Hosea displays his literary skill by using rich imagery and figures of speech to express God's spiritual relationship with Israel. Yahweh is presented here metaphorically as a husband to Israel, as Hosea is to Gomer who becomes the mother of three children. This metaphor portrays God's continuing love and his relationship towards his people.[226]

---

[223] cf. Wolff, H.W., *A Commentary on the Book of the Prophet Hosea,* Philadelphia, Fortress, 1974, 58.

[224] Mays, James Luther., *Hosea: A Commentary,* OTL, Philadelphia, Westminster, 1969, 54;

[225] Beeby, H.D., *Grace Abounding: A commentary on the book of Hosea,* Grand Rapids, Eerdmans, 1989, 28. The first pericope is divided into three sub-units, namely 2:4-15, 2:16-17 and 2:18-25. The second pericope begins with 3:1 where the formula ויאמר יהוה is used as an introduction.

[226] J.B. Gabel, C.B. Wheeler and A.D. York, *The Bible as Literature,* 3rd ed., New York, Oxford University Press, 1996, 31. Cf. L. Ryken, *"How to read the Bible as Literature,"* Grand Rapids, Zondervan, 1984, 201.

3.2.6. Exegesis of Hosea 2:16-3:5

The themes of accusation, judgment and salvation in Hosea are all connected together by the central thread of love, and the husband-wife metaphor of chapter 3 is perhaps the crux of Israel's understanding of the covenant.

Hosea 2:16-3:5 can be divided into two sections. The first one is 2:16-23 which contains Yahweh's promises to His wife, and the second is 3:1-5 which is Yahweh's instruction to love his wife. Yahweh, after condemning Israel for her waywardness, calls her for an everlasting marriage and enacts it through the prophet Hosea.[227] The selected pericope 2:16-3:5 starts in a poetic form and ends in a prose style.

3.2.7. Translation: Hosea 2:16-3:5

Table 2: Translation: Hosea 2:16-25

[16]לכן הנה אנכי מפתיה והלכתיה המדבר ודברתי על־לבה׃	14 Therefore behold I will allure her[228] and bring[229] her into the wilderness and I will speak to her heart.
[17]ונתתי לה את־כרמיה משם ואת־עמק עכור לפתח תקוה וענתה שמה כימי נעוריה וכיום עלותה מארץ־מצרים׃	15 Then I will give to her her vineyards from there and the valley of Achor[230] for a door[231] of hope and she shall sing there as in the days of her young[232] as the day when[233] she came out of the land of Egypt.

[227] Wood J. Leon, *The Prophets of Israel,* Grand Rapids, Baker Academic group, 1979, 278.

[228] The phrase is in the participle form מפתיה and is parsed in the in the following way as Piel participle masculine singular and third feminine singular suffix from the root word פתה, means "to allure." The meaning of the term is "to persuade" or "entice" with the connotation young lovers and patience. It is surely a love word. The following is the characteristic of the particle הנה is translated as "now" and it depicts of an outcome of the result that will take place in the either in the present time or it will happen in the days to come.

[229] Other English versions read in the following mean lead. This refers to the days to come in the future, since it is used in the participle מפתיה; there is a chain of perfects inserted by conjunction waw consecutive that refer to that time to come in the future.

[230] MT has עכור is translated in this way as "the valley of trouble." The name came into being because of the event accompanied with the unfortunate incident that has taken place as cited in Jos. 7:1-26. The term עכור means as trouble or disaster. English translations cite as "the valley of trouble."

[231] The MT means as "door" or "doorway;" the other meaning of the term is also as opportunity. English translation read as "gateway." This phrase refers to the days of Joshua, where the sins of Achan against the people of Israel and how they were brought down. But later on we read that Israel will have a future and promises will be fulfilled.

[232] MT has "as in the days of her youth" English translations as well render as youth.

[233] MT has "as in the day when." English translations read also in the same way.

18 והיה ביום־ההוא נאם־יהוה תקראי אישי ולא־תקראי־לי עוד בעלי:	16 and it shall be on that day[234] says the Lord you shall be called[235] "My husband"[236] and you shall call me[237] no more "My Baal."[238]
19 והסרתי את־שמות הבעלים מפיה ולא־יזכרו עוד בשמם:	17 for[239] I will take away the names of Baalim[240] from her mouth,[241] and they shall not be remembered by their name.[242]

[234] MT translates as "and in that day;" but English translation reads as "in that coming day."

[235] MT understands as תקראי means "you will call;" and it is parsed in the following way as qal imperfect second person feminine singular. Other versions LXX, Vulgate and Syriac versions brings back and study as an alternate reading of תקראי־לי means as "she will call me;" and is parsed as qal imperfect third person feminine singular followed by preposition ל, and first person common singular that refers as suffix. This is because of the variant reading of the term תקראי־לי that is observed here. English translations observe in the following way of MT. other versions reads in the third person as "she."

[236] The word "My husband" has a word play; it combines phrases איש and בעל in Hos.2:16. The phrase אישי is translated as "husband or my man." The term "husband or my man is used as a title for affection in Gen. 2:23; 3:6, 16) to the same as having the same function and characteristic as another is אשה means as "woman, wife" in this context. But the phrase בעלי is translated as "my lord" that draws attention to the husband's as permitted by the law as his possessor in Ex. 21:3; Deut. 22:22; 24:4. The references indicate that the husband will be no more possessor of the woman but there will be a new renewed relationship between them.

[237] The Hebrew תקראי־לי is translated as "you will call me;" qal imperfect second person feminine singular and this is followed by the preposition ל, with first person common singular suffix. The LXX, Vulgate and Syriac versions question this and suggest that an alternate reading of תקרא־לי meaning "she will call me;" qal imperfect third person feminine singular followed by preposition ל first person common singular suffix.

[238] Here we notice wordplay takes place the expression בעלי translated as "my master" and the next term הבעלים means "the Baals:" the above two terms originate from the source בעל which signifies the meaning of "master, lord." The wordplay brings to our notice that the root word לעב refers here specifically to husband and that is referring to the Canaanite god called Baal. In the Canaanite culture Baal is addressed as "husband, master." Similarly the term is used here with איש is "husband, man.

[239] In MT the waw consecutive is added in the beginning to והסרתי translated as "I will remove." The waw consecutive is translated in Hiphil perfect first person common singular explain and make clear as an article.

[240] The word הבעלים is translated as "Baal idols." But MT translates in the following way "the Baals." Because the term appears in the singular form בעל it refers to the Canaanite god Baal whereas the plural form הבעלים refers to the nature and character of the god Baal.

[241] The MT translates this as "from her mouth." But the English versions have "as from your lips." In translation the word it is rendered as second person for consistency.

[242] The Hebrew translates this as "they will no longer be mentioned by their name."

20 וכרתי להם ברית ביום ההוא עם־חית השדה ועם־עוף השמים ורמש האדמה וקשת וחרב ומלחמה אשבור מן־הארץ והשכבתים לבטח׃	18 and on that day I will make a covenant for them with the beasts of the field, and with the birds of the heaven and with the creeping things of the ground and I will break[243] the bow and the sword and the battle[244] out of the land and will make them to lie down in safety.[245]
21 וארשתיך לי לעולם וארשתיך לי בצדק ובמשפט ובחסד וברחמים׃	19 and I will betroth you[246] for myself forever; and I will betroth you for myself in [247] righteousness and in judgment and in steadfast love and in mercies.
22 וארשתיך לי באמונה וידעת את־יהוה׃	20 and I will even betroth to you for myself in faithfulness and then [248] you shall know [249] Yahweh.[250]
23 והיה ׀ ביום ההוא אענה נאם־יהוה אענה את־השמים והם יענו את־הארץ׃	21 and it shall come to pass in that day, I will answer [251] says Yahweh, I will answer the heavens, and they[252] shall they shall hear the earth.
24 והארץ תענה את־הדגן ואת־התירוש ואת־היצהר והם יענו את־יזרעאל׃	22 and the earth shall hear the grain, and the wine, and the oil; and they shall answer Yizrael.[253]

243 English versions translate as "I will destroy," "I will smash," "I will remove."

244 The MT translates the word battle as "bow and sword and warfare." The two words are used in the context of the three similar units וקשת וחרב ומלחמה in a literal sense, "bow and sword and warfare" are used as a figure of speech to refer specifically to bow and sword. In general the word refers to weapons of war.

245 The MT לבטח translates "and I will cause them to lie down in safety." Something to be noted here is that the causative nuance "will make them" is maintained in various English editions. But a few English translations render as "to live securely."

246 The MT has וארשתיך and translates as "I will betroth you to me" there are two occurrences in the verse. However, a few English versions translate in the following way "I will take you for my wife forever."

247 The MT reads וארשתיך לי it is important is note that the preposition ב, clause is repeated in 2:19-20 [21-22], which indicates the meaning of a sign of a price being paid. The MT explains this allusion in terms of the payment of a bridal gift. This reminds that the Lord reminds Israel about her covenant relationship that is explained in this verse.

248 The MT וידעת has waw consecutive and suffix verb. The term is translated as וידעת "then you will know" clause brings an answer and this is supported by other English translations.

249 The MT translates וידעת this term as "you shall know." But a few English versions translate as "acknowledge." MT translates ידע as "know." The word ידע is also rendered as "know, acknowledge." This is applied in the context related to covenant. The ידע refers to the covenant and the suzerain's responsibility to a vassal and also their vassal's covenant irresponsibleness to the suzerain agreement between two parties.

250 The MT reads יהוה but Hebrew manuscripts have כי אני which is translated as "that it is I." Similarly the same idea is prevalent in the Vulgate and Latin texts. But English versions translate as "know who I am."

251 In MT the word ענה is translated as a verb in the following verses 2:23-24. The root word ענה, is translated as "to answer."

252 The MT has "and they." The meaning of MT is that this refers to the "sky," it is used in a dual form in MT for better understanding and for meaning. But English versions translate using the plural term as "heavens" but in this case the plural form has the meaning of "skies."

253 The MT has יזרעאל in this context the name creates a wordplay. יזרעאל as a proper name creates

[25]וזרעתיה לי בארץ ורחמתי את־לא רחמה ואמרתי ללא־עמי עמי־אתה והוא יאמר אלהי׃	23 and I will sow her myself in the earth and I will have mercy on her that had not obtained mercy; and I will say to (them that were) not my people (are). And he[254] will say, You (are) not my people; and they shall say (You are)[255] my God.

Hosea - 3:1-5

[1] ויאמר יהוה אלי עוד לך אהב־אשה אהבת רע ומנאפת כאהבת יהוה את־בני ישראל והם פנים אל־אל˙הים אחרים ואהבי אשישי ענבים׃	1 Then Yahweh said to once again, 'Go again,[256] love[257] a woman[258] who is loved[259] by a friend,[260] and committing adultery,[261] as Yahweh loves[262] the sons of Israel,[263] although they turn other gods and love cakes of raisins.[264]
[2] ואכרה לי בחמשה עשר כסף וחמר שערים ולתך שערים׃	2 So I bought her for myself for fifteen shekels of silver and half barley of homer.[265]

a phonetic wordplay on the similar sounding name ישראל meaning "God will answer Israel."

[254] The MT refers to Hos. 1:8-9, the birth of the son, and translated using the third person masculine singular pronoun. But English versions translate by using third person plural "they," because this reminds us of the meaning in this context: the people of Israel will be re-established.

[255] The phrase "You are" is not found in the MT but the context implies this meaning. This helps the reader to understand the text and the meaning better.

[256] The MT translates as, "and Yahweh said to me, Go again."

[257] Other English versions translate as "give your love to." The Hebrew word אהב has several meanings. In this context the word "love" means for Hosea to use words and acts of love to affirm his marriage with Gomer. Cf. Andersen and Freedman, *Hosea,* 295.

[258] The MT translates as "a woman." The woman refers probable to Gomer. English translations denote that the referent in this case is "your wife." A similar view is proposed by Garrett in his commentary, cf. Garrett, *Hosea, Joel An Exegetical and Theological Exposition of Holy Scripture,* B and H Publishing Group, 1997, 121.

[259] The MT pronounces אהבת as a combining part form of the qal passive participle and carries out ער as a genitive of effect: "who is loved by רע." But LXX, Vulgate and Syriac versions express אהבת as an absolute form of the qal active participle, and take רע as the accusative direct object: "who loves רע." English versions prefers to follow MT. The MT has in a passive participle form, whereas the Greek text translates as "loving evil" which is different from MT translation. So the researcher adopts active participle idea for this research. (Mays, *Hosea,* 54).

[260] The literal meaning of the term רע is "companion." The noun ער has different meaning in different context. רע is translated as "friend," "companion," "another" "lover," "lover; paramour," and "neighbour." Biblical scholars adopt different, contrasting meanings different meanings but the word רע here does not refer to another man, instead it clearly indicates to the reader Hosea himself, as Gomer's husband.

[261] The MT translates as "committing adultery," but the literal meaning of the word is "love a woman who is loved of a lover and is an adulteress."

[262] MT has "Yahweh loves" but it is translated as "like the love of the Lord." It is because the genitive after the construct functions as a subjective genitive.

[263] The MT translates as "sons of Israel," but English versions translate as "children of Israel" and "people of Israel."

[264] MT has "they are lovers of cakes of raisins." Some English versions render literally.

[265] MT has *"lethech,"* meaning a measure for dry things. But the LXX translates as "a homer of barley and a measure of wine." The LXX meaning of "lethech" is adopted by some English versions. Lethech is a measure for dry things about "a homer of barley." The measurement is like this: a homer was about 5 bushels (180 litres) and a lethech about 2.5 bushels (90 liters). Cf. Andersen and Freedman, *Hosea*, 300.

3 וואמר אליה ימים רבים תשבי לי לא תזני ולא תהיי לאיש וגם־אני אליך׃	3 Then I said to her, "you shall wait for me many days. You shall not commit adultery,[266] nor shall have a man;[267] so I will be also toward you."
4 כי ימים רבים ישבו בני ישראל אין מלך ואין שר ואין זבח ואין מצבה ואין אפוד ותרפים׃	4 for the children of Israel[268] will remain for many days without king or prince, without sacrifice, and without an image, and without ephod and teraphim.[269] sacrifice, and without an image, and without ephod and teraphim.[270]
5 אחר ישבו בני ישראל ובקשו את־יהוה אלהיהם ואת דוד מלכם ופחדו אל־יהוה ואל־טובו באחרית הימים׃	5 Then the sons of Israel shall return and shall seek the Lord their God and David their king;[271] and then they shall seek Lord their God and then they will tremble at the Lord and His goodness in the last days.[272]

3.2.8. Text Critical Notes – Hosea 2:16-3:5

Verse 18

תקראי - Footnotes 18a and b (BHS) follows the Septuagint, Syriac Vulgate translation and that replaces the second person singular qal imperfect of female קרא with the third person. Note 18a also adds a לי within line with the rest of the way to come. There is a trend in the LXX to verbal forms that change differences so they match. A text change does not appear to take place here.[272]

Verse 21

וארשתיך לי לעולם - piel perfect, 1st person common, singular with 2nd person feminine sing suffix of ארש (and I will engage you to me forever / I will pay your father's last objections regarding our wedding away by the amount he requires, I will do everything to make your complete and win eternal companionship). וארשתיך לי באמונה:

266 The MT indicates that "she" is the subject of "and you will not be for."

267 The rendering here is that she will not have a husband. The reference to a man as the same word, used in Deut. 21:3, makes clear.

268 The text talks about "sons of Israel" but English versions indicate "children of Israel." Most of the translations prefer to use "children of Israel."

269 The MT תרפים means a standing stone or statue. The word תרפים also means "proclaimer," or 'interpreter.' In some cases תרפים is translated as "household idols."

270 The MT reads as "David their king;" but the English translations as "the king from David's family." This means that a king will come from David's descendants. The meaning of the text is not clear because the prophet predicts that the restoration of Davidic kingship over Israel and Judah (e.g., Jer. 17:25; 22:2) or possibly the phrase refers to the end of the rule of Davidic kings. This could be a reference to the Messiah, who will come and fulfil the Davidic covenant. The promise to David will take place under conditions laid down by Yahweh. This is called the "New David" who will come and fulfil the promise and to retain the covenant. Cf. Walter Kaiser, *Toward an Old Testament Theology,* Grand Rapids, Zondervan Publishing House, 1978, 198.

271 The MT reads as "in the last days." But other translations and English versions suggest "in the end of the days." The confusion is because of the word אחר closes in a simple way. It creates confusion for the reader and the sentence is not clear.

272 Wolff, *Hosea,* 1965, 56; Rudolph, 1966, 74.

repeats an action or statement (and I will engage you to me in kindness and fairness). ובחסד וברחמים : and in grace and mercy / for I will merciful to you and care about you.

Verse 22

וארשתיך לי באמונה : repeats an action or statement in verse 21 (and I shall betroth you in reliability). וידעת qal, pf. 2nd person feminine sing of ידע (and you shall know) (and then you will acknowledge Yahweh).

את-יהוה: Footnotes 22a (BHS) that many Vulgate manuscripts כי אני (for that is I) reading. (Wolff,[273] points out that it is an interpretation from Ezekiel's use of). No change appears to take place here, because the ambiguity of ידע, in the context of the engagement and marriage terminology can completely obscure[274] the meaning.

Verse 23

אענה : Footnotes 23 (BHS) that the first אענה missing in the Septuagint and Syriac translation. There is an argument in favour of its retention in the MT as it depicts Yahweh as being the very cause of the chain reaction that follows, and as the giver of rain and fertility.[275]

Verse 25

וזרעתיה : Footnotes 25a (BHS) suggest that for the female suffix it is possible it can be male. No text changes, however, is needed here, as no textual support exists and as it conceals the sexual reference.[276]

3:1 - Verse 1 (3:1-5)

אהבה: footnote 1a (BHS): the alternative reading אהבת in footnote 1a (BHS) supported by the LXX, Syriac translation and Vulgate takes the participle as active and the subsequent noun זנה (evil) as a homograph רע תם אשה אהבת (she who loves wickedness). It is also in parallel with the active participle מנאפת (an adulterous). The reading of the זנה cannot be correct. When a passive participle is in a construct relationship with a זנה, זנה refer to the acting of the action.[277] Therefore the reading of the MT should be supported.

עוד "again" may be construed also with לך אהב "love again...," though this appears less likely. In consideration of idiomatic, the Hebrew term לך "go" is omitted in translation.

כאהבת יהוה footnote 1b (BHS) suggest that reading in first person singular (first person masculine singular) must be in accordance with chapter 1:2. There is no external evidence for this reading, and it is sufficient to the reading of the MT.

---

[273] Wolff, H.W. *A Commentary on the Book of the Prophet Hosea,* Philadelphia, Fortress,, 1965, 57.

[274] Boshoff. W.S., Yahweh as God of Nature: Elements of the concept of God in the book of Hosea, *JNSL* 18, 1992b, 76.

[275] Breytenbach, *Die verband tussen end die ontwikkeling in die profetiese uitsprake in die boek Hosea,* University of Pretoria, 1979, 47.

[276] Andersen, F.I and Freedman, D.N., *Hosea: A New Translation with Introduction and Commentary,* New York, Doubleday, 1980, 288.

[277] Cf. Andersen, F.I and Freedman, D.N., *Hosea: A New Translation with Introduction and Commentary,* New York, Doubleday, 1980, 296.

Verse 2

ולתך שערים: footnote 2a-a (BHS) indicate the LXX reading καὶ Νεβελ οἴνου (a flagon of wine / and a barrel of wine).[278] There is no external support for the insertion. Therefore it is sufficient to the reading of the MT.

Verse 3

וגם־אני: Footnotes 3a (BHS) indicates a possible insertion of אהוא לא "I will not come in." This reading is supported by Harper. There is no external support for the insertion. Therefore it is sufficient to the reading of the MT.

Verse 5

ואת דוד מלכם and באחרית הימים footnote 5a (BHS) indicates that ואת דוד מלכם and באחרית הימים (belonging to the Jewish eschatology) is probably later additions is.[279] Some manuscripts insert the MT. This study assumes the inclusion in the text as there is no external support to make it.

Hosea 2:16-3:5 reflects God's character and relationship, as it is found in this unit. This passage portrays the intentions of the heart of God towards Israel. Exploring the texture, Hosea 2:16-3:5 examine how marriage as a symbol in this portion is to connote - the gap between the creator and what he has created. The structure stands on its own for the reader to understand. This is followed by an exegesis, called the inner texture, which helps to better understand the text.

3.3. Inner Texture of Hosea 2:16-3: 5

The inner texture is used to analyse and gain a deeper knowledge of words, word patterns, voices, structures, literary devices and modes in the text. To explore the inner texture of the text, it is necessary to use different kinds of sub-textures. These are repetitive, progressive, narrative, argumentative, opening-middle-closing and sensory-aesthetic textures.

3.3.1. Repetitive Texture

Repetitive texture focuses on words, phrases, actions or topics. Macintosh identifies three synonymous parallel phrases in 2:16 that indicate the humiliation and struggle of Israel's wilderness journey, which Yahweh used as an opportunity to address the hearts of the people:[280] This enhances the imagery of love that appears as rhetorical questions in this unit.

אנכי מפתיה

והלכתיה המדבר

ודברתי על-לבה

---

[278] Wine could be used as a commodity of exchange, but MT is the more difficult reading and likely to be original. Wolff. H.W, *A Commentary on the Book of the Prophet Hosea,* Philadelphia, Fortress Press, 1974, 56.

[279] J.L. Mays, Hosea: *A Commentary,* Philadelphia, The Westminster press, 1969, 60; Cf. Wolff, 1970, 63.

[280] Macintosh A.A, *A Critical and Exegetical Commentary on Hosea,* Edinburgh, T and T Clark, 1997, 71.

The word noted here is "the days of her." Leeuwen comments that in 2:17^{Heb} (15^{Eng}) כימי נעוריה (days of her youth), is synonymous with וכיום עלתה מארץ-מצרים (the day she came up out of the land of Egypt / Egypt went up).[281] He continues that the tradition of regarding the time in Egypt as the youth of Israel is hereby idealized as a time of obedience. The desert can be seen as a transition period where Israel had to remember the blessings of Yahweh.[282] The repeated use of the first and third person (you and her) was deliberately chosen to show the contrast in the attitudes of the two parties.[283] Here the punishment changes to love, where Yahweh seeks people to return to him, like a woman saying "I will return to My Husband, for it was better for me than now (cf. 2:9^{Heb} / 7^{Eng})." The idea here is, rather than awarding threat and punishment, repentance and deliverance signify a new start. It is presented as Yahweh's love for Israel. This is indicated as the situation shifts from desert to new life because of Yahweh's love.

The promise of salvation in 2:21-22 is introduced with a threat in the background but it brings out the new conditions of life where Israel makes a new confession to Yahweh to renew her covenantal relationship. The motif here is presented as a parable representing the renewed marriage between a husband and a wife.

Wolff finds that in verses 21 and 22 there are three synonymous parallelisms to the nature of the "marital relationship" which mean לעולם "to be engaged," "to take a woman."[284] For Koehler, these are used to specify the relationship between Yahweh and Israel.[285] The commitment will be צדק (forever). Hobart comments that Yahweh will engage her in משפט (justice), חסד (loving kindness) and רחמים (compassion).[286] In terms of marriage, it also has a sexual connotation.[287]

In Hosea 2:23 and 24, there are five progressive parallelisms used to describe what follows when Yahweh hears his people (אענה). For Stuart, the phrase Yahweh "himself will sow in the land" (וזרעתיה לי בארץ) is loaded with sexual overtones and matches the wedding picture.[288] But according to Freedman, "sow" has an agricultural meaning as well as a sexual reference (cf. Exo. 5:28). The woman is compared to the land in this case.[289] Wolff rightly indicates that this is a reinterpretation of Jezreel with a promise of an increase in the population.[290]

Hosea 3:1-5 presents Hosea's symbolic actions, which are in response to God's command.[291] Stuart points out that this bears a resemblance to the structure of 1:29.

---

281 Van Leeuwen, *Hosea,* 3e aangevuldedruk, Nijkerk, Callebach, 1984, 67.

282 Van Leeuwen, *Hosea,* 3e aangevuldedruk, Nijkerk, Callebach, 1984, 67.

283 Andersen, F.I and Freedman, D.N., *Hosea*: *A New Translation with Introduction and Commentary,* New York, Doubleday, 1980, 262.

284 Wolff, H.W. *A Commentary on the Book of the Prophet Hosea,* Philadelphia, Fortress, 41-42.

285 Koehler, Ludwig; Baumgartner, Walter Richardson, MISS (tra.) *The Hebrew and Aramaic Lexicon of the Old Testament,* Netherlands, Leiden, Brill, 1994-2000.

286 Freeman E. Hobart, *An Introduction to the Old Testament,* Prophets, Chicago, Moody press, 1968, 174.

287 Koehler, Ludwig; Baumgartner, Walter Richardson, MISS (Tra.) *The Hebrew and Aramaic Lexicon of the Old Testament,* Leiden, Brill, 1994-2000.

288 Stuart, Douglas: *Hosea-Jonah, Word Biblical Commentary:* Dallas, Word, Incorporated, 1987, 61.

289 Andersen and Freedman, *Hosea,* 288.

290 Wolff, H.W., *A Commentary on the Book of the Prophet Hosea,* Philadelphia, Fortress, 1978, 54.

291 Stuart, Douglas, *Hosea-Jonah, Word Biblical Commentary:* Dallas, Word, Incorporated, 1987, 63.

The rhetorical question that occurs in 3:1b serves as an introduction to the images of love in the book. Hobart says that the first five verses of the chapter follow the pattern of command, action, and interpretation.[292] However, Stuart finds that this ends with a great hope for the readers, which eventually culminates in chapter 14.[293] To begin with, the inseparable preposition כי in 3:1 brings out the comparison between Hosea and Gomer and God and Israel. Further, the conjunction ו points to the adulterous activities of the people of Israel because the Lord tells Hosea to go and "take" Gomer who has been engaged in adultery. According to Garrett, in 3:2 Hosea's 'buying her' is the action of fulfilling the command.[294] In 3:3, Hosea specifies that the woman he bought should remain faithful to him. Finally, in 3:4-5 he says that Yahweh will put a stop to the Israelites' wicked acts by chastening them. The Israelites were a people who, like Gomer, broke the sacred covenant. Wilkinson says that the "buying back" shows the price God had to pay to get people back. It is also regarded as a purifying punishment that follows restoration of Israel to the Promised Land.[295] This shows the symbolic vision of the people understanding Yahweh's command and the prophet's behaviour. Thus, the binding force of all the repetitive imagery in this section is the covenant.

Table 3: Repetition of words in Hosea 2:16-3:5

v. 1	יהוה	אהב	ומנאפת	ישׂראל	פנים			
v. 1	יהוה	אהבת						
v. 1		אהבת						
v. 1		ואהב						
v. 3			תזני			תשׁבי		ימים
v. 4				ישׂראל		ישׁבו		ימים
v. 5	יהוה יהוה			ישׂראל			אלהיהם	הימים

The recurring theme in Hosea 2:14-23 (MT 16-25) is the covenant and restoration. Wright identifies three key terms associated with this theme: "in that day," "cut" and "covenant." The phrase "in that day," reminds of re-establishing the covenant relationship with Israel and all God's creatures (Hos. 2:18-20).[296] The Lord's promise is that they will be safe and secure in the Promised Land. This symbolises the hope that Israelites and animals will dwell in peace and security. They will not be attacked by anybody anymore. This brings out God's new covenant and reconciliation with the people.

The phrase "in that day" is used frequently in Hosea's writing, (vv. 16, 18, 21), but it is important to note that Hosea also uses another phrase 'last days.' These two

[292] Freeman E. Hobart, *An Introduction to the Old Testament Prophets*, Chicago, Moody press, 1968, 176-177.

[293] Stuart, Douglas, *Hosea-Jonah, Word Biblical Commentary:* Dallas, Word, Incorporated, 1987, 63.

[294] Garrett, *Hosea, Joel An Exegetical and Theological Exposition of Holy Scripture,* B and H Publishing Group, 1997, 125.

[295] Bruce Wilkinson and Kenneth Boa, *The Wilkinson and Boa Bible Handbook,* Nashville, Thomason Nelson publishers, 2002, 233.

[296] Christopher Wright, *An Eye for an Eye: The place of Old Testament Ethics Today,* Downers Grove, Inter Varsity Press, 1983, 18-19.

carry different meanings. In this context, "last days" talks about the relationship to be initiated and preceded with betrothal. For Phillips Anthony, Hosea 2:18ff clearly gives a picture it is Yahweh who directly takes the initiative to talk to Israel.[297] By doing this, Yahweh shows that He is the head of the house of Israel and that Israel had returned in repentance to Him. It also shows that it is God who directly addresses the bride. The promise referred to in 2:21-23 is of the new relationship and life of this world. God's love is restored through the blessings of his natural bounty. According to Harper the heavens will send rain on the earth which will bear fruit and meet the need of Israel.[298] Israel's prosperity comes through the heavens from Yahweh, who is the fountain head of authority. The popular belief is that both rain and dew came as the direct gifts of Yahweh.

ביום תקראי	on that day you will call (18)
ביום וכרתי ברית	on that day I will make a covenant (20)
ביום אענה	on that day I will answer (23)

The phrase "ביום on that day" has several translations. Macintosh translates the phrase as "and so on that day." Vasholz notices that the phrase does not refer to a particular time, and the day will be similar to God's character to Israel.[299] Wolff suggests "on that day," whereas Stuart says that the phrase can be translated "in the future," and continues that Hosea uses this expression to refer to an immediate future (cf. 1:5) or to the future (2:18, 20, and 23).[300] It is significant that Hosea uses this phrase as a synonym for "in the future" (1:5). According to Francis Landy, this reminds us of a new age that is yet to come; it does not refer to an eschatological future. According to Dempsey the phrase "on that day" is about the day of divine blessing and a time of cosmic salvation; both heaven and earth will now answer each other.[301] Hosea did not have any idea of the end times, but it refers to the age that is yet to come. However, Macintosh reminds us of the relationship between Yahweh and Israel through an allegory of the marriage between man and wife and a renewed marriage which will take place "on that day."[302] When that happens, it is in the hands of Israel to choose whether or not she chooses to rely on Yahweh to restore the relationship. God's promise is shown in the form of drawing back Israel through testing of His love and covenantal promises. The reversal takes place in the name of Hosea's children from Jezreel to God plants. The Lord will establish the ecological format and creates relationship between the natural and humankind. This shows the new understanding of the relationship between human beings and the natural world.

[297] Phillips Anthony, *Essays on Biblical Law,* London, T and T Clark, 2002, 123-124.

[298] W.R. Harper, *A Critical and Exegetical Commentary on Amos and Hosea,* Edinburgh, T and T Clark, 1956, 244.

[299] Vasholz Robert I., *English Standard Version Study Bible,* Wheaton, Crossway Bibles, 2008, 1626.

[300] Stuart, Douglas: *Hosea-Jonah, Word Biblical Commentary:* Dallas, Word, Incorporated, 1987, 54-55.

[301] Carol J. Dempsey, *The Prophets: A Liberation-Critical Reading,* Minneapolis, Fortress Press, 2000, 156.

[302] Macintosh, A.A, *A Critical and Exegetical Commentary on Hosea,* Edinburgh, T and T Clark, 1997, 78.

Hosea brings out the idea of anthropocentric forms in nature. The idea of biblical covenant brings out the idea of new global ethic in this context.

God plants her in the land because this brings out a positive answer to the call for God's help. Hosea 2:21: "you will know and they will know," explores the concept of the love of God embracing Israel and including other nations. However it is not certain whether the statement refers to a comparison between heaven and earth. Here, an agricultural metaphor is used in order to communicate the message: that the earth shall hear the fruits and products of the earth. Followed by the "answer" that is the corn, vines and olive trees representing a harvest of crops, and requesting the earth to receive moisture so that it may help grow and produce more and increase and bring more fruits. This communicates the message that fruits will bring more Word to the people and nourishes the people with the message of comfort and hope. The people of Israel will be healed then from their sickness and from their waywardness towards a future, in the days to come. The tender mercies of God are brought out in terms of blessings and spiritual benefits to Israel. Here is the argument that people should not dishonour God as the consequence is disorder. It is the call of God to Israel to return and in response God will show His loving kindness to them. The assurance is that 'you are my people and I am your God.' God thus promises manifold abundance of all gifts to them in their returning to him.

The next term is "cut" which was used as a common term in the Hebrew Bible to describe transactions. This term is commonly understood as 'breaking of the covenant.' Here in this context, "cut" refers to the person who makes a covenant. He is the author and is the one who enforces the entire arrangement and is its guarantor.[303] The term "on that day I will cut a covenant" shows that Yahweh, being the guarantor of this covenant, will create the conditions to make peace and give his blessings for Israel.[304]

The terms "cut" and "covenant" appear together. According to Mays, restoration takes place through the covenant (ברית). Harold points out that this is the first time out of a total of five times that the term "covenant" appears in the book (cf. 12:1 and 10:4).[305] Two of the references refer to the covenant Yahweh extended to Israel and His people after He rescued them from the land of Egypt (6:7; 8:1; cf. 11:1 and 13:4-5). Mays comments, that the covenant is a solemn promise based on an oath between two parties.[306] Here the covenant is called 'new' because the people failed to keep the law that was made on Mount Sinai.[307] Following the regulations and requirements of the covenant bring blessings of peace and security. This promise is extended to God's people and all living things and Yahweh expects the people to

---

[303] Andersen, F.I and Freedman, D.N., *Hosea: A New Translation with Introduction and Commentary,* New York, Doubleday, 1980, 280.

[304] Cf. M. Weinfeld, *TDOT,* vol. 2, 253-279 and Ernest W. Nicholson, *God and His People: Covenant and Theology in the Old Testament,* Oxford, Clarendon Press, 1986

[305] Shank Harold, *Minor Prophets,* Vol. 1, Joplin, Missouri, College Press Publishing co, 2001, 54-55.

[306] Mays, James Luther., *Hosea: A Commentary,* OTL, Philadelphia, Westminster, 1969, 49. Cf. Andersen, F.I and Freedman, D.N., *Hosea: A New Translation with Introduction and Commentary,* New York, Doubleday, 1980, 280-281.

[307] Dearman, J.A, *The Book of Hosea,"* NICOT, Grand Rapids, Wm. B. Eerdmans Publishing co, 2010, 125-126. Cf. Andersen, F.I and Freedman, D.N., *Hosea: A New Translation with Introduction and Commentary,* New York, Doubleday, 1980, 280-281.

renew the covenant and to receive peace and security. God is the source of all living things and preserves His earth and provides life for Israel. The word "creatures" goes beyond preserving the earth, as Yahweh gives life to everyone. The link is noted between creation and Israel as His covenant people. Hosea's conception of a national covenant is influenced by people collectively. This reminds them to move from failure to be faithful to their covenant calling. Thus, the prophet employs ברית in two senses, one is to do with political agreements between peoples, and the other is Yahweh's initiation of a relationship with Israel or other aspects of His creation. The acts of God are presented here to illustrate how God even changes his mind from destruction to discipline, because His purpose is not only for Israel but for the people of all nations.

Finally, the climax of the covenant is seen through the imagery of love which is found in the threefold repetition of the verb ארש "to betroth" in the first person common singular form. Such a repetition recalls an ancient pre-monarchic poetic style.[308] Next, the phrase "in that day" shows that there is a restoration of relationship. Sweeney says that here the marriage metaphor is used to describe a "true husband."[309] Dearman comments that he will not be called "my Baal" any more as Yahweh will be their master.[310] In this case Israel is spiritually restored and she will be revived; Israel will recognize Yahweh as her true husband. Therefore, true covenant relationship is established between Yahweh and those who honestly worship Him. God spoke to His children who worship in truth about His love. His great love proves His great sacrifice, and His great gift of salvation.

3.3.1.1. Repetition of ארש

The second important word in Hosea 2:14-25 associated with repetitive texture is "betrothal." The Hebrew term used for betrothal is ארש used in the piel form in Hosea 1:2 which mean to "go, take in." Hosea uses this term three times in 2:21,22. This refers to his old marriage. It appears later in the passage related to his new marriage.

Table 4: Repetition of Betrothal in Hosea 2:19-20 (21-22 MT)

וארשתיך	I will betroth
וארשתיך	I will betroth
וארשתיך	I will betroth
אענה	I will answer
אענה	I will answer
ויאמרתי	I will say

The translation of ארש is seen by scholars to have two meanings: one of permanent marriage, which will be 'For ever,' and one which will be only 'for now.' However, both can carry the idea of remarriage. Wolff and Macintosh say, "I will betroth you

---

[308] See W. F. Albright, *Yahweh and the Gods of Canaan,* 1-52.

[309] Marvin A. Sweeney, *Tanak: A Theological and Critical Introduction to the Jewish Bible,* Minneapolis, Fortress Press, 1953, 347-348.

[310] Dearman, J.A., *The Book of Hosea,*" NICOT, Grand Rapids, Wm. B. Eerdmans Publishing co, 2010, 124.

and I will make you My own forever," while Tanakh refers to it as "I will espouse you forever" which literally means "to marry." Francis Landy notes that ארש is translated as "I will betroth you My bride" and the piel form denotes the act of legal marriage which refers to a temporary earthly marriage.[311] William Sanford makes clear that the word "I will betroth" appears three times and suggests a binding formula in the book by Hosea.[312] According to Freedman, "I will betroth you" is repeated thrice in 2:19-20 (21-22 MT) and emphasises the new image of marriage.[313] The Hebrew phrase to me occurs three times in line with "betroth." This repetition emphasises the personal relationship between Yahweh and Israel.[314] Harper comments that "I will betroth" is repeated thrice, the statement of betrothal makes it both emphatic and solemn.[315] The term refers directly to the marriage covenant. According to Dearman, the term betroth refers to "I will take you in marriage for myself." For Wolff, ארש is understood as the customary and public act of marriage.[316] For Dempsey the marriage between God and Israel is a covenant, particularly using the analogy for covenant. In the book of Hosea, the concept of marriage is a beginning of a new relationship between God and Israel. It is called a new covenant.[317] In Hebrew culture, a betrothed couple should not sleep together until they are officially married, but in other ways they are officially considered as married. The word "betroth" refers to legal binding or commitment between two parties as they begin a marriage relationship. The theme thus describes the eternal covenant between two parties. "I will betroth you in righteousness" shows God's quality of being consistently good to Israel. He is merciful and compassionate to his people. The consistent goodness shows God's faithfulness (in contrast to Ba'al) is the basis for Israel's salvation.

The ארש guarantees a lasting relationship in marriage (for ever, a long time). Francis Landy says that marriage is a legal term that denotes lifelong commitment between two partners.[318] W. Brueggemann affirms that Yahweh is taking Israel as his bride once again in remarriage, which includes a relationship made right, justice, steadfast love, compassion and faithfulness to each other[319] (cf. Exo. 34:6-7). Exodus 34 is about the breach of covenant, which includes the second commandment of Decalogue (Exo. 20:5-6; Deut. 5:9-10). This shows the completion of the concept of theophany that begun in Exo. 33:19, where Yahweh's expressed intent to show Moses his goodness and that He will be gracious to whom he will be gracious and show mercy to whom he will show mercy. In the future the new marriage between Yahweh

[311] Francis Landy, *Hosea,* Sheffield, Sheffield Academic Press, 1995, 43-44.

[312] William Sanford, *Old Testament Survey: The Message Form, and Background of the Old Testament,* Grand Rapids, Wm. B. Eerdmans publishing company, 1982, 338-339.

[313] Andersen and Freedman, *Hosea: A New Translation with Introduction and Commentary,* New York, Doubleday, 1980, 283.

[314] Andersen and Freedman, *Hosea: A New Translation with Introduction and Commentary,* New York, Doubleday, 1980, 282-283.

[315] W.R. Harper, *A Critical and Exegetical Commentary on Amos and Hosea,* Edinburgh, T and T Clark, 1956, 243.

[316] Wolff, *Hosea* (G. Stansell, Trans.), Philadelphia, Fortress Press, 1974, 45-46.

[317] Carol J. Dempsey, *The Prophets: A Liberation-Critical Reading,* Minneapolis, Fortress Press, 2000, 154.

[318] Francis Landy, *Hosea,* Sheffield, Sheffield Academic Press, 1995, 44-45.

[319] W. Brueggemann, *Theology of the Old Testament,* Minneapolis, Fortress Press, 1997, 222-223.

and Israel in Hos. 2:14-20 [MT 16-22] is predicted on the prior election of Israel in the wilderness (2:14) [MT 16]. The prophet used to identify or reveal something about the present that is rooted in historical tradition and have narrative context.[320] However, for B.S. Childs the betrothal here talks about an event that is going to take place forever (Hos. 2:21.)[321] It appears as though Israel is being reminded that her marriage that began in the wilderness was not going to be permanent.

According to Davies, Israel is expected to renew her relationship and this requires an expectation and requirement in the remarriage.[322] In that case the community of Israel will then become a covenant community again, with Yahweh as her Lord. The new marriage reflects a covenant and a sense of social justice prevails for her and her neighbours. The above terms refer to the character of the faithful husband Yahweh, who will go against the Mosaic command and enter into remarriage. The question that needs to be answered is why God would do such a thing. There seems to be a broader purpose which is only subtly hinted at in the text earlier in 1:4-5 and later in 2:21-22^{Heb} (19-20^{Eng}).

The section ends with an explanation of consummation "and you shall know the Lord" (2:22). In this context, it is noted that both the betrothal and marriage are combined into one form without a gap and this means that the marriage continues. The betrothal involves two important aspects: "righteousness and justice" indicated in legal standards, to meet in betrothal; and "love and compassion" denoted in God's emotional concern for the new bride.[323]

> The repetition of "betrothal" signifies that restoration, not reconciliation, is being discussed. In addition, the qualities given in the marriage appeal are unique and are different from the metaphors of love used by the other Old Testament prophets. The eschatological community of Israel is denoted by the word לעולם "forever."

Charles Dyer and Eugene comment that as the betrothal is followed by a new marriage, it indicates the new relationship mentioned in Hosea 2:16-25.[324] In the previous section, Hosea 2:5 (MT 3), the image indicates that the bride is about to be punished because of her adultery. But the prophet comes out with a strong message that instead Yahweh will renew their relationship through the covenant made with them (Hos. 2:20ff [MT 18]).[325] In the old marriage, everything was lost but now in the new marriage restoration takes place. Now Yahweh promises that Israel will receive what she once lost; all her land and vineyards (Hos. 2:17a [MT 15]). This is

---

[320] Dwight R. Daniels, *Hosea and Salvation History,* BZAW 191; Berlin, de Gruyter, 1990, 130.

[321] B.S. Childs, *Old Testament in a Canonical Context,* Philadelphia, Fortress Press, 1989, 96-97.

[322] Davies, *Hosea, The New Century Bible Commentary,* Michigan, Wm. B. Eerdmans Publishing Co, 1992, 85-86.

[323] Stuart, Hosea, *Hosea-Jonah, Word Biblical Commentary:* Dallas, Word, Incorporated, 1987, 59 and Wood, *Hosea, The Prophets of Israel,* Grand Rapids, Baker Academic group, 1979, 179, Keil, F. Keil, *The Twelve Minor Prophets, Bible Commentary on the Old Testament* by C. F. Keil and F. Delitzsch, trans. By James Martin (2 vols. Grand Rapids, Wm. B. Eerdmans Publishing Company, 1949), I, 43

[324] Charles Dyer and E. Merrill, *Nelson's Old Testament Survey,* Nashville, Thomas Nelson Publishers, 2001, 728.

[325] Leon J. Wood, *The Prophets of Israel,* Grand Rapids, Baker Book House, 1979, 282.

considered as the first step in establishing a new marriage, the gift for the new bride Israel. This gift includes gold and silver, but the special gift is Yahweh's love for his new bride, which brings out the message of renewal of their covenant relationship. It needs to be remembered that God wants to show himself as a faithful 'husband' and go to the extent of breaking His decree of what the Mosaic Law has commanded Looking at this purely from the covenant point of view is like wearing blinkers as there seems be a contradictory 'order' or norm. There may be another explanation.

Beeby notes that the new marriage will have the qualities that the old marriage lacked: fairness, justice, loyalty, mercy, honesty and above all, permanence.[326] But Stuart argues that the use of the preposition ב along with the qualities signifies that this is the "bride price" that Yahweh gives to his wife and thus Yahweh takes the role of a father and husband and pays the bride price himself.[327] However, Garrett's opinion is that the preposition ב indicates that the price paid is doubled, given in both coin and grain.[328] For Dearman, the bride price is in terms of extension of provisions and gifts by Yahweh, which include faithfulness and love. The gifts and building of a family suggest a reference to a covenant community.[329] This marriage is permanent and not temporary (לעולם). The marriage relationship is based on the character of Yahweh himself.[330] The attributes come from the Lord and His divine initiative that represents the community.

In this section, most of the imagery used (for example, bride price and gifts) echoes the salvation message which indeed was for all people, not just for Israel. From this, we see that God's greater purpose in renewing the covenant was far beyond Israel; it was meant for all the peoples of the earth and was to be fulfilled later through the Messiah.

3.3.1.2. Repetition of ענה

In this section, the word associated with the repetitive texture in Hosea 2:14-23 is ענה "I will respond" or "I will answer." This is not a theme, but a significant phrase in this texture. According to Andersen and Freedman, the repetition of ענה "I will answer/respond" signifies covenant restoration.[331] At present, the covenant is broken because of the unfaithful wife. Therefore Yahweh, on renewing it, says that He will respond to the sky and all creation so they will respond to each other as a progressive act. Thus, the whole cosmos will once again be renewed under the new covenant. John Walton comments that the key role is played by Yahweh which is indicated in the repetition of the term, "I will respond."[332] Although it is grammatically

---

[326] Beeby, H.D, *Grace Abounding: A Commentary on the book of Hosea,* Grand Rapids, Eerdmans, 1989, 28.

[327] Stuart, Douglas: *Hosea-Jonah, Word Biblical Commentary:* Dallas, Word, Incorporated, 1987, 58-59.

[328] Garrett, *Hosea, Joel,* NAC, 19A, Nashville, Broadman and Holman, 1997, 80-81.

[329] Dearman. J.A, *The Book of Hosea,*" NICOT, Grand Rapids, Wm. B. Eerdmans Publishing co, 2010, 126-127.

[330] Andersen, F.I and Freedman, D.N, *Hosea: A New Translation with Introduction and Commentary,* New York, Doubleday, 1980, 284.

[331] Andersen, F.I and Freedman, D.N, *Hosea: A New Translation with Introduction and Commentary,* New York, Doubleday, 1980, 276.

[332] John H. Walton, *Zondervan Illustrated Bible Backgrounds Commentary,* vol. 5, Grand Rapids, Zondervan publisher, 1984, 20.

incomplete, it helps in establishing both the rhythm and rhetoric. In the history of Israel so far, Yahweh speaks to His people only through a mediator. In contrast now, the eschatological Israel will experience this same Yahweh talking to them directly because Israel is His wife. The phrase "I will answer" is thus a part of the dialogue between husband and wife which has other phrases like אענה, וענתה, ויאמרתי יאמר. Their significance is noted as the prophet reminds Israel that it is Yahweh who is their God, not Baal, and it is God who provides their needs: grain, new wine and oil (cf. 2:8). It is Yahweh who bestows blessings upon the people with rain.

3.3.1.3. Repetition of יהוה

In 3:1-5, the word Lord (יהוה) is repeated four times.[333] According to Martin J. Buss, 3:1 begins with Yahweh as the speaker.[334] But for Ward the phrase ויאמר יהוה אלי is used to describe a peculiar experience Hosea had.[335] In 3:1, the verse has been slightly adjusted: Andersen and Freedman note that the four occurrences of the term "Lord" in Hosea 3 are a reminder of the Lord's command to Hosea to marry a woman.[336] The significance is the word "Lord" which appears twice in 3:1 and twice in 3:5.

The fact that "Lord" appears four times in this chapter emphasises that the entire chapter is focused primarily on God, rather than on Hosea. The repetition serves not only to move the focus to God, but also to tell the people about God. In this instance, Alice Parmelee notes that Yahweh's vital role is observed, as he shows His love to His people through a symbolic action.[337] Biblical writers use Yahweh as God's name and the word "I" refers to Him as the originator of the covenant with His people.[338] In this case, the name Yahweh reminds Israel that Yahweh is the God of her ancestors, and this is implied in Hosea, under the guidance of the same God.[339]

3.3.1.4. Repetition of אהב - Prominence of love in Marital Relationship

The repeated use of אהב in Hosea 3:1 emphasises the importance of love in the "marital relationship" between Yahweh and Israel. It also serves as a motivation for Yahweh's dealings with Israel. Yahweh Himself pleaded with them not to yield to temptation (cf. Lev. 19:4; 20:6). Here it means that God is the husband and Israel is His wife. Yet even though God has shown his love for the people of Israel, they have turned away from God and sought other gods. This metaphor is an example to explain the state of affairs between God and his people.[340] Rudolph observes that this is the

[333] Stuart, Douglas: *Word Biblical Commentary: Hosea-Jonah,* Dallas, Word, Incorporated, 1987, 65.

[334] Martin J. Buss, *The Prophetic Word of Hosea: A Morphological Study,* Berlin, Verlag Alfred Topelmann, 1969, 50-52.

[335] Ward, James M. *Hosea: A Theological Commentary,* New York, Harper and Row Publishers, 1966, 56.

[336] Andersen, F.I and Freedman, D.N., *Hosea: A New Translation with Introduction and Commentary,* New York, Doubleday, 1980, 295-296.

[337] Alice Parmelee, *A Guide to the Old Testament and the Apocrypha,* Wilton, Morehouse-Barlow, 1979, 84-85.

[338] David Noel Freedman, 1001-1011, New York: Doubleday, 1992. The Hebrew term *el* means god. The term אלהים, is a plural form that serves to emphasize the absoluteness of God.

[339] David Noel Freedman, "Yahweh" in *TDOT,* Vol. 5 eds., J.G. Botterweck and Helmer Ringgren, 500-521, trans. David E. Green, Grand Rapids, Eerdmans, 1986, 500.

[340] Macintosh, A.A, *A Critical and Exegetical Commentary on Hosea,* Edinburgh, T and T Clark, 1997, 97.

fourth use of the verb love (qal, perfect); describing how the Israelites embraced Baal worship,[341] where evil entered into אהב, and created a breakdown in the relationship between Yahweh and his people.

The repetition of אהב denotes a technical covenantal term for a relationship of loyalty. The repetition of various derivatives of the root word אהב provides imagery for Israel. Dearman observes that the idea that Hosea loves a woman but the woman loves another man is parallel to the idea that Yahweh loves Israel but Israel loves 'raisin cakes.'[342] Here it is used as a pun.

Yahweh's love	wife's love	Israel's love
noble, unselfish, generous	evil, selfish	raisin cakes, pleasure oriented
continues as persistent unbroken love	commits adultery	turns to other gods

The use of the chiastic structure in vv. 3

ימים רבים תשבי לי
וגם־אני אליך and
לא תזני
לא תהיי לאיש

indicates reciprocity in the relationship between Yahweh and Israel. The dual use of לא emphasises that זנה (promiscuity) is rejection of Yahweh. The parallelism here increases the instruction not to fornicate and not to belong to any other man. The repeated use of ואין in v. 4 emphasises the removal of Israel's security.

The use of synonymous phrases

ואין שר
אין מלך
ואין מצבה
ואין זבח and
ותרפים
ואין אפוד

focuses on Israel's false securities. The progressive parallelism in v. 5: emphasises the people's intent to return שוב to Yahweh as the one who gives salvation.

אחר ישבו בני ישראל
ובקשו את־יהוה אלהיהם
ואת דוד מלכם
ופחדו אל־יהוה ואל־טובו

In 3:5 MT proposes ובקש "and seek." The word בקש has the same sense of seeking to gain or regain a person or thing. Stuart argues that "seek" implies that the

[341] Here Rudolph's observation is that Hosea here reflects the understanding of his contemporaries within the context of adulterous idolatry is important. Rudolph identifies this kind of love in the Canaanite cult practices.

[342] Dearman, J.A, *The Book of Hosea,*" NICOT, Grand Rapids, Wm. B. Eerdmans Publishing co, 2010, 135.

people of Israel have disobeyed the promise and that they will שוב return one day (in the future).[343] Lewis points out that the word בקש is translated in piel imperfect verb form as "seek," which means Israel's repentance from her rebellious action of going after other gods is envisioned in the future.[344] Mays opinion is that this section closes with hope.[345] The prophet pleads with the people of Israel to return to the Lord.[346] Otherwise, when they disobey again, they will be taken back into bondage as they were earlier. However, the hope is given to Israel that, when she returns/seeks Yahweh, there is healing. The repetitive use of אהב in Hosea 3.1 emphasises the importance of love in the marital relationship between Yahweh and Israel.

3.3.1.5. Theme Repetition

The words below all relate to the concepts of love, compassion and justice, and are used to emphasise the recurrent theme of love in this section. They are:

Table 5: Theme Repetition Hosea 2:16-3:5

פתיה	Persuading	רחמה	compassion
תקוה	Hope	טוב	goodness
ברית	Covenant	עוד	no longer / no more
בטש	Safety	עוד	again
צדק	righteousness	לבה	her heart
משפט	Justice	כרמיה	her vineyard
חסד	loving kindness	נעוריה	her youth
רחמים	tender mercy	מפיה	her mouth
זרע	Sow		

In this section, love takes first place and precedes the return. The prophet is commanded to go again and love a woman (Israel), so love plays an important role in bringing back Israel. Yahweh's love to Israel can be extended to other nations. It is almost a forerunner to the salvation message that came through the Messiah, which was not only for Jews but also for other people.

Yahweh has decided to appeal anew to his wayward bride, not through forceful punishments but through her willingness to repent and return to Yahweh. For Stuart, the wilderness was where she was dependent on and relatively faithful to Him after they were newly "married" in the covenant at Sinai (cf. 13:4–6). Israel will symbolically

---

[343] Stuart, Douglas, *Hosea-Jonah, Word Biblical Commentary:* Dallas, Word, Incorporated, 1987, 67.

[344] Lewis. Jack P., *New International Version Study Bible,* Grand Rapids, Zondervan Bible Publishers, 1985, 1325.

[345] J.L. Mays, *Hosea: A Commentary,* Philadelphia, The Westminster Press, 1969, 59. Cf. Landy, Francis, "In the Wilderness of Speech: Problems of Metaphors in Hosea," *BibInt* 3, 1995, 35-36. Cf. Jobling, David, A Deconstructive reading of Hosea 1-3, in *Relating to the Text,* ed. T.J. Sandoval, *JSOTsup* 384, London, T. and T. Clark, 2003, 206-206.

[346] J.L. Mays, *Hosea: A Commentary,* Philadelphia, The Westminster Press, 1969, 59. Cf. Landy Francis, "In the Wilderness of Speech: Problems of Metaphors in Hosea," *BibInt* 3, 1995, 35-36. Cf. Jobling, David, A Deconstructive reading of Hosea 1-3, in *Relating to the Text,* ed. T.J. Sandoval, *JSOTsup* 384, London, T. and T. Clark, 2003, 206-206.

return there if she is unrepentant. According to Harper *in the days of her youth* refers to bring her back to Him as it was in the days of her youth, Yahweh seduces Israel.[347] Hosea uses rhetoric to show Yahweh's yearning for his wife through repetition of actions such as מפתיה והלכתיה and so on. The emphatic usage of the language of love is found in דברתי על־לבה (speaking to her heart). To "romance her"[348] (לבה על דבר) is a tender expression, used of courtship and winning back love.

The covenantal relationship in the Pentateuch is regained in a much deeper sense, as Yahweh says "You will no longer call me בעלי "My Master" but אישי "My man."[349] The Greek translation is in plural form, Baalim, and means "Baals," or "husbands." Harper translates as my husband; this implies Israel's return to the proper understanding of her relation to Yahweh and of her service acceptable by him.[350] According to Mays, the Hebrew word refers to בעלי "My Master," but אישי "My man" means that the husband is partner and he is the counterpart of the woman (cf. Gen. 2:23; 3:6, 16). Mays continues that the word בעל comes from a verb which means "possessor," "to own" and to "have rights over." The relationship refers to the husband (lord) in marriage, where the husband has rights as possessor of the married woman (cf. the legal rights in the texts of the book of Ex. 21:3, 22; Deut. 22:22; 24:4).[351] For John Walton, the term means an intimate relationship between a husband and wife. It is not the legal bond between a husband and wife but it is more to do with the love between them. Garrett says that the same term also has other meanings like "owner," and "lord."[352] According to Weems, the marriage is a metaphor which the prophet employs here to describe the relationship between Israel and Yahweh and which culminated in covenantal renewal on both sides.[353] The shift takes place that Hosea's love for the woman continues and he will continue to love her, because God has dealt kindly with them and loved them in the wilderness. The fulfilment brings blessing of an everlasting contract, a covenant stands forever and will never be broken.

The term is referred to as "the marriage bond" of the covenant. It shows the peculiarity of Hosea's usage of the imagery of love compared with that of other prophets. This brings out the concept of covenant language that affirms promises and redemption to them. The legal agreement between God and human brings out the idea of relationship. In Hosea it is established as God's covenant with human is the initiative of God. This section highlights one of the strong impressions of covenantal love of God for Israel. The prophet here portrays how God's unfailing love binds the covenantal people.

---

[347] W.R. Harper, *A Critical and Exegetical Commentary on Amos and Hosea,* Edinburgh, T and T Clark, 1956, 240.

[348] J.L. Mays, *Hosea: A Commentary,* Philadelphia, The Westminster Press, 1969, 59.

[349] Stuart, Douglas, *Hosea-Jonah,* Word Biblical Commentary: Dallas, Word, Incorporated, 1987, 54-55. Cf. *NIDOTTE,* H1251 and Davis, *Hosea*, 82.

[350] W.R. Harper, *A Critical and Exegetical Commentary on Amos and Hosea,* Edinburgh, T and T Clark, 1956, 234.

[351] Mays, James Luther., *Hosea: A Commentary,* OTL, Philadelphia, Westminster Press, 1969, 48-49.

[352] Garrett, *Hosea, Joel: An Exegetical and Theological Exposition of Holy Scripture,* B and H Publisher, 1997, 113.

[353] Renita J. Weems, *Battered Love: Marriage, Sex, and Violence in the Hebrew Prophets,* Minneapolis, Fortress Press, 1995, 27.

A few of the prophets, such as Isaiah and Jeremiah have also used the imagery of marriage, but the word used is בעל in Isa. 54:5; Jer. 3:14 and not איש. Therefore, by becoming her man, Yahweh is wiping off all the memories of Baal, so that Israel will know only Yahweh, as she knew Him during her exodus from Egypt. Thus, Yahweh is bringing her back to the faith she had when she started her redemptive journey in the wilderness. The symbolic name emphasises spiritual revival and recognizes God to be the true husband, with Israel as His wife.

In addition to the themes of covenant, restoration, betrothal and the phrase, "I will respond / I will answer" in Hosea 2:14-25, there are repetitive rhetorical phrases used relating to God's love for the children of Israel, and for an adulterous woman and another man, which also appear in 3:1-5.[354]

Repetitive rhetorical phrases are seen in Hosea 3; however, in spite of these, the harmony of this unit is questioned. In Hosea 3:1-5 there is a disconnection at a certain point. The indefinite command *"love a woman"* does not justify the suffix *"I bought her for myself."* The texts produce voices; however, the speaker is Yahweh. He tells her not to play the whore in v. 3. He also binds himself in His covenant with Israel, while dictating terms to her by saying *"so will I also be to you."*[355] In this way he turns the heart of the people to the recollection of their being people of the covenant.

Yahweh dominates the action, removing heterodoxy, instituting his new covenant, betrothing Israel to Himself, ensuring fertility, welcoming the prodigal home - all according to the predictions of the new age in the Mosaic covenantal sanctions.[356] The consistency of Yahweh as speaker and the repetition of "in that day" provide a structural unity for the passage.

3.3.1.6. Betrothal in the New Covenant in Hosea 2:21-22 [19-20^{Eng}]

This section deals with the new order when Yahweh will betroth Israel again. This time in loving kindness, mercy and faithfulness; and finally Israel shall really know Yahweh. It is in this unit that the transformation of the relationship between God and His covenant people takes place; the nature of the covenant relationship between them is shown through the metaphors (2:19-23). The symbolic marriage covenant presents God as the husband and Israel as the covenant people (the bride). According to Vangemeren, renewal takes place in the form of love and creation of the harmony of God's covenant relationship.[357] According to Stuart, the two verses of Hosea 2:19-20 [21-22 MT] form a unit but the verse division is a disruptive one. Yahweh addresses his beloved directly; the metaphor shifts to marriage betrothal, thus bringing in a full circle the allegorical theme that began in 2:4. Stuart remarks that the emphasis now is not merely reconciliation but restoration through the imagery of the new marriage.

---

[354] The chiastic structure indicates reciprocity in the relationship between Yahweh and Israel.

[355] Vasholz. Robert I, *English Standard Version Study Bible,* Wheaton, Crossway Bibles, 2008, 1626-1628.

[356] Beeby, H.D, *Grace Abounding: A Commentary on the book of Hosea,* Grand Rapids, Eerdmans, 1989, 28.

[357] W.A. Vangemeren, *Interpreting the Prophetic Word,* Grand Rapids, Zondervan Publishing House, 1990, 116.

In the ancient Hebrew culture, bride price was either a gift given to the bride's father by her husband[358] or a gift that the husband gives to his bride.[359] Consequently the expression "I will betroth you in righteousness and justice" refers to the bride price, and the betrothal refers to the ancient Israelite practice of formalizing the marriage contract by the groom's payment of the bride-price to the bride's father.[360] This was the final step in the courtship process, virtually equivalent in law to the wedding ceremony.[361] Dearman says that the betrothal metaphor is expressed dramatically via the decisive threefold repetition of the verb "to betroth" in the first person common in singular form. Such repetitive forms recall an ancient monarchic poetic style.[362] Westermann points out that the new marriage will begin with the new affirmation of Israel's covenant and their commitment to their God. God's love and transformation will bring change in the heart and minds of God's chosen covenant people.[363] Here the first marriage is connected with 2:16-19, with the affirmation that God will transform Israel completely as His new partner. The language of the section, as shown in the following chart, emphasises the strength of Israel's commitment to the covenant, both in adhering to her bridegroom (Yahweh) and in turning away from "other gods." The text illustrates how God chose them as the ones to redeem and for that He paid the price to own them as His bride.

Table 6: Terms that portray a dialogue between Yahweh and Israel - Hosea 2:16-3:5

וענתה	she will answer	ונתתי	I will give
יאמר	he will say	והסרתי	I will take away
ימים רבים תשבי	dwell for me many days	וכרתי	I will cut
ימים רבים תשבי	dwell for me many days	אשבור	I will break
מפתיה	I will persuade	והשכ בתים	I will make
ודברתי	I will speak	ורחמתי	I will have compassion

The above terms portray a dialogue between Yahweh and Israel represented by Hosea and Gomer. The words "I will answer," refers to the fact that she will willingly follow by responding to the complaint made against her. Wolff comments that "she will answer" refers to more than an answer in the sense of exchanging words. The woman accepts and is ready to renew her covenantal relationship. The word "answer" implies her response. Garrett comments that this is followed by the condition that she will dwell there for many days.[364] The woman is expected to stay for a long time and

---

[358] *HALOT,* 911.

[359] Davies, *Hosea, The New Century Bible Commentary,* Michigan, Wm B. Eerdmans Publishing Co, 1992, 85-86.

[360] Stuart, Douglas: *Hosea-Jonah, Word Biblical Commentary:* Dallas, Word, Incorporated, 1987, 59.

[361] "The Divorce Formula in Hos. 2:4a," *ITS* 34, 1997, 56-88.

[362] Dearman. *J.A, The Book of Hosea,*" NICOT, Grand Rapids, Wm. B. Eerdmans Publishing co, 2010, 127.

[363] Claus Westermann, *Handbook to the Old Testament,* London, SPCK, 1969, 179.

[364] Garrett, *Hosea, Joel An Exegetical and Theological Exposition of Holy Scripture,* B and H Publishing Group, 1997, 125.

to renew her relationship. Hosea persuades his wife to remain faithful and to sustain the relationship.[365] This is a reminder of the covenant between husband and wife in terms of conditions laid down by her husband.

The negative terms "I will take away," "I will cut," "I will break" turn into positive ones like "I will give," "I will make," "I will have compassion." These terms denote Yahweh's faithfulness to the covenant and His kindness to Israel, presented as steadfast love and kindness to his chosen people. Yahweh's love for His chosen people (cf. Ex. 34:6) is then used by Hosea in the context of married love. The divine love consists of self-giving, trust, a deep affection and submission to each other. Francis Landy identifies the restrictive words "many days" "stay" "dwell" and "return" which are changed into positive ones like "many days stay for me," "do not go commit adultery," "do not be for a man, and also I to you."[366] The terms in the selected passage show how important Yahweh's love and compassion for Israel is, and how Israel can restore the covenant relationship with Yahweh by seeking forgiveness. According to Kohlenberger, Yahweh's assurance is, "many days you shall remain with me if you shall neither prostitute yourself nor be with any man and then I shall be yours" (Exo. 19:9).[367] This shows the covenant made between Hosea and Gomer to be true in intending that their relationship will last for a long time.[368]

3.3.1.7. The Word ברית

Hosea 2:18 [MT 2:20] looks back to previous texts where the oracles are mentioned. Harper comments that the promise of God is that he would make a covenant with beasts of the earth and all creatures.[369] But for McComiskey, the promise also clearly explains about the description of God's creatures in Genesis 1:21, 24.[370] The idea is the restoration of the order of creation. The Hebrew word כרת ברית appears in 12:1 and 10:4. In these references, "covenant" denotes an international treaty made between Israel and other nations. Mays in his argument affirm this; Yahweh will make a covenant with his creation for the sake of Israel.[371] Garrett points out that Hosea 2:18 [MT 2:20] is about the reconciliation of people and Yahweh that will create a new environment of peace and blessings.[372] This may be the reason why the pronouns change from singular "you" (Israel) to plural "them" (people) to infer the covenant has a wider and inclusive connotation. Kevin Vanhoozer says that the concept of the covenant relates here to the fact that God makes a covenant with all

---

365 Gale Yee, *Composition and Tradition in the Book of Hosea: A Redaction-Critical Approach:* SBL Dissertation Series 102, Atlanta, Scholars Press, 1987, 199-220.

366 Francis Landy, *Hosea,* Sheffield, Sheffield Academic Press, 1995, 49.

367 Kenneth L. Barker and John R. Kohlenberger, *Zondervan NIV Bible Commentary,* vol. 1, Grand Rapids, Zondervan publishers, 1994, 1411. Cf. Garrett, *Hosea, Joel An Exegetical and Theological Exposition of Holy Scripture,* B and H Publishing Group, 1997, 126.

368 Garrett, *Hosea, Joel An Exegetical and Theological Exposition of Holy Scripture,* B and H Publishing Group, 1997, 126.

369 W.R. Harper, *A Critical and Exegetical Commentary on Amos and Hosea,* Edinburgh, T and T Clark, 1956, 242.

370 McComiskey, *Hosea,* notes the "covenant" includes the creatures which is free will. See Jeremiah 33:20.

371 Mays, James Luther., *Hosea: A Commentary,* OTL, Philadelphia, Westminster, 1969, 52.

372 Garrett, *Hosea, Joel: An Exegetical and Theological Exposition of Holy Scripture,* B and H Publisher, 1997, 114.

the beasts of the earth.[373] Charles Dyer and Eugene Merrill comment that it is here that Yahweh affirms that he will make a new covenant with the beasts of the earth.[374] It is seen as an act of restoration of creation. This idea brings out the promise of the assurance of peace in the land in Lev. 25:6. The abundant blessing shown earlier is seen in the covenant that God makes with his creation here[375] is seen in the acts of Yahweh indicate ownership, where he will restore creation and the blessing will continue in the future. The covenant thus expands to the eschatological image meant for all people: that they will have a new world (cf. Isa. 11:6-9 and 35:9).

Hosea then illustrates to the Israelites how the marriage represents the covenant relationship between them. Yahweh decides to appeal anew to his wayward wife, not through forceful punishments but through her willingness to return to Yahweh. In order to bring back Israel, Hosea uses rhetoric, saying Yahweh seduces Israel. The language of love is used to win back his love. The covenantal relationship is regained in a much deeper sense as Yahweh says "You will no longer call me Baal (my Master) but I (my Man)." This means an intimate relationship between husband and wife. It is not a legal bond but more to do with the love between them. In Hosea, God's covenant with humans is the initiative of God. In addition to covenant, restoration, and betrothal, the phrase 'I will respond / I will answer' in Hosea 2.14-25, there are repetitive rhetorical phrases relating to God's love for the children of Israel. The expression "I will betroth you in righteousness and justice" refers to the bride price, and the betrothal refers to the ancient Israelite practice of formalizing marriage. The negative terms "I will take away," "I will cut," "I will break" turn into positive ones like "I will give," "I will make," "I will have compassion." These terms denote Yahweh's faithfulness to the covenant and His kindness to Israel, presented as steadfast love and kindness to his chosen people. This shows that covenant between Hosea and Gomer is true, intending that their relationship will last for a long time. Hosea 2:18 [MT 2:20] is about the reconciliation of people and Yahweh that will create a new environment of peace and blessings. The pronouns change from singular "you" (Israel) to plural "them" (people). The phrase "my master" has the meaning of eschatological restoration of Israel (cf. Joel 3:18). The significance is the hope of future salvation as the basis for present reformation. God predicts the restoration of the people and they will be his forever. The concept of covenant relates here to the fact that God makes a covenant with all the beasts of the earth.

3.3.2. Progressive Texture

Progressive textuality emerges out of repetition of words and phrases in the text unit. Progressive texture is a sequence of words and phrases alternating with one another but capable of arranging itself into a systematic diagram.[376] It identifies the sequence of words and phrases throughout the text.

---

[373] Kevin Vanhoozer, *Theological Interpretation of the Old Testament,* Grand Rapids, Baker Academic, 2008, 247.

[374] Charles Dyer and Eugene Merrill, *Nelson's Old Testament Survey,* Nashville, Thomas Nelson Publishers, 2001, 728.

[375] McCmiskey, "*Hosea*," *in The Minor Prophets: An Exegetical and Expository Commentary,* Grand Rapids, Baker books, 1992, 47.

[376] V.K. Robbins, *Exploring the Texture of Texts: A Guide to Socio-Rhetorical Interpretation,* 1994, 9-10.

3.3.2.1. The Word לכן

The first word which shows progressive structure is "therefore." The definition of the word "therefore" means "referring to a sequence of events, introduces the point following another." The word "therefore" normally introduces an oracle of doom, punishment; surprisingly here it leads to hope. Andersen finds that in progressive texture, לכן (therefore) is considered as a logical connector that presupposes discipline and salvation in transformation.[377] Harper also in same opinion with Andersen argues that Israel shall be secluded and retained until the woman has acquired new spirit.[378] According to James Limburg, the word "therefore" refers to a reversal of judgment against the people and the assurance of transformation.[379] Dearman observes that in Hosea 2, "therefore" is used three times to indicate judgment (2:8, 11 and 16).[380] First, it introduces the language of judgment in terms of punishment concerning the wife's adultery; this is a direct reference to Israel. She was like a wandering animal then and but now, must abide with her Lord. The metaphorical idea that is brought out here is that it indicates the contrast when the people were worshipping Baal unlike now.

Garrett notes that secondly, the word "therefore" refers to punishment in terms of disobedience and failures.[381] The second "therefore" is a response to Israel's stubbornness. According to Harper the word "therefore" is consequently understood as that she has gone away after her lovers and it fits well in this context.[382] Here, Yahweh threatens that the people will be stripped naked. Hosea reminds the people of Yahweh's goodness and the covenant that he made with them.[383] Charles Dyer and Eugene Merrill mention that the judgmental language is followed by the promise of restoration and assurance of forgiveness. Hosea 2:2-9 is understood as being in the form of judgmental language.[384] Weems says that the next section 2:14-23 [MT 2:16-25] is followed by the promise of restoration.[385] Finally, in verse 16, a shift takes place to a renewed relationship, betrothal and covenant and announcement of the coming blessings.[386] This view is supported by Dempsey. Hosea 2:14-23 announces

---

377 Andersen, F.I and Freedman, D.N., *Hosea: A New Translation with Introduction and Commentary,* New York, Doubleday, 1980, 269.

378 W.R. Harper, *A Critical and Exegetical Commentary on Amos and Hosea,* Edinburgh, T and T Clark, 1956, 220.

379 James Limburg, Hosea-Micah, *Interpretation A Bible Commentary for Teaching and Preaching,* Louisville, John Knox Press, 2011, 11.

380 Dearman, J.A., *The Book of Hosea,*" NICOT, Grand Rapids, Wm. B. Eerdmans Publishing co, 2010, 118-119.

381 Garrett, D., *Hosea, Joel: An Exegetical and Theological Exposition of Holy Scripture,* B and H Publisher, 1997, 87.

382 W.R. Harper, *A Critical and Exegetical Commentary on Amos and Hosea,* Edinburgh, T and T Clark, 1956, 239.

383 James D.G. Dunn, John William Rogerson, *Eerdmans Commentary on the Bible,* Grand Rapids, Wm. B. Eerdmans publishing, 2003, 677.

384 Charles Dyer and Eugene Merrill, *Nelson's Old Testament Survey,* Nashville, Thomas Nelson Publishers, 2001, 728.

385 Renita J. Weems, *Battered Love: Marriage, Sex, and Violence in the Hebrew Prophets,* Minneapolis, Fortress Press, 1995, 92.

386 James D.G. Dunn, John William Rogerson, *Eerdmans Commentary on the Bible,* Grand Rapids, Wm. B. Eerdmans Publishing, 2003, 677. Cf. Carol J. Dempsey, *The Prophets: A Liberation-Critical Reading,* Minneapolis, Fortress Press, 2000, 156.

Israel's transformation, reminds them of their wilderness experience and affirms that "I will betroth you." This is confirmed by Yahweh.

According to Beeby, לכן appears for the third time to indicate future tense, but this time it refers to future life and not death.[387] Limburg notes that the final "therefore" introduces a brighter side of Israel in the future.[388] Here it is noted that the salvation oracle begins with "therefore." Davies says that the word לכן (therefore) uses two particles (as in v. 6) and refers to the beginning of the unit that connects form as well as content.[389]

For Dearman, לכן is translated as "even so," and he gives the theme to this unit as a reversal of the judgment against Israel and its transformation. For Andersen and Freedman, the word לכן means indictment and penalty, and it is mostly used as a first word in a judgment oracle.[390] Wolff comments however, that לכן appears for the third time to introduce divine speech and people's transgression.[391]

The word לכן generally introduces the action that will take place in response to Israel's return. Garrett points out that Yahweh reminds her to return to him and reminds her that she has nothing to do with Baal anymore.[392] This shows Yahweh's tender love towards Israel and Yahweh's care for her. Stuart says that לכן is used for the third and final time to introduce the divine actions.[393] Here the divine action refers to the fact that people are expected to turn away from their act of adultery to escape from the punishment. As Lewis notes, it is clear that Yahweh has decided to appeal anew to his wayward bride, beginning again with her in response to her willingness to return (Hos. 2:7 cf. Deut. 30:2, 3).[394] This can be understood in terms of restoration, where Yahweh is willing to reverse the punishments and make salvation possible. This symbolises the covenant at Sinai that she will return to. Hosea 2:16 begins with this conjunction and ends with the eschatological formula in Hosea 2:18. The implication of this word "therefore" brings out interest to readers to understand its historical context. The idea is that it is God who chose and established the covenant with Israel with a commitment between God and the fallen people. The word "therefore" is used strategically to show how God knows the situation of Israel and despite knowing that He still continued to love them. It is because of His deep love for them that Hosea was used as an instrument to convey the message of grace of God.

3.3.2.2. The Word עוד

In Hosea 3:1 Yahweh commanded the prophet to go and to love an adulterous woman, to symbolise God's love. עוד (again) frequently brings an effective action (deployed)

---

387 Beeby, H.D, *Grace Abounding: A Commentary on the book of Hosea,* Grand Rapids, Eerdmans, 1989, 27.

388 James Limburg, *Hosea-Micah, Interpretation A Bible Commentary for Teaching and Preaching,* Louisville, John Knox Press, 2011, 12.

389 Davies, G.I. *Hosea.* Grand Rapids, Eerdmans, 1992, 78.

390 Davies, G.I. *Hosea.* Grand Rapids, Eerdmans, 1992, 78-79.

391 Wolff, H.W., *A Commentary on the Book of the Prophet Hosea,* Philadelphia, Fortress, 1974, 41.

392 Garrett, D., *Hosea, Joel: An Exegetical and Theological Exposition of Holy Scripture,* B and H Publisher, 1997, 108-109.

393 Stuart, Douglas, *Hosea-Jonah, Word Biblical Commentary:* Dallas, Word, Incorporated, 1987, 53.

394 L.J. P, *New International Version Study Bible,* Grand Rapids, Zondervan Bible Publishers, 1985, 1324.

in the Hebrew Bible to denote the love of God in Hosea.[395] Davies finds that the author's use of עוד is employed with intention. For Mays, in progressive texture, the repetition of עוד occurs twice in the selected texts: the first is Yahweh's command to Hosea to go and love a woman, and the second is to go and marry an adulterous woman (3:1).[396] Whereas, according to Wolff, Yahweh's command is followed by the prophet.

The word "again" is in first person usage. The word אהב is used as imperative to restore his marriage.[397] It becomes clear that "again" contains a command to renew the relationship and, therefore, the covenant. The character of God can be seen through His love and how he remains faithful to an unfaithful people. This is illustrated through the life of Hosea when he buys back Gomer his wife in Hosea 3:3. The word "again" plays an important role because it shows that God seeks and follows those who do not follow Him.

The aspect to be noted here is that the word "said again," עוד, is adopted by Rowley.[398] There are other scholars who endorse this view: Gordis, Pfeiffer and Robinson.[399] They prefer to keep the word "said again" in 3:1.[400] The word עוד is an adverb intended to limit לך "go" and it can also be translated as "still," "yet" and "again." Garrett notes that the meaning of this term is ambiguous.[401] The question is whether this belongs to the first phrase, "And Yahweh spoke to me again" or it belongs to the second phrase, "Go love a woman again…." The word עוד generally would follow an imperative. The goal of the command is to reacquire or to reconcile with Hosea and enter into relationship.

Here, this research would prefer Garrett's view עוד אהב, "love again," since it portrays God's love for the people of Israel. Here, the paradigm of covenantal relationship can be seen very clearly since the word "love again" talks about God's love in spite of Israel's rejection and waywardness. Further, critical emendations in 3:1b read "I, Yahweh, love the children of Israel," thus denoting the personal involvement of Yahweh and his love. The term "love again" also portrays God's care for the people of Israel, since the word "love again" speaks about God's love, in spite of rejection and disobedience. In this way, the verse talks more about God's love. In this situation the paradigm of covenantal relationship comes through, and, in this concept of love, Yahweh is seen as the centre of the metaphor.

---

[395] Davies, *Hosea, The New Century Bible Commentary,* Michigan, Wm B. Eerdmans Publishing Co, 1992, 98-99.

[396] Mays, James Luther., *Hosea: A Commentary,* OTL, Philadelphia, Westminster, 1969, 54-55.

[397] F.I. Andersen and D.N. Freedman, *Hosea: A New Translation with Introduction and Commentary,* Anchor Bible, New York, Doubleday, 1980, 295-296.

[398] Rowley H.H, "The Marriage of Hosea," *Bulletin of the John Rylands Library 39,* no. 1, September, 1956, 57.

[399] Gordis, R., "Hosea's Marriage and Message," *HUCA* 25, (9-40), 1954, 28-29. R.H. Pfeiffer, *Introduction to the Old Testament,* 2nd edition, London, Harper and Brother Publishers, 1952, 567.

[400] Rowley H.H, "*The Marriage of Hosea,*" Bulletin of the John Rylands Library 39, no. 1, September, 1956, 57-58.

[401] Garrett, *Hosea, Joel An Exegetical and Theological Exposition of Holy Scripture,* B and H Publishing Group, 1997, 121.

3.3.2.3. The Word אהב and the Marriage Metaphor - Covenantal Love of God

Hosea 3.1-5 is interesting in that Hosea suddenly becomes personal-he tells us how much he paid for Gomer and also what he said to her. Wolff observes that the prophets' obedience to God is in the expression of Hosea's love for the unfaithful woman in "I bought her for myself."[402] Harper comments that buying refers to the purchase and entire transaction.[403] We understand that Hosea paid a price to redeem her, and also demonstrated his obedience to Yahweh's command to redeem Gomer. By this Hosea clearly intended to influence the people with the imagery of love between a husband and wife, using this as a parallel to the Yahweh-Israel situation. He uses the marriage symbol, according to Yahweh's instructions, to emphasise the message for the people and then links this with God's love for the people of Israel. Reverting to the personal, we see the "you must not…other men" (Hosea 3:3) concept in the new relationship between Hosea and Gomer, followed by an equally "you must not worship" charge to the Israelites. They must adopt a position of repentance by turning their backs on the worship of Baal. Thus, the two situations-marriage and worship-are parallel. The Hosea-Gomer marriage is used throughout the book as a human image of the love Yahweh has for Israel, and as an image the Israelites can appreciate; 3.5 is one place where the two are brought firmly together in a way the Israelites can understand.

Hosea 3:3 gives a description of the relationship between God and Israel; this can be understood as the covenantal renewal between Yahweh and Israel (cf. 2:8-9, 16). Hosea 3:3 shows the essence of love; that love can be got through obedience, and loving care as God demonstrated for Israel. This approach gives love much importance.

In Hosea 3:5, the Hebrew word אחר is translated as "afterward." This links with the expression "many days" and refers to a future time after the "many days" that is referred in Hosea 3:4a. Expressions of time also explain the covenantal love of God towards Israel. Mays says that here it appears to refer to the time of promise after Yahweh's period of judgment.[404] This in turn points to Israel's return to Yahweh.

Similarly, Charles Dyer and Eugene Merrill notes "in the last days," used at the end of v. 5, shows the literary reference that the Messiah will come from King David's line.[405] Mays points out that it denotes a future event from the author's perspective.[406] Harper comments that this predicts the judgment and the hope that will arise later.[407] According to Lewis Jack, the exact time frame is ambiguous and it carries the idea that Yahweh will judge His people, but after that, following a period,

---

[402] Wolff, *Hosea,* Philadelphia, Fortress Press, 1974, 60-62.

[403] W.R. Harper, *A Critical and Exegetical Commentary on Amos and Hosea,* Edinburgh, T and T Clark, 1956, 218.

[404] Mays, James Luther., *Hosea: A Commentary,* OTL, Philadelphia, Westminster, 1969, 58-59.

[405] Charles Dyer and Eugene Merrill, *Nelson's Old Testament Survey,* Nashville, Thomas Nelson Publishers, 2001, 729.

[406] Mays, James Luther., *Hosea: A Commentary,* OTL, Philadelphia, Westminster, 1969, 59.

[407] Harper, William Rainey., *A Critical and Exegetical Commentary on Amos and Hosea, The International Critical Commentary,* ed. by Samuel Rolles Driver, Alfred Plummer, and Charles Augustus Briggs. Edinburgh: T. and T. Clark, 1905, clix-clxi, 216.

He will restore them. A sense of messianic restoration is implied here.[408] Scholars believe that this must have been a later insertion in the text. These future orientations and time markers are a theological way of asserting Yahweh's knowledge and control over history. Yahweh's judgments therefore must be seen against the bigger picture of Him accomplishing His ultimate goal of fellowship with humankind. Even judgments are parental love (cf. Hosea 11).

Brueggemann identifies עוד which appears twice in the text, as another word. According to him, the prophet accomplished the command of Yahweh, and it is reported that the custom of a prophet was to intermingle rebuke with consolations. This is supported by LXX and reads: ετι πορευθητι, και αγαπη σονγυναικα; and the Vulgate reads in this way: *Adhuc vade et diligemulierem.* For Dearman, עוד (participle, adverb) means the prophet had already been commanded to marry an adulterous woman.[409]

3.3.2.4. The Progression - Love

The progression is God's command to love a woman, which Hosea obeys. The progression in the text is shown by love: the metaphor of love has been included to offer new insights to Israel's understanding of covenant. Campbell Morgan observes that God commands Hosea to go and love an adulterous woman to show he still loves her in progression texture.[410] Mays notes that the expression "her husband" (רע אהבת) denotes she is still the beloved of her husband, though she is an adulterous woman.[411] Andersen comments that Hosea was commanded by Yahweh to "love" in chapter 3, but in Hosea 1:2 "to take a wife;" but the idea here in is to renew conjugal kindness to the woman.[412] Cheyne comments the woman should give up her adulterous life and must enter into proper conjugal life.[413] For Garrett, the command "love a woman" is in contrast to "take a wife" (Hos. 1:2), which refers to the same woman as his wife.[414] According to Harper, the "woman" is unquestionably the same woman, Gomer, described in chapter 1. The reason is that she is later defined as an adulteress, and also she plays the part of parallelism with Israel.[415] The sudden shift of a person brings out the idea of who this woman is in Chapter 3 to support the scholars' view that the woman in chapter 1 and in 3 is the same. The basis is that both women were unfaithful to the prophet. It is evident that Hosea's action is similar to God's, because God loved the Israelites though they were unfaithful to Him. This shows that Yahweh will again love her.

---

[408] L. J. P., *New International Version Study Bible,* Grand Rapids, Zondervan Bible Publishers, 1985, 1325.

[409] Dearman. J.A, *The Book of Hosea,*" NICOT, Grand Rapids, Wm. B. Eerdmans Publishing co, 2010, 133.

[410] G. Campbell Morgan, *Hosea, the Heart and Holiness of God,* Grand Rapids, Baker Book House, 1974, 36.

[411] Mays, James Luther, *Hosea: A Commentary,* OTL, Philadelphia, Westminster, 1969, 55.

[412] Andersen, F.I and Freedman, D.N., *Hosea: A New Translation with Introduction and Commentary,* New York, Doubleday, 1980, 296.

[413] W.R. Harper, *A Critical and Exegetical Commentary on Amos and Hosea,* Edinburgh, T and T Clark, 1956, 220.

[414] Garrette, *Hosea, Joel,* NAC, 19A, Nashville, Broadman and Holman, 1997, 99-100.

[415] W.R. Harper, *A Critical and Exegetical Commentary on Amos and Hosea,* Edinburgh, T and T Clark, 1956, 216-217.

In Hosea 1:2, when God commands Hosea to go and marry a prostitute, there is much conjecture as to the details of this marriage, Gomer's identity and her background. Hosea understands God's agony against the people of Israel. Hosea took an unfaithful wife as commanded so that God could use his marriage as a living example and the main illustration of God's relationship with Israel. It is reasonable to wonder why God wanted the whole marriage saga to take place, and what purpose God had in doing so.

Table 7: Words Related to Love in Hosea 3

1a	ויאמר יהוה אלי עוד לך אהב		אשה אהבת רע	ומנאפת				
1b	כאהבת יהוה		והם פנים אל־אלהים אחרים		בני ישראל	ואהבי אשישי ענבים		
2		ואכרה לי בחמשה עשר כסף						
3a	ואמר אליה תשבי לי		ולא תהיי לאיש	תזני			ימים רבים	
3b		וגם־אני אליך						
4					בני ישראל		ימים רבים	מלך
5a	ישבו ... ובקשו את־יהוה אלהיהם				בני ישראל			
5b	ופחדו אל־ יהוה						באחרית הימים	דוד מלכם

Hosea 3:1-5 is about how God's command to Hosea symbolises God's own persistence in loving Israel despite her unfaithfulness. Yahweh tells Hosea to use the marriage metaphor and this is portrayed through the prophet loving Gomer rather than loving a different woman. In Hosea 1:2, God's command was to "take yourself a wife" but in Hosea 3:1 the command is to "love." The issue is not establishing a relationship but the quality of love that is essential to maintain the relationship in the difficult conditions.

Hosea's phrase in 1:2 "who has a lover" is in MT literally "loving a companion" (cf. Jeremiah 3:1, Song of Solomon 5:16); this shows the guilt of breaking the marriage covenant. The point here is that the symbolic action is made clear in God's command. Harper says that Hosea is to love again "just as the Lord loves the people of Israel, though they turn to other gods and love raisin cakes" (3:1b).[416] Hosea's action is to symbolise the continuity of God's love for Israel. The central issue is exclusively loyalty that God demands from Israel who would be in relationship with God as a covenant partner. The loyalty that God requires is related to marriage, which people knew and could understand. In chapter 3, the additional element comes into focus. When the covenant is broken, a response must be determined. In Hosea 3:1, God suggests through the prophet that love is the ultimate response beyond His anger, pain and judgment that is described in Hosea 2, and Hosea symbolised it by the naming of their children in Hosea 1. The theme of God's love is a major concern of Hosea's message to the people of Israel.

In Hosea 3:1, the verb "to love" is used four times. Hosea is commanded to love, the woman (Gomer), as the Lord loves Israel. But the object of love is different. Here the focus is on Gomer-Israel and on the experiences they have shared. As before, the underlying focus is Hosea 3:3 which clearly bring out a picture of Hosea's renewed commitment to love his wife and to continue to remain as a faithful partner.

The progressive texture of Hosea 3:1-5 is about the symbol of God's love. Harper comments for this, Hosea was commanded to marry an adulterous woman (cf. Deut. 24:1-4).[417] Hosea obeyed the command and married Gomer as his wife. The price paid for Gomer is about thirty shekels, which is the value of a slave (Exo. 21:32).[418] Harper says that the purchase of Gomer brings out the message of the intimacy of God's love for Israel.[419] The idea of restoration is believed to be symbolic of God's redemption and restoration of the unfaithful people of Israel, who had worshipped and sacrificed to other gods. The significance of progressive texture is this (3:1-5): Yahweh's command is to love a woman who is an adulteress, which is portrayed through the names of the children. Mays comments the text continues to say that Israel will not have six things in their lives: a king, a prince, an ephod and teraphim, sacrifice and an altar.[420] This signifies the political realm and the cult of their time where people offered sacrifices at the altar and shrines.[421] Instead, when the people of Israel return with true repentance, Yahweh will provide for their needs. However, the problem was that the people of Israel turned to other gods.

Hosea 3:1 talks about the reclaiming love of God with reference to Israel. This is seen through the command to Hosea, "Go again and love a woman." In this verse, the word "love:" is used four times and in three of these four occurrences, the word love has a different connotation. Here, the verb "love" implies persistence, as to

---

[416] W.R. Harper, *A Critical and Exegetical Commentary on Amos and Hosea,* Edinburgh, T and T Clark, 1956, 217.

[417] W.R. Harper, *A Critical and Exegetical Commentary on Amos and Hosea,* Edinburgh, T and T Clark, 1956, 218-219.

[418] Marten Stol, *Women in the Ancient Near East,* Boston/Berlin, Walter de Gruyter and Company, 2016, 118-119; G. J. Botterweck, Helmer Ringgren, *Theological Dictionary of the Old Testament,* Vol. VII, Grand Rapids, Wm. B. Eerdmans Publishing, 1995, 273; James Orr, *The International Standard Bible Encyclopedia,* Vol. 4, Chicago, Howard-Severance Co., 1956, 289.

[419] W.R. Harper, *A Critical and Exegetical Commentary on Amos and Hosea,* Edinburgh, T and T Clark, 1956, 218-219.

[420] Mays, James Luther., *Hosea: A Commentary,* OTL, Philadelphia, Westminster, 1969, 58-59.

[421] W.R. Harper, *A Critical and Exegetical Commentary on Amos and Hosea,* Edinburgh, T and T Clark, 1956, 221.

pursue. In the second instance, Gomer is said to be loved by a lover. Here it refers to sexual love. And in the final instance, the children of love are said to love the raisin cakes of the idols. This phrase about raisin cakes is translated in various ways. The MT says that they loved the grapes. Some interpret the phrase as a reference to dried grapes that have turned into wine. Scholars believe that this is a reference to dried grapes or "raisins."[422] The "raisin cakes" were often used in pagan worship. This shows the folly of the people of Israel in following idolatry. They have forgotten their faithfulness to their commitment and were following false gods. But God's love is faithful and He loves Israel with an everlasting and redeeming love.

Another aspect of progressive texture in Hosea 3:1-5 is the concept of human married love through the words that appear in the book approximately 12 times, shown in Table 1.2. The human marriage metaphor, used constantly throughout the book, is to make the Israelites understand how, in theological terms, God still loves them and continues to do so. This is how the "parallelism" of human marriage (love) and Yahweh/Israelite covenant (love) is emphasised.

Table 8: the phrases related to love that appear so frequently - Hosea 2:16-25

ותעד	and decorated her with jewels
ותלך	and went after her lovers
ואתי שכחה	and forgot me
מפתיה	persuade her
והלכתיה	and bring her (I will cause her to walk)
וכרתי	and speak to her
ונתתי	and give her
הסרתי	remove from her (I will cause to take away) (Baal)
אכרה	bought her
אמר	said to her

This pericope is divided into two parts: 2:14-23 (16-25 MT) and 3:1-5. In the first part, the progression of the imagery of love is shown in a series of acts described in the table. Heaton identifies the series of words used here as representing the progression of the acts of a lover in order to win back the love of his lady.[423] Here, Yahweh is the lover and Israel is His woman whom He loves. Garrett comments that in such a context, Yahweh will persuade her and bring her to Him and speak to her heart tenderly.[424] He will then give away her vineyards, and the valley of Achor, which was once a dreadful place will become a doorway of hope. This means that Yahweh will restore all that she needs.

The valley of Achor is translated as "valley of trouble" (Hosea 2:15 (MT 2:17). The incident refers to Joshua 7 where Achan disobeyed the word and the result was

[422] W.R. Harper, *A Critical and Exegetical Commentary on Amos and Hosea,* Edinburgh, T and T Clark, 1956, 218.

[423] E.W. Heaton, *The Old Testament,* London, Darton and Longman Press, 1985, 94.

[424] Garrett, D., *Hosea, Joel: An Exegetical and Theological Exposition of Holy Scripture,* B and H Publishing Group, 1997, 108-109.

devastation of the people. But God promised to turn the valley of Achor into a door of hope (לפתח תקוה) for His people.[425] The phrase "door of hope" for Andersen and Freedman is unusually abstract.[426] The word here means "hope" as seen in Proverbs and Job. The word "hope" is understood as promising salvation to the fallen Israel. Here we notice how the prophet is making a wordplay referring to this. The change of name here denotes the renewal of the new covenant. The reversal aspect of restoration and hope is seen as a reality. The restoration speaks about giving back people's land and it is exemplified by people's happiness and joy. The aspect of restoration teaches victory for the people of Israel. The Lord does this for His children who really seek hope, and He will provide them with riches and give back all that they lost. While the doorway of hope was jeopardized by Israel's behaviour and brought darkness to the nation, the promise of God is that Israel's return to the land in the future is marked by a renewed hope and this will become a blessing to many. The important aspect that is noted is that the people of Israel will become a blessing to many in the days to come as God blesses them. The renewal of hope is given to them as they themselves will be renewed; in turn the covenant will be restored as well as the blessing.

In the second division 3:1-5, the prophet performs all that Yahweh said. The progressive texture in the second division is shown here.

Table 9: The progressive texture of Hosea 3:1-5

אהב	loving (3:1)
כרה	buying (3:2)
אמר	giving instruction (3:3,4)
בקש שוב פחד	expecting everlasting fellowship (3:5)

The progression of Hosea's action in this pericope is presented as loving a woman who loves another man. Garrett notes that the actions of the Israelites are directly parallel to those of the adulteress.[427] The term עוד לך אהב־אשה means "Go again love a woman,"[428] and the word אמר is found as a contrast to techillath in the second part of Yahweh's continued discourse with the prophet Hosea. Kimchi brings to our notice that the word is used as opposite to the implication with "אמר (said)." The phrase לי תשבי can be translated as "wait for me." Even the Vulgate prefers the same meaning for this phrase. Hosea 3:3 brings out the idea that תשבי is translated as a period of waiting for Gomer. In the Old Testament, ישבל does not mean "sit in the house." ישב in Hoses 3:4 connects v. 3 and v. 4 and explains Israel's deprivation within the covenant tradition. The word ישב with ל occurs in Jeremiah 3:2 similarly. But Macintosh notices that MT proposes a meaning "shall remain at home."[429] Even if the texts were correct, the usage is unlike that in Hosea 3:3, for the pronoun

[425] Fishbane, *Biblical Interpretation in Ancient Israel,* Oxford, Clarendon Press, 1985, 361.

[426] Andersen and Freedman, *Hosea, Anchor Bible,* Garden City, Doubleday, 1980, 276.

[427] Garrett, D., *Hosea, Joel An Exegetical and Theological Exposition of Holy Scripture,* B and H Publishing Group, 1997, 123.

[428] W. Brueggemann, *Theology of the Old Testament,* Minneapolis, Fortress Press, 1997, 415.

[429] Macintosh, A.A, *A Critical and Exegetical Commentary on Hosea,* Edinburgh, T and T Clark, 1997, 132; cf. Stuart, Douglas: *Hosea-Jonah* Word Biblical Commentary, Dallas, Word, Incorporated, 1987, 66-67.

in Job. 15:28 refers not to a person, but to a house. The usage is much closer to the common לישב "sit upon." LXX, and the translation of the Jerusalem Bible, authored by Harper and Robinson, prefer to use "sit still for me" as in Hosea 3:3 תשבי לי.[430] Thus we find that love dominates in this case and is shown thus because she will sit, remain or dwell.[431]

Wood argues that תשבי לי means "you are to live with me." This shows, Hosea continues to love her. It is in line with God's command in 3:1 to love again.[432] There is no clear picture of why she must wait for Hosea, but the assumption is that he is to show love to a woman loved by others. The word "wait for" in Hosea 3:3b implies that Hosea and Gomer need to wait before having sexual relations with each other. For Garrett, Gomer should remain with Hosea and must not follow any other man (לא תזני or ולא תהיי לאיש).[433] In contrast, the MT says "you shall remain at home as mine." While Macintosh and Stuart translate it as "you shall remain mine," Dearman favours the translation "as mine." Hosea 3:3 gives a description of the relationship between God and Israel; this is described as a sign of a greater relationship in the Bible.[434] This can be understood as the covenantal renewal between Yahweh and Israel (cf. 2:8-9, 16).

Stuart לא תזני or ולא תהיי לאיש translates it as "You will not engage in prostitution, and no one will have you." There was apparently a time of purification for the adulteress.[435] Hosea's priority was completely rhetorical as he intended to influence the people with the imagery of love between a husband and a wife. First, the word "therefore" brings out the connector for progression then the following "you shall remain" is employed with a particular reason to emphasise the message for the people and finally love again, connects God's love with Israel. This is an example of the socio-rhetorical method in progression.[436]

Table 10: example of the socio-rhetorical method in progression

מפתיה	persuade her
והלכתיה	and bring her (I will cause her to walk)
ודברתי	and speak to her
ונתתי	and give her
וכרתי ברית	cutting covenant
וארשתיך לעולם	everlasting marriage
זרע	sow - means Israel is the only generation for Him from now on.

430 Ward, James M. *Hosea*: *A Theological Commentary,* New York, Harper and Row Publishers, 1966, 50.

431 Wolff, *Hosea,* Philadelphia, Fortress Press, 1974, 62-63.

432 Wood J. Leon, *The Prophets of Israel,* Grand Rapids, Baker Academic group, 1979, 181-182.

433 Garrett, *Hosea, Joel An Exegetical and Theological Exposition of Holy Scripture,* B and H Publishing Group, 1997, 125.

434 Victor. H. Matthews, *Social World of the Hebrew Prophets,* Massachusetts, Hendrickson Publishers, 2001, 76.

435 J. Andrew Dearman, *The Book of Hosea,* Grand Rapids, Wm. B. Eerdmans Publishing co, 2010, 139.

436 Robbins, *Exploring the Texture of Texts: A Guide to Socio-Rhetorical Interpretation,* 1994, 87.

The progression of Hosea's action in this pericope is presented as loving a woman who loves another man. Garrett notes that the actions of the Israelites are directly parallel to those of the adulteress.[437] Dearman remarks she commits adultery; they turn to other gods. She loves evil; they love raisin cakes, a synecdoche for heterodox indulgence.[438] Stuart notes that raisin cakes (אשישי ענבים) are sweets made from pressed and dried grapes.[439] Garrett comments that by Hosea's time they were probably associated with cultic worship, and raisin cakes were the fitting metaphorical food of the religious practice seeking spiritual and material gratification from other gods apart from Yahweh.[440] Finally, the progression leads to Yahweh's expectation of Israel's everlasting fellowship with Him through the series of words such as שוב, פחד, בקש. Thus the imagery of love is described in the rhetoric of progressive texture through Hosea's use of words and actions of progression.

The first word which shows progressive structure is "therefore" which means "referring to a sequence of events, introduces the point following another." The word therefore normally introduces an oracle of doom, punishment; surprisingly here it leads to hope. In Hosea 2 "therefore" is used three times to indicate judgment (2:8, 11 and 16). Finally, in verse 16, a shift takes place to a renewed relationship, betrothal and covenant and announcement of the coming blessings. Hosea 2:14-23 announces God's transformation, reminds them of their wilderness experience and affirms that "I will betroth you." This is confirmed by Yahweh to His people. עוד (again) frequently brings an effective action (deployed) in Hosea in the Hebrew Bible to denote the love of God. In progressive texture, the repetition of עוד occurs twice in the selected texts: the first is Yahweh's command to Hosea to go and love a woman, and the second is to go and marry an adulterous woman. The Progression is Love. The progression is God's command to love a woman, which Hosea obeys. The progression in the text is love: It is evident that Hosea's action is similar to God, because He loved the Israelites though they were unfaithful to Him. This shows that Yahweh will again love her. This action indicates the relationship between Yahweh and Israel.

3.3.3. Narrative Texture

A narrative texture deals with the voice or voices through which the words of the text speak.[441] The voice that is represented in the text is the discourse of a particular voice or group.

In this section, it is noticed that Yahweh speaks first. The pattern in the narrative texture is that Yahweh Himself speaks as the judge in a lawsuit.[442] This is confirmed by the formula נאם-יהוה which is repeated in 2:15^{Heb} [13^{Eng}]. It is later found in

---

437 Garrett, *Hosea, Joel An Exegetical and Theological Exposition of Holy Scripture,* B and H Publishing Group, 1997, 123.

438 Dearman, J.A, *The Book of Hosea,*" NICOT, Grand Rapids, Wm. B. Eerdmans Publishing co, 2010, 135.

439 Stuart, D., *Hosea-Jonah,* Waco, Word, 1987, 65. Cf. Mays, James Luther., *Hosea: A Commentary,* OTL, Philadelphia, Westminster, 1969, 56-57.

440 Garrett, *Hosea, Joel An Exegetical and Theological Exposition of Holy Scripture,* B and H Publishing Group, 1997, 123.

441 Robbins, *Exploring the Texture of Texts: A Guide to Socio-Rhetorical Interpretation,* 1994, 90-91.

442 Wolff, H.W, *A Commentary on the Book of the Prophet Hosea,* Philadelphia, Fortress Press, 42.

verses 18 and 23. Concerning this Dearman states the term נאם-יהוה refers to the theme of appearance. The jewellery is presented here to honour Baal.[443]

God is saying that He will punish her; it shows Yahweh's anger towards Israel and that she must completely renounce Baal. Yahweh predicts that "in the day that I punish, I will punish them for their sin" (cf. Exo. 32:34). By this the character of Israel stands exposed (v. 11) as God rejected their festivals, offerings and sacrifices. The voice of God is presented here and warns about their offerings and sacrifices to Baal.

The use of ornament and jewellery in verse 13 is connected with verse 5 in chapter 2. The jewellery refers to a cultic practice here (cf. Exo. 32:2-5). By this the idea presented is that Israel has forgotten Yahweh and followed Baal. Similarly, Stuart points out that this is the metaphor of a promiscuous woman, who is chasing after her lovers.[444] Hosea 2:13 shows the people of Israel had passion for idolatry and they continued participating in the procession at the shrine with other followers. Here, Yahweh reminds Israel through Hosea that they are forgetting the law and facing judgment. He reminds Israel in this verse of His covenant with them that they should not worship Baal but should worship Him alone. There is a progression in the course of the trial and its aftermath, indicative of a narrative texture.

The first-person account by the prophet and his concrete statements are intended to be read as a reference to a real event. Reading this section brings out the importance of the right relationship with Yahweh. The prophet affirms God's gift and enters into a covenant relationship with Yahweh.

Stanley Fish brings to attention that the narrative placement, sequence and structure disregard the unity of the pericope.[445] In order to portray this in v. 4 he fixes the social locations of two groups of people, namely Israelites and Assyrians. Here, Hosea finds a similarity of the Israelites with the Assyrians, who are also under the king, but at the same time differentiates his own people by setting a boundary distinguishing them from the Assyrians by mentioning the sacred pillar, ephod and household idols. Thus, Hosea's intention is not to judge the people but to call them to repentance and healing. The literary form of the text here tells us that Hosea links Israelite and Assyrian culture by bringing in a similarity, which is the rule of a king. Of course, the king of Israel ultimately is Yahweh. Hosea 3:1 (2-5) is entirely narrative. The narration creates a pattern of the prophet's actions, Yahweh's command and drastic responses by the prophet.

Also the previous section focuses on the relationship between Yahweh and Israel (1:9-2:23), it now turns to the relationship between the prophet and Gomer. Macintosh's view of Hosea 3:1-3 is that these verses show Yahweh's action as reflected in the actions of the prophet Hosea by his love for Gomer. Hosea's action

---

[443] Dearman, J.A., *The Book of Hosea,*" NICOT, Grand Rapids, Wm. B. Eerdmans Publishing co, 2010, 118.

[444] Stuart, D, *Hosea-Jonah,* Waco, Word, 1987, 52.

[445] Stanley Fish, *Is There a Text in This Class?* The Authority of Interpretive Communities, Cambridge, MA and London, Harvard University, 1980. The attempt made by Stanley Fish helps to understand the grounding and finds solution. The hermeneutics view brings out the idea of community relativism. For a discussion and critique on Stanley Fish's see Paul R. Noble, *The Canonical Approach: A Critical Reconstruction of the Hermeneutics of Brevard Childs,* Leiden, Brill, 1995, 208-218.

clearly has the idea of redemption and restoration.[446] But Hosea 3:4-5 pertains exclusively to Israel's destiny.

According to Wolff, Hosea 3:4 is merely connected with Hosea 3:3 in a superficial manner. For Alice Parmelee, the combination of this section belongs to the special genre of accounts of the prophet's symbolic actions.[447] The genre is called *memorabile* by Wolff, and Stuart agrees with him.[448] Ehud Ben Zvi calls it a "prophetic monologue."[449] Hosea 3:4 is tied to Hosea 3:3 by the three accented words (כי ימים רבים) and the beginning of v. 4 echoes the vocabulary of v. 3.

In a *memorabile,* a historical event is summarized on one central point. When regarded as a segment of history, a concern for the basic truth suppresses any underlying intention to narrate the story. Therefore, the passage is presented simply, without many autobiographical details. The details in verse 2 and 3 show Hosea's life and they only help in the understanding of a remarkable occurrence into which the individual events merge.

The real marriage illustrates the present situation prevailing in the metaphorical marriage between Yahweh and Israel. It represents the prophesied future event as a present event.[450] The three main elements are: God's command (v. 1) report of its execution (vv. 2f) and interpretation (v. 4). The essential part is its completion.[451]

This is the narrative structure which the book follows:

1. Hosea is charged to love an adulterous woman-Hos. 3:1-3[452]
    a. Most of the scholars take this to be Gomer, who had gone into harlotry.
    b. Hosea takes her back, though with a period of probation.
2. Hosea's action symbolises God's willingness to take Israel back-Hos: 3.4-5.
    a. Also with a probationary period, in which there is no king, altars and sacrifices.
    b. However, Israel would return, and seek the Lord and David her king (the Messiah).[453]

One of the issues in the narrative of Hosea is that there are two women mentioned. One is in Hosea 1 and the other in Hosea 3.[454] But when analysing the passage, it becomes clear that there is only one woman who has been referred to in two different ways.

---

[446] Macintosh, A.A, *A Critical and Exegetical Commentary on Hosea,* Edinburgh, T and T Clark, 1997, 110-11.

[447] Alice Parmelee, *A Guide to the Old Testament and the Apocrypha,* Wilton, Morehouse-Barlow, 1979, 84-85.

[448] Wolff, H.W. *A Commentary on the Book of the Prophet Hosea,* Philadelphia, Fortress, and Stuart, Douglas: *Hosea-Jonah, Word Biblical Commentary:* Dallas, Word Incorporated, 1987, 63.

[449] Ben Zvi, E. *Hosea,* Grand Rapids, Eerdmans, 2005, 97.

[450] Stuart, Douglas, *Hosea-Jonah, Word Biblical Commentary:* Dallas, Word, Incorporated, 1987, 63; cf. Zimmerli, Ezekiel, 103f.

[451] Stuart, Douglas: *Hosea-Jonah, Word Biblical Commentary:* Dallas, Word, Incorporated, 1987, 63.

[452] Stuart, Douglas: *Hosea-Jonah, Word Biblical Commentary:* Dallas, Word, Incorporated, 1987, 65.

[453] Garrett, *Hosea, Joel An Exegetical and Theological Exposition of Holy Scripture,* B and H Publishing Group, 1997, 128.

[454] Sweeney, Marvin A. *Twelve Prophets,* 2 vols. Collegeville, Liturgical Press, 2000, 38-40. Cf. A.A., Mackintosh, *Hosea,* 118-126.

This image is used to represent God's relationship with His people. For Macintosh, God's love for Israel is narrated explicitly in a sequence in 2:14-18, 19-23.[455] In the first scene, Yahweh attracts His lover who has gone astray from Him. In the second scene, the prophet is addressed as a spokesperson for Yahweh. The second section is about Yahweh not forgetting his covenant with the people, and restoration of blessings. It talks about the fulfilment of a promise. The marital imagery itself is present in two places in the second division of the whole structure of chapters 1 and 3. The beauty of the narrational rhetoric is that it is placed between these two marital imageries from 2:14-23.

The narration starts directly and strongly at the beginning of Hosea's marriage. According to Wellhausen the particular theme in Hosea has been its relationship with Deuteronomy.[456] Contrary, Stuart states that Hosea's teaching is based on the covenant curses and blessings as it is in Leviticus and Deuteronomy, though the prophet admits that there is no direct quotation of Hosea (cf. Lev. 26; Deut. 4:25-31).[457] In a similar way, R.R. Wilson argues that Hosea's prophetic tradition is closely linked with the record in Deuteronomy.[458] The prophets used the covenantal forms of punishment or blessing to make reference to what is already incorporated in the Sinai covenant. The texts of Leviticus 26 and Deuteronomy 28-32 provide the materials related to blessings and curses. The prophets concentrated on covenant as main aspect. This is the strongest imagery of Yahweh's covenantal love in the book, since chapter 3 is the focus for conveying this theme of Yahweh's unconditional covenantal love, and this becomes the basis for the narration of Yahweh's restoring love.

In this chapter 3, Yahweh speaks first. The pattern in the narrative texture is that Yahweh Himself speaks as the judge in the lawsuit. God saying that He will punish her shows Yahweh's anger towards Israel and that she must completely renounce Baal. Stuart states that Hosea's teaching is based on the covenant curses and blessings as it is in Leviticus and Deuteronomy, though the prophet admits that there is no direct quotation of the book of Hosea (cf. Lev. 26; Deut. 4:25-31). The narration starts directly and strongly at the beginning in Hosea's marriage.

3.3.4. Opening-Middle-Closing Texture

Opening-middle-closing texture talks about the beginning, body and conclusion of a section of discourse.[459] Opening-middle-closing of a pericope is usually created by repetition, progression and narration.[460] It identifies what is complex in the passage, it helps to refine and improve analysis of the various types of structure that are in the text. In the same way, the middle and closing textures help to bring a passage to conclusion.

In the opening texture, the pericope 2:4-17 begins as a lawsuit, with charges of adultery, and threats that are made by Yahweh in vv. 4-7. Hosea 2:4-17 is about

---

[455] Macintosh, A.A. *A Critical and Exegetical Commentary on Hosea,* Edinburgh, T. and T. Clark, 1997, 106-109.

[456] Wellhausen on Hosea and Deuteronomy in H.L. Ginsberg, Hosea, Book of, in *EncJud* 8, 1972, 23-24.

[457] Stuart, *Hosea-Jonah* (WBC 31), Waco, Word Books, 1987, XXXI-XLH, 15-19.

[458] R.R. Wilson, *Prophecy and Society in Ancient Israel,* Philadelphia, Fortress Press, 1980, 90-91.

[459] Robbins, *Exploring the Texture of Texts: A Guide to Socio-Rhetorical Interpretation,* 1994, 92-93.

[460] Vernon Robbins, *Exploring the Texture of Texts:* 19.

divorce and court proceedings where Yahweh is to help Israel against the accusation. These actions are designed to teach Israelites of the need to return to God. The word לכן is repeated thrice with different meanings in vv. 8-10, where the "therefore" is often used by the prophet to announce action that Yahweh is going to take on the people as a judge. Here the shift is that the punishment 2:11-15 is seen as a second judgment expressing the judge's decision. Israel's wealth and her relationship will be taken away by changing her delight to shame. The Lord uses the marriage symbol to teach Israelites about His covenant relationship. Hosea 2:16-17 offers a new beginning to Israel, showing how Yahweh deals with unfaithful people and also showing how much God loves them. Hosea repeatedly reminds the people of their unfaithfulness. This section presents how a future restoration and reconciliation is promised by Yahweh.[461] God creates circumstances so that the people will not worship heathen gods (v. 8) as they are powerless and weak (v. 12). God delivered His people from Egypt and led them to the Promised Land with love and acts that symbolise the future that means a new beginning for Israel.

Hosea's use of the rhetoric in opening - middle - closing texture is present in this pericope in the use of the following phrases:

ביום	on that day you will call (2:18)
ביום אענה	on that day I will answer (2:23)
באחרית הימים	later days (3:5)

The structure itself emphatically shows Yahweh's love. In these phrases, the prophet as Yahweh's spokesperson narrates what will happen at the time of salvation. It talks about the promise that is going to take place. Israel is addressed in the second person and the announcement for Israel is made in the third person. This analogy is portrayed in the form of a covenant and a marriage between Yahweh and Israel.[462] This section is taken as a collection of sayings rather than as one with a continuous unit of speech. Mays finds that the eschatological formula "it will occur in that day" (vv. 16, 18, 21), is repeated thrice and the oracle formula "a saying of Yahweh" is repeated twice (vv. 16, 21). There is a shift that takes place in personal pronouns referring to Israel: "you" (second feminine. singular) in v. 16, "her" in v. 17, "them" in v. 18, "you" again in vv. 19f, and "her" in v. 23. Scholars' opinion is that Septuagint is consistent in the use of pronouns in its text.

In this pericope, the climax is seen at the opening texture itself (2:18) ביום, on that day you will call me "my man." As repetition, progression and narration work together to create the opening, middle and closing of a unit of a text, the repetition of the phrase ביום denotes successive progression of Yahweh's love towards Israel and Yahweh's eschatological expectations of a redeemed Israel.[463]

Andersen and Freedman find that the sequence of the narration begins with Yahweh persuading and bringing back His wife who has gone astray, and when she

[461] Stuart, Douglas: *Hosea-Jonah, Word Biblical Commentary:* Dallas, Word, Incorporated, 1987, 53.

[462] Renita J. Weems, *Battered Love: Marriage, Sex, and Violence in the Hebrew Prophets,* Minneapolis, Fortress Press, 1995, 13.

[463] Andersen, F.I and Freedman, D.N, *Hosea: A New Translation with Introduction and Commentary,* New York, Doubleday, 1980, 278.

returns to Yahweh, heeding His words, "on that day," she addresses Him as her Man and not as "Baal" thereby denoting Yahweh as master and lord. Israel belongs to Yahweh and is called "my wife" (איש).[464]

This is followed by the middle texture in which Yahweh makes an everlasting marriage covenant. Here the covenant vows will be spoken in truth between two parties, and their marriage will endure forever. The typology of 'marriage' representing 'covenant' is linked to the concept of wilderness; this is to bring to mind the place of making covenant, which serves as the marriage renewal. Hosea's eschatology is used for the concept of Israel's future restoration. This restoration of the covenant takes place as a result of that opening. Harper comments that the Hebrew phrases "return and seek" the Lord literally means "will turn…and will seek."[465] Macintosh points out that this shows that Israel will seek the Lord again.[466] This particular phrase does not refer to returning to the land of Israel, rather it refers to turning the hearts of the people of Israel to the Lord, in order to follow and worship Yahweh. The conclusion of this is that Israel will return and seek the Lord her God, and she shall come in fear to the Lord in the latter days (3:5).

Chester K. Lehman argues that "the formula ביום ההוא "in that day" 1:5; 2:20 [18], 23 [21]) found in the middle texture is eschatological. In the prophetic literature, "the latter days" refers to the coming to the Messiah.[467] But others argue that "latter days" is not synonymous with the "day of the Lord" (יום יהוה) concept mentioned in Amos, Joel, Zechariah and other prophets.[468] There is no hint that it describes a period of change to be expected in the lifetime of Hosea's audience."[469]

Within this pericope, the opening - middle - closing pattern is again inherent in vv. 14-23.

Table 11: opening - middle - closing pattern is again inherent in vv. 14-23

ביום תקראי	on that day you will call (18)
ביום וכרתי ברית	on that day I will cut a covenant (20)
ביום אענה	on that day I will answer (23)

In describing the return to Yahweh as a "turning in fear" (אל־פחד), the oracle makes clear that the Israelites would have learned a lesson prior to their return (cf. Deut. 4:30; and the frequent use of פחד in Deut. 28). However, their God will not be vindictive. When they approach Him, they will find "his goodness" (טובו). Similar

464 Beeby, H.D, *Grace Abounding: A Commentary on the book of Hosea,* Grand Rapids, Eerdmans, 1989, 29.

465 W.R. Harper, *A Critical and Exegetical Commentary on Amos and Hosea,* Edinburgh, T and T Clark, 1956, 223.

466 Macintosh, A.A, *A Critical and Exegetical Commentary on Hosea,* Edinburgh, T and T Clark, 1997, 108; Andersen, F.I and Freedman, D.N., *Hosea: A New Translation with Introduction and Commentary,* New York, Doubleday, 1980, 306-307.

467 Chester K. Lehman, *Biblical Theology,* vol. 2, Scottdale, Herald Press, 1946, 272.

468 Nogalski, J.D., "The Day of Yahweh in the book of the Twelve," in *Thematic Threads in the book of the Twelve,* ed. P.L. Redditt and Schart, BZAW 325, Berlin, Walter de Gruyter, 198-199.

469 Stuart, Douglas: *Hosea-Jonah. Word Biblical Commentary:* Dallas, Word, Incorporated, 2002, 31.

to this is the idea presented in the following verses 2:18–25 [16–23], in which the day of return is proclaimed as a good time.[470] Here Hosea announces that God is bringing his reversal action of exodus and a negation of Mosaic covenant. However, in this context, the prophet promises a new covenant and a "new exodus" in the future. This is because of God's promise to love a wayward people and restore them. The oracle in the middle texture concludes with the adverbial phrase "in the end times" (באחרית הימים), sometimes treated as an addition to the original text. The "end times" are the eschatological ages (cf. Isa. 2:2; Jer. 49:39; Ezek. 38:8, 16; Dan. 10:14; Mic. 4:1), and thus the chapter predicts events that are part of the restoration era, in accordance with the eschatology long revealed to Israel (Lev. 26; Deut. 4 and 30). Sandhya Shency finds that the major elements (return and blessing after deprivation; restoration of Davidic rule; reunification of North and South) would have been recognizable to the Israelites in Hosea's day, whether or not they respected the covenant in which those elements were contained.[471]

According to Mays, in 3:1, the opening texture begins with Yahweh's command to go and love a woman. Here we have a parallel to the Yahweh/Israel relationship; Hosea must take Gomer back and love her; Yahweh is willing to take Israel back because he loves her, despite her turning to false gods. After this command, there is a sudden response of obedience from the prophet.[472] Garrett notes that, in the middle texture, the prophet obeys the command of Yahweh and takes his wife back and says to her "You must dwell as mine for many days; you shall not play the harlot, or belong to another man; so will I also be to you."[473] Harper comments that 'you shall not play the harlot,' is climatic in the prophetic saying. She will not have another husband, things and her own husband will grant her all her needs.[474] This statement brings us to the end of the middle texture and helps us to understand the opening and closing textures.

Finally, the closing texture warns the people that, when they disobey the law and follow other gods, they will be without many blessings. Hosea 3:4 follows: "for the children of Israel shall dwell many days without king or prince, without sacrifice or pillar, without ephod or teraphim." Harper says that "Without king or prince" refers to the time the people of Israel are in exile and the Assyrians will rule them.[475] The phrase clearly explains that they will not be able to govern themselves any more. The Hebrew word "prince" is a generic term for a ruler, a chief, a leader, a captain, an official, or a chieftain.

---

[470] Stuart, Douglas: *Hosea-Jonah, Word Biblical Commentary:* Dallas, Word, 2002, 31.

[471] Sandhya Shency, A Call to Return to the Lord (Hos. 6:1-6), Vol. XXXX, No. 3, September 2014, *Bible Bhashyam,* 146-147 (146-156).

[472] Mays, James Luther., *Hosea: A Commentary,* OTL, Philadelphia, Westminster, 1969, 56.

[473] Garrett, *Hosea, Joel: An Exegetical and Theological Exposition of Holy Scripture,* Nashville, B. and H. Publishing Group, 1997, 128.

[474] W.R. Harper, *A Critical and Exegetical Commentary on Amos and Hosea,* Edinburgh, T and T Clark, 1956, 220.

[475] W.R. Harper, *A Critical and Exegetical Commentary on Amos and Hosea,* Edinburgh, T and T Clark, 1956, 220.

3.3.4.1. Middle texture

3.3.4.1.1. The Command of Yahweh to the Prophet

The middle texture of the pericope 3:1-5 begins with a reference to the command of Yahweh to the prophet: 'remarry' ויאמר יהוה אלי, which is seen in vv. 2-4, and the outcome is אחר in 3:5 with the expectation that a king like David will come.[476] Here, Hosea returns to his own marriage and this is regarded as an image for Yahweh and Israel. The idea is that hope for Israel and Judah is presented in the line of David. Hosea's personal story and command to marry Gomer is a reminder of the origin of Hosea's prophetic ministry. The phrases ואת דויד מלכם *"and David their king"* and באחרית הימים "in the later days," have been regarded by many scholars as a later perhaps exilic hand.[477] This view is supported by Sandhya by saying that the return from exile (11:1) and divided kingdoms will happen at the same time.[478] There are several reasons given for this, because of the use of דויד מלכם. The reason is, בקש may be followed by יהוה but not by דויד.[479] In this connection Garrett identifies that this phrase conveys the reunion of the two kingdoms under one head, the reversal of Israel's pattern of dynastic instability, the rejection of the foreign alliances, and the covenantal continuity of David by Yahweh; all of which were condemned by Amos and the other prophets.[480] The result is Yahweh's love, hope and reconciliation for Israel. Here, Hosea connects Yahweh's future victory to the rebirth of Davidic rule. So, hope is given to the people of Israel that they can return to their Lord from worshipping other gods. The prophet gives them a hope of healing if they turn to the Lord. They can return to the Lord because of His love for them.

W. Brueggemann calls for attention that Hosea connects Yahweh's future victory to the rebirth of Davidic rule. William Standford comments that the prophet reminds the people about the covenant that He made with David, and that the people should remain with God's covenant. Hosea 3:1-3 deals with Yahweh's action reflected in the life of the prophet, but vv. 4-5 exclusively talks about Israel's future life.

3.3.4.1.2. The Male-Female Relationship

In the middle texture, Mays notes that Hosea 3:1 shows a contextual usage with an obvious male-female relationship, for example, Jeremiah 3:1, 20, and Lamentations 1:2.[481] Harper notes that both Jeremiah 3:1 and Lamentations 1:2 refer to an illicit relationship, while Jeremiah 3:20 fits most naturally within the context of the marriage commitment.[482] So "husband" could be a possible rendering of רע in the

---

[476] Sandhya Shency, A Call to Return to the Lord (Hos. 6:1-6), Vol. XXXX, No. 3, September 2014, *Bible Bhashyam,* 146-147 (146-156).

[477] Harper, William Rainey., *A Critical and Exegetical Commentary on Amos and Hosea,* The International Critical Commentary, ed. by Samuel Rolles Driver, Alfred Plummer, and Charles Augustus Briggs, Edinburgh, T. and T. Clark, 1905, 224.

[478] Sandhya Shency, 'A Call to Return to the Lord (Hos. 6:1-6),' Vol. XXXX, No. 3, September 2014, *Bible Bhashyam,* 147 (146-156).

[479] Wolff, H.W, *A Commentary on the Book of the Prophet Hosea,* Philadelphia, Fortress Press, 57.

[480] Garrett, *Hosea, Joel An Exegetical and Theological Exposition of Holy Scripture,* B and H Publishing Group, 1997, 128.

[481] Mays, James Luther, *Hosea: A Commentary,* OTL, Philadelphia, Westminster, 1969, 56.

[482] W.R. Harper, *A Critical and Exegetical Commentary on Amos and Hosea,* Edinburgh, T and T Clark, 1956, 218.

male-female context.[483] The word "husband" is cited in Jeremiah 3:20 in support of this verse. This shows that Gomer is giving her love to another man by her actions (אהבת רע ומנאפת). However, the word רע here could point to Hosea himself.

On the other hand, the Septuagint reads this as "evil." Septuagint takes the participle active and the noun is changed as a homograph רע or evil.[484] The alternative reading אהבת in footnote 1a (BHS) supported by LXX, Syriac translation and the Vulgate takes the participle as active and the subsequent noun (זנה) (רע) (evil) as a homograph אשה אהבת רע (she who loves wickedness). It is also in parallel with the active participle מנאפת (an adulteress). This view is supported by Andersen and Freedman.[485] The word רע continues to state Yahweh's love for Israel.[486] The parallel here is that it is not the love of רע for Gomer, but rather the love of Hosea commanded by God (אהב).[487] Therefore the socio-rhetorical reading here identifies the inter-textuality between LXX and MT to the literary form of this verse. Hosea's programmatic speech as a progression for persuading the people to return to God can be seen clearly.

3.3.4.1.3. The Word רע

Hosea focuses on people's promiscuity because in their context, adultery is punishable by death, though the judgment was an unavoidable one. In this context, the prophet receives the command: to love a woman who lives as a paramour.[488] Limburg comments that רע is described as a relationship with a neighbour or a woman from another community.[489] Macintosh says that רע is a noun and indicates "a lover or paramour (cf. Jer. 3:1)." Dearman renders רע as "a paramour."[490] Stuart translates it as "a woman who loves evil." The word רע can be understood as "other gods." רע is the term (qal, perfect) that Moses used in predicting that the descendants of Jacob would become Canaanite fertility worshipers (cf. Deut. 31:18, 20).[491] Yahweh Himself pleaded with them not to yield to this temptation (cf. Lev. 19:4; 20:6). Here it means that God is the husband and Israel is His wife.

This is the fourth use of the verb love (qal, perfect), describing how the Israelites embraced Baal worship. Small delicacies like cakes of raisins were given to the worshippers after a time of sacrifice (cf. 2Sam. 6:19).[492] They are also referred

[483] T.K. Cheyne, *Hosea: With Notes and Introduction,* Cambridge, Cambridge University Press, 1892, 58.

[484] Scott, *The Message of Hosea, London,* SPCK, 1921, 127.

[485] Andersen, F.I and Freedman, D.N., *Hosea: A New Translation with Introduction and Commentary,* New York, Doubleday, 1980, 296.

[486] C. F. Keil, *The Minor Prophets,* translated by James Martin, vol. 10 in Commentary on the Old Testament, 10 vols. Edinburgh, Tand T Clark, 1866; reprint, Peabody, Mass.: Hendrickson Publishers, Inc.: 2001, 45-46.

[487] Macintosh, A.A., *A Critical and Exegetical Commentary on Hosea,* Edinburgh, T and T Clark, 1997, 94.

[488] James Limburg, *Hosea – Micah,* Interpretation Commentary, Westminster, John Knox Press, 1988, 13-14.

[489] James Limburg, *Hosea – Micah,* Interpretation Commentary, Westminster, John Knox Press, 1988, 14.

[490] Dearman, J.A., *The Book of Hosea,*" NICOT, Grand Rapids, Wm. B. Eerdmans Publishing co, 2010, 64.

[491] Mayes. A.D.H, *Deuteronomy,* New Century Bible Commentary, Grand Rapids, Eerdmans, 1979, 367.

[492] Mays, James Luther, *Hosea: A Commentary,* OTL, Philadelphia, Westminster, 1969, 57.

to in Isa. 16:7 and Jer. 44:19 as objects of fertility worship (cf. Jer. 48:31).[493] The love of the רע for Gomer is parallel to the love of Israel for raisins cakes. Here the command to Hosea is to continue to love her though she is an adulterous woman.[494] Philip King points out that not only were cakes of raisins delicacies associated with fertility worship, they were also apparently distributed at times of celebrations, as in 2Sam. 6:19. Socio-rhetorical reading here brings to light the mixture of two cultures of Hosea's time and the use of cakes as offerings in their sacrifices. Here the command of Yahweh is seen in Hosea's action and symbolises Yahweh's love for Israel who has turned away to worship other gods. The characteristic of the divine love that Yahweh has for Israel are an important factor. In this way, they embraced other gods. God's love for his people is undeserved and is shown through Hosea's life.

3.3.4.2. Closing texture of Hosea 2:16-3:5

In the closing texture, Hosea 2:18-25^{Heb} / 16-23^{Eng} points to the restoration of the marriage relationship between Yahweh and Israel.[495] Wolff calls 2:18-25^{Heb} the day of the new covenant.[496] The main charge (v. 15) is that Yahweh is ignored (forgotten) and considered to be part of court law proceedings. Dearman comments that 2:18ff is about the metaphor of marriage and covenant is renewed again. The idea is that in the future Yahweh will be gracious to them.[497] Charles Dyer and Eugene Merrill comment that the new covenant emphasises new conditions in all areas of people's lives. The previous verses (cf. 18-19, 21-22) remind us of Yahweh's intimate relationship with Israel.[498] The intimacy between Yahweh and Israel brings out a new relationship and new order. People's apostasy brought national disorder and now the new covenant reminds them of things that will make everything new. The new covenant carries hope and the gift of life. Here, two aspects are noticed: re-establishment of agricultural blessing and future promises of restoration in the new covenant.

3.3.4.2.1. They Will Come Trembling to the Lord

In the closing texture, ופחדו אל־יהוה *("they will come trembling to the Lord")* is an idiom אל פחדו. This verb (qal, perfect) is used in a similar way, and in the same form, by Hosea's contemporary eighth century prophet in Judah, Micah (cf. 7:17). This element is described as a movement for return to the Lord. Similarly, Harper comments that trembling here refers not only Yahweh, but his goodness and blessings when they return to the Lord.[499] By doing this, the people escape from judgment and try to re-establish the political kingdom.[500]

---

[493] S. R. Driver, *An Introduction to the Literature of the Old Testament,* New York, Meridian Books, 1960, 43.

[494] Robert B. Chisholm, *Jr., Handbook on the Prophets,* Grand Rapids, Baker Academic, 2002, 346.

[495] Stuart, Douglas, *Hosea-Jonah: Word Biblical Commentary, Dallas,* Word, Incorporated, 1987, 54.

[496] Wolff, Hosea, 55-56.

[497] Dearman, J.A., *The Book of Hosea,*" NICOT, Grand Rapids, Wm. B. Eerdmans Publishing co, 2010, 122-123.

[498] Charles Dyer and Eugene Merrill, *Nelson's Old Testament Survey,* Nashville, Thomas Nelson Publishers, 2001, 728.

[499] W.R. Harper, *A Critical and Exegetical Commentary on Amos and Hosea,* Edinburgh, T and T Clark, 1956, 224.

[500] Wolff, H.W, *A Commentary on the Book of the Prophet Hosea,* Philadelphia, Fortress, 63.

Dearman translates פחד as a verb, which means 'to fear,' 'to reverence.' The idea here is true repentance from the people and to remain faithful.[501] By returning to Yahweh, people get back their status and become self-reliant. The status in this context includes returning and becoming holy by themselves and for others, they are channel of blessings to others. It reminds them about their bondage and who brought them out of bondage.[502]

Although "last days" is mentioned earlier, it appears here again. באחרית הימים (*"in the last days"*[503]) throughout the book of Hosea is a message for the future though it was conveyed at a time in which the prophet lived.[504] In the last days the covenant relationship between God and people of Israel will be restored-renewed. The people of Israel will look for the messianic king and the king will come from David's root (Hos. 3:5).[505] This shows that God-Hosea will love their people-wife and they will bless and renew their covenant relationship (Hos. 2:21-23).

In the opening, middle and closing texture, there is the fourth use of the verb love (qal, perfect), describing how the Israelites embraced Baal worship, and ate sacrificial cakes, (cf. 2Sam. 6:19),[506] which were also objects of fertility worship (cf. Isa. 16:7, Jer. 44:19 and Jer. 48:31),[507] and eaten during celebrations (2Sam. 6:19). The opening-middle-closing texture helps to understand the repetitive, progressive and narrative texture of the text. The opening-middle-closing texture also progresses with the text and allows us to see how God's love is applied and elaborated.

Opening texture begins with "the formula ביום ההוא ("in that day" 1:5; 2:20 [18], 23 [21]) found in the middle texture is eschatological. In the prophetic literature "the latter days" refers to the coming of the Messiah.[508] But others argue that "latter days" is not synonymous with the "day of the Lord" (יום יהוה) concept mentioned in Amos, Joel, Zechariah and other prophets. The middle texture of the pericope 3:1-5 begins with a reference to the command of Yahweh to the prophet: 'remarry' ויאמר יהוה אלי, which is seen in vv. 2-4, and the outcome is אחר in 3:5 with the expectation that a king like David will come. Here Hosea returns to his own marriage and this is regarded as an image for Yahweh and Israel. The idea is that hope for Israel and Judah is presented in the line of David. Hosea's personal story and command to marry Gomer is a reminder of the origin of Hosea's prophetic ministry. The phrases ואת דויד מלכם *"and David their king"* and באחרית הימים "in the later days," have been regarded by many scholars as a later perhaps exilic hand. This calls for attention that Hosea

---

[501] Dearman, J.A, *The Book of Hosea,*" NICOT, Grand Rapids, Wm. B. Eerdmans Publishing co, 2010, 141.

[502] Wolff, H.W. *A Commentary on the Book of the Prophet Hosea,* Philadelphia, Fortress, 62-63.

[503] Wolff, *Hosea,* 63, compare with Isa 2:2; Mic 4:1; Jer. 23:20; Eze. 38:16. Deut. 4:30 text uses the phrase to refer to the Babylonian Exile, which will motivate the people "to return to Yahweh," cf. Hos. 3:5. Cf. for Lewis verses 3-5 are depicts of exile and return, Lewis. Jack P., *New International Version Study Bible,* Grand Rapids, Zondervan Bible Publishers, 1985, 1325.

[504] Derek Kidner, *Love to the Loveless: The Message of Hosea,* Illinois, Intervarsity Press, 1981, 43.

[505] Sandhya Shency, A Call to Return to the Lord (Hos. 6:1-6), Vol. XXXX, No. 3, September 2014, *Bible Bhashyam,* 147 (146-156).

[506] Mays, James Luther., *Hosea: A Commentary,* OTL, Philadelphia, Westminster, 1969, 57.

[507] S. R. Driver, *An Introduction to the Literature of the Old Testament,* New York, Meridian Books, 1960, 43.

[508] Chester K. Lehman, *Biblical Theology,* vol. 2, Scottdale, Herald Press, 1946, 272.

connects Yahweh's future victory to the rebirth of Davidic rule. Hosea 3:1-3 deals with Yahweh's action reflected in the life of the prophet, but vv. 4-5 exclusively talks about Israel's future life. In the closing texture, Hosea 2:18-25^{Heb} / 16-23^{Eng} points to the restoration of the marriage relationship between Yahweh and Israel. Hosea focuses on people's promiscuity because in their context, adultery was punishable by death, though the judgment was an unavoidable one. In this context, the prophet receives the command: to love a woman who lives as a paramour.

3.3.5. Argumentative Texture

Argumentative texture and pattern investigates multiple kinds of inner reasoning in the text.[509] In argumentative texture, the reasoning is discussed either as logical or qualitative, and persuades the reader to think and act a certain way. This text displays a qualitative pattern, in which the quality of the images and descriptions convince the reader to accept the portrayal as true. The argumentative texture deals with prophetic speech and legal proceedings. This section discusses prophetic speech.

The prophetic speech contains reference to Israel as a wayward and adulterous wife, who is expected to return to Yahweh. Hosea 2:16-17 talks about the promise of recovery and 2:18-25 assures of actual restoration that will take place in the future. Yahweh's test of her repentance, followed by Yahweh's love, is compared with gifts that the people received. The twist is that punishment turns into His loving grace and is expressed in the parable of return to the covenantal relationship with Yahweh. This means that the restoration takes place in this context.

3.3.5.1. The Cause-Effect Symbolic Act

When Yahweh commands *"Go again love a woman,"* the prophet obeys the command. Some interpreters ask why Hosea would marry another woman other than Gomer, as the name of the woman is missing in Chapter 3. However, the word *again* makes it clear that Hosea has to love one whom he has already married. Mays points out that the command is a peculiar experience that involves the consciousness and concentration of both the prophet and divine agent.[510] The command brings out the analogy between the prophet and the adulterous woman on one side, and Yahweh and the faithless people on the other. The comparison brings out the symbolic act of the woman to leave her companion (cf. Jer. 3:1; Song of Songs 5:16). After commanding the prophet, Yahweh expects him to obey and follow.

Apart from cause and effect, the argumentative texture contains opposites and contradictions. Philip King notes that Yahweh in 2:17 says that he will give her vineyards and the valley of Achor as a doorway of hope,[511] which means he will persuade her and bring her back and will give her possessions to her. According to Macintosh, the phrase "valley of Achor" is used as a figure of speech that symbolises

---

[509] V.K. Robbins, *Exploring the Texture of Texts: A Guide to Socio-Rhetorical Interpretation,* 1994, 94-96.

[510] J.L. Mays, *Hosea,* Westminster, John Knox press, 1969, 56.

[511] Philip King, *Amos-Micah: An Archaeological Commentary,* Philadelphia, Westminster, 1988, 25-26. Cf. Macintosh, *A Critical and Exegetical Commentary on Hosea,* Edinburgh, T and T Clark, 1997, 74-75.

the entire nation.[512] The prophet assures the people that the Lord will change Israel as a nation as she experienced trouble and now hope is offered to her. The "valley of Achor" was in the past a "valley of trouble" but Yahweh will change the place into a doorway of hope. The change of name is understood as the renewal of the covenant.[513] Andersen and Freedman note that the use of "valley of Achor" refers to a time span though they appear in reverse historical order in relation to the name.[514] According to Cross's interpretation, this is an ancient route to Jerusalem and as in the promise in Isa. 65:10, the valley of Sharon to the east and the valley Achor to the west will be given as rich pasture land to those who seek God.[515] The valley becomes the source of great fertility the trouble becomes hope. This shows the door of hope is a promise of success. The valley of Achor is here mentioned because of its fertility and the prediction that Israel was to return.

Some of the internal arguments in the discourse are logical articulations which give explanations and support with reasons, brightened by opposites and contradictions, and give possible short or extended counter arguments. Others are more qualitative in nature. Because of the quality of the images and descriptions, the portrayal is accepted as sincere and true. This is where the analogies, examples, and quotes from ancient evidence have a persuasive function.

The prophetic speech contains reference to Israel as a wayward and adulterous wife, who is expected to return to Yahweh. Hosea 2:16-17 talks about the promise of recovery and 2:18-25 assures of actual restoration that will take place in the future. Yahweh commands "Go again love a woman" and the prophet obeys the command. The argumentative texture is seen in the cause-effect symbolic act of Yahweh. The cause is buying or ואכרה (I will buy her), and the desired effect is seen in the command to תשבי (sit) which is the expected result שוב (to return) in v. 5.

3.3.6. Sensory-Aesthetic Texture

The sensory-aesthetic texture forcefully evokes the various senses of thought, feeling, sight, sound, touch, smell, and the way in which the text develops reasoning, intuition, imagination and humour. Attention to sensory-aesthetic texture reveals the dimensions, sound and range of the given discourse. Sometimes the discourse is so rich and vivid, with images that it is dramatically evoked as emotion. One way to search for sensory-aesthetic texture in every aspect of a text is to identify and group a part of the body that is referred to, as well as actions or perceptions related to a part of the body (sight, hearing, smell).

Sensory-aesthetic texture is divided into three zones; the three important aspects of zones are: a. Thought, b. Emotion, c. Action. The first aspect, thought, is treated as thought in the text. The second aspect talks about emotion while the third type is more active, leading to action. In sensory-aesthetic texture and pattern, the thought is an idea. For example, the word love is related to thought, and love is expressed through action.

---

[512] Macintosh, *A Critical and Exegetical Commentary on Hosea,* Edinburgh, T and T Clark, 1997, 74-75.

[513] W.A. VanGemeren, *Interpreting the Prophetic Word,* Grand Rapids, Zondervan, 1990, 118.

[514] Andersen, F.I and Freedman, D.N., *Hosea: A New Translation with Introduction and Commentary,* New York, Doubleday, 1980, 269.

[515] F. M. Cross, *Canaanite Myth and Hebrew Epic,* Massachusetts, Cambridge, 1973, 110.

There are different ways in the discourse to identify the "body zones." Bruce Malina identifies three such zones.[516]

In the zone of emotion, fused with thought, the author brings out the emotions of the characters. In exegesis, the author brings out different kinds of emotions shown within the text. This is called emotion texture and the pattern where importance is given to emotional thought shows how it proceeds to the next level.

The second aspect in this texture is called the zone of self-experience or self-expressive speech. In this texture, the author deals with emotional self-experience, which is verbal. This self-expression is more to do with self-revelations and deals more with the communication aspect, which is also called the dialogical aspect.

The third aspect is the zone of purposeful action. In this texture, importance is given to more specific action. It proceeds step by step, where thought develops and moves into emotions and ends with actions.

3.3.6.1. Action zone / Emotion zone (Hosea: 2:14-3:5)

The words below show the actions and emotions related to this zone.

Table 12: Action zone / emotion zone - Hosea 2 :14-3 :5

בטש	Safety
זרע	Break
ארש	Betroth
ענה	Answer
זרע	Sow
אמר	Say
אהב	Love
כרה	Bought / Purchase
ישב	Dwell

There are several emotional phrases found in Hosea 2:14-3:5. Weems says that one of the major ways in which both action and emotion are shown is through the idea of compassion and love.[517] Earlier in Hosea 2, Yahweh disowns His people. However, in Hosea 2:25 Yahweh shows the reverse of this in ורחמתי (and I will have compassion), the word *have pity* cancels 1:6 and 2:6, by fulfilling the promise of 2:3. *You are my people* withdraws 1:9, by fulfilling the promise of 2:3.[518] In the reversal of the names at 2:1, *"Not-my-people"* was changed to *"Children of the living God."* 2:25b returns to the title drawn from the covenant vows.[519] Andersen and Freedman identify that the singular pronoun *"he will say"* refers to the individual members of

[516] Malina. B.J, *The New Testament World: Insights from Cultural Anthropology,* rev. ed. Atlanta, John Knox Press, 1993, 73-77.

[517] Renita J. Weems, *Battered Love: Marriage, Sex, and Violence in the Hebrew Prophets,* Minneapolis, Fortress Press, 1995, 50.

[518] Andersen, F.I and Freedman, D.N., *Hosea: A New Translation with Introduction and Commentary,* New York, Doubleday, 1980, 187-188.

[519] Charles Dyer and Eugene Merrill, *Nelson's Old Testament Survey,* Nashville, Thomas Nelson Publishers, 2001, 728.

the family and highlights them particularly. In the immediate context, the speaker is the former לא עמי, whose name in the previous clause changed to עמי: *"You are my people."*[520] It is appropriate that עמי should respond by affirming the matching title "My God." The balancing pronouns, "You," and "He" support the connection. My God matches the name isi in 2:18. The various rituals and pronouncements connected with adoption, marriage, and covenant-making in general show that dual affirmation was usually made by one person, not antiphonally. Such an exchange of similar statements matches the reciprocal affirmations made in vv. 23-24, whose statement was not specified. The פקדתי (visit) of Yahweh is described in verse 15, which connotes dialogue. 2: 15 indicates that Israel has שכחה (forgotten) Yahweh.

Another area in which both action and emotion are shown is through the idea of love. The MT emendations of אני to לא אביא (qal, imperfect, first common singular), imply the personal nature of this relationship. The verse explains the essence of love;[521] love that is shown through Israel's obedient response to God's loving care and protection. Hosea 3:3 describes the relationship between God and his people Israel as a sign of a greater relationship.[522]

Beeby points out that the command of Yahweh in v. 1 לך (again) with the aim to אהב־אשה (to love or choose a woman), requires a thoughtful decision that leads to an action.[523] The אהב (love) is an outstanding example of "emotion-fused" thinking. To love is a thoughtful decision with the element of choice. The required actions are ישוב (they will return), ובקשו (and they will look) and ופחדו (and fear approaching). Zones of "emotion-fused" thinking are eyes, heart, eyelids, pupils, and the activities of these organs enable one to see, know, understand, think, remember, choose, feel, and consider watching.

3.3.6.2. Imagery of Love - Covenant with all Creation

In this discourse, the text presents Yahweh as the character who presents no emotion-fused thoughts (in both instances this is through his words to the prophet Hosea) or self-expressive speech (in both instances this is shown in his command to Hosea). The prophet responds to the command with purposeful action.

3.3.6.3. The Zone of Self-Expressive Speech

In chapter 2, the means of verbal activity by ריבו (twist) in verse 4; אמרה (she said) in verse 7, 9 and 14; ידברת (I speak) in 2:16, and in 17 ענתה (she will answer) indicate the importance of advocacy in the lawsuit. The word ענתה can mean both answer and following after. The ענתה is an adverb used for directional purpose and the additional ה is added for better meaning and for particular purpose.[524] Wolff says that an additional ה is used as the verb for motion. The תקראי (call) in 2:18 is used as 3rd person singular *"she will call Me."*

[520] Andersen, F.I and Freedman, D.N., *Hosea: A New Translation with Introduction and Commentary,* New York, Doubleday, 1980, 187-189.

[521] Mays, James Luther., *Hosea: A Commentary,* OTL, Philadelphia, Westminster, 1969, 58.

[522] Mays, James Luther, *Hosea: A Commentary,* OTL, Philadelphia, Westminster, 1969, 58.

[523] Beeby, H.D., *Grace Abounding: A Commentary on the book of Hosea,* Grand Rapids, Eerdmans, 1989, 38-39.

[524] Wolff, H.W., *A Commentary on the Book of the Prophet Hosea,* Philadelphia, Fortress, 1974, 42-44.

Similarly LXX supports MT reading to retain the third person throughout. In 2:18 the wife calls her husband by a new name. With the new name "my husband," the activation takes place by taking away the name Baal and replacing it with the title "my husband." This refers to the domestic setting in the framework of wife calling her husband "my husband" but in the case of Israel it is Yahweh who is addressed as husband. In Andersen's opinion, the prophet tries to abolish the name Baal from the mouths of the people of Israel and their culture, and asks them to remain with the true God Yahweh.[525] Stuart translates this as "You will call me."[526] This indicates the idea of speaking to and returning to Yahweh; Baal will not be their master, rather they will call Yahweh "my master." It belongs to the zone of "self-expressive speech." It is therefore a pertinent speech activity where Yahweh as "man" is recognized. According to Mays, the name of Baal should not be pronounced by Israel but Yahweh himself will act to fulfil the covenant demand.[527] It says that "you shall call down/forth" (used in passive of the Hiphil form) זכר the name should not be spoken (Exo. 23:13).[528] The idea here is that Yahweh himself will act and will bring the people into the necessary fulfilment of the covenant.[529] The same reference follows in verse 19, where the Baals' names are to be removed from Israel's mouth מפיה. Her activity is therefore accursed ולא-יזכרו עוד בשמם (so their names should not be mentioned).[530] The ולא-יזכרו עוד בשמם (and לא עמי) and the resulting ואמרתי ללא-עמי (and then she would say) in verse 25 is a pertinent speech activity and speaks of her infidelity.

In Hosea 2:18-25 (16-23 MT), Wolff finds that comparison is made with the old covenant. It is Yahweh who provides everything for the people of Israel, including establishment and faithfulness that includes mercy for the guilty (cf. Hos. 2:25).[531] Harper points out that here the restoration of the old covenant takes place and there is an announcement of a marriage that establishes a new covenant and communion between God and His people (cf. Jer. 31:31-34).[532] Here, we observe that Hosea went and took Gomer again, shows election. God's love for Israel is because of His loving kindness. The divine election is not for individual but for countless millions and it is very special concern for His loved ones. Here we notice God's purpose in His electing love. The new covenant introduces the overall conditions for a new life. The new covenant helps Israelites to grow more in faith and hope for the future and to depend upon God. Stuart concludes that this section is about re-establishment and agricultural abundance. Both re-establishment and abundance refer to eschatological themes in the book that characterize the promises of restoration in the new covenant.[533]

---

[525] Andersen, F.I and Freedman, D.N., *Hosea: A New Translation with Introduction and Commentary,* New York, Doubleday, 1980, 278-279.

[526] Stuart, Douglas: *Hosea-Jonah, Word Biblical Commentary:* Dallas, Word Incorporated, 1987, 45-46.

[527] Mays, James Luther., *Hosea: A Commentary,* OTL, Philadelphia, Westminster, 1969, 49.

[528] Cf. M. Noth, *Exodus,* Old Testament Library, London, SCM Press, 1962, 16.

[529] See *THAT,* vol. I, 513.

[530] Andersen, F.I and Freedman, D.N., *Hosea: A New Translation with Introduction and Commentary,* New York, Doubleday, 1980, 279.

[531] Wolff, H.W., *A Commentary on the Book of the Prophet Hosea,* Philadelphia, Fortress, 1974, 54-55.

[532] W.R. Harper, *A Critical and Exegetical Commentary on Amos and Hosea,* Edinburgh, T and T Clark, 1956, 242.

[533] Stuart. D, *Hosea-Jonah,* Waco, Word, 1987, 61.

Harrison and Greenspahn emphasise that the prophet gave symbolic names to his children; *Jezreel* a son, called after the place where Jehu's dynasty came to power (2Kgs. 10:11), served as a warning that Yahweh was going to punish Jehu's line. לא-רחמה or "not-pitied," a daughter, signified Yahweh had no more pity for his people, and לא-עמי or *"not-my people"* a son, symbolised the broken relationship between Yahweh and Israel.[534] Westermann notes that the change of names indicates the ownership and dominion or the person's identity.[535] In this context, it is noted that Israel has now become a new people and Yahweh is their Lord. Here both God's naming and re-naming of Hosea's children are significant.

In chapter 3, the advocacy activities ויאמר יהוה (and Yahweh said) in 3:1 and ואמר אליה (I told her) in 3:3 depict the importance of speech in the form of a symbolic act.[536] Wolff points out that ויאמר יהוה recounts of a specific command from Yahweh to the prophet, which includes people's responsibility for their sins. Hosea reminds them of broken marriage and pleads with Israel to work for reconciliation with God. The requirement is that the woman should continually be faithful to her husband, just as Hosea is with Gomer and Yahweh is with Israel.

3.3.6.4. The Zone of Purposeful Action

In the text, both Yahweh and Israel show purposeful action through which they try to attain their goals. First, Israel keeps Yahweh away from her with her actions. This is indicated by זנוניה מפניה (of her promiscuity her face) and ונאפופיה מבין שדיה (from her adulteries and her breasts away).[537] Yahweh comes in verse 14 with His purposeful action of his generosity in forgiving and re-accepting Israel back to covenant.[538] He says והלכתיה מפתיה which means "I will allure her, and guide her," but verse 16 says נתתי which is "I give."[539] The language used here is passionate; מפתיה is used in the piel verb form meaning to allure, to romance, to seduce as in Exo. 22:16[540] (cf. Hos. 7:11). על דבר-לבה is a tender expression, used for courtship (Gen 34:3) and winning back love (Jud. 19:3), and also kind considerate favour not necessarily involving romantic intentions (Ruth. 2:13).[541] The verb "allure" (מפתיה) is used in a different way: that is, a seduction of a virgin (Ex. 22:15 [16]). In this context the word "allure" is a bold word, powerfully echoing the longing of God for Israel. William Sanford interprets Gomer to be like any other virgin in Israelite culture: she has participated in the Canaanite ritual and sexual acts prior to her marriage.

---

[534] R.K. Harrison, *Introduction to the Old Testament,* London, The Tyndale Press, 1969, 861. Cf. Greenspahn F.E., Hosea in Paul J. Achtemeir, *Harper Bible Dictionary,* 406-407. Cf. Matthews H. Victor, *Social World of the Hebrew Prophets,* Massachusetts, Hendrickson Press, 2008, 75-76.

[535] Claus Westermann, *Handbook to the Old Testament,* London, SPCK, 1969, 179.

[536] Andersen, F.I and Freedman, D.N., *Hosea: A New Translation with Introduction and Commentary,* New York, Doubleday, 1980, 294.

[537] Renita J. Weems, *Battered Love: Marriage, Sex, and Violence in the Hebrew Prophets,* Minneapolis, Fortress Press, 1995, 47.

[538] W. Brueggemann, *Theology of the Old Testament,* Minneapolis, Fortress Press, 1997, 261.

[539] Walter Kaiser, *Toward an Old Testament Theology,* Grand Rapids, Zondervan Publishing House, 1978, 198.

[540] Dearman, J.A., *The Book of Hosea,*" NICOT, Grand Rapids, Wm. B. Eerdmans Publishing co, 2010, 121. Cf. Vasholz. Robert I., English Standard Version Study Bible, Wheaton, Crossway Bibles, 2008, 1626.

[541] Wolff, H.W. *A Commentary on the Book of the Prophet Hosea,* Philadelphia, Fortress, 41-42.

Mays conclude that the meaning of persuading is for overwhelming the resistance and the will of another.[542] Similarly, the word "allure" indicates persuasion by means of attractive benefits. Charles Dyer argues that in this context it looks as though it is a strong statement but it can be compared with the phrase "speak to her tenderly" (Hos. 2:16), which does not imply any force.[543] But Leon Wood finds that the statement refers to implying the persuasion by means of attractive benefits.[544] This interpretation corresponds to the context in the light of the following (2:17): The expression is of winning back love, kindness and favour. Hosea 2:17 continues והסרתי את־שמות הבעלים מפיה *"I will take away the names of Baalim out of her mouth;"*[545] Harper continues that Hosea regularly use the plural form for *Baalim* when he speaks in relation to Canaanitish elements in the Yahweh worship.[546] Verse 19 says, וכרתי להם ברית meaning "and I include them in a covenant;" 2:20 says וקשת וחרב ומלחמה אשבור מן-הארץ meaning *"yes bow and sword, and war will break out of the country"* and finally אענה is *"I will betroth you to,"* emphatically stated in 2:21 and 22.[547] The marriage bond is created between Yahweh and Israel, characterised by covenant keeping, righteousness, tender mercy and steadfast love. Here we find how God used Hosea to explain their future reality to His people. Harper comments that the reason is God would "allure her," "speak to her tenderly," God will remove the name Baal from their mouth (Hos. 2:14, 17).[548] This is to remind them *"I will betroth you forever." I will betroth you in steadfast love, righteousness and in justice.* This is to make known to His people that He is their God.

Garrett notes that in chapter 3, there is a purposeful action again by Yahweh when He gives commands in 3:1 to his prophet: לך אהב־אשה which is *"go and love a woman."*[549] Andersen notes that the prophet's actions in 3:2 ואכרה meaning *"and I will buy her"* is a purposeful response to Yahweh's command.[550] The consequential actions, namely the command תשבי and not to commit whoredom (לא תזני) 'and you will not belong to any man' (ולא תהיי לאיש), are focused actions by the command of the prophet to meet Yahweh's instruction.[551] The expected and desired outcome

542 Mays, James Luther, *Hosea: A Commentary,* OTL, Philadelphia, Westminster, 1969, 43-45.

543 Charles Dyer and Eugene Merrill, *Nelson's Old Testament Survey,* Nashville, Thomas Nelson Publishers, 2001, 728.

544 Leon Wood, "Hosea," *The Expositor's Bible Commentary,* vol. 7, ed. F.E. Gaebelein, *Four Minor Prophets,* Grand Rapids, Zondervan Publishing Co, 1985, 178-179.

545 Andersen, F.I and Freedman, D.N., *Hosea: A New Translation with Introduction and Commentary,* New York, Doubleday, 1980, 279.

546 W.R. Harper, *A Critical and Exegetical Commentary on Amos and Hosea,* Edinburgh, T and T Clark, 1956, 234.

547 Ortlund Raymond C., *Whoredom: God's unfaithful wife in Biblical Theology,* Grand Rapids, Wm. B. Eerdmans, 1996, 70, cf. Beeby, H.D., *Grace Abounding: A Commentary on the book of Hosea,* Grand Rapids, Eerdmans, 1989, 2-29. Cf. B.S. Childs, *Old Testament in a Canonical Context,* Philadelphia, Fortress Press, 1989, 96-97.

548 W.R. Harper, *A Critical and Exegetical Commentary on Amos and Hosea,* Edinburgh, T and T Clark, 1956, 239.

549 Garrett, *Hosea, Joel An Exegetical and Theological Exposition of Holy Scripture,* B and H Publishing Group, 1997, 124.

550 Andersen, F.I and Freedman, D.N., *Hosea: A New Translation with Introduction and Commentary,* New York, Doubleday, 1980, 295.

551 Wolff, H.W, *A Commentary on the Book of the Prophet Hosea,* Philadelphia, Fortress, 62. Cf. Stuart, Douglas: *Hosea-Jonah, Word Biblical Commentary:* Dallas, Word, Incorporated, 1987, 136.

is given in 3:5, namely ישׁוּב *(they will repent)*, ובקשׁו *(and they will look)* and ופחדו *(and approach respectfully)*. Yahweh's command of love is portrayed in the life of Hosea. Hosea is a messenger of the word of God and becomes a witness to the people because the people disobeyed and broke the covenant. The consequence of breaking the covenant is explained by the message he received from God. When the people disobeyed the covenant, punishment followed them. But the assurance of God's love is proclaimed and that will lead them from judgment to salvation.

The word 'allure' Hosea 2:14 (MT 16) refers to the event taking place in the immediate or near future. The prophet prophesied that the event refers to a future when God will have mercy on His people. Here Hosea used the word 'return' to describe what Gomer did, what the Lord wanted His people to do and what the Lord would do when Israel truly repented of their sin (cf. 5:15; 14:4). The assurance is that the Lord will speak to them tenderly and He is going to invite them to return to Him and change their hearts.

Yahweh's purposeful action is connected with restoring the covenant relationship through love, whereas Israel seems bent on breaking the covenant to satisfy her desire for other gods. Yahweh expects repentance as a purposeful action from Israel, but she does not heed this. In spite of this waywardness, God remains faithful. For the other nations, Yahweh's love is astonishing, for other nations as well as his people. God is presented as a passionate lover who cares for Israel and others. God's gracious love is presented in the form of a metaphor that leads to God's sacrifice for the people. The covenant in Hosea states God is committed to His nations and to all creatures/creation. The book reveals clearly how God accomplishes and declares the renewal of the covenant. The central theme in this section is God's covenant. The restoration is clearly through discipline.

The zones deal with several emotions and phrases in Hosea 2:14-3:5. The action and emotions bring out the idea of compassion and love. The zones express the feeling that Israel is God's chosen people. Yahweh affirms that He will have compassion on her. This can be seen through the change of names of children from negative to positive. This highlights that Israel will be Yahweh's chosen people. For this, God uses love as an instrument in redeeming His people. The love in this case means for Israel and for others. The idea changes from lawsuit to compassion. The purposeful action that this brings is forgiving and reaccepting Israel. This section is all about Yahweh's command and love for her.

There are several emotional phrases found in Hosea 2:14-3:5. One of the major ways in which both action and emotion are shown is through the idea of compassion and love. Earlier in Hosea 2, Yahweh disowns His people. However, in Hosea 2:25 Yahweh shows the reverse of this in ורחמתי (and I will have compassion), the word 'have pity' cancels 1:6 and 2:6, by fulfilling the promise of 2:3. 'You are my people' withdraws 1:9, by fulfilling the promise of 2:3. In the reversal of the names at 2:1, *"Not-my-people"* was changed to *"Children of the living God."* In this discourse, the text presents Yahweh as the character who presents no emotion fused thoughts or self-expressive speech. The prophet responds to the command with purposeful action.

The next section deals with inter-textuality and is followed by other textures: social, cultural, historical texture and theological texture.

3.4. Inter-textuality

Inter-textuality compares similar sections in other parts of the Old Testament to reveal how one theme is found in other events. The reconfiguration technique places the wilderness time (verse 16) and Egyptian time (verse 17) in the foreground. The new desert time is foretold as the ideal humiliation time in which there is a willingness to listen to Yahweh. Coming out of Egypt at the command of the Lord becomes the ideal image of obedience. The covenant (verse 20) leads to a new understanding between Yahweh and his people. The warning comes in the form of Hosea abandoning his wife as God abandoned him. Instead God promises new tender courtship of the adulterous woman (Israel) and the change takes place during a return into wilderness. This is predicted by Jeremiah who foresees the new covenant written on the heart (Jer. 31:31-34), similarly, Ezekiel who promises that God would remove their hard heart and replace it with a new heart touched by the Spirit of God (Ezek. 36:26-27). Harper notes that in this context, Hosea sees God who speaks tenderly to his beloved by promising to restore the possessions and giving her back her vineyards.[552] Hosea 2:16^{Heb} (14^{Eng}) predicts Yahweh's response towards Israel. Dearman comments that the unit is a reminder of the restoration that the wife of the prophet will be transformed into the kind of wife that she had failed to be in the past (Deut. 30:6).[553] This section looks at the wilderness and conquest experience that constituted the basic foundational experience of Israel.[554]

Two themes from Israel's wilderness experience are selected to represent the recollection of those days.[555] First, according to Matthews, the gift of the land is alluded to in the promise to give Israel back "her vineyards from there" (cf. Josh. 24:13). The second example is the valley of Achor ("trouble valley" cf. Josh. 7:24-26).[556] The Hebrew word Achor is translated as "trouble or disturbance."[557] The reference to Achor in Joshua 7 is well known. This valley, which was a source of disappointment early in the conquest, would now be a gateway of hope.[558] Andersen and Freedman argue that the word Achor brings out the meaning of לפתח תקוה *"door of hope."*[559] According to Harper *"the valley of Achor"* refers to the time period and is reminiscent of a chronological order reaching out and achieving its hope.[560] Garrett notes that the people of Israel's future hope will be in thanksgiving

---

552 W.R. Harper, *A Critical and Exegetical Commentary on Amos and Hosea,* Edinburgh, T and T Clark, 1956, 239-240.

553 Dearman, J.A, *The Book of Hosea,*" NICOT, Grand Rapids, Wm. B. Eerdmans Publishing Co., 2010, 121-122.

554 S. Talson, "The Desert Motif in the Bible and the Qumran Literature," in *Biblical Motifs.* Ed., A. Altman, Cambridge, Harvard, 1966, 31-64.

555 Dearman, J.A, *The Book of Hosea,*" NICOT, Grand Rapids, Wm. B. Eerdmans Publishing Co., 2010, 122.

556 Victor. H. Matthews, *Social World of the Hebrew Prophets,* Peabody, Massachusetts, Hendrickson Publishers, 2001, 75. Cf. Sweeney, Marvin A. *Twelve Prophets,* 2 vols. Collegeville, Liturgical Press, 2000, 1257.

557 BDB, TWOT.

558 Literally, "I will make the valley of Achor a door of hope," (לפתח תקה) *HALOT,* 10282.

559 Andersen, F.I. and Freedman, D.N., *Hosea: A New Translation with Introduction and Commentary,* New York, Doubleday, 1980, 275-276.

560 W.R. Harper, *A Critical and Exegetical Commentary on Amos and Hosea,* Edinburgh, T and T Clark, 1956, 240.

filled with happiness and blessing as they enter into the Promised Land from Babylonian captivity.[561] This memorial place will not be a thing of the past but a gateway for hope as the Israelites better their future in the land where they are going to dwell. The future days will be greater when the people return to their land, and the Messiah is their king.

Another example of inter-textuality is by ענה, which means "to reply." Andersen and Freedman note that Israel will now ענה "respond," just as she did for the first time in Deuteronomy. ענה sums up the series of positive relationships and actions which follow God's salvation. Things will thus be as they were during the Exodus from Egypt; the original situation being repeated in the eschatological situation.[562] Israel had foolishly chosen to depend upon the Baals; now she will learn to depend only on Yahweh, and the Baals will be nothing to her, as it was before she ever knew them.[563] The Pentateuchal restoration promise that eschatological Israel would again benefit from the blessings given to the first generation in the original Mount Sinai covenant (Lev. 26:45), including "ownership" by Yahweh *(I will be their God)* will be fulfilled. Garrett identifies how the shift from לא־עמי to *"not my people"* changes according to Mosaic tradition and it is noted that Yahweh called Israel 'עמי' *"my people."*[564] Here however, the relationship is assumed and so also the hope: that Israel will obey the command of Yahweh and she will continue to remain in their covenant (cf. Exo. 6:7 and 19:5). If they return to him Hosea reminds us that God called Israel "my people," but because of her unfaithfulness she was called "not my people." However, the message to Israel is that God will in future say to them 'I am your God.'

The phrases "without King or prince," אין מלך ואין שר and *"David their king"* דויד מלכם are synonymous and can be taken as repetition. The phrases *"and David their king"* and *"in the later days"* have been regarded by many scholars as marks of a later, perhaps exilic hand. The meaning of this phrase conveys the reunion of the two kingdoms under one head, the reversal of Israel's pattern of dynastic instability, the rejection of the foreign alliances which served as a buffer against their own political weakness and the covenantal continuity to David by Yahweh that was violated by Jeroboam I and all his successors and which was condemned by the prophets like Amos and the other great prophets who followed him. Here Hosea connects Yahweh's future victory to the rebirth of Davidic rule. The idea of hope is given to the people of Israel that they will return to their Lord from worshipping other gods. The prophet gives them the hope of healing if they turn to the Lord. They can return to the Lord because of His love for them.

Hosea 3:4 continues with the narration of the story. The narrational voice is seen in v. 4. The prophet enacts the command and gives voice to the statement and

---

[561] Garrett, *Hosea, Joel: An Exegetical and Theological Exposition of Holy Scripture,* Nashville, B. and H. Publisher, 1997, 112-113.

[562] Andersen, F.I and Freedman, D.N., *Hosea: A New Translation with Introduction and Commentary,* New York, Doubleday, 1980, 275-276. Cf. W.R. Harper, *A Critical and Exegetical Commentary on Amos and Hosea,* Edinburgh, T and T Clark, 1956, 239.

[563] Wolff, H.W, *A Commentary on the Book of the Prophet Hosea,* Philadelphia, Fortress, 80.

[564] Garrett, *Hosea, Joel An Exegetical and Theological Exposition of Holy Scripture,* B and H Publishing Group, 1997, 117.

connects the statement to show how God's love is brought out or portrayed through a metaphor. The metaphor is used to show God's love towards his people through the imagery of husband and wife and the statement connects this with the people of Israel in verse 4, "for the children of Israel shall dwell many days without king or prince, without sacrifice or pillar, without ephod or teraphim" (Hos. 3:5). Afterward the children of Israel will return and seek the Lord their God, and David their king; and they will come in fear of the Lord and know his goodness in the latter days. When the people go after other gods these are the things they will lose. But the love of God tries to get people back by giving them everything. This shows the love between God and his people. In verse 5, the text clearly brings out that the narrator himself is a speaker as in verse 1 and 3. The speaker is the one who takes the initiative and continues his speech to the prophet to communicate his message to his people. Here we find the separation between the two speeches in verse 1 and 3. The first one is of the Lord, and the second is of the prophet Hosea.

Chapter 3 exhibits other texts that are important passages within the Pentateuch. For example the interplay between Hosea 1:9 and Exodus 3:14 the concept of "I am." The name of the Lord was revealed and the Lord says "I am who I am." The term God is used in order to communicate the message to Israel. In this context, God discloses his name to Moses in commissioning Moses to be his representative before Pharaoh. The statement of the phrase in Hosea indicates that Israel's special relationship with God has been abolished. Stuart explains the Hosean reference in light of Exo. 3:14 that Yahweh himself refers here to the first person form of the name, referring back to the ancient original use of the first person from Exo. 3:1, the first person form was that associated with the tradition of initiation of the covenant. Yahweh was withdrawing the very covenant he created and then in an impressive manner via the revelation of his name was using the same form of the name he used to Moses.[565] The revealing of the name implies the meaning of his deliverance of the Israelites at the exodus; it meant God would henceforth reside with the Israelites. The explicit reference to the exodus deliverance include Hos. 2:15 [MT 17] and the phrase "I am the Lord your God from the land of Egypt;" this alludes clearly to the exodus. For Hoffman the significance of the abundant reference to the exodus-wanderings theme in Hosea is in reference to the hope motif in Hos. 2:14-15 [MT 16-17].[566] Similarly, in Hosea 3:5 the phrase "in the last days" occurs in Genesis 49:1, Numbers 24:14 and Deuteronomy 31:29. The text goes like this; afterward the people of Israel will return and seek the Lord their God and David their King. This demonstrates the prophet's awareness of a significant messianic phrase from the Pentateuch and intends the usage in a corresponding way.

Ezekiel 34:22-24 speaks about One Shepherd which refers to David, who will feed them and take care of them. This identifies David to be Israel's King and Messiah in that day. Ezekiel 34:22-24 summarizes David as the ruler of Israel: David will be ultimately subservient to God/Christ. The relationship between David and God is seen in this passage. Ezekiel 37 speaks about David's identity as an anointed one and he will be Israel's King and Messiah at the resurrection from the dead. The prophet speaks of the literal resurrection of the whole house of Israel in the first five

[565] D. Stuart, *Hosea-Jonah,* Waco, Word, 1987, 33.

[566] Hoffman, "The Exodus in Hosea and Amos," *VT* 39, (1989), 170-73, 171.

verses (37:1-5). David himself will return to rule. In Jeremiah 30:9 (7-9) "but they shall serve the LORD their God and David their king, whom I will raise up for them." The name "David" appears as the new representative of the house of Israel who is going to restore the kingdom. The kingdom will be united. Jeremiah speaks about the restoration of Israel and Judah. God will raise up David to them - that great day is compared with Isaiah 9:4 and 6, the time when "unto us a child is born," the people will not give obedience to strangers but to their Lord (David as their king). (Isaiah 11: David to return and rule the kingdom) Zech. 12:8 refers to David. "In that day" God saves the people of Judah and Jerusalem. David shall be as God. Those who follow the house of David will be prudent and leads people more strongly. This shows the people of Jerusalem will be mighty men of valour. The phrase "the house of David..." is a striking metaphor used in the sense of God's empowering of His people.

Isaiah is one of the most unified poems in the Hebrew Bible.[567] The chapter is centered on the theology found in verse 3, where God promises a covenant life to the exiles of Israel. "I will make an everlasting covenant with you; (the mercies of David,") emphasises for one who hears the Lord, God promises a covenant. From Isaiah's perspective, this covenant is still in the future (I will make). The covenant characterizes the mercies of the Lord, in the following ways: God spared David's life though he committed sin, because God had promised to bless him. Isaiah 55:1-5 is a call to life itself by means of a covenant Yahweh is willing to make. These verses refer to the exiles, commanding them to come (5x), buy (2x), eat (2x), and listen (2x).[568] In Isaiah 55:3, the prophet says that Yahweh will make a covenant with Israel along the lines of the covenant he made with David. David is shown here as witness and leader of the peoples (v. 4) and Israel (v. 5). Here the covenant is referred to as "eternal" which demonstrates God's loving-kindness to David. Isa 55:4 clearly refers to what Yahweh had done for David and what he gave him as a witness to people and as a leader and commander for the peoples.[569] The prophet says that Yahweh offers the covenant directly to the nation as a whole and not just to the Davidic line within the nation.[570] The imagery that we see in this section (1-5) describes the blessing awaiting the exiles if they return to Yahweh. This is followed by abundant blessings of life and obeying God's word and listening to the Lord (v. 2). Here we note that the specific content of the promise which is given to the people and here emphasised concerns the Davidic king's relationship to the world in v. 4 and 5.[571] The parallel noticed here is: what was done for David will be done for the nation.

The text makes clear that it talks about the restoration of Davidic kingship over Israel and Judah (cf. Jer. 17:25; 22:2) and continues to say that the Messiah who will fulfil the state of the Davidic covenant will be fulfilled in the blessings of the Davidic

---

[567] Richard J. Clifford, Isaiah 55; In the Word of the Lord shall Go Forth: Essays in Honor of David N. Freedman, ed. C.L. Meyers and M. O'Connor, Winona, Esenbrauns, 1983, 33.

[568] BDB, הוֹי, 222, Clements, *Isaiah 1-39.*

[569] Kaiser, *"The Unfailing Kindnesses Promised to David,"* 94.

[570] M. A. Sweeney, "The Reconceptualization of the Davidic Covenant in Isaiah," in *Studies in the Book of Isaiah:* ed. J. Van Ruiten and M. Vervenne, Leuven: Leuven University Press, 1997, 42-47.

[571] Otto Eissfeldt, "The Promises of Grace to David in Isaiah 55:1-5," in *Israel's Prophetic Heritage: Essays in Honor of James Muilenburg,* ed. Bernhard W. Anderson and Walter Harrelson, London: SCM Press, 1962, 203.

covenant for Israel. Harper points out that here the idea of Messiah is pictured as the "New David" because he would fulfil the ideals of the Davidic covenant and that will be followed to Davidic descendants as they were commissioned to be (Isa. 9:7, 16:5; Jer. 23:5-6, 33:15-16, Eze. 34:23-24, 37:24-25).[572] The idea presented in this context is that the children of Israel would repent and return and seek the Lord. The idea noted is that God often uses deprivation to bring back the lost children to return to the Lord and the hope is given that they will have a new King.

Inter-textuality deals with how the similar theme occurs in the Bible. The idea of covenant between Yahweh and his people and warning comes in the form of the prophet through Hosea's wife. Similar idea is found in the books of Jeremiah 31:31-34 and Ezekiel 36:26-27 promises that God would remove their hard heart and replace it with a new heart. Hosea 2:16^{Heb} (14^{Eng}) predicts Yahweh's response towards Israel. Two themes from Israel's wilderness experience are selected to represent the recollection of their past history. The shift from לא־עמי to "not my people" changes according to Mosaic tradition and it is noted that Yahweh called Israel 'עמי' "my people."

3.5. Social Texture

In terms of social and cultural categories, the pericope is part of a lawsuit warning about the opposition. This is a cultural rhetoric. It is taken as a firm stand against the perverse cult of idolatry. The worship is criticized by making use of harsh words and concepts of adultery and זנה (promiscuity). This idea is altered in verses 4 and 18 by the use of terms like אש (man) and אשה (woman), the connotation of marriage and the "provision of livelihood" (verse 10) as well as "wedding gifts" (vv. 21-22).[573] The promiscuity referred to in verses 4, 6, 7, 10, 13, 14 and 15 seems to refer to the fertility rites in the cult and foreign alliances during the government of the various kings of the Northern Kingdom.

Despite the description of Jeroboam's reign as "a rule of each, prosperity and power" it is a fact that his reign saw the breakdown of the Israelite social structure into one of a small rich ruling class living in luxury and the majority of the population, especially the poor artisans, craftsmen, labourers and farmers, crushed beneath heavy taxes and injustice. Inevitably, Israel began to lose its social character.[574] It was against this background of social injustice that Hosea preached a return to Yahweh. Here we see a reference to Hosea's marriage to a harlot creeping in where Hosea 1:2 draws a parallel between the literal "harlotry" (זנונים) in Hosea's family life and the figurative sin that "the land has committed in flagrant harlotry" (הארץ תזנה). Here the term "land" is used in its broad sense to mean the nation itself the people who have turned away from Yahweh to worship foreign gods (harlotry), because it was during this time that the Israelites started to follow their neighbours' gods, which was against the covenant law, and ignored Yahweh. Although Hosea preached Yahweh's anger, it is noticeable that he also preached Yahweh's forgiveness if it was sought.

---

[572] W.R. Harper, *A Critical and Exegetical Commentary on Amos and Hosea,* Edinburgh, T and T Clark, 1956, 223.

[573] Dearman, J.A, *The Book of Hosea,*" NICOT, Grand Rapids, Wm. B. Eerdmans Publishing Company, 2010, 127.

[574] N.K. Gottwald, *The Hebrew Bible: A Socio-Literary Introduction,* 356.

There are diverse interpretations regarding the marriage of Hosea. Scholars of the Old Testament differ in their opinions with regard to the woman in Hosea's life, while sketching the biography of Hosea that is found in chapters 1 and 3. One interpretation pertaining to Hosea's marriage is that of the "adulterous wife" (1:2), which probably could be a title given in a rhetorical way. Under the guidance of Yahweh, the prophet takes for himself a woman who will become an adulterous wife involved in harlotry. Robinson contends that Hosea married a woman whom he knew at the time to be impure,[575] which the prophet interprets in a rhetorical way. In chapter 3, Hosea is specifically commanded to take an adulterous woman. However, there is no data mentioned in chapter 3 to prove that Gomer is to be identified with the promiscuous wife. Although it has often been suggested, there is nothing mentioned about Gomer's profession. There is nothing mentioned about Gomer's marital infidelity and this is only learned metaphorically.[576] She is called אשת זנונים meaning *"prostituting woman"* in 1:2. However, this cannot be taken as a literal statement of her profession or practise, even though there is an understanding that the prophet married at God's command a woman who was or who became a prostitute. This matter of Gomer being a prostitute is blunted by the fact that the marriage remained unconsummated. Perhaps the term may just mean that Gomer is an Israelite; there is a reference to all of Israel being a prostitute because it has broken Yahweh's covenant and gone after false gods.

Scholars such as Wolff, Macintosh, Mays, Andersen and Freedman, and Harper comment that although Gomer was originally a faithful bride; she subsequently committed adultery underwent divorce and perhaps fell into slavery. She was taken back by Hosea as a symbol of Yahweh's love for apostate Israel. Rhetorical studies in the early twentieth century have completely changed such a biographical understanding of Gomer. Some of the earliest interpretative trends questioned whether Gomer was involved in sexual misconduct before, or only after, her marriage to Hosea.[577] On the other hand Rowley states that the imagery of Hosea 1-3 suggests that Gomer was a professional prostitute whom Hosea felt divinely compelled to marry as part of his message to apostate Israel.[578] This research also takes the view that both Gomer and the 'adulterous woman' are one and the same. However the notion of Gomer taking part in a Baal fertility cult characterizes the majority of biographical interpretations throughout the second half of the twentieth century. Other views refuse to ascribe any personal misconduct to Gomer. Recent studies offer a very different approach to biography; the characters in the text are imaginatively recreated. Many interpreters, however, prefer to say that biographical questions ultimately miss the point of the theology, metaphor, and rhetoric at work in Hosea 1-3.[579]

---

[575] Robinson, "Hosea," in *Die Zwölf kleinen Propheten,* HAT 1/14, Tübingen, 1948, 13.

[576] Robinson, "Hosea," in *Die Zwölf kleinen Propheten,* HAT 1/14, Tübingen, 1948, 13-14.

[577] Abma, R., *Bonds of Love: Methodic Studies of Prophetic Texts with Marriage Imagery (Isaiah 50:1-3 and 54:1-10, Hosea 1-3, Jeremiah 2-3),* SSN 40, Assen, Van Gorcum, 1999; Brad E. Kelle, Hosea 1-3 in the Twentieth-Century Scholarship, 190-192; James Mays, *"Hosea"* The Old Testament Library, Philadelphia, Westminster Press, 1969, 9.

[578] Andersen and David Noel Freedman, "Hosea," *The Anchor Bible,* New York, Doubleday, 1985, 44. Cf. Andrew Dearman, *The book of Hosea,* NICOT, 2010.

[579] Brad E. Kelle, *Hosea 1-3 in the Twentieth-Century Scholarship,* 190-192.

There is also an indication of dyadic agreements. The principle of reciprocity in the patron-client relationship between Yahweh and Israel will come to the forefront in the broken "marital relationship" (v. 1), and end in the relationship with Yahweh (v. 3). The reference to an agricultural subsistence economy and an industrial technology based economy is clearly presented in v. 2 בחמשה עשר כסף וחמר שערים ולתך שערים *(fifteen shekels of silver and half barley homer).*[580] The phrase ימים רבים תשבי לי *(you need a long time to sit still for me)* in v. 3 is indicative of a purity used in terms of the purity codes (pure-impure) referring to Israel because of her 'adultery.' If she did not become "clean," she will have another desert experience.[581]

Social and cultural textuality refers to the ability of the text to indicate social reform, or to withdraw or oppose support of cultural perceptions of dominance, submission, difference, or exclusion and retaliation. The specific social issues in the text help to destroy or recreate social practices. Common social and cultural topics in the discourse deepen the exegete's understanding of the range of usual practices, core values, forms of relationships and transitions, perceptions of the source of life and well-being, and presuppositions about purity and taboos that the text presents.

In social and cultural categories, the pericope is part of a lawsuit warning about the opposition. The worship is criticized by making use of harsh words and concepts of adultery and זנה. A reference to Hosea's marriage to a harlot creeps in where Hosea 1:2 draws a parallel between the literal זנונים in Hosea's family life and the figurative sin that "the land has committed in הארץ תזנה. In chapter 3, Hosea is specifically commanded to take an adulterous woman. She was taken back by Hosea as a symbol of Yahweh's love for apostate Israel.

3.6. Historical Texture

Historical texture brings out an idea of the historical context of the text. An example of this is the name Jezreel, which means 'scattered' and it, can be used in the negative sense (cf. Hos. 1:4-5). Matthews is of the opinion that Jezreel in Hosea 2:25 is one of the examples of how the passage fits into the historical texture. There is a reference to Jezreel as the main centre of the fertile land.[582] This stands in stark contrast to Jezreel as the place of the bloody coup of Jehu (1:4).[583] In this context, Samuel Schulz says that the Valley of Jezreel was one of the most fertile agricultural regions of the state and a major source of royal cash crops: corn, wine and oil (cf. 2:24 [22]).[584] It was also an important region in Solomon's redistribution of the kingdom into twelve districts, which had provided enormous resources to the two kingdoms enabling them

[580] W.R. Harper, *A Critical and Exegetical Commentary on Amos and Hosea,* Edinburgh, T and T Clark, 1956, 219.

[581] Cf. Van Leeuwen, *Hosea,* PredOT, Nijkerk, 1968, 85-86; Mays, J. L., *Hosea: A Commentary,* OTL, Philadelphia, Westminster, 1969, 58.

[582] Victor. H. Matthews, *Social World of the Hebrew Prophets,* Massachusetts, Hendrickson publishers, 2001, 75.

[583] R.K. Harrison, *Introduction to the Old Testament,* London, The Tyndale Press, 1969, 861. It is noted that in the prophecy of Hosea preserves only one name that is to reference to Israelite king Jehu. This refers for the purpose of interpreting the prophecy. This indicates the political event occurred in those days and the play of monarchs.

[584] Samuel J. Schulz, *The Old Testament Speaks,* New York, Harper and Brothers publishers, 1960, 388. Cf. Wolff, H.W., *A Commentary on the Book of the Prophet Hosea,* Philadelphia, Fortress, 43.

to provide valuable resources to the royal court (1Kgs. 4:12, 22-28).[585] It had become an important trade route and contained a strategic military highway that Israel had committed to its foreign trading partners.[586] Jezreel had, therefore, played a critical economic, political and military role in Israel's tributary mode of production.[587] This would be the place where Yahweh would "break the bow of Israel" (Hos. 1:5), in other words, where the elite's military power would be destroyed.[588] The corn, wine and oil will return to Israel, Israel is restored with their land and the gift is from the Lord. All the scattered Israelites will return to the land of their ancestors. The purpose of sowing is that they may bring forth fruit.

The word Jezreel is used here as positive sense to describe the good scattering of seed, means "sowing." Here the Lord promises glorious redemption of the name Jezreel which was given as a serious reminder of scattering in judgment. In this context in the positive sense, it becomes a prophecy of the promise. The verb זר (Hos. 2:23) appears in the name of יזרעאל and means *"I will sow."* The pronoun "her" refers to Israel as wife or mother. How does Hosea compare Jehu with Jezreel? Samuel Schulz points out that the symbolic name of the child Jezreel, has three symbolic messages of Yahweh's judgment reversed (1:4, 6, 9) and it has a new meaning for the new covenant (cf. 2:10).[589] Garrett adds that God will not judge the people of Israel but she will be sowed afresh; the promise is that when God sows there will be plenty of harvest in the land of Israel.[590] The agricultural metaphor shows that the people will enjoy their fertility and the promise made by Yahweh. The reminder is that Israel will be once again nurtured and protected by God's compassion. The dialogue here is between two people, where confession and prayer takes place. Yahweh forgives and takes them back as his people, judgment is overlooked and this reaches the final climax of the covenant ceremony which involves both parties.

Authors have argued this image indicates God's relationship with His people. For Andersen and Freedman, the final word of 2:24, *"Jezreel"* and the first word of 2:25, *"I will sow her,"* share the root "to sow/plant."[591] Here the Lord promises to restore His people and to abundance and blessing. The scattering here turns into transforming. The two verses are connected by the continuing themes of the name of Hosea's children. *"No compassion"* and *"not my people"* are used as vehicles for the transformation of the messages once conveyed by these names. Thus "agricultural bounty," *"compassion"* and *"peoplehood"* are returned to the nation from which they had been withdrawn. To the new Israel, Yahweh once again becomes "my God."

---

585 Williamson, H.G.M., "Jezreel in the Biblical Texts," TA 18, 1991, 72-92; Yee, *"She is not my wife and I am not her husband," New Approaches in Biblical Studies,* Minneapolis, Fortress Press, 2001, 35-36.

586 Stuart, Douglas: *Hosea-Jonah, Word Biblical Commentary:* Dallas, Word, Incorporated, 1987, 49.

587 Yee, *"She is not my wife and I am not her husband," New Approaches in Biblical Studies,* Minneapolis, Fortress Press, 2001, 36.

588 Cf. Yee, *"She is not my wife and I am not her husband:" A materialistic analysis of Hosea 1-2,* Leiden, Koninklijke Brill, 2001, 37.

589 Samuel J. Schulz, *The Old Testament Speaks,* New York, Harper and Brothers Publishers, 1960, 388.

590 Garrett, *Hosea, Joel: An Exegetical and Theological Exposition of Holy Scripture,* B and H Publishing Group, 1997, 117.

591 Andersen, F.I and Freedman, D.N., *Hosea: A New Translation with Introduction and Commentary,* New York, Doubleday, 1980, 287-288.

The old curse of rejection is withdrawn. The new blessing of Yahweh's favour replaces it.[592] God will establish new blessings in terms of crops. Here the significance of Hosea's children's names and their symbolic meaning brings out a powerful message of God's love to Israel. The assurance that God is going to do this follows. The people of Israel will have a great hope. This message is confirmed by a positive note: that God is to have mercy on his chosen and on the land of the people. The declaration "not my people" changes to "my people" which affirms that Yahweh will be the God of all nations. The theme is that Yahweh will extend his mercy to all. Yahweh confirms that there is a time of restoration, renewal and transformation that is predicted for Israel and other nations. The shift takes place in this context from punishment (1:4, 6, 9) to a new covenant with Yahweh.

3.7. Cultural Texture

The book of Hosea attacks the entanglement of the Baal cult and the worship of Yahweh. Hosea carried on his fight against the beliefs and practices in contemporary Yahwistic worship of Israel, and not so much against foreign gods or religions.[593] Hosea used the terminology of religion to express his views on Yahweh. So the word זנה is substituted in the pericope by שוב, ידע and אהב.

There is an allusion in the pericope to the degenerate cult, for example the phrase ואהבי אשישי ענבים (and love raisins cakes) in verse in 1. The worship is criticized in v. 1 by using graze in ומנאפת (but she committed adultery), by placing a moratorium on cult objects being used to worship Yahweh (v. 4). The ultimate desired correction; שוב, בקש and פחד are presented in v. 5.

Susan Ackerman identifies in v. 1 that the Israelites have been living in a covenantal culture. Covenantal culture depends completely on Yahweh for the provisions for living. Assyrian culture, unlike that of the Israelites, is a fertility culture; fertility being the product of appeasing their god Baal. In Hosea the mixture of these two cultures is seen. The result of such a mixture is shown in the economic status of the country.

Israelites feared losing their prosperity, and v. 1 give a glimpse of their economic condition. The intersection of their culture with the cult of Baal has economic consequences and that is indicated in v. 1. אשישי ענבים raisins cakes. The mixture is seen in the same verse when they turn to other gods. The application of a socio-rhetorical reading in v. 1 involves a mixture of Israelite and Baal cultures. The various terms, like raisin cakes, (אשישי ענבים) are indicative of the culture.[594]

For the people in the eighth century, the family formed a base for a strong society.[595] This social institution[596] was valuable for Hosea's community. Hosea

---

[592] Stuart. Douglas, *Hosea-Jonah, Word Biblical Commentary,* Dallas, Word, Incorporated 1987, 60-62.

[593] Boshoff. W.S, "Yahweh as God of Nature: Elements of the concept of God in the book of Hosea," *JNSL* 18, 1992b, 239.

[594] J. Andrew Dearman, The Book of Hosea, Wm. B. Eerdmans publishing co, Grand Rapids, 2010, 135; see Andersen, F.I and Freedman, D.N., *Hosea: A New Translation with Introduction and Commentary,* New York, Doubleday, 1980, 298.

[595] Eric M. Meyers, *The Oxford Encyclopaedia of Archaeology in the Near East,* vol. 2, Oxford University Press, 1997 137.

[596] Originally published in *New Perspectives on Ancient Judaism,* ed. Paul. V. M. Flesher, Lanham, New York, University Press of America, 1990, 220-223.

picked up a language that had a conventional base for the society which he was addressing. To address the economic status of the society, Hosea merges the social institution called family into his language, the imagery of love between husband and wife. The text also merges the people of Israel into Assyrian culture.[597]

3.8. Ideological Textuality

Ideological textuality refers to the specific alliances and conflicts which the language of a particular text evokes. Ideological textuality extends to specific ways in which people express their own interests and well-being through action, emotion, and thinking. It is not just about the way the language of the text and the interpretation of the text speaks to the reader or to other individuals and groups but about the nature of the specific view that the language itself evokes and feeds. Each specific method of interpretation has its own set of ideological structures. Therefore, there are visible approaches which feminist scholars use to approach Hosea 2-3 in a radical and different way. They argue that Gomer is portrayed as a victim.[598] Other scholars maintain that she has been abused sexually in 2-3.[599] Dijk-Hemmes develops a radical interpretation that the prophet gives biased fragments of Gomer's poetry, love songs that were analogous to the woman's part in the book of Song of Songs.[600] In this case, the power against women is seen as oppressive. The story of marriage brings out the sad experience of the covenant people. The theological understanding of Hosea 2-3 is that the faithless wife is symbolic of Israel's apostasy, and that this is expressed through the naming of the children and the meanings of their times. The theological aspect of bringing out God-husband and Gomer-Israel link is explained through the marriage metaphor.[601] Historically chapters 1-3 are considered to be a parable or an allegory. Calvin calls chapters 1-3 a vision with no relation to actual marriage and family life.[602] Another interpretation is that the story of Gomer is real and she is presented as a faithful wife in chapter 1 whereas chapter 3 indicates Israel's sin. In this account Hosea shows his mercy and kindness to his promiscuous wife. The prophetic symbol is seen here as God's compassion on Israel.[603]

Historically "the woman" is referred to as Gomer. From an anthropological view, God is presenting pathos and emotions to his message: *I bought her and I will have compassion, and have pity by adopting them as My people.* Harper comments that the shift takes place from "not my people" to "my people."[604] The assurance

---

[597] Susan Ackerman, "The Personal Is Political: Covenantal and Affectionate Love (אהבה, אהב) in the Hebrew Bible," *VT* 52 (2002): 437-458.

[598] Carol J. Dempsey, *The Prophets: A Liberation-Critical Reading,* Minneapolis, Fortress Press, 2000, 155.

[599] Cf. R J. Weems, "Gomer: Victim of Violence or Victim of Metaphor?" *Semeia* 47 (1989) 87-104, and T D. Setel, "Prophets and Pornography: *Female Sexual Imagery in Hosea,*" in L. Russell, Feminist Interpretation of the Bible, Philadelphia, Westminster, 1985, 86-95.

[600] Evan Dijk-Hemmes, "The Imagination of Power and the Power of Imagination: An Intertextual Analysis of Two Biblical Love Songs," *JSOT* 44 (1989) 75-88. Cf. Mays, *Hosea*, 11-12.

[601] Renita J. Weems, *Battered Love: Marriage, Sex, and Violence in the Hebrew Prophets,* Minneapolis, Fortress Press, 1995, 32.

[602] J. Calvin, *Commentaries on the Twelve Minor Prophets,* Grand Rapids, Baker, 1:43-45.

[603] R H. Pfeiffer, *Introduction to the Old Testament,* New York: Harper and Brothers, 1941, 567-70.

[604] W.R. Harper, *A Critical and Exegetical Commentary on Amos and Hosea,* Edinburgh, T and T Clark, 1956, 244.

comes in the form of a blessing that *"I will sow"* them in the land. The shift from stubbornness to compassion is brought out vividly.[605] The name is reversed here by Israel's confession. The repetition of word is for the sake of rhetorical effect, followed by rhythm of the passage.

Ideological textuality refers to the specific alliances and conflicts which the language of a particular text carries. Ideological textuality is about the way the language of the text and the interpretation of the text speaks to the reader or to other individuals and groups but also about the nature of the specific view that the language itself evokes and feeds. Ideological texture portrays Gomer as a victim.

3.9. Theological Texture

Theological texture in general deals with the relationship between man and a divine entity, communication with gods, holy persons, spirit beings, divine history, human redemption, human commitment, religious community, and ethics. In the selected text, the theological theme of divine love is twofold. It is the love and discipline of God towards Israel to stress ungratefulness of Israel and future restoration. God's care and love is brought out in terms of a covenant relationship designed to continue. Although this has been highlighted previously, the deeper motivations behind the love, discipline, and continuation of the covenant despite repeated rejection are yet to be explored.

Theology in strict sense is related to the image of God. Hosea prefers the divine name 'Yahweh' much more than 'God.' Israel knows Yahweh as a Liberator. Israel does not know any other God or saviour besides Yahweh (13:4b). Hosea indicates a negation of the old covenant formula and, in this respect, similar to the interpretation of Yahweh in Ex. 3:14, he proclaims anew that Yahweh, the ancient God of Israel is 'the God.'

Hosea's theology, nevertheless, develops openly in dialogue with the mythology of his day and is marked by a remarkable process of adaptation and polemic against this mythology. Hosea's best known allegorised metaphor of Yahweh is the loving yet rejected husband, hence, the idea of Yahweh as the husband and Israel as a wife. This then leads to the use of this metaphor having its roots in the recognition of Israel's specific guilt of 'whoredom' and adultery because the people had given themselves to cultic practices and worship of Baal. They also depended much on the Canaanite mythology and thought, and this made them unfaithful to Yahweh. Hosea's adaptation of the divine husband concept to Yahwism is commendable. It represents Yahweh as the only God and it vividly states the exclusive claims of Yahwism. It directly expresses the genuine profession of faith in Yahweh and carries its opposition to syncretism.

Yahweh as a marriage partner is set against certain historical conceptions. Yahweh is not just another god or goddess, but rather is understood within the legal categories of the Covenant. He replaces the mythico-cultic fertility conception that is rooted in the '*ierosgamos*' (sacral marriage, cf. l: 19, 2:4). During the eighth century BCE, there was a spiritual decline within the nation. In Hosea's time, the worship of Yahweh had gradually fallen into decline as the Canaanite god Baal

---

605 J. G. Janzen "Metaphor and Reality in Hosea 11," *Semeia* 24, 1982, 7-44.

became popular with the Israelites. Hosea preached against the worship of Baal and carried Yahweh's message of anger. His call for repentance is through drawing parallels between his own marriage and the Yahweh/Israel "marriage" through the covenant. Hosea addressed in a plain way the moral, spiritual, and political life of the Israelites. Yahweh is using Hosea as a vessel to win his people from idolatry. The entire book of Hosea fights against the cult and mythology of the god Baal. This gradual unfolding of Hosea's theology in polemic dialogue with the existing culture and mythology of Canaan provides us with a fundamental example of faith's dialogue with contemporary ideology.[606] Hosea uses the key words employed in myth, and these remain dominant themes throughout. Yahweh is the Lord of Israel's history. Hosea views Israel's present and future through this history. It is remarkable how Israel's history is thoroughly embedded in his proclamation.

In the beginning, God threatens to punish Israel by withdrawing blessings, but because of His covenant, the relationship is restored. Here, discipline brings promise and hope for their eternal relationship. It is a way in which she may continue to be in communion with Him. If she repents, her transformation will create a new covenant relationship with her God (Hos. 2:18, 20-21). This reminds people that God is a covenant partner (Hos. 2; 20, 23). Chester K. Lehman in his writing says that the unfaithfulness will turn to faithfulness and covenant relationship, and promises that they will become "sons of the living God" to other nations (Hos. 1:10).[607] In this context the prophet talks about a new era when the people will turn to God and become His beloved.

This is where Hosea introduces the marriage covenant theme the comparison here is between Hosea and Gomer (the marriage) and Yahweh and Israel (the covenant). Due to the fact that Israel had lusted after Baal, she is in effect a prostitute as well.[608] So Yahweh calls Hosea to take Gomer back; again the parallel is with Yahweh calling Israel back, with Hosea as messenger. His action symbolises Yahweh's love for Israel-as Hosea can "take back" his adulterous wife, so Yahweh is willing to "take back" the adulterous Israelites provided they ask for forgiveness.

In supporting this view, David B. Wyrtzen argues that the purpose of Hosea's message is to present an intensely personal divine restorative confrontation with Israel. He continues to argue that God's continuing confrontation with His people is to establish a new covenant.[609] Brueggemann has the same opinion: that blessing come because Yahweh gives them but those blessings are promised in connection with obedience to the covenant (Lev. 26; Deu. 28). But in Hosea, blessings do come to the disobedient (Hos. 2 and 14). As stated by Walter C. Kaiser, the theology of Hosea has a dual emphasis: the righteousness of God and the love of God. Because He is righteous, men should turn to the Lord and seek him. The Lord's gracious call

---

606 Wolff, *Hosea, Biblical Commentary,* Philadelphia, Fortress Press, 1974, p.16

607 Chester K. Lehman, *Biblical Theology,* vol. 2, Scottdale, Herald press, 1946, 27.

608 For discussion of different views by biblical scholars: refer to Leon J. Wood, "Hosea," *EBC* 7:164-166; Lasor, *OTS*, 335-336.

609 David B. Wyrtzen, "The Theological Center of the Book of Hosea," *Bibliotheca Sacra* 141, 564, 1984, 315-329.

to repentance does include judgment, but not without grace and restoration.[610] Robert B. Chisholm Jr recognizes that the Lord's covenantal relationship with the people of Israel is central to the message of Hosea. The prophet preached repentance to inform the chosen people to return to their covenant. The prophetic messages speak about teachings, warnings and promises to the descendants of Israelites in the coming days as a continuation of an inclusive aspect of the blessing.

An overview of Hosea's prophetic role indicates that Hosea's rhetorical and theological purpose was to serve as God's covenant enforcement mediator. In this role, Hosea enforced God's covenant mandates by accusing the people of sin, announcing imminent judgment for continued covenant violation, and announcing the nation's future restoration and salvation.[611] Most of the oracles which God spoke through Hosea were of judgment and not blessing.[612] Harper points out that Hosea held a theology which saw Yahweh as Israel's God "from the land of Egypt" (12:9; 13:4).[613] God chose Israel, brought her out of Egypt, cared for her and gave her the land with its fruits (9:10; 11:1-4; 12:13; 13:4-5; 2:8). She stood in a covenant relationship with Him (6:7; 8:1), like a wife with her husband (2:7), and this should have involved observance of His law (4:6; 8:2, 12). However, this did not happen as God's wrath came upon Israel. However, Israel had a hope and future if it turned to God in repentance; the symbolic action changes from God's wrath to future restoration of all their things. Though the people had forgotten the Mosaic Law God still remembered the covenant He made with Abraham and promised that one day He would restore them from their disobedience.

However, it is not enough to look at the aspect of covenant merely through the eyes of Israel. From God's perspective, there seems to be a greater purpose in all this: other nations. It can be argued that He wanted to keep the covenant not just because of His love for Israel, but because of His love for the other nations. They were chosen for a specific purpose: 'If the people obey and keep my covenant, they will be the treasured possession.' The mention of them in Hosea 1:10 is the first hint we get of this divine purpose. It is not explicitly stated, but because it is mentioned, it cannot be ignored.

The second aspect of theological texture is a polemic monotheism: Yahweh is the true God among all Baals. Yahweh is not equal to Baal but above other gods. He provides all the necessities for existence every day. He is the one who called the people back and spoke to their hearts. He is truly the God who cares and remains loyal even when people do not recognize him as the one who cares. In this context of trying to recapture a wayward people's attention, it is almost as if Yahweh wants to show Himself superior to Baals as a testimony not just for Israel but for the followers of all the other Baals. He wants them to know that He is not a wayward God who will desert His people because of their fickleness; He is a God who remains true, loves, provides and disciplines.

---

[610] Walter C Kaiser, *Toward an Old Testament Theology,* Michigan, Zondervan Publishing House, 1980, 198.

[611] Wood J. Leon, *The Prophets of Israel,* Grand Rapids, Baker Academic group, 1979, 282.

[612] D. Stuart, *"Hosea-Jonah,"* WBC, Vol. 31, ed. by Bruce M. Metzger, David. A. Hubbard and Glenn W. Barker, Nashville: Thomas Nelson Publishers, 1987, 7.

[613] W.R. Harper, *A Critical and Exegetical Commentary on Amos and Hosea,* Edinburgh, T and T Clark, 1956, 241.

It is to be noted here that the theology of Hosea differs from other contemporary prophets of his time. The disintegration of patriarchal Yahwehism in the Canaanite fertility cult, and the peculiar political and governmental system which existed there, meant that even a prophet's intervention in public affairs and their problems took on an essentially different aspect from that of the eighth century prophets in the southern kingdom.[614] The basic message of Hosea is that God is love; however, the Israelites sinned so grievously that He is forced to punish them. Nevertheless, He has not given up on them and will restore them to Himself again, provided they seek forgiveness. This was the message of Hosea; hope is offered for a repentant nation.

The theological texture shows that Yahweh is the only God among all other gods (Baals) who is "adored" (v. 1). He is the one who truly loved (v. 1), and who is truly good (v. 5). This implies that a faithful marriage is the base to serve as a vehicle for a monotheistic religion. There are certain theological terms used to describe God's love for the Northern and Southern Kingdoms. The terms are חסד, רחם, ידע, שוב, הנז, בקש, משפט, אמת and אהב.

The key words in Hosea's theology are אהב, חסד, דעת אלהים and other terms which could be translated as "faithful love" and "knowledge of God." According to Freedman, חסד denotes loyalty and devotion that is perhaps expected in a relationship of love.[615] This view is supported by Lalmuankima and continues with the idea that Yahweh demands complete loyalty and expects to fulfil the demands of justice and righteousness.[616] Therefore, חסד is used for God's attitude towards Israel, as well as the response for which He hopes from Israel. Hosea interprets God's judgment upon sin and unfaithfulness not as arbitrary acts, but as a consequence which stems from the nature of sin itself. The disruption of the covenant relationship results in the disappearance of דעת אלהים, and faithful love. Unlike some of the Minor Prophets, Hosea ends his message with a clear word of hope. The major purpose of this book is to proclaim God's compassion and love.

Through Hosea God describes his relationship with His people not as that between a master and slave, but as that between a husband and wife in 2:16. God's love is expressed in intimate language with Israel as His wife. It depicts God's gracious act and his love for the wayward people. God remembers His covenant and promise made them that give hope and salvation.[617] God's character is presented in the form of His righteousness, justice, love, compassion, covenant and faithfulness to Israel.[618] These qualities are the core of God's covenantal relationship with the people of Israel and with all of His creation, providing hope for the future. In chapter 11, God describes Israel as his child whom he loved and cared for. Like Gomer, however, Israel was a wife engaged in prostitution; God would know that his chosen people would betray Him. Yet He chose and loved them anyway with unconditional love which convinces one more of the greater purpose of His love.

---

[614] Gerhard von Rad, *The Message of the Prophets,* London, SCM Press, 1968, 110-111.

[615] Freeman E. Hobart, *An Introduction to the Old Testament Prophets*, Chicago, Moody press, 1968, 174; Ucheawaji G. Josiah, *"Hosea's Perspective on the Knowledge of God and its Relevance to Rivers State, Nigeria,"* Vol. 11, No. 1, March, 2014, 9.

[616] C. Lalmuankima, Challenges from the Book of Hosea in Understanding the Kindness of God, *Bangalore Theological Forum,* Vol. XL, No. 1, June 2008, 154 (149-160).

[617] B.S. Childs, *Old Testament in a Canonical Context,* Philadelphia, Fortress Press, 1989, 96-97.

[618] Gary V. Smith, *Hosea, Amos, Micah,* Grand Rapids, Zondervan publishers, 2001.

In addition to the theme of love, there is the theological theme of repentance through progressive parallelism in v. 5, which notes a call to return, and to seek Yahweh. The people are afraid to approach Yahweh because they had broken the covenantal relationship. Therefore, repentance finds its climax when Yahweh is fearfully approached. Hosea 2-3 brings out the final result when Hosea describes God's grace and the restoration of the covenant relationship with his chosen people and creation (Hosea 2:16-23).[619] According to Weems, the promise is restored when there will be peace and harmony.[620] The portrayal in vv. 16-23 talks about restoration of peaceful ecological order and cosmic order. These promises will take place in the eschatological future through transformation and assurance of God's promise of restoration.

Theological texture talks about divine love. God's care and love is explained in terms of a covenant relationship. Hosea preached against the worship of Baal and carried Yahweh's message of anger. His call for repentance is through drawing parallels between his own marriage and the Yahweh/Israel "marriage" through the covenant. Hosea introduces the marriage/covenant theme the comparison between Hosea and Gomer (the marriage) and Yahweh and Israel (the covenant).

The inner texture with its sub-textures allows us to expose the meaning and significance of the text. The socio-rhetorical method helps us to understand why the author has used rhetorical techniques. Reading the text rhetorically provides a dialogue between the reader and the text. Here the dialogue becomes a bridge to bring out the real meaning of the text. Inter-textuality, social and cultural texture, historical texture and ideological texture have been briefly discussed; however, they may not be considered as fundamental to the need for exegesis of the selected passage.

3.10. Love of God

3.10.1. The Marriage Metaphor

The marriage metaphor is used in the text to describe God's love for his people and to make them understand.[621] The metaphor suggests the covenant relationship between God and Israel. Garrett notes that Hosea 3:1 "to once again, love a woman who is loved by a friend," and the response "I bought for myself" is a demonstration of "love in action."[622] According to Harper, the love of a friend is omitted because of the narrative of the prophet's relation to Gomer in chapter 1[623] Hosea's response (v. 2) shows how costly love can be. It is love that endures all that is necessary to accomplish the divine purpose. The metaphor of husband - wife remains central in

---

[619] W. A. VanGemeren, *Interpreting the Prophetic Word,* Grand Rapids, Zondervan, 1990, 118.

[620] Renita J. Weems, *Battered Love: Marriage, Sex, and Violence in the Hebrew Prophets,* Minneapolis, Fortress Press, 1995, 51.

[621] Macintosh, A.A, *A Critical and Exegetical Commentary on Hosea,* Edinburgh, T and T Clark, 1997, 97.

[622] Garrett, *Hosea, Joel an Exegetical and Theological Exposition of Holy Scripture,* B and H Publishing Group, 1997, 124.

[623] W.R. Harper, *A Critical and Exegetical Commentary on Amos and Hosea,* Edinburgh, T and T Clark, 1956, 215.

this chapter 3: 1- 5.[624] The focus that we find in this chapter is complete dependence on Yahweh's love, which is used as imagery to help Israel understand how much God loves her. The opening v. 1 begins with a simile that portrays Yahweh as the ideal lover. God loves even when the object of his love deserts him. The important aspect is that Yahweh's all-enduring love becomes the model for and the standard of Hosea's love. Hosea's use of a symbolic action brings out the idea of family customs and metaphors which are proclamations of his time.[625]

3.10.2. God as Lover

Hosea 2:16-3:5 portray God as a spurned lover. The prophet uses legal language to confront Israel.[626] This chapter talks about the divorce proceedings between God and Israel, where God is presented as a plaintiff and Israel as the defendant. Hosea comes out very strongly and compels Israel to listen to the message or warning that he has received from Yahweh. Elliott argues that Israel's idolatry is viewed as adultery. Because of this, the prophet's message is that "Yahweh will no longer favour them nor will he look upon them as his chosen people."[627] In Eastern culture, if a woman is found guilty of adultery, she will be stripped in public and put to shame. In this case, death penalty was prescribed.[628]

According to Hubbard, 2:12-3:5 "rings with overtones of love."[629] Hosea could have completely divorced Gomer, but although his love was spurned, he pursued her and she remained with him as God did with Israel. Brueggemann notes that the prophet is wounded and shamed, he is rejected by his wife by her going with another man, his honour is violated and the act of the woman is noted as wrong.[630] Furthermore, the prophet is the one who speaks of the people's relation with Yahweh by using the marriage metaphor.[631] Wyrtzen argues that the marriage between Hosea and Gomer was broken because of her sexual promiscuity, but the husband's love continues.[632] From this we understand that Yahweh's love continues towards his people, despite their "adultery" in worshipping other gods.

Hosea 2:16-3:5 looks at the future, and even predicts it. This is prophetic foretelling. However, the first principle of foretelling is that it concentrates with a message for the existing generation. In this case, the message is directed to the faithful few in Israel. It is designed to give them hope for an eternal home. By revealing the future restoration of Israel through Hosea and his wife, God is instilling eternal hope in the godly of the last generation of the Northern Kingdom before their destruction. As the faithful see the kingdom fall around them, and the utter destruction of their own people, they will be able to endure knowing the present God, and the future for their nation.

---

[624] King P.J, *Amos, Hosea, Micah–An Archaeological Commentary,* Philadelphia, Westminster Press, 1988, 26.

[625] Braaten Laurie, *Parent and Child Imagery in Hosea,* Boston University, 1987, 73.

[626] Brueggemann, W. *Tradition for Crisis: a Study in Hosea.* Richmond, John Knox, 1968, 86.

[627] Elliott, *"Hosea,"* 197.

[628] Vander Hart, *"Warning,"* 118.

[629] Hubbard David Allan, *With Bands of Love* (Hosea), Grand Rapids, Wm. B. Eerdmans Publishing co, 1968, 87.

[630] Brueggemann, W. *Tradition for Crisis: a Study in Hosea.* Richmond, John Knox, 1968, 86.

[631] Bowman, *"A Special Kind of Grief,"* Minnesota, St. Paul, 1994, 235.

[632] Wyrtzen, "The Theological Center of the book of Hosea," *Bibliotheca Sacra* 141, 564, 319-321.

3.10.3. Love in Action

The main theme of the chapter is "love" in action. This highlights Yahweh's love as a model for Hosea's love. It stands in contrast to that of the fickle lovers who do not remain true. The overpowering strength of God's true love becomes clear as it is reflected in the prophet's symbolic action. The specific command "to love" that came to Hosea is humiliating even as a personal request-to bring home someone who has gone into another's possession. The law says one thing but God does the impossible according to the law He forgives.

Here, Hosea is a witness not only as a messenger of God's word, but also as the one who experiences the consequences of the message he has received. By his obedience, he confirms that the proclaimed love of Yahweh leads Israel through judgment to salvation. Chapter 1 showed Israel's judgment and her ruin, whereas chapter 3 talks about reconciliation and restoration of the people.

3.11. Summary of Hosea 2:16-3:5

The exegetical study of the selected passage has brought out the important idea that, in this text, Hosea brings out a remarkable narrative about God's steadfast love and how he wants to deliver and redeem His elected people. Yahweh's redemption includes not just Israel but also all humanity and creation. For this purpose, through his love, God liberates and recognises Israel. This redemption is explained through God's assurance to renew life for the people of Israel and reestablish them as a nation. The prophet lived in the midst of a time of political, economic, and social chaos. Hosea clearly signifies the theme of God's redemption and deliverance. Yahweh offers His love to Israel in order to redeem and bring reconciliation. This redemptive love is expressed in the form of a divine imperative to Hosea to love an adulterous woman. The study brings out the important aspect of God's love which is demonstrated through the people's right relationship with their God.

The inner texture of Hosea 2:16-3:5 explain the courtship that leads to restoring a relationship in Hosea 2:16b and 17a. The text is a reminder of a new Exodus and Israel's journey in the wilderness (v. 16a and 17b). The inner texture discusses the fornication/promiscuity of the people who committed adultery in the context of marriage relations by forgetting and not acknowledging Yahweh as their God. Stanley Jose notes that then the new Exodus brings out the idea of restoring a new relationship through a new marriage and love of the natural gifts.[633] This reminds the people of Israel to recognize Yahweh as their true God, and God is then ready to bless them by forgetting their promiscuity and leaving away their אמונה (v. 21-22). Hosea 2:16 begins with the broken relationship and ends (v. 25) with revival and restoration of the promise.

In 3:1-5 the word אהב is repeated four times in verse 1 itself. In v. 2 and 5 the sign of Yahweh's אהב is worked out. Furthermore, other words such as שוב, בקש and פחד are deployed here. Yahweh's love is compared structurally in verse 1 with the love of the woman's beloved. In chiastic structure, mutual relationship is explained between Yahweh and Israel. It is Yahweh's love that delivers in the form of אהב to the

[633] Stanley Jones, *"Exodus Motif in the Book of Hosea and its relevance to the Socio-religious Context of India,"* Faith Theological Review, Vol. 16, No. 1, March 2015, 36.

people of Israel. The progressive parallelism brings out the people's return to Yahweh by approaching Him in trembling.[634] In parallelism, it is noted that repentance is understood in terms of return to Yahweh. In this context, it is indicated that אהב is explained through the relationship between a man and a woman as the account makes clear. The sociological aspect brings out the shameful act of Israel; she was stripped of her religious rites and securities and challenged to restore her (Israel) honour. The desired response is explained as true repentance and return to the Lord. The passage deals with the patron-client relationship between Yahweh and Israel through the broken relationship. The final aspect that is to be noted here is the return of the people of Israel.

In relation to the above discussion, the text brings out the following terms and nuances that were investigated: אהב, חסד, צדק, משפט, אמונה, שוב, שכח, ידע, פחד, בקש. The terms serve as strategic catchwords in introducing the literary units in the book while the theme of the return serves as a unifying factor. Hosea stands and proclaims the restoration of Israel and her relationship with Yahweh. Hosea 2:16-3:5 shows Yahweh's powerful love that is expressed through the marital relationship by calling His people back as his "wife." Here, God's graciousness and the covenant with His people are shown through hope and salvation. The various textual examinations detailed above in this study help to identify the core message of Hosea 2-3, which is about Yahweh's faithfulness towards His people and the significance of the covenantal relationship.

Conclusion

In conclusion, the research has established that God's love is demonstrated through his willingness to redeem the people from their apostasy. The concept of restoration plays a vital role in restoring the relationship by maintaining values and honour in the marital relationship. This leads to the idea of seeking and restoring the brokenness. The central concept of this chapter is love. Love is an important theme that is sought and maintained in the covenantal relationship that is defined through the marriage concept. Hosea clearly brings out the message that both partners must value the marriage bond and seek for restoration of the relationship and reconciliation between them. Hosea 2-3 emphasises the power of love, covenant relationship, and commitment through the metaphor of marriage. Hosea 2:16-3:5 talks specifically about the marriage image and how it is used to show the covenantal relationship between Yahweh and Israel, as symbolised in the life of the prophet Hosea and his adulterous wife. This is the first occasion in the entire Bible where we see Yahweh using human relationships to draw parallels with His covenantal relationship with Israel. It is also a clue to show how God wants other nations to perceive Him: as a loving and faithful God who draws His people to Himself.

Therefore, the undergirding purpose of restoration and renewal used in the marriage metaphor is that it would serve as a "light to the nations," rather than the one-sided view that it was meant only for Israel. Although apparently designed to call

---

[634] W.R. Harper, *A Critical and Exegetical Commentary on Amos and Hosea,* Edinburgh, T and T Clark, 1956, 224.

Israel back from its worship of false gods, by demonstrating Yahweh's love through human emotions, Hosea's message is actually designed to redeem the people of Israel so that they will be God's people and that they will become witnesses to bear the glory of God's name among other nations. Hosea 1-3 sets an eschatological plan for the entire twelve minor prophetic books. Yahweh's aim is to spread His name among the nations, not just Israel and His concern is to bring His wandering tribe back into a right relationship with Him by using Hosea as his messenger. Yahweh uses human emotions and relationships to bring home His message. It is also important to note that rather than the thundering and angry God as traditionally depicted in many Old Testament stories, Yahweh in this context is the opposite. Through Hosea, He has first shown Himself as the loving husband. In the next chapter, the research examines how Yahweh demonstrates the second metaphor of human love that of the caring father (Hosea 11:1-11) and its importance in Yahweh's demonstration of His "steadfast love." The chapter will also consider the Exodus event and its relevance to the father-son, parent-child metaphor.

Chapter 4

Hosea 11:1-11: Wayward Israel and God's Love: A Metaphor of Parental Love

Introduction

The second theme used in Hosea to make the Israelites understand Yahweh's attitude to the covenantal relationship is the nature of a father's love manifested towards a rebellious son. This theme is set out in Chapter 11. While the husband-wife relationship is used in the previous chapter to emphasise the implications of the Yahweh-Israel relationship, Chapter 11 considers another aspect of that relationship, not just the human father-son situation but also its connection to the Exodus event and the journey out of Egypt and through the wilderness to the Promised Land. It must be remembered that the parent-child relationship is not based on a covenant in the same way as a marriage covenant is, although it is still grounded on the unconditional love of God, which is the foundation of the covenant between Yahweh and Israel. But it is also in keeping with the other two human themes, of marriage and the physician-patient relationships. How the "parental love" theme examined in this chapter uses the very human father and son relationship and how that connects well with the covenantal relationship and Yahweh's overwhelming love for Israel?

Contrasting emotions of anger parental punishment for misconduct in Chapters 9 and 10, and love-parental love that forgives in Chapter 11, are used in Hosea to help urge Israel to seek forgiveness. As a father loves and forgives his son, so Yahweh loves and is ready to forgive Israel for breaking the Sinai Covenant, provided Israel seeks forgiveness. To make the message clear, Hosea uses strong parental style language of caring and loving to manifest Yahweh's love using the imagery of a responsible father and showing what it implies to the people of Israel. Hosea 11 is about a continuous speech which is presented in the form of rhetorical "I." The language that is noted is the personal "I" statements: *"I love, I called, I taught Ephraim to walk, I took them up in my arms, I healed, I led, I lifted them, I bent down, and I fed.*" The book focuses on this personal aspect of God's love for His people (2-3,) as a compassionate parent, and emphasises the call 'to share the love of God and be truthful to that love' (11:1). The message of the book is love, and it also offers the forgiveness of sin and reconciliation to God and compels them to turn to God, reflecting and executing love in action (6:1, 6:11, and 14:1).

4.1. Context of Hosea 11:1-11

Hosea 11 shows Yahweh as a father lamenting for his rebellious son. Prior to that, Chapter 10 talks about Israel's judgment and its past life of disobedience. For this, the warning given was in the form of an announcement to destroy. They were reminded of their wilderness and Egyptian experience of bondage followed by the message of God's judgment over Israel.[635] In vv. 1, 3 and 5, Israel/Ephraim is described as a rebellious son who deserves to be punished while Yahweh is the loving father who cares for his son despite his rebellion.[636] The idea presented here is of Hosea urging them to sow righteousness, when they are expected to turn and reap kindness. Chapter 11 then shows the father-son relationship; here we have a parallel situation a father's attitude to his rebellious son and Yahweh's faithfulness to his rebellious people through the covenantal relationship. In this passage, we see a shift, i.e., the composition changes from Israel's punishment to God's love, in spite of his people's persistent apostasy.[637] This is clearly shown in v. 1-9, and acknowledged by Patrick Miller.[638] But we then find a change in v. 10-11, which reverts to the primary idea of the record of Israel's unfaithfulness to God.[639] It picks up the theme that Israel has "bitterly provoked him to anger" through her extensive sin. Sandhya Shency then concludes this section with the argument that the prophet is presented here as a "prophet of love" emphasizing the "father-son" relationship created as an image of the covenantal Yahweh-Israel relationship love on one side and rebellion on the other.[640]

The book of the prophet is characterized by its fresh and varied metaphors to describe God and His actions. Two of the most powerful and personal metaphors are: first, God as a faithful lover (chapters 1-3); and second, God as a loving parent (both male and female; chapter 11).[641] God has revealed himself to a fallen humanity by choosing things that humans have experienced; things which are deeply personal and powerfully moving and He has said, "I am like that to you."[642] Through these experiences God has clearly revealed the depth of His love and loyalty (cf. 11:8-9).

4.1.1. Poetic Structure of Hosea 11:1-11[643]

An examination of Chapter 11 shows how strongly the chapter is characterized by its varied metaphors describing God and His loving attitude, enforcing the idea of Hosea as a "prophet of love."

---

[635] Wolff, H.W, *A Commentary on the Book of the Prophet Hosea,* Philadelphia, Fortress Press, 1974, 193 -194.

[636] D.J. Wiseman, *Tymdale Old Testament Commentary,* Downers Grove, Inter Varsity Press, 1989, 179-180.

[637] Frank Gaeblein, ed., *The Exposition Bible Commentary,* Vol. 7, *Daniel and the Minor Prophets,* by Leon Wood, Grand Rapids, Zondervan Publishing House, 1985, 212.

[638] Hosea 11:10-11 reverts to the primary idea of the record of Israel's unfaithfulness to God. Patrick D. Miller, ed., *Old Testament Theology Essays on Structure, Theme and Text,* Minneapolis, Fortress Press, 1992, 39.

[639] Patrick D. Miller, ed., *Old Testament Theology Essays on Structure, Theme and Text,* Minneapolis, Fortress Press, 1992, 39.

[640] Sandhya Shency, "A Call to Return to the Lord (Hos. 6:1-6)," Vol. XXXX, No. 3, September 2014, *Bible Bhashyam,* 146-147 (146-156).

[641] Gloria L. Schaab, "I Will Love Them Freely:" *A Metaphorical Theology Of Hosea* 14, 7.

[642] Mays, James Luther., *Hosea: A Commentary,* OTL, Philadelphia, Westminster, 1969, 151.

[643] Cf. the motivation for the poetic structure at 4.3 and 4.4 below

God has revealed himself through various images like "*loving Israel as a child,*" "*calling him my son,*" "*taking him in my arms,*" "*I healed them, I fed them, I lifted the yoke.*"[644] But the chapter also reminds Israel of Yahweh's anger "*he shall roar like a lion,*" "*the children shall tremble.*" Yet even then Yahweh's love shines through "How shall I give you up, O Ephraim?" and "I will not execute the fierceness of my anger."

Table 13: Poetic Structure of Hosea 11:1-11

Stanza	Strophe	Strings		Translation	Parallelism
1	A	1 כי נער ישראל ואהבהו	1aA	When Israel was a child, then I loved him,	Synonymous Parallelism
		וממצרים קראתי לבני:	1aB	and out of Egypt I called my son.	
		2 קראו להם	2a	I called them	
		כן הלכו מפניהם		So they went from me	
		לבעלים יזבחו	2bA	they sacrificed to the Baals	Synonymous Parallelism
		ולפסלים יקטרון:	2bB	and burnt incense to the idols	
	B	3 ואנכי תרגלתי לאפרים	3a	I taught Ephraim to walk	Synonymous parallel phrase
		קחם על־זרועתיו		I took them upon in my arms	
		ולא ידעו כי רפאתים:	3b	but they did not know that I healed them.	
		4 בחבלי אדם אמשכם	4a	With cords of humanity, I drew them	Synonymous parallel phrase
		בעבתות אהבה		with bonds of love	Synonymous parallelism
		ואהיה להם כמרימי על על לחיהם	4b	I became to them the one who lifts the yoke upon their jaws[645]	
		ואט אליו אוכיל:	4c	and I bent down to him, and fed them.	
II	C	5 לא ישוב אל־ארץ מצרים	5a	He shall not return to the land of Egypt	
		ואשור הוא מלכו	5b	but Assyria shall be his king,	
		כי מאנו לשוב:	5c	because they refused to return.	

[644] W.R. Harper, *A Critical and Exegetical Commentary on Amos and Hosea,* Edinburgh, T and T Clark, 1956, 364.

[645] Mays, James Luther, *Hosea: A Commentary,* OTL, Philadelphia, Westminster, 1969, 151-152.

	D	6 וחלה חרב בעריו	6aA	And the sword shall abide their cities	
		וכָלתה בדיו	6aB	it will demolish his strong men	Progressive parallelism
		ואכלה ממעצותיהם:	6aC	and it will consume them and their gate bars because of their counsel.	
	E	7 ועמי תלואים למשובתי	7a	And my people are bent on turning away from me	
		ואל־על יקראהו	7b	and upwards they call together,	
		יחד לא ירומם:	7c	he does not rise them at all.	
III	F	8 איך אתנך אפרים	8aA	How shall I give you up, O Ephraim?	
		אמגנך ישראל		How shall I give you up, Israel?	
		איך אתנך כאדמה	8aB	How shall I make you as Adama?	Synonymous parallelism
		אשימך כצבאים		How shall I set you as Zeboiim?	
		נהפך עלי לבי	8bA	My heart is turned within me	
		יחד נכמרו נחומי:	8bB	my repenting are kindled together at the same time raised my compassion.	Synonymous parallelism
		9 לא אעשה חרון אפי	9aA	I will not execute the fierceness of my anger,	
		לא אשוב לשחת אפרים	9aB	I will not return to destroy Ephraim;	
		כי אל אנכי ולא־איש	9bA	for I am not a man;	Synonymous parallelism and chiasm
		בקרבך קדוש	9bB	the Holy One in the midst of you	
		ולא אבוא בעיר:	9aC	and I will not enter in wrath.	

		[10]אחרי יהוה ילכו	10aA	They shall walk after Yahweh;	Chiasm and Synonymous parallelism
		כאריה ישאג	10bA	He shall roar like a lion;	
		כי־הוא ישאג	10bB	Yes, he will roar,	
		ויחרדו בנים מים:	10aB	then the children tremble from the west.	
		[11] יחרדו כצפור ממצרים	11aA	They shall tremble as a bird from Egypt,	
		וכיונה מארץ אשור	11aB	and as a dove from the land of Assyria;	
		והושבתים על־בתיהם	11b (10aC)	and I will place them in their houses[646]	
		נאם־יהוה:	11c	says Yahweh.	

It is notable that in Hosea 11:1-4 stanza I, a contrast is made, namely what a person does and what Yahweh does (1AA-1AB, 3a, 4a, 4b, 4c)-and this is enacted in synonymous parallelism, with Israel's response phrases (2a-2bb). The unit 11:1-4 is written in the first person masculine singular. God is directly accusing Israel, who is addressed in the third person. Stanza I (vv. 1-4) serves as an explanation of Yahweh's historical association with and care of his son. Stanza II (vv. 5-7) shows the results of the people's unfaithfulness towards Yahweh and their subsequent punishment.

In stanza II, God judges Israel, citing exile by the use of a progressive parallelism in D. Israel-Ephraim is directly addressed, but this time the accusation is brought before the court. The proposal for a settlement is directed to the accused, particularly during a simulated dispute.[647] Stanza III (vv. 8-11) deals with salvation and the consequences of reconciliation and the reaching to a settlement.

Chapter 11:8-11 is Stanza III (stanza F), but v. 10 is considered by some scholars to be an insertion. Hosea 11:10 speaks about people scattered to Egypt and Assyria. The Assyrians took Israel into exile after the death of Tiglath-Pileser III. This makes it seem as if v. 10 is not part of this section, because v. 10 speaks of Yahweh in the third person. Philip King notes that v. 10 speaks of how the punishment will turn into promise.[648] The message to Israel is that Yahweh himself will proclaim the return of the people. Here Yahweh is portrayed as a lion in a positive way. This symbolises calling people to hear Yahweh's judgment. Yahweh extends an invitation to the people to return and it is the people's responsibility to acknowledge God as the only God.[649] Re-establishing a right relationship with God creates hope for the people.

[646] Cf. Kakkanattu, J.P, *God's Enduring Love in the Book of Hosea. A Synchronic and Diachronic Analysis of Hosea 11:1-11,* Tubington, Mohr Siebeck, 2006, 97.

[647] H.W. Wolff, *Hosea,* Philadelphia, Fortress Press, 1974, 194.

[648] Philip King, *Amos-Micah: An Archaeological Commentary,* Philadelphia, Westminster, 1988, 129.

[649] Samuel J. Schulz, *The Old Testament Speaks,* New York, Harper and Brothers publishers, 1960, 389.

The other verses of Stanza III highlight a number of synonymous parallelisms and a chiasm indicating Yahweh's change of heart. Stanza G hints at Israel's desired response, from 11b being attributed to Yahweh's intervention. It is He who returns. Chapter 11:1-11 should be seen as a rhetorical unit. Yahweh's first person discourse is interrupted in v. 10 and is resumed in v. 11. The promise of change of redemption (second person) for an explanation of salvation is used in the third person. Verse 11 also can be considered as a rhetorical unit. Vv. 10 and 11 should be seen as a traditional comment, especially on the word יחרדו.[650] The keyword in the pericope, i.e., אהב, is found in vv. 1 and 4, and שוב is found in vv. 5 (twice),[651] in vv. 7 and 9. There is a poetic rhythm in 11:1-9 and 11, but it is not obvious in v. 10.

4.1.2. Chiastic Structure of Hosea 11:1-11

A' 1a When Israel was a child, I loved him, and out of Egypt I called my son 11:1

B' He shall return to the land of Egypt, and Assyria shall be his king 11:5

B' My heart is overwhelmed; my pity is stirred 11:8

Ba' Out of Egypt they shall come trembling, like sparrows 11:11

A' (11:1-0-11) from the land of Assyria, like doves (11:11)

4.1.3. Discussion of the Structure of Hosea 11:1-11 - Parallelism, Poetic, Chiastic

The unit vv. 1-7 is internally connected by a copulative structure (v. 3, 6, 7), by the use of personal pronouns in the singular (v. 1, 4b, 5a, 6a) or plural (v. 2, 3, 4a, 5b, 6b, 7) for "Israel" (v. 1): "Ephraim" (v. 3), or "my people" (v. 7A) The unity of the theme of Israel begins with the definite rejection of response to Yahweh's love (v. 2, 3, 5, 7).[652] The key words in the pericope are אהב (vv. 1a and 4a) and שוב (vv. 5a, 5c, 7a and 9a).

The analogical legal objection from a father to his disobedient son is preceded by Yahweh's reverting back to his אהב needed for the rescue from Egypt as evidence in 11:1.[653] The references in v. 3 and 4 provide further evidence of Yahweh's care for the nation in the desert. The depth of Yahweh's אהב is uncovered in v. 8, where Yahweh declares that his heart is הפ and כמר, with the consequent withholding of judgment (v. 9).

The pericope displays a strong poetic rhythm by making use of parallelism. This serves to emphasise clarification and continuance. In v. 1, כי נער ישראל ואהבהו is parallel to וממצרים קראתי לבני. Thereby the nation's נער ישראל (childhood) marked the time when Yahweh brought them out of Egypt.[654] It shows that Yahweh reveals himself through love. Israel as his adopted son inherits this love.

[650] Wolff, H.W., *A Commentary on the Book of the Prophet Hosea,* Philadelphia, Fortress, 1974, 194-195.

[651] Dearman, J.A., *The Book of Hosea,"* NICOT, Grand Rapids, Wm. B. Eerdmans Publishing co, 2010, 286.

[652] Cf. Wolff, H.W., *A Commentary on the Book of the Prophet Hosea,* Philadelphia, Fortress, 1974, 193.

[653] Landy. F, *Hosea,* Sheffield, Sheffield Academic Press, 1995, 136-138.

[654] Kakkanattu, *God's Enduring Love in the Book of Hosea: A Synchronic and Diachronic...,* Moherbeck, 2005, 38-40.

In v. 2b, לבעלים יזבחו is parallel to ולפסלים יקטרון, through the Baals unmasked as לפסלים (human-made gods/idols).[655] The statement of synonyms

בחבלי אדם אמשכם בעבתות אהבה to
ואהיה להם כמרימי על על לחיהם and

ואט אליו אוכיל in v. 4a-c expresses Yahweh's אהב as protection and care.[656] The synonymous phrases in 4a such as בחבלי אדם (people with bonds) and בעבתות אהבה (with cords of love) express the same meaning and also refer to Israel's' experiences in the desert. Hos. 11:6 is parallel to וחלה חרב בעריו and progressively worked with וכלתה בדיו and to continue to ואכלה. The expression תיהם ממעצו relates to all the three lines of the parallelism.

Hos. 11:8 is particularly poetic in that it is built with a number of synonymous parallelisms that depict Yahweh's inner struggle for his people. Ephraim is synonymous with his people. The surrender of Ephraim, איך אתנך אפרים, is synonymous with the abandonment of Israel, מגנך ישראל. Ephraim and Israel are considered alike. This commitment has further been equated to איך אתנך כאדמה and אשימך כצבאים and thus the judgment of אדמה כצבאים is consummated.

Yahweh's struggle for אהב in His heart is exposed through the use of a parallelism in v. 8b: נהפך עלי לבי with יחד נכמרו נחומי. The נהפך עלי לבי gives more expression to the intense inner tension. It describes the will and sense of Yahweh before a fundamental decision. This is instead of changing a decision, as the analysis of the parallel phrase (i.e., יחד נכמרו נחומי) demonstrates.[657] Janzen argues that in v. 8 the change of heart brings out transformation. But Mays argues that all analogies represent feelings, thoughts and change in the attitude of a person.[658] The change of heart, feelings and emotions of Yahweh are seen here. His struggle is highlighted in this case to show his justice and love.

11:9a holds a synonymous parallelism as follows:

לא אעשה חרון אפי to
לא אשוב לשחת אפרים

These words can refer to Yahweh's withholding judgment and punishment of Ephraim. The reason for withholding the judgment in v. 9b is spelled out by a parallelism; כי אל אנכי ולא־איש is due to the fact that Yahweh is God and not man.[659] It is because He is בקרבך קדוש - the Holy One among you.[660] This parallelism is the key

---

[655] See the excursus below

[656] Cf. Landy F., *Hosea,* Sheffield, Sheffield Academic Press, 1995, 138; Kakkanattu, *God's Enduring Love in the Book of Hosea: A Synchronic and Diachronic...,* Moherbeck, 2005, 60.

[657] Kakkanattu, *God's Enduring Love in the Book of Hosea: A Synchronic and Diachronic...,* Moherbeck, 2005. Mays *Hosea,* 81, 1982, 48 new questions as rhetorical questions and that Yahweh's decision anticipate.

[658] Mays, Metaphor and Reality in Hosea 11, *Semeia* 24, 1982, 46-47. This is a response to Janzen's view of my heart turned…. is changed to my mind had changed.

[659] W.R. Harper, *A Critical and Exegetical Commentary on Amos and Hosea,* Edinburgh, T and T Clark, 1956, 370.

[660] Kevin Vanhoozer, *Theological Interpretation of the Old Testament,* Grand Rapids, Baker Academic, 2008, 247-248. Cf. Patrick D. Miller, ed., *Old Testament Theology Essays on Structure,* Theme and Text, Minneapolis, Fortress Press, 1992, 41.

point of the chiasm and serves to focus attention on the true identity of Yahweh as בקרבך קדוש. This is followed by ולא אבוא בעיר because of the chiastic structure in 9a, i.e. לא אעשה חרון אפי to לא אשוב לשחת אפרים.

Hos. 11:10 reinforces the strong poetic rhythm of the pericope by the continued use of a chiasm (10b), where אחרי יהוה ילכו is used in parallel to ויחרדו בנים מים to כאריה ישאג and ישאג כי־הוא.

The synonymous parallelism within the chiastic structure (v. 10) continues in v. 11a and that brings out a fresh idea, יחרדו כצפור ממצרים and וכיונה מארץ אשור. It stresses that the nations are afraid of returning to Yahweh, even though He would lead them back to dwell in safety. In Hosea 3:1-5, there is an indication of reconciliation that takes place. In that case Yahweh was approached with trembling.[661]

4.1.4. Exploring the Text of Hosea 11:1-11

Hosea 11:1-11 is part of the second major unit of chapters 4-14 and, more specifically, is part of the sub-unit in 9:10-11:11. The latter unit refers to historical events he lost innocence of Israel's youth.[662] It is a historical-theological accusation,[663] as the summary judgment ועמי תלואים למשובתי in 7a indicates. This is structured using the analogy of a legal objection of a father to his disobedient son.[664]

Hosea 11 is a reminder of the covenant between God and the faithless Israel and this has been described as one of the most poetic writing uses in literary conventions.[665] In order to remind Israel of the covenant, Hosea uses references to Egypt. Harper notes that Hosea had both Egypt and Assyria in mind as places of exile, because both countries are regarded as powers and threatening invasion.[666] Kakkanattu refers to Yee's work on Hosea 11, which describes the Exodus (7, 16; 8, 13; 9, 3, 6) and the wilderness experience.[667] His interpretation refers to the return from Egypt. He highlights the use of various Deuteronomist concepts in this chapter. These include the use of אהב in the sense of the covenantal love of God (11:1) and a God who corrects his son (11:5). The concept of God's love that teaches them to walk is taken from Deuteronomy.[668]

Hosea 11:8-9 describes Yahweh's emotion as follows: "How can I give up my son?" and His unwillingness to see the death of his son. Yahweh cannot completely forsake the covenant that he had made with Israel and He reminds her to remain in it.[669]

---

[661] H.W. Wolff, *Hosea,* Philadelphia, Fortress Press, 1974, 194; Kakkanattu, *God's Enduring Love in the Book of Hosea: A Synchronic and Diachronic...,* Moherbeck, 2005, 78.

[662] Cf. Composition and structure of the book referred to the beginning of Chapter-3.1 above.

[663] H.W. Wolff, *Hosea,* Philadelphia, Fortress Press, 1974, 193-194; Jeremias, *'Der Prophet Hosea', Das Alte Testament Deutsch* 24(1), 1983, 139.

[664] Landy. F, *Hosea,* Sheffield, Sheffield Academic Press, 1995, 136.

[665] Landy. F, *Hosea,* Sheffield, Sheffield Academic Press, 1995, 136-137.

[666] W.R. Harper, *A Critical and Exegetical Commentary on Amos and Hosea,* Edinburgh, T and T Clark, 1956, 366.

[667] Kakkanattu.J. P., *God's Enduring Love in the Book of Hosea: A Synchronic and Diachronic,* Moherbeck, 2006, 151.

[668] Gale Yee, *Composition and Tradition in the Book of Hosea: A Redaction-Critical Approach:* SBL Dissertation Series 102, Atlanta, Scholars Press, 1987,216.

[669] Gale Yee, *Composition and Tradition in the Book of Hosea: A Redaction Critical Investigation.* SBLDS, 102, Atlanta, Scholars, 1987, 226-227.

Here compassion and redemption are considered to be synonymous. Hosea 13:14 can be regarded as a negative counterpart to 11:8-9. According to Brueggemann, the terms compassion (נכם) and redemption introduce two verbs which employ rhetorical questions that epitomize Yahweh's character towards his people.[670] Though Hosea has some of the harshest language; it also has some of the most compassionate expression.[671]

4.1.5. Demarcation of the Unit of Hosea 11:1-11

Hosea 11:1-11 is a homogeneous unit, defined by the preceding and subsequent literary contexts. There is no conjunction with 10:9-15 and the direct address of Israel is almost entirely absent here.[672] Hosea 11:1-11 starts with a complete story and a much more intensive historical retrospect. A new segment starts at 12:1, where a new subject is addressed, and the theme changes. The first person is to prosecute in the oracle in v. 8. The figures of the metaphorical personification in v. 1, 3a, 4b, 5a, 6a are addressed in the singular. The content, which is לא אשוב לשחת אפרים, of the judgment in v. 9 are only understandable against the background of the previous disciplinary measures against Israel (cf. vv. 1-7). Thus, Hosea 11:1-11 is a rhetorical unit.[673]

Yahweh's first person statement is continued in v. 11. Israel is addressed in the third person (as in vv. 2-4a, 5b, 6b, 7), instead of a direct address as in v 8a, 9b, which has been interrupted by the third person (see v. 9a). Therefore, the promise of redemption (second person) is changed after the declaration of redemption (third person). Hosea 11:11 share the rhetorical unity of vv. 1-9. In this chapter only v. 10 makes statements about Yahweh in the third person.[674] The content in Hosea 11 is understandable on the basis of the comment in v. 11; especially the term יחרדו, which the traditional analysis considers a substitution.

---

[670] W. Brueggemann, *Theology of the Old Testament,* Minneapolis, Fortress Press, 1997, 246. Similar view is presented by J. A. Dearman, *The Book of Hosea,* NICOT, Grand Rapids, Wm. B. Eerdmans Company, 2010, 328-329.

[671] W. Brueggemann, *Theology of the Old Testament,* Minneapolis, Fortress Press, 1997, 246. Similar view is presented by J. A. Dearman, *The Book of Hosea,* NICOT, Grand Rapids, Wm. B. Eerdmans Company, 2010, 329-330.

[672] H.W. Wolff, *Hosea,* Philadelphia, Fortress Press, 1974, 193.

[673] H.W. Wolff, *Hosea,* Philadelphia, Fortress Press, 1974, 194, 178, 193-194.

[674] James D. Nogalski, *The Book of the Twelve: Hosea-Jonah,* Smyth and Helwys Publishing, Macon, 2011, 155.

4.1.6. Translation: Hosea 11:1-11

Table 14: Translation: Hosea 11:1-11

[1]כי נער ישראל ואהבהו וממצרים קראתי לבני׃	1 When Israel was a child, then I loved him,[675] and out of Egypt I called him my son.[676]
[2] קראו להם כן הלכו מפניהם לבעלים יזבחו ולפסלים יקטרון׃	2 I called them,[677] so they went from me[678] to the Baals. They sacrificed and burnt incense to the idols.
[3] ואנכי תרגלתי לאפרים קחם על־זרועתיו ולא ידעו כי רפאתים׃	3 I taught[679] Ephraim to walk. I took them upon[680] in my arms,[681] but they did not know that I healed them.[682]

[675] The term "like a son" is not found in the MT but it is used to clarify what kind of love is meant.

[676] The MT translates the term בני as "My son;" even so, the LXX suggests that בניו here refers to "his sons." The researcher adopts the MT phrase for the reason that it supports the internal evidence and it looks more appropriate in this context and brings meaning to the reader.

[677] The MT reads as קראו which means "they called" qal perfect third person common plural. The root word comes from קרא, is translated as "to call." In a similar way, LXX and Syriac translations read in the following way כקראי is "as I called"; the word 'I called' is translated as a preposition because of כ qal infinitive construct from קרא first person common singular suffix. The Hebrew text translates as 'as they called, they went away:' this word does not express the meaning in a clear way. The reason that is found here is that the phrase 'as they called, they went away' does not make it clear to whom the text refers.

[678] The MT text has מפניהם "from them" is a preposition and masculine plural noun and third person masculine plural suffix. Nevertheless the other versions, LXX and Syriac, translate as in this way ekproswpoumouautoi הם that reflect and suggest an alternative to the MT: that מפניהם means "they went away from me / my face"; this is translated as preposition masculine plural noun and first person common singular suffix. Here the MT renders that the speaker in this context is Yahweh himself.

[679] The word תרגלתי is rendered as "taught Ephraim to walk." However, the verb תרגלתי means "I taught him to walk, I led him"; Tiphil perfect first person common singular from רגל, "to walk."

[680] Other translations in LXX, Targum the Syriac read in the following way: ואקהם = "I took them upon," the reason is that the subject should be in first person for the progression of the passage.

[681] LXX, Vulgate and Syriac, read as follows: זרועתי = 'in my arms.' The translation of the phrase is correct and the researcher prefers this translation. The reason for adopting this is that the subject here is in the first person to agree with what is said above of Yahweh's speech.

[682] Other translations suggest, "but they did not know that I healed them."

[4] בחבלי אדם אמשכם בעבתות אהבה ואהיה להם כמרימי על על לחיהם ואט אליו אוכיל:	4 with cords of humanity,[683] I drew them with bonds of love.[684] I became to them the one who lifts the yoke[685] upon their jaws.[686] And I bent down to him and fed them.[687]
[5] לא ישוב אל־ארץ מצרים ואשור הוא מלכו כי מאנו לשוב:	5 He shall not return to the land of Egypt,[688] but Assyria shall be his king,[689] because they refuse to return.[690]
[6] וחלה חרב בעריו וכלתה בדיו ואכלה ממעצותיהם:	6 And the sword shall abide their cities, it will demolish his strong men,[691] and it will consume them[692] and their gate bars because of their counsel

683 The word בחבלי אדם is translated as "human cords" or "cords of human kindness." In this context the word אדם is used as a noun that relates to man. This word either literally or figuratively conveys the meaning to the reader. This refers to compassion and is sometime used as parallelism to אהבה.

684 The word אהבה refers sometimes to "ropes of love." This is because the noun אהבה is traditionally related to אהבה "love."

685 The MT implies "and I became to them the one who lifts the yoke." The suggestion is followed and is read as כמרימ עול since it agrees with the construction of cords and ropes in this sense.

686 The MT translates this as "their jaws." But it is also translated as "their neck." Most of the English translations endorse the use of "their jaws."

687 The MT text translates in singular form as "him." But this is regarded as a collective singular by most English versions and is translated as a plural pronoun.ואט אליו אוכיל should be read as ואט אליו ואוכיל לו. This corresponds with the LXX reading, "I bent down to them and fed them" is more meaningful than "and I bent down to him and fed him" as translated by MT, because it was Yahweh who took care of them during their journey and fed them in the wilderness journey. Here Yahweh's love is depicted as parent's/father's love for his child.

688 The other rendering is that "they shall not return to the land of Egypt?" this is followed by LXX and MT, the MT reads in this way as לא ("not") rather it should be read in the following way as לו ("to him") and this connects with the close of 11:4 rather than commencing of 11:5. Here we find a textual confusion within the use of לא and לו is considered as probably an unintentional scribal error while the scribe was taking down his notes while hearing (for example *Kethib/Qere* in Ps. 100:3 it is noted similar scribal error in the text).

689 The MT translates in the following way make us to understand that "Assyria, Assyria shall be his king over Israel."

690 The MT translates שוב as "return." The origin of the root word שוב means "to turn, return" comes in the beginning and ends with the word return. This creates an inclusion in this context. The repetition of such word produces an ironic wordplay in this context and especially in this verse. The reason is that the people of Israel refuse to "return" to God or "turn" from their wickedness, if they do not return to Yahweh the punishment is warned that will be taken back to Egypt again. This is called as punishment for them when they do not return to Yahweh.

691 The MT reads in the following way that בדים is "gate bars" which can be translated in the following way as "defenders," but the literal meaning of the MT is "gate bars" or "barriers" employed in this context relates to idols that the people of Israel had chosen idols as their security and they believed that they will be protected from all their dangers and defensive structure (cf. Hos. 4:18). The phrase בדיו is read in the following way by the LXX ἐν ταίς Χερσίν αὐτοὺ. At the same time Syriac understands as "*E manibus*." However, the Targum reads "*Proceres*." Vulgate reads "*Electos ejus*."

692 The MT reads "consume them" 'and will devour them in their fortresses.'

7 ועמי תלואים למשובתי ואל־על יקראהו יחד לא ירומם:	7 And my people are bent[693] on turning away from me,[694] and upwards they call together, he does not rise them at all.
8 איך אתנך אפרים אמגנך ישראל איך אתנך כאדמה אשימך כצבאים נהפך עלי לבי יחד נכמרו נחומי:	8 How shall I give you up, O Ephraim? How shall I make[695] you as Adama? How shall I set you as Zeboiim? My heart is turned within me, my repenting are kindled together at the same time raised my compassion.
9 לא אעשה חרון אפי לא אשוב לשחת אפרים כי אל אנכי ולא־איש בקרבך קדוש ולא אבוא בעיר:	9 I will not execute the fierceness of my anger, I will not return to destroy Ephraim for I am not a man; the Holy One in the midst of you: and I will not enter in wrath.[696]
10 אחרי יהוה ילכו כאריה ישאג כי־הוא ישאג ויחרדו בנים מים:	10 They shall walk after Yahweh: he shall roar like a lion: yes, he will roar, then the children shall tremble[697] from the west.
11 יחרדו כצפור ממצרים וכיונה מארץ אשור והושבתים על־בתיהם נאם־יהוה:	11 They shall tremble[698] as a bird from Egypt, and as a dove from the land of Assyria, and I will place in their houses, says Yahweh.

4.1.7. Text Critical Notes - Hosea 11:1-11

Verse 1

לבני Footnote 1a (BHS): The alternative reading of the LXX τα τεκνα αυτου supports the Targum following the plural in v. 2. The masculine singular that Israel was behind in v. 1 is referred here, corresponds to the masculine singular used in v. 8. Reading of the text is therefore unchanged.

Verse 2

קראו Footnote 2a (BHS): The alternative reading of the LXX καθωζ μετεκαλεσα αυτους corresponds to 1st masculine singular קראכי. Within the context of v. 1 and v. 3 is expected a judgment of Yahweh. So the alternative reading of the LXX maintained.

מפניהם Footnote 2b (BHS): The alternative reading of the LXX (supported by the Syriac version) εκ προσωπου μου αυτοι correspond with מפני הם.

---

693 In MT the phrase תלואים (qal passive participle masculine plural from תלא, "to hang") is translated in the following way "[My people] are hung up."

694 In MT the phrase משובתי is translated as first person common singular suffix as the noun משובתי meaning "turning of me" serves here as an objective genitive: "turning away from me."

695 The MT reads אמגכד meaning "abandon." The meaning of the word is as used in Gen. 14:20. The old version means "shielding" which connects with מגן. LXX reads: ὑπερασπιώσου, Vulgate has: "*Protegam te*," Syriac "*Juvarem te*." and Targum has "*Exterminabo te*."

696 The meaning of the clause is "against the city." Yahweh presents as the Holy One of Israel. Yahweh continues that He will consume them with his anger. This seems to be the real meaning of the expression of this passage. However, Ancient versions read: בעיר which is translated in general and interpreted as "in wrath": the root word comes from עור.

697 The MT translates the verb as חרד "to tremble." In this case the rendering refers to prepositions of direction. The meaning of the verb is "to go or come trembling." In this context perhaps the verb referred ויחרדו מים means to come trembling.

698 The MT reads this way: the word חרד means "to tremble" as a preposition.

The reading the LXX is maintained in accordance with the amendment adopted in footnote 2a (BHS).

Verse 3

קחם footnotes 3a (BHS): The Masoretic text is incomprehensible. The reading of the LXX as subject is in the first person masculine and to a third person masculine object correctly. It also enjoys the support of the Syriac version and the Targum.

על־זרועתיו footnotes 3b (BHS): The reading of the Syriac translation, Targum and Vulgate changed the subject after the first person masculine singular. This is in line with the amendment adopted in footnote 3a (BHS). The amendment to זרועתי is therefore maintained.

Verse 4-5

אדם footnotes 4/5a (BHS): The Masoretic text reading is probably corrupted. The alternative אמת or חסד deserves consideration as בעבתות אהבה with a closer analysis of it.

כמרימי על footnotes 4/5b (BHS): the reading כמרים עול before. The amendment fits better within the metaphor of Israel to Yahweh as Father as a child. The reading of the text is very unusual in the context because it represents an animal metaphor.[699] The alternative reading is therefore accepted.

לחיהם footnotes 4/5c (BHS) The LXX changes the reading to לחייו. The reading of the text, however, is in sufficient sense within the context of the amended text in footnote 4/5b (BHS) to maintain it.

ואט אליו אוכיל לא footnotes 4/5d (BHS) The Septuagint reads δυνησομαι αυτω compared to the alternative reading ואט אליו ואוכיל לו. The text reading is maintained as it is sufficient to make sense within the context of worship *Yahweh to Israel to give him food.* The לא should be as amended to לו as this object represents.

כי מאנו לשוב footnotes 4/5e: (BHS) The critical comment in footnote 4/5e the possibility that כי מאנו לשוב is an insertion. However, there is no evidence to support it, and the phrase fits within the context as a reason why Israel returned to Egypt and Assyria and the king. The reading of the text is therefore maintained.

Verse 6

בדיו footnotes 6a (BHS) The alternative reading בנדיו without evidence is suggested. However, there is no sufficient reason to change the text. The reading of the text is therefore maintained.

ואכלה ממעצותיהם footnotes 6b (BHS) A possible variation of some manuscripts on the reading of the text is presented as ואכלה ממעצותיהם. Another variation is ואכלתם ממי. However, no sufficient external evidence is offered for this alternative reading. The reading of the text is therefore maintained.

Verse 7

תלואים למשובתי footnotes 7a the reading of the text is shown as corrupted. The following alternatives are proposed נלאה ממשובתו (supported by the LXX επικρεμαμενος);

[699] Macintosh. A.A, *A Critical and Exegetical Commentary on Hosea,* Edinburgh, T and T Clark, 1997, 446.

חולאים למשובתם and תלואים למצבים. The reading of the text can be maintained because Yahweh is the object of Israel's apostasy. The other alternative reading also provides no external confirming evidence.

ואל־על יקרא הו footnotes 7b: (BHS) The text is puzzling.[700] Another possible reading ואל־בעלי קרא (הוא) ואל יקראהו is proposed. It is, however, difficult to read in connection with the enforcement of the text to footnote 7a. No external evidence is presents a fair amendment.

הו יחד לא ירומם footnotes 7c (BHS): An alternative reading is האחדל ארחם which is suggested without external evidence. The reading of the text is translatable and should therefore be maintained.

Verse 8

נחומי footnote 8a (BHS) The alternative reading רחמי supported by the Syrian translation and the Targum is proposed. The reading of the text is maintained for the purpose of parallelism that is found here.

Verse 9

אבוא בעיר footnote 9a (BHS): Two possible alternative readings are presented without external evidence, that אבער and אובה בער. The LXX reads εις πολιν πολιν. The reading of the text is translatable and understandable. The text reading of the text is here maintained.

Verse 10-11

Footnote 10/11a: Footnote 10/11 set whether the entire verse 10 and 11 are taped. However, there is no external evidence to allow the fresh way. The text is, therefore, maintained.

כי־הוא ישאג footnote 10/11b (BHS) suggest that כי־הוא ישאג is omitted from it. The reading of the text, however, is maintained for the sake of the chiastic structure which כי־הוא ישאג part.

והושבתים footnote 10/11c (BHS): the LXX reads και αροκαταστσω αυτου. The alternative reading of the text would be introduced as והשבתים. The reading of the Masoretic text is maintained, as not enough internal motivation exists to edit the text.

4.2. Inner Texture

Here, the researcher examines the text of Chapter 11, looking at it under the different factors: Repetitive, Argumentative, Progressive, Open-Middle-Closing, Sensory-Aesthetic textures and inter-textuality.

The overall pattern of Hosea11:1-11 develops in the form of a diatribe as the narrator foregrounds Yahweh the protagonist against the people of Israel. The "I and They" expressions within the narrative framework introduce an imaginary dialogue between Yahweh and Israel.

4.2.1. Repetitive Texture

In this section of Hosea 11, three main elements of repetitive texture can be distinguished: the parent-son metaphor, the love between them and calling.

[700] Wolff, Hans Walter, *Hosea,* Philadelphia, Fortress Press, 1974, 192.

4.2.1.1. Parent-Son Metaphor

The importance of Yahweh's use of Hosea through human love relationships to emphasise the covenantal relationship is described strongly here in the love images throughout Chapter 11. While these images occur in other sections as well, they are emphasised strongly here, suggesting the importance Yahweh places on both the covenantal relationship and his use of Hosea's human relationships to draw the Israelites' attention to what He is trying to tell them."

In Hosea 1-3, female imagery describes the relationship between a husband and a wife, but in chapter 11, male imagery is used in order to depict the relationship between a father and a son, which in turn refers to God and Israel.[701] In this context, Yahweh became Israel's parent when He called them out of the land of Egypt. As a parent, he taught and guided his children, and as a parent he both punished and forgave them when they chose to do wrong. Hosea is not the only book in the Bible where the image of God as father occurs. (cf. Deut. 14:1a; 32; 6b; Isa. 1:2, 4, 9; Jer. 3:19, 22; 4:22; 31:9, 20),[702] Kakkanattu says that Yahweh's words in 11:1 are reminiscent of the expression in Ex. 4:22-23 which means "Israel is my firstborn son. . . let my son go..." The reason is that since Israel is the first born son, God had chosen and elected the nation as His own child (Gen. 12:2-3; cf. Matt. 2:13-15).[703] In this context the important aspect to notice is that in Chapter 11, Israel is being characterized as a son instead of a wife. Hosea 11:1 is understood in the context of Exo. 4:22-23 where the command came to Moses from Yahweh at the very beginning of his journey out of Egypt.[704] Macintosh notes that "from Egypt I began to call my son..." the phrase refers to Exo. 4:22 where Yahweh tells pharaoh that He wants His people to be delivered *"My son, My first-born."*[705] But Dearman translates in the following way: *"and from Egypt I called My son."* This phrase appears for the first time in the Old Testament where the theme of God's love is given as reason for His electing Israel as His people. The idea is elaborated in the book of Deuteronomy (Deut. 4:37; 7:7-9 and 10:15).

The other theme בחר 'elect' as the outcome of the divine love and עם 'people, nation' is unfolding the limits of that love. Out of many nations Yahweh loved one עם. The context shows God's exclusive and elective love of Israel and surprisingly the statement that God also loves the גר *'stranger'* (10:18). The notion is that Israel is called to love God as the proper response to God's love and to love the stranger. The book clearly presents that the history of Israel is based on the exodus event. The question is whether this event brings out Hosea's knowledge of the patriarchal period. Wolff observes that it is Yahweh who elected Israel and called His son from the land of Egypt. Yahweh's love extended to redeeming His covenant people and delivering His people from Egypt. At the same time one important aspect to be noted is that Yahweh's call to His son shows covenantal intimate relationship of care and

---

[701] Wolff, H.W. *A Commentary on the Book of the Prophet Hosea,* Philadelphia, Fortress, 1974, 193-194.

[702] Stuart, Douglas, *Hosea - Jonah*, Waco, Texas, Word Books, 1987, 177. Cf. Dearman, J.A., *The Book of Hosea,"* NICOT, Grand Rapids, Wm. B. Eerdmans Publishing co, 2010, 277.

[703] Kakkanattu, *God's Enduring love in the book of Hosea,* 40.

[704] Stuart. Douglas, *Hosea - Jonah,* Waco, Texas, Word Books, 1987, 277.

[705] Macintosh, A.A, *A Critical and Exegetical Commentary on Hosea,* Edinburgh, T and T Clark, 1997, 437.

protection. The purpose that we find here is that Hosea was called for a special reason in reaching out to his people in that particular time. The book especially brings out the idea of God's love where Israel is regarded as a person, Yahweh's chosen child, who is called to accomplish a special purpose that is to live as Yahweh's son for other nations.

This thought rhetorically links the Exodus with the statement in Ex. 4:22-23.[706] The concept that is noted here is that God is the one who called his child to him (Hos. 11:1) and taught him and reminded him that God's call and election came up solely out of his love. God is the one who calls and takes the initiative; it is not because of what we have done. Briefly then, God had a message for His people. For this particular message, He needed a messenger whose heart ached and yearned as His did for Israel. This messenger needed to know from personal experience just how He felt. But there was none, so God chose Hosea. God told him to marry a prostitute, knowing that his experience with her would mould Hosea into the messenger He needed.

Mays states that this verse shows God's love as a father for His people.[707] Israel is portrayed as Yahweh's נער (boy).[708] While the Hebrew translates it as "lad" or "youth,"[709] English versions translate it as "child." Davies says that the word "child" is used figuratively.[710] Dearman understands Israel as a youth who is obedient and completely dependent at any age, which best describes the narrative of Israel as a son in 11:1.[711] This shows how much God loved His people from the beginning and made a covenant with them as his people.

4.2.1.2. Prominent Theme of Parental Love

The next aspect is the theme of love repeated three times in 11:1 and 4. Macintosh considers "love" as the predominant theme of chapter 11 and describes how the love relationship between Yahweh and Israel existed even when the people were suffering in slavery in the land of Egypt. God reminds Israel of her former relationship with Him.[712] Here, the relationship between Yahweh and Israel is expressed in the first person (i.e., "I loved him"). There are several references in the Old Testament which beautifully describe Yahweh's love for Israel and this section reinforces this idea.[713]

Wolff concludes that the word אהב is used for Israel as the loved one of Yahweh. This means that Hosea is the first prophet who uses the word "אהב" (i.e., love).[714] He says that the prophet was the first to affirm Yahweh's love in relation to Israel.

[706] William Rainey Harper, *A Critical and Exegetical Commentary on Amos and Hosea,* T and T Clark, Edinburgh, 1979, 361.

[707] Mays, James Luther., *Hosea: A Commentary,* OTL, Philadelphia, Westminster, 1969, 152-153.

[708] Wolff, H.W. *A Commentary on the Book of the Prophet Hosea,* Philadelphia, Fortress, 1974, 197-198.

[709] Dearman, J.A, *The Book of Hosea,*" NICOT, Grand Rapids, Wm. B. Eerdmans Publishing co, 2010, 276-277.

[710] Davies, *Hosea*, 254. Cf. Wood J. Leon, *The Prophets of Israel,* Grand Rapids, Baker Academic group, 1979, 278.

[711] Dearman, *The Book of Hosea,* NICOT, Grand Rapids, Wm. B. Eerdmans company, 2010, 277.

[712] Macintosh, A.A, *A Critical and Exegetical Commentary on Hosea,* Edinburgh, T and T Clark, 1997, 437.

[713] Deut. 7:8, 13; 10:15; 26:6 (MT 5); Isa. 43:4; 63:9; Jer. 31:3; Hos. 9:15b, 11:1, 4a; Zep. 3:17.

[714] Wolff, H.W., *A Commentary on the Book of the Prophet Hosea,* Philadelphia, Fortress, 1974, 198.

Dearman agrees with Wolff that Yahweh's love/call of Israel was by election and that further affirms Yahweh's love (אהב) for them.[715] The people are reminded of this in Deut. 7:6-8 which discusses God's choice of an insignificant people to love and the resultant commitment to אהב.[716]

The next question is of God's drawing them to Him as a parent would rescue his/her child from a difficult situation. Davies suggests "I drew them ... or I sought to draw them, and this is translated in terms of the imperfect."[717] The Hebrew word משך is translated as an animal pulling a load (cf. Deut. 21:3; Isa. 5:18), but if the word is translated metaphorically (cf. Ex. 12:21; Judg. 4:6; Job 21:33), it includes a lover. Wolff comments that because of his love he elected and called his son out of Egypt.[718] But Dearman says that the reference to his son who is called out from Egypt actually belongs to Hosea's generation.[719] In contrast, Macintosh argues that Yahweh's gracious love and compassion brought the people from the land of slavery and showed his love to the people. However, the reasons for returning to Egypt were rebellion, involvement in vassal policies and idolatry (v. 2b).[720]

Garrett finds that the image in 11:4 brings out the metaphor of father and son and the shift takes place to an animal metaphor in verse 4.[721] The other term in repetitive texture is 'cords' which, according to Davies, is a tool Yahweh uses to show *compassion* to them. The parallel expression found is *bands of love* for humans rather than beasts in this place.[722] Harper says that "with bands of love" is parallel and first time the word "human" is made synonymous with "love."[723] It is noted here that both אדם and אהבה (love) resemble Arabic words for leather.[724] For Zenger, 11:4 refers to punishment for humans, but logic suggests that Yahweh drew Israel to him and loved them with bands of love. Zenger takes Yahweh's love as an instrument to his people.[725] Jeremias understands the bands of love as an expression to show that it was Yahweh who educates Israel.[726] The Hebrew word אהבה means love in this case. The idea that is brought out is that Yahweh treated Israel with cords of love to draw her to Him. His parental love motivated Him to do this. The cords of humanity also can be understood as "cords of love" in this case Yahweh, who educates Israel. God associates himself with bands and cords in animal imagery, as bull cart and farmer.[727] This is understood

---

[715] Dearman, *The Book of Hosea,* NICOT, Grand Rapids, Wm. B. Eerdmans company, 2010, 278.

[716] Kakkanattu, *God's Enduring love in the book of Hosea,* 40.

[717] Davies G. I. *Hosea, New Century Bible Commentary,* Grand Rapids, Wm. B. Eerdmans pub co, 1992, 256. Cf. Wood J. Leon, *The Prophets of Israel,* Grand Rapids, Baker Academic group, 1979, 256.

[718] Wolff, H.W., *A Commentary on the Book of the Prophet Hosea,* Philadelphia, Fortress, 197-198.

[719] Dearman, *The Book of Hosea,* NICOT, Grand Rapids, Wm. B. Eerdmans company, 2010, 280

[720] Macintosh, A.A., *A Critical and Exegetical Commentary on Hosea,* Edinburgh, T and T Clark, 1997, 437.

[721] Garrett. *Hosea, Joel,* NAC, 19A, Nashville, Broadman and Holman, 1997, 255.

[722] Davies G. I. *Hosea, New Century Bible Commentary,* Grand Rapids, Wm. B. Eerdmans pub co, 1992, 256. Cf. Wood J. Leon, *The Prophets of Israel,* Grand Rapids, Baker Academic Group, 1979, 282.

[723] W.R. Harper, *A Critical and Exegetical Commentary on Amos and Hosea,* Edinburgh, T and T Clark, 1956, 364.

[724] Driver, *JTS* 39, 1938, 161-162. Cf. J. Barr, *Comparative Philology and the text of Old Testament,* Oxford, 1968, 153-154.

[725] Zenger, *Durch Menschen zog ich sie...,* (Hos. 11:4), 191-193.

[726] Jeremias, *Der Prophet Hosea,* 142; cf. Seifert, *Metaphorical Study*, 193.

[727] W.R. Harper, *A Critical and Exegetical Commentary on Amos and Hosea,* Edinburgh, T and T Clark, 1956, 364.

as a metaphor for father-son and farmer-animal. The farmer metaphor brings out the idea of leaving a bloody mark on the neck, and injuries that turn to human cords of bands of love. The metaphorical language shows that Yahweh's love and compassion brought Israel out of slavery and reminds her of her covenant with Yahweh.

The Lord is presented here in the form of illustrative analogies: according to Dempsey Yahweh loves people as a father, as a husband and as a shepherd.[728] In these images God's love is portrayed in the form of Father's love for His children (cf. Jer. 31:2, 3, 20). Here God is heartbroken, people are deserted; the broken heart presents the pain of a parent. The prophet insists that there is a fundamental and an important way God likes humanity as He loves His children. The reason is that God is similar to humans. God loves them and loves in a way that a human being can experience and understand love. This is because of God's love. God's love can help in understanding the language of humanity. The language is understandable because life is filled with emotions, feelings, pain and suffering that help to understand who God is.

4.2.1.3. Repetition of קראו

An important term in this section is "calling." Hosea uses the verb "to call" which denotes the geographical notion "from Egypt." The same word has a special meaning "to call with a name" that applies status or position to people. "Calling" indicates Yahweh's role as a liberator in the history of Israel. Wolff comments that in v. 2 קראו להם indicates the people's apostasy and Yahweh's liberating act.[729] In this instance Eidavell points out that the people followed other gods, specifically referring to Baal and thought that they need to be liberated for following other gods.[730] Wolff's argument is that v. 1 and 3 are statements of Yahweh.

The Hebrew word קראו means "they called." Greek translates καθως μετεκαλεσα, (even as I called), which reflects that the Hebrew word כקראי is translated as *"I called."* The Septuagint renders the Greek word καθως μετεκαλεσα meaning *"just as I called"* instead of the Hebrew word קראו, meaning *"they called,"* which again describes the intensity of the relationship. The LXX reading is supported by Nyberg and it suggests that the plural form refers to the messenger sent by God.[731] Targum recommends that the meaning of the word "they" refers to the prophets who "called them." But Israel disobeyed and fled from the presence of God, and she continues to sacrifice to idols.[732] Wolff, Stuart and Dearman prefer to use the Greek translation "I called" rather than the Hebrew rendering. This research agrees with the opinion of the scholars that the LXX rendering suits this context.

Macintosh brings to our notice the verbs of v. 2 (הלכו...קראו) that function similarly to 7:11b. The above statement refers to the prophets (cf. LXX translation and

---

[728] Carol J. Dempsey, *The Prophets: A Liberation-Critical Reading,* Minneapolis, Fortress Press, 2000, 154

[729] Wolff, Hans Walter, *Hosea,* Philadelphia, Fortress Press, 1974,199.

[730] Goran Eidevall, *Grapes in the Desert: Metaphors, Models and Themes in Hosea 4-11,* Stockholm, Almqvist and Wiksell International, 1996, 169.

[731] H.S. Nyberg, *Studien zum Hoseabuche,* 1935.

[732] F. Tilney Bassett, *The Book of the Prophet Hosea,* London, Paternoster Row, 1869, 67-68.

2Kgs. 17:13-18; Isa. 6:10; Jer. 7:25-26). In Mays' opinion, Israel acted like teenagers.[733] The more God called them, the Septuagint and Syriac have "God" instead of "they", the more they did just the opposite (cf. v. 7b).[734] Hubbard re-divides line 2 and thinks that "they" refers to tempters here, meaning the Baal of the fertility worshipping women in Num. 25.[735] Here the lines become *"the more they called them, the more they went from me."*[736] To a wayward son, bent on self and sin, the call of idolatry was louder and stronger than the call of a loving parent.[737] The loving parent describes God's care for them. The care God took indicates His character of loving. The rebellion is contrasted with Yahweh's love and His election. Here, the prophet repeats these for a stronger emphasis. But in 9:6 the literal translation of the phrase הלכו משד is "they walked," which reminds the reader of Yahweh's call to his people.

The word קרא "to call someone" is presented in the form of God's love in calling his son from Egypt. Consideration is needed to determine the reason why Yahweh chooses his son and how Egypt relates to the narrative. The implication of parent-child metaphor in relation to Yahweh-Israel also needs to be determined. The word is בן used in the singular form to show the identity of Israel used rarely in the Old Testament. But the plural form בנים "sons" speaks more of Yahweh's relationship with Israel (cf. Hos. 11:10).[738] In two places in the Bible, Yahweh addresses Israel as "my son" (Exo. 4:22-23). Hosea presenting Israel as Yahweh's son describes the relationship between Yahweh and Israel as being one of parental love.

The בן is important in understanding Hosea 11, because the chapter utilises the metaphor between parent and child to demonstrate the relationship between Yahweh and Israel. Hosea uses parent-child metaphor to bring out anthropological meaning that it refers to household, a social institution whose importance is preserved in the kinship and its relationship in the ancient world.[739] In the Hebrew language the exact word for family is not found, but the extended form of the word means to three or four generations and its possessions. The prophet uses household metaphor to link related members in the family. Through this the prophet brings out the imagery of parental love to express God's love in dealing with Israel.

But modern exegetes agree that the reason behind the parent-child metaphor is the concept of the covenant.[740] Fensham notes that "when the Lord says according to the prophet, that Israel is His son," it links this with the event of the Exodus.[741] This shows the author clearly refers to the covenantal relationship. In a similar way, Moran and McCarthy strongly prove that אהב is a covenantal term, though Hosea

---

[733] J.L. Mays, *Hosea,* London, SCM Press, 1969, 154.

[734] Macintosh, A.A., *A Critical and Exegetical Commentary on Hosea,* Edinburgh, T and T Clark, 1997, 439.

[735] David A Hubbard, and Glenn W Baker, Vol. 31, Nashville, Thomas Nelson Publishers, 1987.

[736] David A. Hubbard, *Hosea,* Tyndale Commentary Series, 187.

[737] J.L. Mays, *Hosea,* London, SCM Press, 1969, 154.

[738] Fohrer, υἱός, υἱόθεσία *TDNT* 8, 351-352.

[739] L.E. Stager, "The Archaeology of the Family in Ancient World," *BASOR* 260, 1985, 1-35.

[740] Carol J. Dempsey, *The Prophets: A Liberation-Critical Reading,* Minneapolis, Fortress Press, 2000, 157.

[741] Fensham, *"Father and Son,"* 121-135.

speaks merely of the love of Yahweh to Israel.[742] However, Fohrer notices that two facets of relationship are communicated-the concept of subordination of Israel to Yahweh and the steadfast love of Yahweh, which dominates in Hosea 11.[743] This love of Yahweh is the basis for Israel to be called "son" and it is a reminder of the exodus event.

The reference to Yahweh's son called from Egypt is in Hosea 11:1. It conveys the message to Hosea's own generation. That means the fundamental historical event of exodus communicates Yahweh's saving acts to Israel as Israel is called out of Egypt, as 'son.'

The subject is קרא which means "to commission, to call someone, to call someone over." The love of God is presented in the form of a loving parent who called them out of Egypt and gives them commission, which indicates a personal relationship between God and the called one.[744] The verb here is understood that it applied to the person, especially in the context of the prophets; they are called for a reason. In Hosea 11:1 Israel is believed to be a person that is Yahweh's son, who is called to fulfil a particular task that is to live as a Yahweh's son.[745] The term indicates a personal relationship between Yahweh and the called one.[746] The context shows that Israel was called for a specific purpose. Israel is presented as Yahweh's son to fulfil that task.[747] Here, "קרא" denotes an indication of election and adoption as the chosen one. This shows that while Israel was in Egypt, Yahweh sent this message to Pharaoh, *"Thus says the Lord: Israel is my firstborn son"* (Exo. 4:22). That reference in Exodus and this one in Hosea are two of the few places in Masoretic Text that refer to Israel as "my son."

Israel went into Egypt as an extended family-not as a nation. Israel became a nation in Egypt, and was able to come out of Egypt only by virtue of Yahweh's intervention. The metaphor teaches that love of God for Israel here expresses divine election. Garrett notes the quote "I called my son out of Egypt" is quoted in Matt 2:13-15 as being fulfilled in the life of Jesus. The gospel of Matthew describes Jesus during His life and revives the idea of the life of Israel, especially its beginning.[748] Matthew concludes that story by saying, 'that it might be fulfilled which was spoken by the Lord through the prophet, saying, "Out of Egypt I called my son.' Dearman remarks here that the reference to God's son and calling out of Egypt in Hosea 11:1 may not be applicable to Hosea's time and their generation. According to Harper Matthew 2:15 is understood in terms of predictive messiah, to represent Israel as type of Christ, this furnishes the historical event which the gospel writer was describing.[749] But Matthew's use of Hosea 11:1 is an example which portrays the linkages between both the Testaments.

---

[742] Moran, "The Ancient Near Eastern Background of the Love of God in Deuteronomy," *Catholic Biblical Quarterly,* Vol. 25, (72-87), 1963," 77.

[743] Fohrer, υἱός, υἱόθεσία *TDNT* 8, 352-353.

[744] *TLOT* 3; 1161

[745] *HALOT,* 1127-1128.

[746] *HALOT,* 1127-1128.

[747] Kakkanaatu, *God's Enduring love in the book of Hosea,* 39-40.

[748] Garrett, *Hosea, Joel,* NAC, 19A, Nashville, Broadman and Holman, 1997, 220-221. Cf. Michael Eschelbach, *Called to Be God's people: An Introduction,* Oregon, Wipf and Stock Publishers, 2006, 481.

[749] W.R. Harper, *A Critical and Exegetical Commentary on Amos and Hosea,* Edinburgh, T and T Clark, 1956, 362.

In this case, two entities are specified-Israel as God's son and Jesus as God's Son who will bring salvation to His people as well as for Gentiles.[750] Macintosh summarizes Hosea 11:1 by saying Yahweh's action is presented in the form of love. In bondage, Israel was like an incapable child. In this condition, Yahweh chose to show His love to the people of Israel and liberate them from slavery; this follows the adoption of Israel as His own son. From that moment, Israel's distinctive relationship with Yahweh is instituted, whereby they become chosen as Yahweh's son.

Matthew writes that-God called his son out of Egypt to fulfil his purpose to be a light to the nations (Matt. 2:15) in the same way God called Israelites out of Egypt for the sake of the nations. Israelites were called to fulfil their identity as God's people and therefore showcase the covenantal love of Yahweh to the nations. When they broke their covenant, this identity was at stake. Therefore, God salvages the covenant by offering restoration. It was for his name's sake and Israel's identity as God's chosen ones that he remained faithful in spite of their waywardness. The chosen people become the witness for God to others in order to bring salvation to all other people, other nations.

Table 15: Overview of Repetitive Texture Table - Hosea 11:7-8

Hos. 11:7	יחד	all together
Hos. 11:8	יחד	all together

The previous sections emphasise punishment if God's chosen people do not return to God they must change their behaviour or face the consequences. The other important aspect of repetitive texture is noted because of unity in the text. יחד basically means "unity and togetherness," because of its adverbial and adjectival usages which brings out the connotation of "together" and "all my compassion."[751] The construction of the word יחד shows that Yahweh is going to bring punishment to the people and reminds them of Israel's unfaithfulness (v. 2 and 3). According to Janzen, the adverb form means to bring the many into one. It is all about the components of divine life.[752] Here יחד reaffirms the concept of the people's complete loyalty by leaving their apostasy and following Yahweh not Baal. That means, they will not continue to follow Baal again and they will call on the Most High and they will exalt Him. The word יחד brings out the meaning of togetherness in this context.

Hos. 11:5a	לשוב	He shall return
Hos. 11:5b	ישוב	They refuse to return
Hos. 11:7	למשובתי	On turning from me
Hos. 11:11	והושבתים	I will place

[750] Dearman, J.A, *The Book of Hosea,*" NICOT, Grand Rapids, Wm. B. Eerdmans Publishing co, 2010, 280.

[751] W.R. Harper, *A Critical and Exegetical Commentary on Amos and Hosea,* Edinburgh, T and T Clark, 1956, 369. Cf. Fabry, יחד, 45.

[752] Janzen, 'Metaphor and Reality in Hosea 11,' *Semia* 24, (7-44), 1982, 29-30.

The focus moves from punishment to return. The concept of return is understood as the central theme conveyed by the verb שוב.[753] The context shows the theme of Israel's unfaithfulness and return to God. This verb שוב is translated in four different ways. First in v. 5a שוב the possibility is that return to Egypt as punishment. Secondly in v. 5b, it is translated as Israel's refusal to return to Yahweh. Third, it refers to the people of Israel turning away from המשוב as stated in v. 7. Finally, the word is used for Yahweh helping them to return to their own homes (v. 11). The suffix verb שוב should be taken in the objective sense "apostasy from me." The phrases "turning from" means to "turn back" or "apostatize" (cf. 14:5; in Jer. 3:6 of Israel; in Jer. 2:18; 3:22; 5:6; 8:5; 14:7 of Judah, often translated "faithless"). Macintosh comments that instead of turning to God in repentance they turned away from Him in apostasy.[754] Wolff notes that the opening words "My people" is an allusion to 1:9 (i.e., "לא עמי"), but with the future hope of the full hope of 2:23 (that is המחר, cf. 1:6 and עמי).[755] The covenant between Yahweh and Israel is echoed here. When Israel fulfils the requirements of Yahweh, the covenant blessings will be renewed.

The text brings out the contrast that Israel was cared for tenderly, but in the future days; God's promised wrath will be upon her. The central point is that the people rebelled against the father's love and this led them to captivity.

This can be read in line with the previous statement, the translation of which is "He will return to Egypt land." But Wolff and Stuart interpret "He will return to the land of Egypt." If the people of Israel will not return to Yahweh, who is their healer and the source of their being, they will return to bondage. This verse talks about God's deliverance from Egypt and his caring for his people in the wilderness. It is God who elected them and saved them from bondage. This shows a clear picture that God is not only the deliverer of the people of Israel, but because of His love towards them, He saved them from bondage and gave them an identity.

Hos. 11:8	איך אתנך	How shall I give you up
Hos. 11:8	איך אתנך	How shall I make you
Hos. 11:8	איך אתנך	How shall I set you

The repeated use of parallelism throughout the pericope is a poetic pattern for the sake of emphasis and continuum. The repeated use of איך אתנך within the parallel structure in v. 8 emphasises Yahweh's inner struggles to preserve Israel: The rhetorical question in v. 8 is a lament. Hoass notes that the rhetorical question is used to bring out the emotions, accusations and contempt involved therein. The exclamation is understood as a mockery, and lament.[756] The drama is enacted here to show how Yahweh feels the pain at the behaviour of a faithless child.

---

[753] W.R. Harper, *A Critical and Exegetical Commentary on Amos and Hosea,* Edinburgh, T and T Clark, 1956, 371. Cf. Frank Gaeblein, ed., *The Exposition Bible Commentary,* 1985, 216-218

[754] Macintosh, A.A., *A Critical and Exegetical Commentary on Hosea,* Edinburgh, T and T Clark, 1997, 455-456.

[755] Wolff, *Hosea,* Philadelphia, Fortress Press, 1974, 200-201.

[756] Hoass, "Passion and Compassion of God in the Old Testament: A Theological Survey of Hosea 11:8-9," *SJOT* 11, 1987, 146-148.

איך אתנך אפרים
אמגנך ישראל
איך אתנך כאדמה
אשימך כצבאים

The fourfold repetition and emphasis on איך accentuates the poetic technique of ellipses, the passionate tone of the question.[757] The repeated use of the denial לא in v. 9 indicates Yahweh's determination not to punish.[758] The subsequent use of לא־איש indicates that it is a divine act, not a human one. The chiasm in v. 9 with framing synonymous parallelism indicates the depth of the revelation of God:[759]

כי אל אנכי ולא־איש

בקרבך קדוש

The highlight of this parallelism is that Yahweh is God, the Holy One (completely different from humans), and that He is in their midst. The function of the repetition of יחרדו in 11:10-11 is to indicate the intended result of Yahweh's act of love to refrain from punishing without the loss of fear of Yahweh. The terms symbolise the continuing relationship between Yahweh and Israel. To express Yahweh's love, Hosea employs terms to express God's decision and personality, to show that He loves them though they continued to reject Him and follow other gods.

'They shall return to the land of Egypt,' talks about the return. The root word שוב appears at the beginning and at the end of this chapter that creates inclusion in reading. According to Harper, the word repetition produces word play to understand that the people of Israel refuse to return to God or turn from their sin; if they do not return to God they will return to Egypt.[760] The idea of punishment is presented here. Their choice could be to return to Egypt or continue to remain in sinful life. The emotional sense is presented in the form of heart where the idea of reversal can be seen here. The idiom describes a decisive change of heart from destruction to make blessing to others. The emotional change and heart's decision of God changes from wrath to future restoration. The function of the prophetic announcement of future restoration is found in 11:10-11. The important aspect found here are the divine intention and God's care and love for the people of Israel. God's tender affection and love is demonstrated by His compassion. Yahweh's love for Israel is to stand firm with their God and be ruled by God. The message ends with a positive connotation that God will restore them.

The importance of Yahweh's use of Hosea through human love relationships to emphasise the covenantal relationship is described strongly here in the love images throughout Chapter 11. God had a message for His people. The theme of love is repeated three times in 11:1 and 4. The theme "love" as the predominant of chapter 11 and describes how the love relationship between Yahweh and Israel existed even

---

[757] H.W. Wolff, *Hosea,* Hermeneia, Fortress Press, 1978, 194; Kakkanattu, *God's Enduring Love in the Book of Hosea: A Synchronic and Diachronic...,* Moherbeck, 2005, 78.

[758] Andersen and Freedman, *Hosea,* Anchor Bible, Garden City, Doubleday, 1980, 589.

[759] W. Brueggemann, *Theology of the Old Testament,* Minneapolis, Fortress Press, 1997, 289. Cf. W. Eichrodt, The Holy One in Your Midst: The Theology of Hosea, *Interpretation* 15, 1961, 259-273.

[760] W.R. Harper, *A Critical and Exegetical Commentary on Amos and Hosea,* Edinburgh, T and T Clark, 1956, 367.

when the people were suffering from slavery in the land of Egypt. Dempsey points out that the image in 11:4 brings out the metaphor of father and son.[761] The idea that is brought out is that Yahweh treated Israel with cords of love to draw her to Him. His parental love motivated Him to do this. The cords of humanity also can be understood as "cords of love," in this case Yahweh.

4.2.2. Progressive Texture

In progressive texture (Hosea 11), there are four main elements: "when / because," "from me," "taking Him by His arms" and the "theme of election." Each of these helps to unfold the progressive texture.

Table 16: Progression texture table

v. 1	נער ישראל	Israel was a child
	וממצרים קראתי	(Israel) was called out of Egypt
v. 2	הלכו מפניהם	(Israel) went from me
	לבעלים יזבחו	(Israel) kept sacrificing to Baals
	ולפסלים יקטרון	(Israel) burning incense to idols
v. 3	ולא ידעו	(Israel) did not know
v. 5	לא ישוב אל-ארץ מצרים	(Israel) shall return to the land of Egypt
	ואשור הוא מלכו	Assyria shall be their kings
	מאנו לשוב	(Israel) have refused to return to me
v. 6	וחלה חרב בעריו	The sword shall rage against (Israel's) cities
	וכלתה בדיו	Consume the bars of (Israel's) gates
	ואכלה—ממעצותיהם	Devour (Israel) is their fortress
v. 7	ועמי תלואים למשובתי	(Israel) are bent on turning away from me
		(Israel) are appointed to the yoke
		(Israel) none shall remove it

4.2.2.1. The Role of כי

In progressive texture, Hosea 11 begins with the rhetorical question of כי ("when"). The first part of Hosea11:1 begins with the verbal clause כי.[762] The usage brings out perplexity, but this clause introduces rich possibilities of understanding the biblical text. Hosea 11 begins with the rhetorical question of כי ("when"). Macintosh identifies כי in his work by comparing it with Isa. 43:2. Ancient versions translate the conjunction in a causal sense ("because") which is connected to the phrase in

[761] Carol J. Dempsey, *The Prophets: A Liberation-Critical Reading,* Minneapolis, Fortress Press, 2000, 157.

[762] Williams, 'Annotated Bibliography on Hosea,' *RevExp* 72, 1975, 495-501.

10:15, "I loved him from his childhood."[763] According to Harper כי is temporal, not causal.[764] However, Ibn Ezra and Kimchi argue that כי is used here in the temporal sense and interpreted as the discipline of a child applied to Israel (cf. Deut. 8:5), and they continue that the connection is between punishment and parental love. God's attitude to Israel is compared to a father's protective care and disciplining love in his dealing with his son. The father-son metaphor indicates dependency and a sure relation of belonging and fellowship with God.

On the other hand, Macintosh quotes Jerome's argument that the conjunction conveys the meaning that Yahweh loved Israel, but because of her helplessness, she was taken as captive to Egypt.[765] The Greek translation is οτι / διοτι, meaning "because." The conjunction helps to see the varied possibilities of understanding the biblical text. If the preposition כי is taken in the temporal sense, it facilitates the reference where God considers Israel as His *first-born*. This further refers to Ex. 4:22, where Pharaoh is reminded that Israel is God's son with the temporal sense (see כי). Kimchi confirms the use of the preposition מן "from (the time) of Egypt I began to call him "My son."[766] The rhetorical question denotes a positive outcome from future captivity.

In Hosea 11:1, כי is translated in Greek as "when," or "that," or "because," but the exact Greek translation is διοτι "because." This makes it difficult to understand. Since Hebrew has לבני *(i.e., "to my son")*, the Greek translation τα τεκνα αυτου *("I called the children of His")* refers to Israel's children. In the ICC commentary, the author notes that Rudolph's readings of the Greek and Targum translations both have plural form "His children," and this is understood to be a Christological interpretation.[767] Hosea uses comparative particle כי to refer to images that refer to God. The reason is that Hosea wanted to avoid any misunderstanding that God will not be compared with the nature of any other gods. Here, verbal metaphors present God metaphorically as father.

4.2.2.2. From Me - מפניהם

The following progressive texture follows with the phrase "from me," because it further develops Hosea's redemptive theme, in which the repetitive terms "love" and "calling" are initiated. The most common textual variant is מפניהם, which is usually translated "from their faces." The variant texts of the MT cf. Vulgate פנים reads, "The more they called to them, the more they went away from them." If the second reading of the MT is to be followed, the question is who called whom? McComisky notes that it was God's prophets who were calling the Israelites; Garrett[768] however, says, the

763 Macintosh, A.A, *A Critical and Exegetical Commentary on Hosea,* Edinburgh, T and T Clark, 1997, 435-436.

764 W.R. Harper, *A Critical and Exegetical Commentary on Amos and Hosea,* Edinburgh, T and T Clark, 1956, 361.

765 Macintosh, A.A, *A Critical and Exegetical Commentary on Hosea, Edinburgh,* T and T Clark, 1997, 435-436.

766 Macintosh, A.A, *A Critical and Exegetical Commentary on Hosea,* Edinburgh, T and T Clark, 1997, 436-437.

767 Macintosh, A.A, *A Critical and Exegetical Commentary on Hosea,* Edinburgh, T and T Clark, 1997, 439.

768 Garrett, *Hosea, Joel,* NAC, 19A, Nashville, Broadman and Holman, 1997, 88-91.

prophets were calling the Egyptians, and Sweeney argues it was the Israelites who were calling the Egyptians.

But Sweeney's proposal has the advantage of scriptural precedent in Israel's repeated complaints against the leadership in the days of the Exodus and during the wilderness wanderings.[769] As Sweeney observes, "Insofar as the passage later highlights the issue of the return to Egypt in v. 5, there is a problem that the passage refers to Israel's continuous expression of the desire to return to Egypt and its seeking foreign gods in the wilderness."[770] But the more the prophets appealed to the people to follow the Lord, the more the people turned aside from following Him. The image concept brings out that the 'worship of idols' means going away from Yahweh's loving act and adopting cultic practices. Hosea reminds the people of their election and Exodus to encourage them to return to Him. Thus, the reading of "from me" as refusing to Yahweh better fits the context and clearly brings out the meaning of the text.

4.2.2.3. Taking Him by His Arms

Another important aspect is found in the progressive texture in Hosea 9:10, this version of the second line is accepted almost universally by scholars although the word "taking him by his arms" (JPS) is additional to line one and is as close to the MT as an alternative. MT has *"I took them by or upon in his (my) arms"* in qal perfect third person masculine singular with the third person masculine plural suffix, and is translated as "he took them up." The Hebrew word has "he took them, here we note the unusual form of קחם (cf. Ezek. 17:5) and a similar abbreviated form of *laqah "in his arms."*[771] This term appears in the middle of the passage which shows that the use of the first person is not right here. The LXX translation reads as ἀνέλαβον αὐτόν means "I took him up." Wolff is of the opinion that the MT text קחם על-זרועתיו is not clearly understood and expressed in the text. Van Rooy investigates whether the text refers to the names of "Israel" "Ephraim" and "Jacob" in the book. The text (11:10) argues that it reflects the traditions of Exodus and Israel's journey in the wilderness (cf. 9:10; 10:1-2; 12:10; 13:4-5).[772] The LXX translates it in the following way: ἀνέλαβον αὐτὸν ἐπὶ τὸν βραχίονά μου means *"I took him up upon the arms of Mine."* Eidavell observes a shift that takes place from *"His arms"* to *"My arms."*[773] The LXX reading however, is adopted and supported by modern English translations.

The key word in this verse is "love," and so the apostasy to the Baals becomes quite unclear: Wolff says that Yahweh helped the people of Israel to grow independently. Dearman points out that here Yahweh is referred to as a parent extending His arms זרועות and this is as a rich image in order to show how much Yahweh loves his people.[774] Macintosh says that MT translates it in the third person singular suffix.

---

[769] Sweeney, Marvin A. *Twelve Prophets,* 2 vols, Collegeville, Liturgical Press, 2000, 113.

[770] Sweeney, Marvin A. *Twelve Prophets,* 2 vols, Collegeville, Liturgical Press, 2000, 113.

[771] Davies G. I. *Hosea, New Century Bible Commentary,* Grand Rapids, Wm. B. Eerdmans pub co, 1992, 256. Cf. Wood J. Leon, *The Prophets of Israel,* Grand Rapids, Baker Academic Group, 1979, 255.

[772] H. F. Van Rooy, The Names of Israel, Ephraim and Jacob in the book of Hosea, *VT* 6, 1993, 138. H.W. Wolff, *A Commentary on the book of the Prophet Hosea,* Philadelphia, Fortress Press, 1982, 44.

[773] Goran Eidevall, *Grapes in the Desert: Metaphors, Models and Themes in Hosea 4-11,* Stockholm, Almqvist and Wiksell International, 1996, 171.

[774] Dearman, *The Book of Hosea,* NICOT, Grand Rapids, Wm. B. Eerdmans company, 2010, 282.

The MT reading is incorrect and there is a corruption in the text itself with the preceding and following third person plural suffix, and this is supported by other translations.[775] The argument here is that the MT term did not use the written form of the language but used the spoken form; more precisely, from a comment spoken by the prophet himself, or by a later editor. James Limburg writes: "Yahweh taught him to walk and he took them by His arms," showing the divine statement from Yahweh who continues to care for them and protects them.[776] Wolff reads it in this way: *"and I who took them in My arms,"* but Stuart makes it clear that any pronoun that is translated here means "taking them by the arms." This view is supported by Garrett and other English translations prefers emendation to "taking them in arms."[777] The picture presented here is that of Yahweh as a father teaching his child to walk, bending down to hold her hand. The metaphor of teaching a child (Israel) to walk depicts the past event of Israel when they walked out of Egypt.

Eidavell notes that the meaning of this phrase is God's loving care and protection is obviously the point that is stressed here.[778] Dearman brings out the contrast with Israel's lack of knowledge of God's concern "but they did not know that I healed them."[779] Israel could not see that Yahweh had been the key to Israel's well-being as he "taught them to walk" through their history, holding them by the hand.[780] In the same way, Limburg describes the imagery of parent-child to emphasise how God loved, taught to walk and healed, all of which denote a parent's care.[781] The progression of the term is קחם helps to understand the texture: Yahweh who taught Israel to walk took them by his arms.

4.2.2.4. The Theme of Election

God's love is visible through the saving acts in leading Israel out from the land of Egypt. God's love further showed in delivering the people and saving them during their journey. Because of God's love, curse was turned into blessing. From punishment and judgment, the theme culminates in election. The concept of election is an integral part of the progressive texture because God loved His people, delivered them from Egypt and brought them to the Promised Land.

According to Wolff, the characteristic of Deutronomic idea occurs first in Hosea. Thus, we find reminiscences of the exodus from Egypt that there is Yahweh's love.[782] Wolff states that the prophet makes use of the concept of love in order to interpret God's election of his people. Hosea's catch אהב word passes through his circle of traditionists into Deuteronomy. Thus, the strong focus in Deuteronomy on God's love

---

[775] Macintosh, A.A, *A Critical and Exegetical Commentary on Hosea,* Edinburgh, T and T Clark, 1997, 443.

[776] James Limburg, *Hosea-Micah,* Westminster, John Knox press, 2011, 39.

[777] Garrett, *Hosea, Joel,* NAC, 19A, Nashville, Broadman and Holman, 1997, 223.

[778] Goran Eidevall, Grapes in the Desert: Metaphors, Models and Themes in Hosea 4-11, Stockholm, Almqvist and Wiksell International, 1996, 167-168; *NIDOTTE*, Vol. 3, 401.

[779] Dearman, *The Book of Hosea,* NICOT, Grand Rapids, Wm. B. Eerdmans Company, 2010, 282-283.

[780] Macintosh, A.A., *A Critical and Exegetical Commentary on Hosea,* Edinburgh, T and T Clark, 1997, 435-436.

[781] James Limburg, *Hosea-Micah,* Westminster, John Knox Press, 2011, 39-40.

[782] H.W. Wolff, Hosea: A Commentary on the Book of Hosea, Philadelphia, Fortress Press, 1974, xxxi.

has its roots in Hosea's prophesying on this topic. Zobel speaks about the relationship between Hosea and Deuteronomy in his monograph and this is one of the major contributions to the study where he goes through the texts about God's love of Israel. He argues that the theological aspect of Yahweh's love of Israel is due to Hosea's work, and in the eighth century prophets it is found only in him. Not until several generations later did Deuteronomy take this theological idea into the very centre of its theology.[783]

The development of the theological concept of Yahweh's love follows the path from Hosea in the eighth century BCE to the later Deuteronomy in the seventh and sixth century BCE. According to Zobel, the predominantly image loaded and emotional portrayal of God's love in Hosea is transformed into a more universal theological concept in Deuteronomy.[784] God's divine love in both Deuteronomy and Hosea concentrates on God's election of His people and His choosing to enter into a relationship with Israel. The basis of God's love is not found in the merit of the people but exclusively in God alone. The table shows the progression of the theme of election in the passage.

Table 17: Progression table 2

v. 1	ואהבהו	I loved him
	קראתי	I called my son
v. 2	קראו	I called them
v. 3	תרגלתי	I taught
	קחם	I took them up
	רפאתים	I healed them
v. 4	אמשכם	I led them
	ואהיה	I became to them
	ואט אליו	I bent down to them
v. 8	אתנך	I give you up
	אמגנך	I hand you over
	אשימך כצבאים	I treat you like Zeboiim
v. 9	לא אעשה	I will not execute
	לא אשוב לשחת	I will not again destroy
	לא אעשה	I will not destroy

In Hosea 11, the prophet goes further back into the first stages of Israel's history. He specifically mentions Israel's very beginning. According to Harper chapter 11 is in contrast to the tradition taken up in 9:10 and 10:11.[785] Israel's history begins

[783] K. Zobel, *Prophetie und Deuternomium: Die Reception Prophetischer,* BZAW 199: Berlin, de Gruyter, 1992, 49.

[784] K. Zobel, *Prophetie und Deuternomium: Die Reception Prophetischer,* BZAW 199: Berlin, de Gruyter, 1992, 49-50.

[785] W.R. Harper, *A Critical and Exegetical Commentary on Amos and Hosea,* Edinburgh, T and T Clark, 1956, 364.

with the concept of election, an election out of bondage, because of God's love. Philip King affirms that historically, Israel's beginning was with the Exodus, an event which has roots in the past; but theologically, the beginning was rooted in love and election.[786] Israel's whole existence, present, past and future, depended on God's continuing love and the perpetual election expressed in the covenant. Bosh says that God considered that the eschatological act brings other nations to Jerusalem to worship Him through the covenant He made with the universe.[787] In the biblical language, imagery is applied in regard to the purpose. C. Wright rightly puts Israel in the Old Testament image that they were not chosen against other nations but for the sake of rest of the nation.[788] Calling Israel into existence affirms them for a reason. In Hosea it is clear that God has elected them for a specific commission and action. The people of Israel thus become an embodiment of proclamation of the message of inclusivity to other nations.

The significance of Israel's election is Yahweh's love (11:1, 4). This love proves God's divinity in electing them as His own people. Yahweh's love combines calls and actions, though the people disappointed Him by following other gods. At this time, the prophet reminds them of the Deuteronomic law (Deut. 21:18-21) which says that a rebellious son is to be stoned to death. However, in Hosea 11, the stubborn son learns how the father struggles within himself, and how the father's wrath turns into a new expression of divine love. God's love is presented as a powerful and liberating action that makes Israel free and makes it His son. The divine love holds the whole life of Israel as God's people from the beginning and into future which means Israel survives only because of love of God. Hosea clearly brings out the message to Israel that Yahweh has purpose in the lives of Israel. This love is genuine and becomes channel of life for many and for all humankind. Here, we notice that God's nature is loving and cares for Israel's welfare. Israel had the personal experience of being cared for by God and experienced God's love and care for them as well as for strangers. The love of God thus is the basis and reason for the whole existence of Israel.

According to Gaeblein, Hosea is a prophet of judgment to Israel for her unfaithfulness to God's covenant with her, and the overall message to this point has been judgment on Israel.[789] In this passage, a shift takes place and the theme changes from Israel's punishment to God's love in spite of Israel's persistent apostasy.[790] אהב in Hosea 11:4 is used as a metaphor for wild beast and discusses the Exodus and wilderness experience of the Israelites that shows how God cared for His people.[791] God's loving care is obviously the point that is stressed here. Contrasted with this is Israel's lack of the knowledge of God's concern: *"But they did not know that I healed them."*

---

[786] Stanley Jones, *"Exodus Motif in the Book of Hosea and its relevance to the Socio-religious Context of India"* Faith Theological Review, Vol. 16, No. 1, March 2015, 36-37.

[787] Bosch J. David, *Transforming Mission: Paradigm Shifts in Theology and Mission,* Maryknoll, Orbis, 1991, 1718-1719.

[788] C.H. Wright, *Knowing the Holy Spirit Through the Old Testament,* Downers Grove, Inter Varsity Press, 2006, 99-100.

[789] Frank Gaeblein, ed., *The Exposition Bible Commentary, Vol. 7, Daniel and the Minor Prophets,* by Leon Wood, Grand Rapids, Zondervan Publishing House, 1985, 212.

[790] Wood J. Leon, *The Prophets of Israel,* Grand Rapids, Baker Academic group, 1979, 278.

[791] Stanley Jones, *"Exodus Motif in the Book of Hosea and its relevance to the Socio-religious Context of India"* Faith Theological Review, Vol. 16, No. 1, March 2015, 36-37.

Progressive texture explains the role of כי and its function as a rhetorical question in the progressing text. The word כי can be translated as 'when, because' to understand the text in a better way. The progression of the term is קחם, this helps to understand the texture: Yahweh who taught Israel to walk, took them by his arms.

In progressive texture, the first part of Hosea11:1 begins with the verbal clause כי. The following progressive texture follows with the phrase "from me," because it further develops Hosea's redemptive theme, in which the repetitive terms "love" and "calling" are initiated. Another important aspect is found in the progressive texture in Hosea 9:10. This version of the second line is accepted almost universally by scholars although the word "taking him by his arms." Reversal from punishment and judgment, as the theme culminates in election. The concept of election is thus an integral part of the progressive texture because God loved His people, delivered them from Egypt and brought them to the Promised Land. The prophet's use of the word wilderness is to make it clear what is being discussed. The word wilderness refers to the place between Egypt and the Promised Land where Yahweh's concept of marriage to Israel is presented. Wilderness represents metaphorically God's divine care upon His people (Hos. 2:3 [MT 5]).

4.2.3. Narrative Texture

The narrative texture presents God's love for Israel. God reminds the people to forsake their sins and return to him.

Hosea 8-10 talks about Israel's apostasy of sin and her punishment. Now the shift in chapter 11 speaks of God's love and compassion. According to W. Eichrodt, the Hebrew word "love" in Hosea 11 is about passion accompanied with strong emotion. This love is based more on covenantal relationship. Hosea 11 is considered to be "one of the great chapters of the Old Testament," where the text explains Yahweh's love which "reaches an explicit tenderness with details unmatched in the Old Testament."[792] Philip King notes that chapter 11 is portrayed as a poem of God's love for the people of Israel despite all her failings and lack of repentance.[793] There is a close link to the curses of Deuteronomy 4:20-31, where God was prophesied to enforce the terms of his covenant.[794] Hosea would have expected his hearers to realize their disobedience to the broad terms of the covenant.[795] Love is free and involves caring for one another, forgiving others and protecting one another without any precondition. The concept of divine love brings out the acts of God and the response in a positive way. The prophet uses the husband-wife and father-son relationships to portray divine love in both ways: to Israel as well as to other nations Hosea 2-3, 11.

Hosea 11 contains the most poignant yet touching words in all of Hosea. It features a sharp contrast between God's tender reminiscences of His early relationship with Israel and His sorrow at their rejection of Him for Baal despite all that He had

---

[792] Knight, George A. F, *Hosea: Introduction and commentary,* London, SCM Press, 1960, 108.

[793] Philip King, *Amos-Micah: An Archaeological Commentary,* Philadelphia, Westminster, 1988, 25-26.

[794] Gale Yee, *Composition and Tradition in the Book of Hosea: A Redaction-Critical Approach:* SBL Dissertation Series 102, Atlanta, Scholars Press, 1987, 216.

[795] Stuart, Douglas, *Hosea - Jonah,* Waco, Texas, Word Books, 1987, 10.

done for them (11:1-4).[796] The Lord is concerned at their constant lack of fidelity, which now necessitated their coming judgment (11:5-7). Eidavell points out that in a second display of His compassion, the Lord reveals that His abiding love for Israel would mean that His judgment could not and would not spell the end for His people (11:8-9).[797] In a future day, Israel would respond to His call and they will return to their homes and receive His blessings (11:10-11).[798]

4.2.3.1. Exodus Motif

The first portion of Hosea 11 deals with Israel's historic past at a time when God's people were in bondage in Egypt. Guenther notes that it was then that God called His people out of Egypt, redeemed them with a mighty show of force, and led them on their journey toward the Promised Land (v. 1).[799] According to Garrett, Hosea's citation of the Lord's words is in harmony with the familiar Exodus motif that runs throughout the Scriptures (e.g., Ex. 3:8; 12:37-13:19); which when included has both warnings to the people for covenant disobedience (e.g., Jer. 2:5-9; 7:21-29; 11:14-17) and promises of restoration through repentance and surrender to God's will (e.g., Isa. 42:5-7; 61:1-4; Jer. 16:14-15; Ezek. 20:32-38).[800] The Exodus motif reaches its climax in the prophesied New Covenant (Jer. 23:7-8; 31:31-37; 32:40-41; Ezek. 37:21-28). In the Lord's adaptation of the exodus motif, He portrays Himself as a parent to His child Israel. The metaphor of God as a father to his son Israel, is common enough in the Old Testament (e.g., Ex. 4:22; Deut. 14:1-2; Isa. 1:2; Jer.3:19; 4:22), but here it is connected to the theme of deliverance.[801] As Vos notes, "the Exodus from Egypt is the Old Testament redemption…[802] This view is supported by Stanley Jose: that it is Yahweh who called Israel out of Egypt and brought them to Promised Land.[803] In a very real sense Israel's deliverance from the power of the Egyptians was an act of redemption both physically and spiritually.

4.2.3.2. Imagery of Father - Son Relationship

In chapters 9 and 10 Yahweh recounted Israel's sin and punishment, but now the tone becomes personal and affectionate. Chapter 11 clearly portrays that the speech is by Yahweh himself since chapter 11 contains elements of a court case with evidence (vv. 1-4), judgment (5-7), insights into judge's mind and reconsideration (8-1),[804] Wolff calls it a "historical theological accusation" in respect of a child's rebellion, breaching Deuteronomy 21:18-21.[805] The text of Hosea 11 can be seen as a working

---

[796] Goran Eidevall, *Grapes in the Desert: Metaphors, Models and Themes in Hosea 4-11,* Stockholm, Almqvist and Wiksell International, 1996, 167-168.

[797] Goran Eidevall, *Grapes in the Desert: Metaphors, Models and Themes in Hosea 4-11,* Stockholm, Almqvist and Wiksell International, 1996, 178.

[798] Ben Zvi, E, *Hosea,* Grand Rapids, Eerdmans, 2005, 226. Cf. Allen R. Guenther, *Hosea-Amos,* Scottdale, Herald Press, 1938/1997, 177.

[799] Allen R. Guenther, *Hosea-Amos,* Scottdale, Herald Press, 1938/1997, 178-179.

[800] Garrett, *Hosea, Joel,* NAC, 19A, Nashville, Broadman and Holman, 1997, 253-254.

[801] Dearman, *The Book of Hosea, NICOT,* Grand Rapids, Wm. B. Eerdmans company, 2010, 277.

[802] Geerhardus Vos, *Biblical Theology,* Grand Rapids, Eerdmans, 1954, 124.

[803] Stanley Jones, *"Exodus Motif in the Book of Hosea and its relevance to the Socio-religious Context of India"* Faith Theological Review, Vol. 16, No. 1, March 2015, 36-37.

[804] Allen R. Guenther, *Hosea-Amos,* Scottdale, Herald Press, 1938/1997, 177.

[805] Wolff, Hans Walter, *Hosea,* Philadelphia, Fortress Press, 1974, 193.

out of the threatened curse, with the difference that the judge decides to partly lift the curse at the end despite any mention of repentance. This section, a divine speech, begins with a reference to Israel's history in order to contrast the past with the present (cf. 9:10; 10:1, 9). "The passage at its outset has similarities with the form of the legal complaint made by parents against a rebellious child (Deut. 21:18-21; cf. Isa. 1:2-20 where hope is held out that the child [Israel] may yet repent and receive compassion rather than death)."[806]

Though the son acts as if he had no father, Yahweh's love towards him is continuous; this is steadfast love. The rebellious son (cf. Hos. 4:16, 9:15, 13:16), according to the law, is to be stoned to death (Deut. 21:18-21). But in this passage, Israel, the stubborn son, was redeemed by Yahweh's love (v. 8). Mays comments that the oracle could well belong to the middle years of Hosea's life when Israel's king had provoked the retribution of Shalmaneser V (727-722 BCE) by withholding tributes and appealing to Egypt (2Kgs. 17:4), and the final end of the nation was all too obvious.[807]

Hosea 11:1-4 serves as an explanation of Yahweh's historical association with and care of his son. The accused party is addressed in the third person. Hosea 11:5-7 shows the results of the people's unfaithfulness towards Yahweh and their subsequent punishment. Hosea 11:8-11 deals with salvation and the consequences of reconciliation and the reaching of a settlement.

Hosea 11:1-4 serves as an explanation of Yahweh's historical association with and care of his son. But in this passage, Israel, the stubborn son, was redeemed by Yahweh's love.

4.2.4. Opening-Middle-Closing Texture

Opening-Middle-Closing texture is about the beginning, body and conclusion of a selected pericope. The opening-middle-closing texture section explains Yahweh as father. Hosea reminds the Israelites of the message conveyed by Moses and how they were elected by Him when they were in Egypt.

4.2.4.1. Opening Texture and Imagery

The pericope 11:1-11 begins with Yahweh's reference in v. 1 proving his love when he called Israel out of Egypt. Verse 11 ends with the promise of the love of Yahweh: והושבתים על־בתיהם describes Yahweh as a judicial and righteous father, (vv. 2-4); the people's refusal (vv. 2-3, 7); threat to punish (vv. 5-6); Yahweh's inner struggle (vv. 8-9) and prophecy of the return of Israel (vv. 10-11).

4.2.4.1.1. Parental imagery - When Israel was a Child I loved Him

The opening texture begins with the statement כי נער ישׂראל ואהבהו *"When Israel was a child I loved him."* This phrase is reminiscent of the opening verse in Hosea 9:15 where Israel is portrayed as Yahweh's son and they are reminded God delivered them from Egypt.[808] According to Kuhnigk, "patriarch" refers to Israel, and Israel's sons

---

[806] Stuart, Douglas, *Hosea - Jonah,* Waco, Texas, Word Books, 1987, 175.

[807] Mays, James Luther., *Hosea: A Commentary,* OTL, Philadelphia, Westminster, 1969, 152. Cf. Stuart, D, *Hosea - Jonah,* Waco, Word, 1987, 182.

[808] Allen R. Guenther, *Hosea-Amos,* Scottdale, Herald Press, 1938/1997, 178.

are mentioned in the plural form in v. 1b[809] The LXX reading misses the connection between Israel and a historical person (perhaps Jacob) whose sons are delivered from the land of Egypt.[810] MT makes it clear that it refers to Egypt, and Targum endorses it. The Hebrew term נער means "child, young man, lad" (cf. Jer. 1:6) and refers to Israel, whom Yahweh loved ואהבהו.[811] Garrett suggests that נער connotes no precise age but it could mean adolescence.[812] Kuhnigk translates this as "slave, servant."[813]

Macintosh considers this phrase the main clause. For him "I set my love upon him" reiterates that the relationship focuses on Yahweh's love and (cf. Deut. 4:32-40) that He had chosen them to be His people[814] (cf. Amos. 3:2, which reflects Ex. 19:5-6). This is very similar in relation to 9:10 and 10:1. The verb ואהבהו is translated as *"I came to love him"* and marks a beginning of life of the people of Israel.[815] The term אהב in this context implies Yahweh's care, affection, protection and guidance.

The opening texture reiterates the covenant between God and Israel by reminding her that he has chosen them to be his covenant people. He has brought her out of Egypt and has proven that he is Israel's deliverer and protector. That means their history is determined by God's constant effort and intervention to bring them back within his fold and to make them to be witnesses to others.

4.2.4.1.2. Parental imagery - Yahweh Taught Ephraim to Walk

Here, the tender figure of a parent teaching a child to walk shows God's care, love and compassion in disciplining them (Israel). ואנכי תרגלתי לאפרים *"it was I who taught Ephraim to walk."* תרגלתי is a rare verb form Tiphel, perfect, first person singular with an unusual meaning for the root "foot." Harper calls "I" in contrast with the Baalim, and introduces another description of Yahweh's act of parental love.[816] Wolff calls it an "anomalous form."[817] Macintosh agrees with Wolff on the verb תרגלתי. Vv. 3 and 4 show the love of God expressed in the metaphor or analogy of Yahweh as a loving parent, both father and mother (emendation of v. 4b, c).[818]The father either (1) went before His child to walk or (2) went before His child as an example of protection.[819] The Hebrew תרגלתי is generally understood to be a rare tiphel form of a denominative verb from the noun רגול ("foot"). The unusual קחם is qal perfect third person masculine

---

[809] Kuhnigk, *Biblica Orientalia* 27, Rome, Biblical Institute Press, 1974, 127.

[810] Andersen, F.I and Freedman, D.N., *Hosea: A New Translation with Introduction and Commentary,* New York, Doubleday, 1980, 577.

[811] H.W. Wolff, *Hosea,* Hermeneia, Fortress Press, 1974, 197-198.

[812] Garrett, D., *Hosea, Joel: An Exegetical and Theological Exposition of Holy Scripture,* B and H Publisher, 1997, 249.

[813] H.W. Wolff, *Hosea,* Hermeneia, Fortress Press, 1974, 197-198.

[814] Macintosh, A.A, *A Critical and Exegetical Commentary on Hosea,* Edinburgh, T and T Clark, 1997, 437.

[815] Mays, James Luther, *Hosea: A Commentary,* OTL, Philadelphia, Westminster, 1969, 153.

[816] W.R. Harper, *A Critical and Exegetical Commentary on Amos and Hosea,* Edinburgh, T and T Clark, 1956, 363.

[817] Wolff, Hans Walter, *Hosea,* Philadelphia, Fortress Press, 1974, and Andersen, F I and Freedman, D N, *Hosea: A New Translation with introduction and commentary,* Garden City, Doubleday, 1980, 578

[818] J.L. Mays, *Hosea,* London, SCM Press, 1969, 154.

[819] Lewis. Jack P, *New International Version Study Bible,* Grand Rapids, Zondervan Bible Publishers, 1985, 1334.

singular with the third person masculine plural suffix and is perhaps to be taken as a rare infinitive from the verb קחם ("to take"), hence to be understood as "taking them."[820] Here, a shift is seen where Yahweh speaks in the first person. Dearman comments that ל "is to do with Yahweh's parental arms (זרועות)." He stretches His arm (cf. Ex. 15:16; Deut. 4:34; 11:2) to preserve the people from Egypt and to enable them to enter the Promised Land.[821] However, Macintosh states that the MT has a third person singular suffix. The shift from the plural "them" to "his own" (MT) may emphasise God's instructions for not only corporate Israel but individual Israelites.[822] Ephraim refers to the Northern Kingdom (Jeroboam I). Hosea uses "Ephraim" more than any other of the prophets in prophetic literature. The frequent use of the term "Ephraim" is almost equal to "Israel."[823] Among Biblical scholars, there is a general opinion that Hosea's name appears to be an Ephraimite name and also there is a suggestion that perhaps Hosea himself was an Ephraimite.

The covenant between God and Israel plays a determinant factor in the care and discipline of Israel by God. He has taken care of them and disciplined them like a Father. He has shown them his gracious compassion and loving protection even though they do not deserve it. It is the model of a Father dealing with his child in a gentle and patient manner to keep them in the covenantal relationship. His love and discipline become an example for corporate Israel and for others to follow.

4.2.4.2. Middle Texture

The major part of the middle texture consists of the concept of election. The phrase that shows this is "Israel… called my son out of Egypt," which Bengel translates as *"From the time that he (Israel) was in Egypt, I called my son."* This has a definite parallelism with a reference in Matthew 2:24. John Walton identifies the idea that this has a relationship with the concept of the Messiah and relates to the people.[824] Stanley Jose comments that Hosea 12:9 and Hosea 13:4 use the words "from Egypt," to mean, from the time that they sojourn in Egypt."[825] Exodus 4:22 also shows that Israel was called by God, "My son," from the time of his Egyptian sojourn (Isa. 43:1). God is always said to have led or brought forth, not to have "called," Israel from Egypt. God included the Messiah and because of the Messiah, Israel was included, in one unit, as the head and the body. Isa. 49:3 calls Him "Israel." The same general reason, danger of extinction, caused the infant Jesus, and Israel in its national infancy (cf. Gen. 42: 1-43:34 45:18 46:3, 4; Eze. 16:4-6, Jer. 31:20) to sojourn in Egypt, so He, and His spiritual Israel, are already called "God's sons" while yet in the Egypt of the world.

---

[820] Andersen, F I and Freedman, D N, *Hosea: A New Translation with Introduction and Commentary,* Garden City, Doubleday, 1980, 578.

[821] Dearman, *The Book of Hosea,* NICOT, Grand Rapids, Wm. B. Eerdmans Company, 2010, 282.

[822] Macintosh, A.A, *A Critical and Exegetical Commentary on Hosea,* Edinburgh, T and T Clark, 1997, 443.

[823] Andersen, F I and Freedman, D N, *Hosea: A New Translation with Introduction and Commentary,* Garden City, Doubleday, 1980, 579.

[824] John H. Walton, *Zondervan Illustrated Bible Backgrounds Commentary,* vol. 5, Grand Rapids, Zondervan publishing house, 1984, 31.

[825] Stanley Jones, *"Exodus Motif in the Book of Hosea and its relevance to the Socio-religious Context of India"* Faith Theological Review, Vol. 16, No. 1, March 2015, 36-37.

The shift of status occurs when Israel was delivered from slavery; Jeremias says that calling refers to God's action.[826] The reference is to do with the Exodus event of travelling from Egypt to Canaan and settling into the Promised Land where their status is changed from slavery to sonship. The important aspect noted is love as a covenantal term which symbolises election. Apart from the concept of election, the conjunction "כי" is a significant part of the middle texture.

4.2.4.3. Closing Texture

The closing texture begins with the verse: ואל־על יקראהו יחד *"and to upon they call him together"* which can also be translated as "determined to turn away from Yahweh." This further stresses refusal to repent. Wolff modifies the text and reads it as לא בעלו meaning "and to Baal they call." Similarly, Stuart modifies the text to read "and to Baal they call." However, JPS translates it as "and though they call them upwards," Stuart translates it as "all together they exalt him." Here it is important to note that the change of negative particle לא "not" to לו "to him," a call to the "Most High" is relevant - not Baal (who does not exist) but Yahweh (who has decided on punishment). Macintosh comments on "call" which recurs in v. 1. God once "called" kindly and now Israel "calls" in vain. In addition, "turn from" recurs in v. 2 for emphasis and also to stress the consequence in v. 6 return to Egypt.[827]

God's pain of unrequited love after Israel's revolt is shown by the repetition of "my" and "me." Wolff says that the Hebrew text of the last part of v. 7 is very difficult to understand.[828] The Greek translation differs slightly. Where the MT says "And my people turning away (from) me," the Greek has καὶ ὁ λαὸς αὐτοῦ ἐπικρεμάμενος ἐκ τῆς κατοικίας αὐτοῦ "and His people are being hung up out of His dwelling place." יחד לא ירומם translates as "none at all exalts Him." This phrase expresses the problem of fallen humankind, especially the covenant people (e.g., Isa. 53:6), who are not ready to repent.

The Hebrew word רפא used for "healing" is better understood in its connection with the liberation from the land of Egypt than as refereeing to Yahweh's care of Israel in the wilderness. Yahweh is the one who brought the people from bondage, not Baal. רפא is translated as "that Yahweh healed." Dearman says that the Hebrew term רפא means nurture, and divine healing is metaphorically explained.[829] This term appears five times in the book (Hos. 5:13; 6:1; 7:1; 14:4).[830] According to Lohfink, healing twice refers to the physical aspect of healing, transferred from the family to the whole nation as a community.[831] But Dearman says that healing refers to Yahweh's healing,

---

[826] Jeremias, *Der Prophet Hosea,* 141-142.

[827] Macintosh, A.A., *A Critical and Exegetical Commentary on Hosea,* Edinburgh, T and T Clark, 1997, 457.

[828] Wolff, Hans Walter, *Hosea,* Philadelphia, Fortress Press, 1974, 192.

[829] Gale Yee, *Composition and Tradition in the Book of Hosea: A Redaction-Critical Approach:* SBL Dissertation Series 102, Atlanta, Scholars Press, 1987, 132-133.

[830] Allen R. Guenther, *Hosea-Amos,* Scottdale, Herald Press, 1938/1997, 178-179. Goran Eidevall, *Grapes in the Desert: Metaphors, Models and Themes in Hosea 4-11,* Stockholm, Almqvist and Wiksell International, 1996, 171. Cf. W.R. Harper, *A Critical and Exegetical Commentary on Amos and Hosea,* Edinburgh, T and T Clark, 1956, 363.

[831] Lohfink, "*Ich bin Jahwe dein Artz,*" 46-47.

which is the restoration of the relationship between Yahweh and Israel.[832] Macintosh comments that the verb "healed," qal perfect is often used for God forgiving sin, as seen in Hosea 5:13, 6:1; 7:1; and Ex. 15:26. The parallelism of Ps. 163:3 and Isa. 1:5-6 are examples of national sin described in terms of a physical disease that is healed and also protection from danger and threat.[833] Yahweh points out the unthinkable in v. 3, that his people, despite His love act, ולא ידעו כי רפאתים did not acknowledge that He healed them. Hosea uses the father-son image to highlight this.

The opening-middle-closing texture section thus explains Yahweh as father. Hosea reminds the Israelites of the message conveyed by Moses and how they were elected by Him when they were in Egypt. The opening texture opens with the statement *"When Israel was a child I loved him,"* the tender figure of a parent teaching a child to walk shows God's care, love and compassion in disciplining them (Israel). The covenant between God and Israel plays a determinant factor in the care and discipline of Israel by God. The major part of the middle texture consists of the concept of election. The closing texture begins with "and to upon they call him together."

4.2.5. Argumentative Texture

The argumentative texture deal with sacrificing to Baal and for this Hosea warns Israel about the judgment and punishment. The text displays characteristics of a historical-theological accusation.[834] Therefore, it recalls the historical Exodus from Egypt (v. 1), the subsequent care of Yahweh in the wilderness (vv. 3-4); the action of the prophets (v. 2); the Baal worship of Israel (v. 2); the disregard towards Yahweh (v. 3); and Yahweh's persuasive love (vv. 8-9). The prophecy regarding Israel's return (vv. 10-11), is the desired outcome of the father's accusation.[835] In order to make escape from punishment, the prophet uses figurative language of an affectionate father to persuade them to return to Him in true repentance.

The term "Baal" in the book plays an important role. The term occurs both in singular and plural forms. The plural form *Baalim* is a focus mainly on polytheism and deities of their cults.[836] לבעלים is here translated in the verbal form. The literal meaning is "to the Baals." The "Baal" here means the master or the husbands. This refers to the male Canaanite fertility god. "They kept sacrificing to the Baals and burning incense to idols."[837] These two lines of poetry occur in parallel. Nothing is known of animal sacrifices to Baal; therefore, the sacrifices (piel imperfect) may refer to offering incense (piel imperfect).[838] The association of *qtr* and *zbh* (sacrifice) is

---

[832] Dearman, *The Book of Hosea,* NICOT, Grand Rapids, Wm. B. Eerdmans company, 2010, 282.

[833] Macintosh, A.A, *A Critical and Exegetical Commentary on Hosea,* Edinburgh, T and T Clark, 1997, 444-445.

[834] H.W. Wolff, *Hosea,* Hermeneia, Fortress Press, 1974, 193; cf. Stuart, D., *Hosea - Jonah,* Waco, Word, 1987, 175.

[835] Allen R. Guenther, *Hosea-Amos,* Scottdale, Herald Press, 1938/1997, 177.

[836] W.R. Harper, *A Critical and Exegetical Commentary on Amos and Hosea,* Edinburgh, T and T Clark, 1956, 463.

[837] Dearman, *The Book of Hosea,* NICOT, Grand Rapids, Wm. B. Eerdmans Company, 2010, 280-281

[838] Andersen, F I and Freedman, D N, *Hosea: A New Translation with Introduction and Commentary,* Garden City, New York, Doubleday, 1980, 578.

common in Kings (cf. 1Kgs. 22:44).[839] There was however a practice of sacrificing children to Molech, the fertility fire god. This practice is referred in Hosea as the "slaughter of children." Macintosh brings to notice that it echoes the earlier judgment and people's suffering under the Assyrian power. The people of Israel turned to other nations for help instead of turning to Yahweh.[840] According to Haran, the verb is used in the P source and Pentateuch in terms of hiphil conjugation that refers to incense burning (2:15; 4:13; 11:2).[841] But Heger differs from Haran and says that the word "sacrifice" has nothing to do with flesh sacrifice in connection with incense.[842] The verb *qtr* in Hosea (2:15; 4:3; 11:2) refers to illegitimate alien worship and sacraments that are offered to the false gods during the time of Hosea.

Dearman brings to notice the failure of Gomer and her children in chapters 1-2. Here it denotes the failure of Israel in not responding faithfully to Yahweh, and the people are reminded about their waywardness. It reminds the listener of the story of Gomer who betrayed her spouse in a similar way to that in which the Israelites violated sonship.[843]

Other nations are mentioned in Hosea 11:2: Israel sacrificed to Baal, and this means that the people's identity, at least in the eyes of other nations who saw them making these sacrifices, was perhaps under question. It is in this context that Yahweh uses the parent-child metaphor to speak to His people.[844] He wanted them, and others who saw them making these sacrifices, to know that He was indeed a god who would not leave them, even though they themselves had forsaken their own children in the fires of Molech. That means, even though the Israelites had sacrificed their own children, sinned or turned away Yahweh would not break His covenant with his own children: Israel.

The text displays characteristics of a historical-theological accusation. The prophet uses figurative language of an affectionate father to persuade them to return to Him with true repentance. The term "Baal" in Hosea plays an important role. Here it denotes the failure of Israel in not responding faithfully to Yahweh, and the people are reminded about their waywardness. Yahweh uses the parent child metaphor to speak to His people.

4.2.6. Sensory-Aesthetic Texture - three "body-zones"

According to Malina, there are three "body-zones"[845] in the sensory-aesthetic texture that can contribute to the understanding of the text. They are the zones of emotion-fused thinking, self-expressive speech and purposeful action.

---

[839] Davies. G. I, *Hosea, New century Bible commentary,* Grand Rapids, Wm. B. Eerdmans pub co, 1992, 256. Cf. Wood J. Leon, *The Prophets of Israel,* Grand Rapids, Baker Academic group, 1979, 255.

[840] Macintosh, A.A., *A Critical and Exegetical Commentary on Hosea,* Edinburgh, T and T Clark, 1997, 440.

[841] M. Haran, The use of Incense in the Ancient Israelite Ritual, *VT* 10, 1960, 116.

[842] Heger. Paul, *Development of Incense Cutl in Israel,* Berlin, De Gruyter, 1997, 33.

[843] Dearman, *The Book of Hosea, NICOT,* Grand Rapids, Wm. B. Eerdmans Company, 2010, 280-281.

[844] Carol J. Dempsey, *The Prophets: A Liberation-Critical Reading,* Minneapolis, Fortress Press, 2000, 157.

[845] Malina. B.J, *The New Testament World: Insights from Cultural Anthropology,* Atlanta, John Knox Press, 1993, 73-77.

4.2.6.1. Zone of "Emotion-Fused Thinking"

In v. 8f an emotional speech (indicated by the repetitions and the tone) is recorded. Although the word belongs to "lamentation," it can also introduce a "self-accusation" and can follow the first person imperfect, especially when there is a transition to "self-caution." In Hosea 11, the caution that immediately follows the accusations gives "the proposal to reach a settlement, a definite form of a declaration of amnesty."[846] Thus, the sudden shift need not be an indication of a separation of these verses. Yahweh's self-caution and remission of punishment (vv. 8-9) makes it necessary to discuss Israel's former deeds in vv. 1-7, which have a summary statement in 7a: "my people are bent on apostasy from me."

In emotion - fused thinking, Yahweh recalls the Exodus: when out of "love" he made himself manifest and rescued Israel from unjust oppression in Egypt.[847] "Son" emphasises adoption of the nation by God, which forms a permanent bond.[848] The use of אהב refers to covenant fidelity in Deuteronomy (6:5; 7:8; 10:15; 23:6 [5]).[849] This has two different meanings "to have deep affection" and "to be loyal to."[850]

Eidavell notes that the emotions of Yahweh in 1a show the people how much He loves Israel. His struggle in His heart, as uncovered by the use of v. 8b 2 words is parallel to נהפך עלי לבי (My heart is turned within me) and יחד נכמרו נחומי (together my condolences raised); the synonymous parallelism לא אעשה חרון אפי (I will not let wrath take away) to לא אשוב לשחת אפרים (I will not destroy Ephraim again) in v. 9a, are thoughtful decisions that culminated in acts of care and grace.[851] Israel לא ידעו (not recognized) in v. 3b; they מאנו לשוב (refusing to turn) in v. 5c; תלואים למשובתי (they keep getting away from me once) in v. 7a, on the other hand, signify the decisions of the people going away from Yahweh.

The desired response, that is אחרי יהוה ילכו (they will go back to Yahweh) and אחרו (they will come with trembling) in v. 10 and 11, with Yahweh's intention and response that is desired, plays a determining role.

4.2.6.2. Zone of "Self-Expressive Speech"

The advocacy activities קרא (call) in v. 1a, 2a and שאג (roar) in v. 10b indicate the importance of speaking in the historical-theological accusation.[852] It is precisely Yahweh's accusation that Israel does not listen to when He speaks. In fact, Israel did not know that Yahweh healed them.[853] There is an emphasis on the fact that this whole unit of "self-expressive speech" of Yahweh in v. 11 ends with נאם־יהוה, 'It is a burden.'

---

846 H.W. Wolff, *Hosea,* Hermeneia, Fortress Press, 1974, 193-194.

847 Mays, *Hosea,* London, SCM Press, 1969, 153.

848 Dearman, *The Book of Hosea,* NICOT, Grand Rapids, Wm. B. Eerdmans company, 2010, 280.

849 Stuart. D, *Hosea - Jonah,* Waco, Word, 1987, 178.

850 Stuart. D., *Hosea - Jonah,* Waco, Word, 1987, 178-179.

851 W.R. Harper, *A Critical and Exegetical Commentary on Amos and Hosea,* Edinburgh, T and T Clark, 1956, 369.

852 H.W. Wolff, *Hosea,* Hermeneia, Fortress Press, 1974, 193; cf. Stuart, D., *Hosea - Jonah,* 1987, 175.

853 Goran Eidevall, *Grapes in the Desert: Metaphors, Models and Themes in Hosea 4-11,* Stockholm, Almqvist and Wiksell International, 1996, 171.

4.2.6.3. Zone of "Purposeful Action"

Yahweh's purposeful actions are reflected in his קרא (call) in v. 1a, 2a, and שאג (roar) in v. 10b as shown in His messages through the prophets. Garrett comments that He is the one who taught תרגלתי לאפרים (Ephraim to walk); He is the one who carried them in His arms קחם על-זרועתיו (have them on my arms);[854] He is the one who will heal their apostasy רפאתי (they heal) verse 3a. 11:4 states that he continues to love by his caring acts, namely: בחבלי אדם אמשכם בעבתות אהבה (people with ties, with cords of love He drew them); על על לחיהם (I was like them that the child against the jaw picks); ואט אליו אוכיל (I bent down to him or and I fed him with food).[855] This section shows the picture of Yahweh who bends down lift them in his arms and cares for His own people.

The word sword will whirl refers to the coming devastation, and destruction. For Harper Hosea 11:6a is a sign of Yahweh's drastic actions to gain his people's attention, namely בדיו וכלתה (the sword will fall upon their cities).[856] Salvation prophecy in v. 11b, והושבתים על־בתיהם (and I will settle them in their homes), is a purposeful act of love, which Yahweh promised if his people return to him with true repentance. Hosea 11: 2a-bb shows a series of Israel's purposeful actions which can be seen from Yahweh's response, that is הלכו מפניהם (they were aware of my presence) and לבעלים יזבחו (they offered to Baals), and ולפסלים יקטרון (for they brought incense to idols).

The nation's תלואים למשובתי (they went away from Yahweh and he asks them to return to him) in v. 7a and ואל־על יקראהו (and calling them to come to him) in v. 7b, shows more purposeful actions in turning away from Yahweh. His expectation in v. 10a and 11a that his people אחרי יהוה ילכו (they will follow Yahweh) and יחרדו (they will come trembling), are Yahweh's acts of love and hope in purposeful actions.

Israel was inattentive to God's love and protection but God did not distance himself from them. They had gone away from God but he called them to return to him. They were aware of his presence but they offered sacrifices to Baal and brought incense to the idols. But God did not waver from the covenant He had made with them. He persisted in calling them back and warned them not to remain in their sins. God expected Israel to remain faithful in his covenant and return to him with fear.

In emotion - fused thinking, Yahweh recalls the Exodus: when out of "love" he made himself manifest and rescued Israel from unjust oppression in Egypt. The emotions of Yahweh in 1a show the people how much He loves Israel. This section deals with how much Yahweh struggles in His heart. Yahweh's purposeful actions are reflected in his קרא in v. 1a, 2a, and שאג in v. 10b as shown in His messages through the prophets.

4.3. Inter-textuality

Inter-textuality refers to oral-written texture of the people of Israel here, and is considered in five sections, examining specific textures and patterns under the headings of Social, Cultural, Historical, Ideological and Theological textures.

[854] Garrett, *Hosea, Joel,* NAC, 19A, Nashville, Broadman and Holman, 1997, 254.

[855] G.I. Davies, *Hosea, New Century Bible Commentary,* Grand Rapids, Wm. B. Eerdmans publishing co, 1992, 257.

[856] W.R. Harper, *A Critical and Exegetical Commentary on Amos and Hosea,* Edinburgh, T and T Clark, 1956, 367

The use of the singular form בן represents Israel's identity and this term is rarely used in the Old Testament. The plural form בנים "sons" refers to the relationship between Yahweh-Israel (Hos. 11:10).[857] In the Old Testament there are two occurrences where Yahweh declares Israel *"my son"* (Exo: 4:22-23). Hosea presents Israel as Yahweh's son, depicting Yahweh's relationship with Israel as parental. The parental image of God is used by the prophet to demonstrate God's love for them and to help them to understand the relationship between God and Israel. Here the text explains about God's remembrance of His love for Israel before they were delivered from the land of Egypt. This is called unexpected prophecy fulfilled later and is quoted in Matt. 2:15. The concept of son plays an important role in showing how God helped them to come out of Egypt.

The context of Hos. 11:1 speaks of the relationship between the Lord and Israel. The analogy that we find here is that of God as the father and Israel as the child. The parallelism noted here is Israel-child/son/loved/called. In this instance the pronoun "I" is the one who initiates the action.

Yahweh reminds Israel that He was the one who brought them out of Egypt and brought them to the Promised Land. 11:11b serves as a reminder of the covenant and the Mosaic love referred to earlier in the chapter. It encourages them to return to Yahweh in true repentance.

Hosea 11:3-4 is about the father testifying about rebellious children (in v. 1 singular is used for son, but most of the verses use a plural pronoun for Israel). God narrates his love for them, through mentioning actions such as calling them out of Egypt (v. 1), teaching them to walk (v. 3a), and comforting them in their troubled times (v. 3b-c). But the response was continued rebellion and ingratitude.[858] This shows the paternal fondness, keeping them on their feet and care for them when they were child. It is Yahweh who did this, but Israel failed to recognise their God. Yahweh is the one who healed them and led them from bondage.

Chester K. Lehman points out that there are references in the Bible to Yahweh's love for Israel (Deut. 7:8, 13; 10:15; 23:6 MT [5^{Eng}]); Isa. 43:4; 63:9; Jer. 31:3; Hos. 9:15b, 11:1, 4a). ואהבהו is waw consecutive and it connects expression in the text.[859] The *waw* here completes the sense of the temporal כי which is translated as "then…when." Paul in his work treats "loved" as an act of election that means Israel is Yahweh's child.[860] To continue, Act 1 ends to a great extent with evidence of the father's love, leading them and making their life easier, and providing their needs. These actions show of the father's self-defence, indicating the loving act of a parent and that the son's rebellious act was not caused by poor parenting. This is followed by softening the emotional feeling from accusation to love. The comparison is that punishment changed to compassion. According to John Walton, the words

---

857 Fohrer, *TDNT* 8, 351-352. According to the author there is difference between Israel as the son or the Israelites as the sons of Yahweh both the expressions are seen in Deut. 32:5-6, 18-19 and the parallelism can be seen between 'my people' and 'sons' in the book of Isaiah 63:8; Jer. 4:22.

858 W.R. Harper, *A Critical and Exegetical Commentary on Amos and Hosea,* Edinburgh, T and T Clark, 1956, 363.

859 Chester K. Lehman, *Biblical Theology,* vol. 2, Scottdale, Herald press, 1946, 209.

860 Paul, *Adoption Formulae*, 180-185. Andersen, F I and Freedman, D N, *Hosea: A New Translation with Introduction and Commentary,* Garden City, Doubleday, 1980, 576.

that Hosea employs 'when Israel was a child' are used as a metaphor to describe the act of adoption into a family and the love of a father as he adopts a son and his obligation by agreement.[861] Similarly, Dearman argues that when Israel was a child *"I loved him"* refers to adoption.[862] Andersen and Freedman continue that there is also an opinion that this idea is relevant in the political context of the suzerain and a vassal.[863] In the *ANET* texts, loyalists are described as those whom the king loves. Emphasis is on the favour shown by the king as a benefactor.[864] The use of Israel here is deliberate and it reminds one of Yahweh's descriptions of Israel as his son at the time of Exodus (Exo. 4:22f cf. Deut. 14:1; 32:5-6).[865] For Harper "my son" implies the call out of Egypt to become Yahweh's son (Exo. 4:22f; Deut. 14:1; Jer. 3:19; 31:9, 20) in these references no such statement appears, because he is already represented as Yahweh's son.[866] In Hosea, the prophet everywhere represents Israel and Yahweh as husband and wife, not as father and son (cf. 11:8ff). This shows the contrast with v. 1, where Yahweh mercifully loved Israel and helped them to come out of Egypt.[867] The context makes it clear that it is a father's affection, care, protection and love that bring a child into a family. The prophet's testimony brings out God's action and is fulfilled in the parental obligation. The aspect of care is given importance and it becomes a testimony that a child is received with parental care, as illustrated in the Babylonian traditions. A similar idea is presented in this section. In this context loving is referred to as choosing (cf. Gen. 12:2-3). God chose the people of Israel for a special purpose and to be a blessing among the world's nations and in this context we see how much God loved him.

The use of the singular form בן represents Israel's identity and this term is rarely used in the Old Testament. In the Old Testament there are two occurrences where Yahweh declares Israel "my son" (Exo: 4:22-23). Hosea presents Israel as Yahweh's son, depicting Yahweh's relationship with Israel as parental. This is called unexpected prophecy fulfilled later and is quoted in Matt. 2:15. The concept of son plays an important role in showing how God helped them to come out of Egypt.

---

[861] John H. Walton, *Zondervan Illustrated Bible Backgrounds Commentary,* vol. 5, Grand Rapids, Zondervan Publishing House, 1984, 31.

[862] Dearman, *The Book of Hosea,* NICOT, Grand Rapids, Wm. B. Eerdmans company, 2010, 277.

[863] Andersen and Freedman, *Hosea,* 576. The term love is frequently used in the treaties level; this can be seen equal rulers or suzerain and vassal. Cf. William L. Moran, The Ancient Near Eastern Background of the Love of God in Deuteronomy, *CBQ* 25, 1963, 77-87. McCarthy is in support of this argument the vassal is to love the king as he does the Great King. From this the author's conclude that the expression of a relationship of love is connected with metaphors of family, and it is connected between God and Israel as we find in Deuteronomy. Cf. M. Weinfeld, "The Covenant of Grant in the Old Testament and in the Ancient Near East," *JAOS* 90, 1970, 194.

[864] ARM 10:7 line 13, ANET, 630; ARMT VIII 1:1-3; cf. Andersen, F I and Freedman, D N, *Hosea: A New Translation with Introduction and Commentary,* Garden City, Doubleday, 1980, 576-577.

[865] Andersen, F I and Freedman, D N, *Hosea: A New Translation with Introduction and Commentary,* Garden City, NY, Doubleday, 1980, 577.

[866] W.R. Harper, *A Critical and Exegetical Commentary on Amos and Hosea,* Edinburgh, T and T Clark, 1956, 362.

[867] Stuart. Douglas, *Hosea – Jonah,* Waco, Texas, Word Books, 1987, 178.

4.4. Social Texture

Hosea 11 shows that there is awareness of social memories reflected in the book. There are metaphors used as devices to bring awareness to post-monarchic communities. Neef finds that the reference to Admah and Zeboiim points to a tradition reflected in Deut. 29:22[868] that associate Israel's doom with Sodom and Gomorrah (Gen. 10:19; 14:2, 8).[869] Brueggemann points out that this brings out an idea that qualifies them as paradigmatic examples of total destruction.[870] Here the paradigm is that the people of Israel disobeyed the covenant.[871] God's tender mercy and compassion are part of his divine love for his sinful people. God's intimate relationship is communicated through the people's lives in a contractual way rather than in a legal way. The father-son relationship is presented in the form of caring as God cares for others.

According to Hosea southern king's experienced military importance and economic prosperity.[872] Unfortunately, experiencing such prosperity did not last for a long time; in their spiritual welfare the people began to attribute their prosperity to Baal instead of God.[873] The northern kingdom followed the Baal worship and the prophet denounces Baalism and warns of the covenant curses that are doomed to come upon the nation because of its violation of the terms of the Mosaic Covenant (Deut. 28:15-68). The nation sacrificed to Baals and burned their incense to carved images. Hos. 11:2 is a reference to dealing with the nations' rejection of God's order and instead they follow Baal. The people of the Northern Kingdom were more influenced by the Canaanite cult than the more remote Southern Kingdom of Judah.[874] The accusation in 11:2 is that Israel directly offered their sacrifices to Baal לבעלים יזבחו *and they burnt incenses to idols* ולפסלים יקטרון, despite the prophet's warning.[875] Hos 11:2 affirms the events of the nation which followed the Exodus experience. Despite several warnings about the nation's sacrificing to Baals and burning incense, the prophet calls the wayward nation, but the people went after other gods. The nation's continued sacrificing and disobedience must be seen against the backdrop of God's ever present fatherly love.

The pericope highlights the repentance, return of Israel (יחרדו) to Yahweh. Israelite religion was syncretistic in adapting to cultural changes in the ancient Near East. It adapted to Assyrian religious expressions (Amos. 5:16). The practices led to the rapid decay of the essence of Israel's existence as the people of God.[876] In Hosea 11:8 the Lord asked four rhetorical questions to show how hard for God it was to hand over Israel to other nations for punishment. The verse depicts the nature of judgment and how God will ultimately restore the nation. One main aspect of the

---

[868] Neef, *Die Heilstraditionen Israels,* 9.

[869] Brueggemann, *Genesis,* Interpretation, Westminister, John Knox Press, 1982, 18-19.

[870] W. Brueggemann, *Theology of the Old Testament,* Minneapolis, Fortress Press, 1997, 539.

[871] Stuart. D, *Hosea-Jonah,* Waco, Word, 1987, 181.

[872] Chisholm. R.B, "Hosea," *in The Bible Knowledge Commentary: Old Testament,* ed. John F. Walvoord and Roy B. Zuck, 2 Vols, Colorado Springs, Chariot Victor Publishing, 1985, 1377.

[873] Dietrich Ritschl, "God's Conversion," *Interpretation* 15, 1961, 288.

[874] W.R. Harper, *A Critical and Exegetical Commentary on Amos and Hosea,* Edinburgh, T and T Clark, 1956, 363.

[875] Boshoff, *Die boek Hosea en die Jahwe-Baal stryd, The Prophet,* University of Pretoria, 1994, 239.

[876] David Noel Freedman and William Foxwell Albright, eds., *Hosea,* vol. 24, *The Anchor Bible,* Doubleday Company Inc., 100.

verse is concern to Israel's restoration. The idea of divine discipline for Israel is the assurance that God will punish her permanently, but there is hope by saying that when they obey and return to God, there is hope and restoration. For this the prophet use two similes "as a bird" and "as a dove" to depict and to accelerate future return that will occur soon. This shows that the return will be from their former place of exile, that is Egypt and their future exile, Assyria. Here the prophet gives Assyria in a figurative way to portray a "new Exodus." The new exodus will result in future national obedience and people will return from the global dispersion. God's action changed from punishment to compassion. He assures them that He will not destroy them completely but will have compassion and will place them in the cities. This brings out strong expressions of divine emotion, particularly *love*, for His chosen nation.

Social texture talks about the reference to *Admah* and *Zeboiim* and points to a tradition reflected in Deut. 29:22 that associate Israel's doom with Sodom and Gomorrah (Gen. 10:19; 14:2, 8). The pericope highlights the repentance of Israel to Yahweh.

4.5. Cultural Texture

Israel's apostasy began soon after leaving Egypt. Moses was the key figure in bring out Israel from Egypt, the crossing of the Red Sea and journey through the wilderness and the reception of the Law. Davies notes the point and portrays the same pattern as the central figure and the New Covenant Law.[877] Before crossing the Red Sea, the Israelites complained, "For it were better for us to serve the Egyptians, than that we should die in the wilderness" (Ex. 14:12). After the deliverance from the hands of Egyptians Israelites made and worshipped a golden calf (Ex. 34). Even before entering the Promised Land, Israelites quickly yielded to Baal worship (Jud. 2:11-13; 3:7; 8:33; 10:6).

Hosea 11 contains touching words in the book. It is all about the sharp contrast between God's tender recollection of His early relationship with Israel and still His sorrow for them because they followed other god Baal, remembering all that he had done for the people of Israel (11:1-4). The reason is that the people have taken for granted God's love and care for them. But, the Lord is concerned over them and constantly warns them to escape from coming judgment due to the fact they had turned to other gods. This shows the clear violation of the standards in God's law that was given to them to follow. The MT text reads "The more they called to them, the more they went from them." There is confusion here over who was calling and to whom. God's prophets were possibly calling the people of Israel or the Egyptians or the Israelites called for the Egyptians. The Scripture quotes Israel's repeated complaints against the leadership in the days of exodus and during the wilderness wanderings. According to Sweeney the passage highlights the issue of the return to Egypt in verse 5; the passage refers to Israel's continuous expression of the desire to return to Egypt and seeking foreign gods while they were in the wilderness.[878]

---

[877] Davies, *The Setting of the Sermon on the Mount,* 78; Howard, *"The Use of Hosea 11:1 in Matthew 2:15;* An Alternative Solution," 328, No. 40.

[878] Sweeney, *Twelve Prophets,* vol. 1, Collegeville: Liturgical Press, 2000, 113.

The idea is that Israel went away from them refers to the former days in Egypt rather than looking forward with eager anticipation where Yahweh is going to place them in the Promised Land. The image of Yahweh is presented here as Israel's father, who called them and protected them and gave them spiritual liberty and healed their wounds and lead them to the Promised Land (cf. Hos. 6:1; 7:1).

The cultural inter-texture talks about the nation ignoring the love and care of Yahweh. They are accused of honouring the Baals and the cultural customs associated with Baal worship. The Baals means "the master" or "the husbands." The honouring is Baal by sacrificing יזבחו and burning יקטרון (incense). Stuart notes that in v. 2b there are direct references to rebellion and rejection of Yahweh's call.[879] This was one of the problems of the emergence of the Baal cult that the people adopted and they became a "rebellious child" in v. 2. The contrast is seen in v. 1. Even in the story of Gomer a similarity is found, where she offered sacrifices to Baals (cf. 2:13^{Eng} / 2:15^{Heb}). This shows the clear violation of the standards in God's law that was given to them to follow.

4.6. Historical Texture

The book of Hosea consists of several cycles (Hos. 1:2-2:1; 2:2-23; 3; 4-14) each cycle saying something about sins of the nation and forthcoming judgment. The ultimate restoration awaits for the nation upon her repentance that results in her return to the terms of Mosaic covenant.[880] Hosea 11:1 is found in the final cycle, which consists of covenant lawsuit against Israel. In this final cycle it is noted that God takes Israel to court for violating the terms of its covenant.[881] Hosea 11 focuses upon God's love and element of plan to restore the nation. God called Israel out of Egypt, redeemed them with His mighty show of force and led them to the Promised Land.[882] Hos. 11:1-4 is about God's tender love for the nation that a father has for his son. Such a love was expressed when God called His people out of bondage. There is a direct reference in v. 1 to the historical Exodus from Egypt. Hosea 11:2 is about fatherly love not being reciprocated by the nation. The prophets called to the wayward nation but the people moved away from the prophetic message into sin.[883] The קרא (call) of Yahweh in v. 2 can be interpreted as Yahweh's continuing call of Israel by the prophets.[884] Hosea 11:3-4 is about the theme of God's love for Israel. God's love is established after the deliverance of Israel from the bondage by the analogy of the parent training a child to walk, carrying in his arms and removing the yoke. This shows God's care for Israel and healing of the nation.[885] Patrick D. Miller points out there is also a reference to the

---

[879] Stuart, D., *Hosea-Jonah,* Waco, Word, 1987, 177-178.

[880] Dyer and Merrill, *Old Testament Explorer,* Swindoll Leadership Library, ed. Charles R. Swindoll and Roy B. Zuck, Nashville, Word Publishing, 2001, 723.

[881] Dyer and Merrill, *Old Testament Explorer,* Swindoll Leadership Library, ed. Charles R. Swindoll and Roy B. Zuck, Nashville, Word Publishing, 2001, 729.

[882] W.R. Harper, *A Critical and Exegetical Commentary on Amos and Hosea,* Edinburgh, T and T Clark, 1956, 363.

[883] Chisholm, R.B, Hosea, In *The Bible Knowledge Commentary: Old Testament,* ed. John F. Walvoord and Roy B. Zuck, 2 Vols, Colorado Springs, Chariot Victor Publishing, 1985, 1402.

[884] Davies. G I, *Hosea,* London, Marshall Pickering, 1992, 255; Buck, 1953, 163.

[885] Chisholm, R.B., Hosea, In *The Bible Knowledge Commentary: Old Testament,* ed. John F. Walvoord and Roy B. Zuck, 2 Vols, Colorado Springs, Chariot Victor Publishing, 1985, 1402.

Assyrian Exile in v. 5 and the destruction of אדמה כצבאים (sister cities of Sodom and Gomorrah) in v. 8. אדמה is identified as a Canaanite town and צבאים is unidentified.[886] Harper points out that these two villages in Hosea 11: 8 are two places mentioned that shared the same fate as Sodom and Gomorrah.[887] Mays argues that the Hosea tradition shares what was recorded in Deuteronomy 29: 21ff.[888] To sum up, despite God's love and expression of love through Yahweh's deliverance of Israel from Egypt, the nation ignored the prophet's warning and continue to worship another god. By worshipping other god, nation committed idolatry and hence violated the basic religious dogma of the Mosaic covenant (Exo. 20:3, 23; 22:20; 34:17). The message of Hosea is based on the Mosaic covenant that God made with Israel after their deliverance from Egypt. The exodus event is called as God's rescuing of the patriarchs from the captivity in Egypt. This is based on God's gracious act of redemption, God called out the rescued people for His very own possession to represent God among the nations. The historical texture shows that the passage may be dated near the end of Hoshea's reign around 727-723 BCE. Hoshea had cut off tribute payments to Assyria and was seeking an alliance with Egypt (2Kgs. 17:4), because of which Shalmanessar V (727-722) was angry with him.[889] Assyria then became an enemy of Israel and it was a matter of time before the wrath of God, through Assyria, struck Israel (vv. 5-6).[890] Thus, the passage shifts from past to present to the future and then to the eschatological future in the following verses: vv. 1- 4: *Past* - God's calling and people's rebellion; vv. 5-7: *Present and future* - Threat to Israel for their continuing rebellion; vv. 8-11: *Eschatological future* - refusal to destroy and promise of restoration.[891] The present condition of Israel is articulated in the form of prophecy and the future is declared in repentance toward God that will bring faithfulness and restoration to His people. God is gracious and a new beginning takes place for the people of Israel. God's love brings promises, forgiveness and restoration.

The book of Hosea consists of several cycles (Hos. 1:2-2:1; 2:2-23; 3; 4-14) each cycle saying about sins of the nation and forthcoming judgment.

4.7. Ideological Texture

Restoration is a key part of the embedded ideology of chapter 11. Hosea reminds Israel that the Lord's words are in harmony with the familiar exodus event that we find throughout the scriptures. This includes both warnings to Israel for covenant disobedience and the promise of restoration through repentance and complete surrender to God's will. The prophet expands God's pronouncements by revealing God's future plans for them. This includes the concept of restoration of repentant

886 Kakkanattu, *God's Enduring Love in the Book of Hosea: A Synchronic and Diachronic...,* Moherbeck, 2005, 78-79.

887 W.R. Harper, *A Critical and Exegetical Commentary on Amos and Hosea,* Edinburgh, T and T Clark, 1956, 369.

888 J.L. Mays, *Hosea,* London, SCM Press, 1969, 156-157.

889 Marvin A. Sweeney, *The Prophetic Literature: Interpreting Biblical Texts Series,* Nashville, Abingdon Press, 2005, 150.

890 Macintosh, A.A. *A Critical and Exegetical Commentary on Hosea,* Edinburgh, T and T Clark, 1997, 450-452.

891 Stuart, D., *Hosea-Jonah,* Waco, Word, 1987, 173-174.

people who will renew fellowship with the Lord. Hosea 11:8-11 is about Israel's restoration. These verses introduce the theme of divine chasteness. God says that He will discipline them and will not permanently destroy them. Hos. 11:10-11 describes about Israel's future obedience and return to land from global scattering. Philip King comments that Hosea 11:10-11 talks about Israel's return from their exile, trembling before their God.[892] The punishment turns into a promise, the message of which will be proclaimed by Yahweh himself. The message is that Yahweh will declare the words of return and the transformation should take place in the hearts of the people. According to Harper Hosea use striking similar imagery of the lion. Earlier there is other figure of a raving lion, which would bring judgment in the form of destruction. In Hosea 5:14 and 13:7, there are two terms, לחש and ריפכ that portray Yahweh as a "lion."[893] Here the term הירא is used for lion in a similar way. Here the God is portrayed as a compassionate and concerned parent lion calling for its young to follow him. By doing this the Israel will choose to respond to their God. This will bring new exodus for Israel and the people will return to their land and settle down.

חרד is translated as "hurry" (also translated as "tremble") and is used for the exile, and eschatological return of the people from different directions. The people of Israel are in a hurry to return to their home. The language that is used in v. 11 reflects the vocabulary that has already been used in this book (חרד "to hurry" in v. 10 and הנוי "dove" in v. 11) which denote Egypt and Assyria. The verb שוב brings out a positive note to the people in this verse. Here the return is promised and the people will inherit their lands, possessions and covenant blessings made with Yahweh (cf. 2:18 [16], 20 [18]). In the following verses, the promise will be fulfilled (cf. 2:25 [23]). Hosea 11:11 points out that the return will be from their former place of exile that is Assyria. Here the prophet uses Egypt and Assyria in a figurative way as "New Exodus." Unless like the former exodus this resulted in national disobedience (Hos. 11:1-4), the new exodus will bring outcome in future national obedience. The covenant brings renewal of blessing and assurance of return from their exile and repossession of the land to Israel. God's people in that day will respond in faith to his calling and his will shall be fulfilled by returning to the place of blessing.

The punishment turns into a promise, the message of which will be proclaimed by Yahweh himself. The message is that Yahweh will declare the words of return and the transformation should take place in the hearts of the people. Here the return is promised and the people will inherit their lands, possessions and covenant blessings made with Yahweh (cf. 2:18 [16], 20 [18]).

4.8. Theological Texture

The metaphor of Israel as a rebellious son is presented in this chapter; the accusation and legal proceedings take place in this section. The theological significance of this chapter discloses Israel's election and protection in their journey, based on Yahweh's love (vv. 1-4). This characteristic of love shows that God's love cannot be set aside. His love calls people and is expressed in action.

---

[892] Philip King, *Amos-Micah: An Archaeological Commentary,* Philadelphia, Westminster, 1988, 129.

[893] W.R. Harper, *A Critical and Exegetical Commentary on Amos and Hosea,* Edinburgh, T and T Clark, 1956, 371.

Eidavell stresses that Hosea 11:8-9 describes Ephraim/Israel's potential to be a blessing in the eschatological future.[894] This includes return from exile, and but it does not talk about the end of days in this context.[895] In this section, the important thing to note is the use of anthropomorphic terms to show Yahweh's relationship with His people through irrepressible love (cf. Isa. 49:15). Yahweh reminds the people that though they have renounced their God, He cannot reject them. Here Yahweh is presented as the judge but He never forgets His people, and his heart is full of compassion, tender mercy and love for them. Hosea preaches again and again reminding the people of their sins and warning them of God's judgment.

Stuart notes that the sudden shift of hope for Israel takes place here. The punishment for disloyalty of Israel is Assyria taking them to exile, and Yahweh will bring them back to the Promised Land (cf. Deut. 4:25-31).[896] Dearman notes that this is expressed in a poetical form by the prophet in 8-9. In v. 8 there are six clauses, and three bicola of parallel expressions. The first two are presented in the form of questions, but they are not rhetorical questions. In this verse Yahweh asks a question and expects an answer. George Adam Smith rightly points out that Hosea 11 is all about Yahweh's love. The concept of covenant with son / child is made clear in this context. The very nature of God is to show love, compassion, mercy and justice.

After studying all these textures, it is clear that Hosea 11 emerges as an entirely "homogenous unit, separate from the previous and the following context."[897] The unit begins with a more historical retrospect and the subsequent new passage (Hos. 12:1) introduces a totally different subject and the theme changes accordingly. There are several pointers within the internal structure towards considering 11:1-11 as a unit. First, vv. 1-7 are characterised by:

1. copulae (vv. 3, 6, 7);
2. the use of personal pronouns in singular (vv. 1, 4b, 5a, 6a) or plural (vv. 2, 3a, 4a, 5b, 6b, 7) and
3. the unity of the theme: "Israel has responded to Yahweh's love with obstinate renunciation from the very beginning (vv. 2, 3, 5, 7)."[898]

The theological significance of this chapter discloses Israel's election and protection in their journey, based on Yahweh's love. The concept of covenant with son is made clear in this context. The very nature of God is to show love, compassion, mercy and justice.

4.9. Summary of Hosea 11

Hosea 11 is all about the divine complaint and God's anger over His rebellious son. It contains an oracle from Yahweh because of the apostasy of Israel. Hosea 11:1-5

---

[894] Goran Eidevall, *Grapes in the Desert: Metaphors, Models and Themes in Hosea 4-11,* Stockholm, Almqvist and Wiksell International, 1996, 178.

[895] Stuart, D., *Hosea - Jonah,* Waco, Word, 1987, 179-180.

[896] Stuart, D., *Hosea - Jonah,* Waco, Word, 1987, 180-181.

[897] Beeby, H.D, *Hosea: International Theological Commentary,* Grand Rapids, Wm. B. Eerdmans publishing company, 1989, 41.

[898] Wolff, Hans Walter, *Hosea,* Philadelphia, Fortress Press, 1974, 193.

talks about the Exodus event and reminds them of the destruction of Sodom and Gomorrah. The first unit begins with the Exodus narrative and ends with a warning that they will be sent to a new Egypt, that is, Assyria. The next section, Hosea 11:6-11, is about Israel becoming unfaithful, their punishment and restoration. To illustrate God's love, the text is built on the metaphor of a father's love for a rebellious son.

The inner texture of Hosea 11 discusses important terms of repetition: אהב, קראו, ידע and שוב and חרד. This is presented in the form of a parent-son metaphor. In the progressive texture, key terms like "כי" "from me," "taking him by His arms "are discussed and followed by the theme of election. In the narrative texture, the importance of God's love for Israel is brought out to remind them of their sins, and God expects them to return to Him. Then other textures bring out the idea of the Exodus motif and how God loved Israel when they were in Egypt. For this, the prophet uses parental imagery to help them understand.

Conclusion

The main metaphor used to describe the love of God in this section is that of father-son. God's love is portrayed in the form of a compassionate parent in Hosea 11:1-11. Hosea conveys a human and divine image of God. The central message of this text is about language of this relationship, it talks about care and compassion with the promise of future restoration. The exegetical study reveals the love of God that is portrayed here as grieving love over the rebellious son, who has gone astray from God. Yahweh's complaint is that Israel, His child, had turned away from Him, despite the fatherly love and care that was showered on the nation of Israel. God's expectations as a father and Israel's failure as a son is shown through a chain of images. Yahweh is a "parent" grieving over Israel, the "rebellious child." In fact, the figure of speech is more personal in this passage. However, God's compassionate love endures to restore the covenantal relationship. The text brings out an aspect of a parental discipline towards his child as a response to the child's rebellious actions. God's love is stated to be a "tough-tender" love. God's discipline is rooted in love, and it is because of His love that He sets out to discipline. This 'tough tender' father-son relationship is characteristic of parenthood. The lessons drawn from Hosea 11 can be a model for parents in the present day.

Hosea 11:1-11 highlights the message of God's unconditional love in both the present and past life of Israel. Yahweh continues to love His covenant people Israel and looks forward to restoring the covenant. As with the previous marital imagery, it brings a message of hope instead of a message of judgment. Hosea 11:1-11 is the theological climax of the book of Hosea as it sets the stage for the powerful call to repentance which then concludes the prophecy. It also provides the impetus for the movement of the story to Chapter 14 where the appeal for Israel's return and restoration is shown through the third imagery: the physician-patient medical relationship. The next chapter will examine this relationship in detail, consider the "curing" of the patient - Israel and deals with the healing methods and results of the "treatment" for the people of Israel. It looks to the future and the rewards Israel will receive, especially in agricultural terms, for its return to Yahweh in repentance.

Chapter 5

Hosea 14:2-9: Return to God as a Pre-Condition for Restoration of God's Love and Renewal of Covenant Relationship

Introduction

The final chapter of Hosea (Chapter 14) concludes the prophecy of Hosea wherein Israel's repentance plays a pivotal role. In previous chapters, the research has shown how the human emotions involved in marital and parental events parallel the Yahweh and Israel relationship? This chapter is directed towards the people as words of hope, rather than works of judgment. God's message through the prophet is that God is ready to ignore their apostasy and heal their wounds and is ready to take them back, if they return with true repentance. God becomes their healer and by extension, Israel becomes his patient. In this chapter the research emphasises the final theme, the importance of the relationship of 'physician-patient' (healer-sufferer) as belonging to the concept of the covenant relationship. It details the affirmation of healing in the form of prosperity which comes in the form of restoration and transformation, if people return to Yahweh seeking divine forgiveness. The focus is on the spiritual healing of Israel.

While the previous chapters consider forms of Israel's apostasy, Yahweh's anger and His predicted punishment, Chapter 14 emphasises the 'love' element in Yahweh's attitude to Israel. The research shows how this offers hope for the future once genuine repentance has been made and details how the only one condition Yahweh imposes is that Israel must repent and seek forgiveness before a hope for the future could be promised. To enforce this message, emphasis is placed on the three themes which forms the bedrock of the whole book - The Covenant, Yahweh's Forgiveness, and most importantly, Yahweh's Love for Israel. The research also develops an argument for the extension of the concept of the blessings conferred on Israel to other nations as well. Israel will be a model for the nations through whom God's purpose is carried outward to the rest of the world. The chapter will examine these themes of healing, return-restoration and forgiveness in detail and also the words "apostasy," "forgiveness" and "return" used to convey their meanings.

5.1. Context of Hosea 14:2-9

Just as Chapter 11 was preceded by two chapters speaking of punishment for Israel, so here the final chapter, Chapter 14, is preceded by Chapters 12 and 13, covering Israel seeking help from Assyria and Egypt and worshipping idols, plus God's judgment against them. Against this background, there is a change in chapter 14 where God's message comes through the prophet that, if they return in true repentance, God is ready to ignore their apostasy and heal their wounds and is ready to take them back.[899] In addition He offers them restoration in glowing agricultural terms. God's anguish at Israel's wrong choices in response to His love is apparent. In this chapter, we find three dominant themes the importance of the covenantal relationship, Yahweh's willingness to forgive in the face of Israel's apostasy, and through it all, his love. It is his love that links the covenantal relationship and forgiveness to his all embracing and overwhelming love that will see all and yet forgive all, if only Israel will repent. If all this can be combined within the circle of Yahweh's love, then restoration will follow.[900] This promise is painted in glowing agricultural terms, with images of plentiful harvests and rich wine. But the metaphorical symbol at this point is healing-the physician heals the patient, with the promise of a physical gain the farmers' hope of harvests and wine as well as a spiritual gain. Hosea concludes his efforts at returning Israel to Yahweh with the comforting message of her future destiny.

5.1.1. Origin of Hosea 14:2-9

There are four theories about the origin of Hosea 14:2-9: first, scholars argue that the text originated from Hosea himself.[901] Second, Hosea's disciples composed this unit.[902] Third, the text may belong to a post-exilic composition of salvation.[903] Fourth supposes exilic redactional composition.[904]

Most scholars believe Hosea 14:2-9 is a post exilic composition by Hosea or by a group of his disciples.[905] For example, the scholars opine thus based on the passage concerning the reign of the Assyrian king Shalmaneser V (726-722), shortly before the description of Samaria, which leaves the origin of the

[899] Mays, James Luther., *Hosea: A Commentary,* OTL, Philadelphia, Westminster, 1969, 187.

[900] W.R. Harper, *A Critical and Exegetical Commentary on Amos and Hosea,* Edinburgh, T and T Clark, 1956, 408.

[901] Wolff, *BK* 14/1, XXXf; Rudolph, W. *Hosea*, KAT, XIII/1. Gütersloh, Gütersloher Verlagshaus Gerd Mohn, 1966, 249f; and Mays, James Luther., *Hosea: A Commentary,* OTL, Philadelphia, Westminster, 1969, 16.

[902] Jörg Jeremias, *Der Prophet Hosea, Überstzi und erklärt,* ATD 24/1, Göttingen, Vandenhoeck and Ruprecht, 1983, 170.

[903] Marti, *HAT* 105; H. Nowack, *Die Kleinen Propheten,* HKAT, Gottingen, Vandenhoeck and Ruprecht, 1903, 79.

[904] Gale A. Yee, *Composition and Tradition in the Book of Hosea: A Redaction Critical Investigation.* SBLDS, 102; Atlanta: Scholars, 1987. B.S. Childs, *Introduction to the Old Testament as Scripture,* Philadelphia, Fortress Press, 1979, 382; E. Kelley, "The Holy One in the Midst of Israel: Redeeming Love: *Review and Expositor* 72, 1975, 472."

[905] Beeby, H.D., *Grace Abounding: A Commentary on the book of Hosea,* Grand Rapids, Eerdmans, 1989, 185.

passage undecided. The date (726-722) helps to indicate that this unit contains primarily pre-exilic information and background.[906]

There is a common consensus among biblical scholars that Hosea 14:2-9 are the words of Hosea himself but with some minor additions which were probably added later. But recent theological studies prove that chapter 14 is a genuine work of Hosea.[907]

Most biblical scholars divide the structure of the entire book in the following way:

- Hosea 1-3
- Hosea 4-14.[908]

The first division of the passages shows that there is an alternation between the passages of judgment and of salvation (1:2-9 with 2:1-3; 2:4-15 with 2:16-25; and 3:1-4 with 3:5).[909] Most scholars treat 4-11 and 13-14 as major separate thematic blocks. Other scholars argue that the chronology of the materials in chapters 4-14 plays some role in its organization and structure.[910] Chapters 4-14 deal more with an accusation of a threat to salvation than chapters 1-3.

5.1.2. Exploring the texture

Hosea 14 is an elaborate dialogue between Yahweh and Israel. First, God speaks to Ephraim in the first few verses. Then the nation responds by saying "What have I to do with idols anymore?" In this context, Gordis and Harper identify an example similar to Hosea 14: in Jer. 50:7 where Yahweh is the speaker and there is a similar rhythm in the text.[911] The word אני (I say) introduces the function in this context to show that the allegory conveys the relationship between Yahweh's heart and Israel as His son. The healer-sufferer relationship is defined clearly the sufferer must take certain actions which will then through the healer bring relief. This is made clear throughout the entire chapter, which begins with Hosea's last plea to the people of Israel to forsake their sinful and self-centred ways. His plea is a double layered one, which also contains some sound spiritual and practical advice.[912] Sweeney proposes that "by appealing to Israel to 'return' to Yahweh and to reject its alliance with Assyria, Hosea 14:2-9 recounts the primary theme of the book: Israel's rejection of Yahweh in favour of relations with Assyria, followed by Yahweh's call for Israel to turn back to him."[913]

---

[906] D.J. Wiseman, *Tyndale Old Testament Commentary,* Hosea (David Hubbard), Downers Grove, Inter Varsity Press, 1989, 22-23. Wolff, *BK* 14/1, XXV, 303; Rudolph, *Kommentar zum Alten Testament,* 13/1, 250; and Mays, James Luther., *Hosea: A Commentary,* OTL, Philadelphia, Westminster, 1969, 185.

[907] Jörg Jeremias *"Zur Eschatologie des Hoseabuches,"* in Die Botschaft und die Boten. Festschrift fur Wolff, Neukirchen, Neukircher Verlag, 1981, 217-34.

[908] Except Gale Yee, *Composition and Tradition in the Book of Hosea: A Redaction-Critical Approach:* SBL Dissertation Series 102, Atlanta, Scholars Press, 1987.

[909] James Nogalsk *Literary Precursors to the Book of the Twelve,* Berlin, Walter de Gruyter, 1993, 58.

[910] Wolff, BK 14/1, XXIIIff; Jeremias, Der Prophet Hosea, *ATD* 24/1, Gottinham, Vandenhoeck and Ruprecht, 1980, 18f; and Rudolph, W. *Hosea,* KAT, XIII/1. Gütersloh, Gütersloher Verlagshaus Gerd Mohn, 1966, 26

[911] Gordis, R., "Hosea's Marriage and Message," *HUCA* 25, 9-40, 1954 and Gordis, 1971, 114-116. W.R. Harper, *A Critical and Exegetical Commentary on Amos and Hosea,* Edinburgh, T and T Clark, 1956, 414.

[912] Allen R. Guenther, *Hosea-Amos,* Scottdale, Herald Press, 1938/1997, 206.

[913] Sweeney, Marvin A. *Twelve Prophets,* 2 vols. Collegeville: Liturgical Press, 2000, 136.

5.1.3. Poetic Structure of Hosea 14:2-9[914]

Table 18: Poetic Structure of Hosea 14:2-9

Stanza	Strophe	Strings		Translation	Parallelism
1	A	שובה ישראל עד יהוה אלהיך	2a	return, O Israel, to Yahweh your God	Climatic
		כי כשלת בעונך:	2b	For you have stumbled by your iniquity	Climatic
		קחו עמכם דברים	3a	Take words with you	Grammatical
		ושבו אל-יהוה		Return to Yahweh	
		אמרו אליו כל-תשא עון	3b	Say to him, take away all iniquity,	Grammatical
		וקח-טוב		And receive us graciously,	Climatic
		ונשלמה פרים שפתינו		So we will offer the fruit of our lips	Climatic
	B	אשור לא יושיענו	4a	Assyria shall not save us	Synonymous parallelism
		על־סוס לא נרכב		We will not ride upon horses,	Grammatical
		ולא-נאמר עוד אלהינו למעשה ידינו	4b	We will not say again to our God to the work of our hands,	Grammatical
		אשר־בך ירחם יתום:		For in you the orphans find mercy	Synthetic
II	C	ארפא משובתם	5a	I will heal their apostasy	Synonymous parallelism
		אהבם נדבה		I will love them freely	Synonymous parallelism
		כי שב אפי ממנו	5b	For my anger is turned away from him	
		אהיה כטל לישראל	6a	I will be as the dew to Israel,	Synonymous parallelism
		יפרח כשושנה	6b	He shall grow as the lily,	Synonymous parallelism
		ויך שרשיו כלבנון		And cast forth his roots as the forests of the Lebanon	
	D	ילכו ינקותיו	7a	His branches shall spread out,	Synonymous parallelism
		ויהי כזית הודו	7b	His splendour shall be like the olive tree	Synonymous

[914] Francis I. Andersen and David Noel Freedman, *Hosea, The Anchor Bible Series,* vol. 24, New York, Doubleday, 1980, 642-643.

		וריח לו כלבנון:		and his fragrance as that of Lebanon.	Synonymous
	E	ישבו ישבי בצלו יחיו	8a	They who dwell in his shadow shall return again	Synthetic
		דגן ויפרחו		As they shall grow grain	Synthetic
		כגפן זכרו	8b	And they shall blossom as the vine, his remembrance	Synonymous
		כיין לבנון:		Shall be as the wine of Lebanon	Synonymous
	F	אפרים מה־לי עוד לעצבים	9a	Ephraim what I have to do any more with you,	Synthetic
		אני עניתי ואשורנו		I have heard and observed you.	Synthetic
		אני כברוש רענן	9b	I am like a green tree	Climatic
		ממני פריך נמצא:		From me is your fruit found.	Climatic

5.1.4. Discussion of the Structure of Hosea 14:2-9 Divisions, Poetic, Chiastic

The literary structural analysis describes the divine promise in Hosea 14:2-9. This passage is termed a call to repentance and the final verse concludes with the motif (14:10) of the entire chapter.

Hosea 14:2-4: prophetic call to repentance

- Verse 2: Call to Israel to return to Yahweh
- Verse 3a: Call to the people
- Verse 3b-4: Prayer for the people

Verses 5-9: Divine Promise of healing with botanical imagery

- Verse 5a: Decision of Yahweh to heal the apostasy of the people
- Verse 5b: Removal of Yahweh's anger from Israel
- Verse 6-7: Yahweh's promise to be like dew to Israel
- Verse 8b: Metaphorical description of dew's effects on Israel
- Verse 8a: Parenthetical statement about the inhabitants' return to Israel
- Verse 9a: Rhetorical question of Yahweh to Ephraim
- Verse 9b: Yahweh answers a question

Verse 10: The concluding motif

- Verse 10a: A double rhetorical question
- Verse 10b: A three-fold statement about the ways of Yahweh[915]

[915] James Nogalsk., *Literary Precursors to the Book of the Twelve,* Walter de Gruyter, Berlin, 1993, 65.

The above is the format Garrett uses.[916] Jeremias notes that the first two units are combined to bring out the idea of a call to repentance. In this section, 14:2-4, Hosea talks about a prophetic call to repentance, and in this prophetic speech, the prophet addresses Israel regarding Yahweh.[917] The subsequent section, 14:3-4, deals with the cultic language and its relationship with other passages in the Bible (Isa. 30:16; Deut. 17:16). These passages support the arguments of a post-Hoseanic composition,[918] as the description of Assyria in these verses presupposes the destruction of Samaria.

The next subsection, 14:5-9, deals with Yahweh's speech, and his message is communicated through the prophetic call to repentance in verse 2-4. This section is considered as a separate unit that contains several elements that are related to Israel. Verse 5 explains Yahweh's salvific action using divine speech. In the following section, the use of a metaphorical language about Israel (14:6-8) is situated. Here Yahweh is the speaker and we find a shift in persons. Yahweh is addressed in the second person masculine singular, while in other times he is addressed in the third person masculine singular.

5.1.5. Chiastic Structure of Hosea 14:2-9

A return, O Israel, to Yahweh your God, for you have stumbled by your iniquity (14:2)

  B I will heal their apostasy I will love them freely, for my anger is turned away from him (them). (14:5)

A Ephraim what I have to do any more with you (idols) (14:9)

The present section explains the important role played by chapter 14. According to Childs, Hosea 14 is about the oracles of salvation.[919] Hosea 14 is divided into two main units: The first part - Hosea (MT 2-9) is an oracle of salvation, poetry, and admonition.[920] The next unit - Hosea 14:9 is about an oracle of salvation, poetry, followed by the instruction.[921]

A great speech is made by Yahweh in Hosea 14:5-9. Here we notice that a kind of chiastic alternate addresses take place which do not happen elsewhere in the book. First Yahweh speaks to Israel ("them") about his attitude (v. 5a), next is "him" (vv. 5b-7) and then "them" (v. 8). The chiasm in verse 9 opens and closes with a second person address but contains the third person. The persuasion "you" in the plural finds its reply in vv. 3b-4a. The opening verse urges "you" (Hos. 14:3a) in singular form

---

[916] Garrett, *Hosea, Joel, An Exegetical and Theological Exposition of Holy Scripture,* Nashville, Broadman and Holman, 1997, 303. cf. Allen R. Guenther, *Hosea-Amos,* Scottdale, Herald Press, 1938/1997, 206-207.

[917] Mays, James Luther., *Hosea: A Commentary,* OTL, Philadelphia, Westminster, 1969, 186.

[918] Ina Willi-Plein, *Vorformen der Schriftexegese innerhalb des Alten Testaments. Untersuchungen zum literarischen Werden der auf Amos, Hosea und Micha züruckgehenden Bücher im hebräischen Zwölf prophetenbuch.* BZAW 123, Berlin, DeGruyter, 1971, 231.

[919] B. S. Childs, *Introduction to the Old Testament as Scripture,* Philadelphia, Fortress Press, 1979, 382.

[920] G.I. Davies, *Hosea-New Century Bible Commentary,* Grand Rapids, Wm. B. Eerdmans publishing co, 1992, 298-299.

[921] Kidner, Derek. *Love to the Loveless: The Message of Hosea,* BST, Downers Grove, Inter Varsity, 1981, 124-125.

and finds its response in v. 9. The passage addresses Israel (Hos. 14:2) and Ephraim (Hos. 14:9) both in the singular form and constitute an important inclusion in this passage.[922] The plural passages in the text refer to the nation as a whole both Israel and Ephraim.

5.1.6. Translation - Hosea 14:2-9 [1-8^{Eng}]

Table 19: Translation - Hosea14:2-9

[2] שובה ישראל עד יהוה אלהיך כי כשלת בעונך:	1 return, O Israel, to Yahweh[923] your God, for you have stumbled by your iniquity.[924]
[3] קחו עמכם דברים ושובו אל־יהוה אמרו אליו כל־תשא עון וקח־טוב ונשלמה פרים שפתינו:	2 Take words[925] with you return to Yahweh, say to him, take away[926] all iniquity, and receive[927] us graciously,[928] so we will offer[929] the fruit of our lips.[930]
[4] אשור לא יושיענו על־סוס לא נרכב ולא־נאמר עוד אלהינו למעשה ידינו אשר־בך ירחם יתום:	3 Assyria shall not save us, we will not ride upon horses, and we will not say again to our God to the work of our hands, for in you the orphans find mercy.[931]
[5] ארפא משובתם אהבם נדבה כי שב אפי ממנו:	4 I will heal their apostasy[932] I will love them freely,[933] for my anger is turned[934] away from him.

922 Mays, James Luther., *Hosea: A Commentary,* OTL, Philadelphia, Westminster, 1969, 189.

923 MT reads as "to Yahweh:" the word עד is translated as "up to," and not as merely אל, meaning "towards." In this context the summons is to total conversion.

924 English translations read as "because of your iniquity."

925 MT reads "words." The meaning is about open confession of the sins of the people and their utterance of broken-hearted prayers of penitence.

926 In MT the placement of the word כל־תשא עון is not correct. The MT reads in the following way by rearranging the phrases as follows: תשא כל־עון means "Forgive all iniquity. However, Gesenius proposes that כל does not fit in this context. The word כל־עון is used in a genitive phrase and modifies the verb as תשא is understood as "completely forgive."

927 In MT it is noticeable that the repetition of the word לקח becomes an important wordplay in Hos.14:2. The meaning of the word is that God expects confession from Israel and is ready to accept them and ready to forgive them.

928 The MT translates טוב as graciously receive us. Here the word "good" contains prayer within it and God is ready to accept Israel with the condition of confession of their wickedness and true repentance from the people (cf. Hos. 3:5).

929 The MT translates טוב as good. However, the word טוב can mean "word, speech." The verb בבט is "to speak." And in this context means word, or speech. There are other meanings such as "confession of sins," "acceptance of prayer" and "receive us graciously."

930 The MT translates the word פרים as "bulls," whereas LXX suggests פרי means "fruit." Here two readings are found "that we may offer the fruit of [our] lips [as sacrifices to you]." Cf. Gale Yee, *Composition and Tradition in the Book of Hosea: A Redaction-Critical Approach:* SBL Dissertation Series 102, Atlanta, Scholars Press, 1987, 132-133. The LXX suggests καρπὸν χειλέων as in 13:15, which is translated as "the fruit of lips.

931 The MT translates "mercy" as "compassion." The next word "orphan" is used in a figurative way for better understanding and refers to Israel.

932 In MT משובתה is used as noun means "waywardness." The root word is שובה meaning "return" (cf. Hos. 14:1 [MT 2]). The word שוב repeated as wordplay stresses and brings to attention, and expect the response that Israel will return to the Lord from their apostasy.

933 In MT the נדבה is used as a noun mean free-will offering by voluntarily.

934 The MT refers שוב as verb meaning "will turn" and is used as wordplay in 14:1-4[2-5].

6 אהיה כטל לישראל יפרח כשושנה ויך שרשיו כלבנון:	5 I will be as the dew to Israel, he shall grow as the lily, and cast forth his roots as the forests[935] of the Lebanon.
7 ילכו ינקותיו ויהי כזית הודו וריח לו כלבנון	6 His branches shall spread out, his splendour shall be like the olive tree and his fragrance as that of Lebanon.
8 ישבו ישבי בצלו יחיו דגן ויפרחו כגפן זכרו כיין לבנון:	7 They who dwell in his shadow shall return again[936] as they shall grow grain,[937] and they shall blossom as the vine, his remembrance shall be as the wine of Lebanon.
9 אפרים מה־לי עוד לעצבים אני עניתי ואשורנו אני כברוש רענן ממני פריך נמצא:	8 Ephraim what I have to do any more with you,[938] I have heard and observed you. I am like[939] a green tree.[940] From me is your fruit found.[941]

5.1.7. Text Critical Notes: Hosea 14:2-9 [1-8^ENG]

1a - a - והריותיו יבקעו - this is probably an insertion; however there is no evidence to support it and the phrase fits the text. The reading of the text is maintained.

2a - יהוה אלהי - the full version is found in 12: 10; 13:4; BHS raises the question whether one of these words is an insertion.

3a - a - אמרו אליו - this is possibly an insertion. But since the phrase fits and has no evidence to support it, the reading of the text is maintained.

3b - תשא - The Masoretic text reading is probably corrupted. However, there is no proper evidence from to support this. Thus the text is maintained as it is.

3c - וקח - Targum reads with 1 c. p.

3d - פרים - the LXX and Syriac pronounce as "fruit." The LXX and Syriac likely seek to simplify somewhat the complex figure of speech in MT.

5.1.8. The Themes in detail

The imagery of the three themes mentioned above play an important role in helping us to understand God's message of love to the Israelites. Before discussing the texture of the Chapter, it is useful to examine the details of the imagery used.

This means that one day Israel will return to the Lord with true confession of their sins and apostasy, and God will heal their wickedness and show his mercy upon them. Cf. Gale Yee, *Composition and Tradition in the Book of Hosea: A Redaction-Critical Approach:* SBL Dissertation Series 102, Atlanta, Scholars Press, 1987, 132-133.

935 The MT translates "like Lebanon." MT use "as forest," the word "a cedar of" is not found. The word is altered to make the meaning more clearly. The English versions translate as "the forests of Lebanon."

936 The word "shall return" emphasises the term which sound in a similar way: ישבו ישבי means as "the dwellers will return." The wordplay helps emphasise the meaning of ישבו ישבי.

937 The MT translates as "they will cause the grain to live" or "they will revive the grain." Other English versions translations treat this as a suggestion for a comparison.

938 MT is מה־לי עוד used as a formula for emphatic purpose, to show the reader that Yahweh nothing to do with idols (Judg. 11:12; 2Sam. 16:10; 1Kgs. 17:18; 2Kgs. 3:13; 2Chr. 35:21; Jer. 2:18; Ps. 50:16).

939 In MT "like" is not found, rather it is used in the translation to make the meaning clear.

940 Some English translations translate as "a green tree"; "a green pine tree"; "an evergreen cypress."

941 The MT translation is "your fruit is found in me" but other English translations have "your faithfulness comes from me."

5.1.8.1. Covenant Relationship

Hosea 1-3 depicts Yahweh's covenant in various ways, in particular by using the image of the marriage between Hosea and Gomer. In this section, Hosea uses the word "love" to depict an affection which involves the concentrated dynamism and energy of a person. This word denotes close relationships between the partners. He has deliberately used the word "love" to give a more intensive meaning to the covenantal relationship that Yahweh has for Israel.[942] This feeling is established through His covenantal relationship with the people of Israel by electing and redeeming them from the land of Egypt (11:1). In doing so, it is important that the covenant demands faithfulness from both parties. Yahweh emphasises this by using the image of Hosea's marriage to Gomer, when Gomer breaks the marriage vow by her harlotry. In a similar way, the prophet depicts Israel's apostasy and breach of the covenantal relationship where the people turned away from Yahweh to worship other gods (11:2, 5, 7). The whole story of the prophet's message is Yahweh's desire to renew this relationship by Israel turning back Him and forsaking the foreign gods.

It is to restore the covenantal relationship that Yahweh, through Hosea as his prophet, uses the three strong metaphors describing love in human terms marital, parental and healing in an effort to make Israel understand what He has done. Through these metaphors, He emphasises His love for Israel, and His willingness not to punish but to restore the relationship.

5.1.8.2. Forgiveness

The concept of forgiveness runs as a thread through the three metaphors used by the prophet. In the marital metaphor, Hosea is commanded to redeem his wife, who has played the harlot, thus emphasizing the concept of forgiveness. The parallel to this marriage relationship is the renewal of the covenantal relationship between Yahweh and Israel-Yahweh is willing to forgive the people's 'harlotry' caused by worshipping false gods and, by virtue of His forgiveness, Israel will be restored and reconciled.

In the metaphor of the father-son relationship (11:1-11), Hosea presents Yahweh's explicit act of forgiveness in 11:8-9. The people of Israel had deliberately rebelled and rejected Yahweh by worshipping false gods (11:2, 5). By using the father-son metaphor, he is able to contrast Yahweh imposing justice for wrongdoing (the angry father) with Yahweh offering reconciliation (the loving and forgiving father). The ultimate result is that Yahweh does not punish Israel, though He is entitled to, but instead holds out His arms in loving forgiveness with the offer of salvation. All He asks is that Israel should return to Him and abandons the false gods. As a loving father, Yahweh does not want to destroy His own child. The thought of this causes Yahweh's heart to shrink within him (11:9). What we find here is that Yahweh refrained from destroying Israel not because of their goodness but because He is their God (11:9) and because of His parental nature. God's nature of forgiveness spared the life of Israel from punishment. His sovereign authority shows that He will not punish them but forgives them as a father forgives his child.

---

[942] Renita J. Weems, *Battered Love: Marriage, Sex, and Violence in the Hebrew Prophets,* Minneapolis, Fortress Press, 1995, 13.

In the metaphor of healing as a physician, Yahweh has 'diagnosed' Israel's sins (7:1). This shows that Israel as a patient is 'sick' and should in fact receive Yahweh's punishment (treatment). But because of Yahweh's grace He has forgiven them by healing their sickness using love (14:5) not punishment. Israel broke the covenant and they were not up to Yahweh's expectation, for example, their repentance was not genuine (7:1). Yahweh as doctor could still punish them by withholding His 'treatment,' but instead He forgave their sins and sickness and healed them and provided a life of reconciliation and restoration.

5.1.8.3. Love

Hosea portrays Yahweh's love in these three metaphors-each of which represents a human relationship and each parallels the Yahweh-Israel relationship. Yahweh's love is the basis that underpins all three metaphors; without His overwhelming love the Israelites would have been abandoned.

In the marital scenario, the parallel is between Hosea and Gomer and Yahweh and Israel. Hosea takes Gomer back after her harlotry; Yahweh is willing to take Israel back after her 'harlotry' through worshipping false gods. Only Yahweh's great love for Israel lets Him do this.

In the father and son scenario (Hosea 11), the prophet presents Yahweh's love as caring for Israel as a son He called the people out of Egypt and loved them like a parent, teaching, guiding, serving and nourishing them for their growth (11:1-4). Though Israel rejected Yahweh by worshipping other gods, and though He would be justified in punishing them as a father would punish a rebellious son, He ultimately does not do so. Justice requires punishment but love, His redemptive love, requires forgiveness. The God of justice is also the God of love. This gives hope for the people that they can continue to remain in His love forever.

The third metaphor Yahweh as a physician shows Yahweh's love through the metaphor of the physician healing the patient (Israel). Israel had become weak and sick due to the people's dependence upon other nations and their worship of false gods instead of putting their trust in Yahweh. But because of His love (14:5), He was prepared to heal His people, using the healing physician metaphor to help them understand.

Yahweh's great love for His people is the basis on which Israel's fortunes have rested since the days in Egypt. Through the wanderings in the desert, the Sinai covenant, and the people's apostasy, Yahweh's love for them has never failed. Using Hosea and the three great images of love is His strongest effort yet to bring the people back into the fold of the Sinai covenant, even though they did not really deserve it.

It is now important to turn to the actual texts in which Yahweh emphasises His love for Israel. These are considered under the headings Repetitive, Progressive, Open-Middle-Closing, Sensory-Aesthetic textures and Inter-textuality.

5.2. Inner Texture

The unique characteristic of this passage is that the entire discourse is expressed by Yahweh. There is one issue of prime importance to God: Israel's return to Him (vv. 2-3a) in response to the speeches (vv. 3b-4).[943] Ehud Ben Zvi considers Hosea 14

[943] Allen R. Guenther, *Hosea-Amos,* Scottdale, Herald Press, 1938/1997, 206.

as one of the restoration passages in the book, where there is an open call for Israel to repent and follow Yahweh.[944]

5.2.1. Repetitive Texture

While the metaphor shifts from husband-wife and parent-child to physician-patient, the two terms "return" and "stumbled" establish the pattern of repetition in this section.

5.2.1.1. Physician-Patient Metaphor

In chapter 14, the prophet invites Israel to repent in order to return to Yahweh.[945] To convey this, the main metaphor used is healing.[946] The prophet urges the people to confess (vv. 2-3) their backsliding and says that God will respond to them with healing, love, and promises of prosperity and security (vv. 4-8).[947] This is supported by Harper and says that return, backsliding and pity as a father which Yahweh has for the people is presented in the prophet's message that brings Israel from weakness to restoration.[948]

Hosea wants people to return to Yahweh and reminds them that everything will not be changed immediately. He pronounces oracles of judgment but informs them that God does not want to punish them if they return.[949] Though the people of Israel were warned earlier concerning the upcoming punishment several times (3:5; 5:4; 7:10; 11:5), they continued in their activities of sin and pride. But now things have changed.

5.2.1.2. Significance of the Word שוב

The word "return" is introductory utterance. The imperative is predictive, consisting of prediction with the announcement to that effect followed by the no hope reference is not made. The text (Hosea 14) begins without hope because they are faithful. To overcome Israel's apostasy, return is first step to be taken toward reconciliation. Here Hosea appealed to "Israel" using the honoured name for the nation. The repeated word in this section, שוב, refers to Israel. The prophet issues several reminders to Israel to persuade them to leave their sinful life and seek forgiveness from Yahweh.[950] According to Sweeney, the prophet appeals to Israel to return to Yahweh by forsaking their alliance with Assyria.[951] The usage of repetition exemplifies the twofold idea of Yahweh's calling for people to return and repent (v. 2). The word שוב is used as an imperative in verse 1 and indicates a new beginning, that introduces the final three-part chapter (vv. 1-3; 4-8; 9).

---

[944] Ehud Ben Zvi, *Hosea FOTL,* Grand Rapids, Wm. B. Eerdmans Publishing co, 2005, 288.

[945] Daniel J. Simundson, *Hosea-Micah: Minor Prophets,* Abingdon Old Testament Commentaries: Abington Press, Nashville, 2005, 111.

[946] Gale Yee, *Composition and Tradition in the Book of Hosea: A Redaction-Critical Approach:* SBL Dissertation Series 102, Atlanta, Scholars Press, 1987, 132-133.

[947] Stuart. D, *Hosea-Jonah,* Waco, Word, 1987, 211-212.

[948] W.R. Harper, *A Critical and Exegetical Commentary on Amos and Hosea,* Edinburgh, T and T Clark, 1956, 409.

[949] Mays, James Luther., *Hosea: A Commentary,* OTL, Philadelphia, Westminster, 1969, 184-185.

[950] Dearman, J.A, *The Book of Hosea,*" NICOT, Grand Rapids, Wm. B. Eerdmans Publishing co, 2010, 334-336.

[951] Mays, James Luther., *Hosea: A Commentary,* OTL, Philadelphia, Westminster, 1969, 186.

The prophet uses a twofold aspect of calling for both a return to the Lord and repentance. Hosea's use of two imperatives for "return" and a third for "repent" is a kind of familiar threefold style. This means to return and repent, addressed to all Israel. Here the promise of divine acceptance, forgiveness, and restoration is realised; now it is imperative that Israel should act immediately to seek His forgiveness. Macintosh suggests that the word שובה means "go back," but the literal meaning of the term שובה is *"return,"* and "go / come back." It can mean repentance in this context[952] (cf. 6:1: שובה means "return").[953] Stuart comments that this refers to a repentance of the future and is not to be understood in the immediate context of the audience. This repentance refers to the people who are taken into exile.[954] According to Andersen, the word שוב is from a context of political exile and is symbolically expressed here.[955] He comments that the prophet used the term "return" a great deal in the book.

According to Limburg James, the prophet uses two imperatives for "שוב" (vv. 1-2) and a third imperative for "repent," which is one of the characteristics of Hosea.[956] The double pleas to return and repent are meant for all Israel.[957] The imperatives emphasise the necessity of Israel's return to Yahweh. The imperatives are also meant to make them respond faster and to compel them. The people are informed through the prophet that a true repentance is expected from them.

The main emphasis focused on the word שוב is due to the love of God which compels them to return. As the people of Israel stumbled in their iniquities Hosea reminds them to return to their God. When they come with true repentance, He is ready to accept them as His own people. The prophet reminds them again of God's unfailing love for the faithless people and his willingness to heal them. The imagery of healing describes the loving heart of God towards Israel.

5.2.1.3. The Repetition of שוב

The repetition of term שוב has a semantic trajectory of forms.[958] The root word occurs twenty-five times in Hosea.[959] The trajectory has a central message for the reader. The first two expressions (that is שובה ישראל *"Return, O Israel"* in v. 2 and האל־יהוו שובו "return to Yahweh" in v. 3) show that the people of Israel must return to Yahweh.[960] The next form that is found here is the expression of ארפא משובתם in v. 5a. Here the important theme is משובתם "their turning away."

---

952 Macintosh, A.A, *A Critical and Exegetical Commentary on Hosea,* Edinburgh, T and T Clark, 1997, 559.

953 G.I. Davies, *Hosea-New Century Bible Commentary,* Grand Rapids, Wm. B. Eerdmans publishing co, 1992, 301.

954 Stuart. D, *Hosea-Jonah,* Waco, Word, 1987, 213.

955 Andersen, F.I and Freedman, D.N., *Hosea: A New Translation with Introduction and Commentary,* New York, Doubleday, 1980, 645.

956 James Limburg, *Hosea-Micah, Interpretation: A Bible Commentary for Teaching and Preaching,* Westminster, John Knox Press, 2011, 51.

957 LeCureux, Jason T., *The Thematic Unity of the book of the Twelve,* HBM 41, Sheffield, Sheffield Press, 2012, 64.

958 Ben Zvi, Ehud, *Hosea,* FOTL, Grand Rapids, Wm. B. Eerdmans Publishing Co, 2005, 288.

959 Garrett. *Hosea, Joel, An Exegetical and Theological Exposition of Holy Scripture,* Nashville, B and H Publishers, 1997, 304.

960 Zvi, Ehud Ben, *Hosea,* FOTL, Grand Rapids, Wm. B. Eerdmans Publishing Co, 2005, 288.

The word ארפא mean 'healing' of Israel's apostasy השובה (this can allude to Yahweh as a physician).[961] The word שב in verse 5b says that Yahweh's anger is turned away from Israel.[962] The final form of ישבו in v. 8 reminds the people to return to Yahweh as he is the life giver and the protector, and this applies even to the future.[963] When Israel repents, they will escape from the coming judgment and will enjoy healing. In chapter 14, in both 2 and 3, the word שוב refers to Israel.[964] The prophet adds further to the above discussion that the people's confession should also contain an expression of their realisation that they should not rely on military powers, especially the foreign nations and their gods. The command is to worship Yahweh alone as the one true God and the Lord of the covenant. This should be reflected in both their attitudes and their actions.

Dearman notes that in verse 2 Hosea appeals to Israel to return to Yahweh, and this is repeated in verse 3 with a slight variation in the text. The word repeated here is שובה which in this context means repentance, where Yahweh is presented as the object. Stuart summarizes the structure in the following way:[965]

Program for repentance	v. 1-3 (MT 2-4)
Invitation to return to Yahweh	v. 1 (MT 2)
Suggested prayer of repentance, including vow of penitence and confession of trust	v. 2-3 (MT 3-4)
Divine promise of restoration	v. 4-9 (MT 5-9)
Healing will replace divine anger	v. 4 (MT 5)
Israel's future prosperity in Yahweh	v. 5-8 (MT 6-9)

Israel is reassured of healing through the following repetition of the terms that Hosea uses:

ארפא משובתם	I will heal their apostasy (faithlessness) 14:5a
אהבם נדבה	I will love them freely
כי שב אפי ממנו	For my anger has turned from them

Mays notes, that שוב is a qal imperative. For Allen Guenther "return" is a theme that is repeated throughout Hosea (e.g. 3:5; 5:4; 6:1; 7:10, 16; 11:5; 12:6; 14:1-2).[966] McConville finds that repentance is about turning to God (14:1) and turning away His anger (14:4) that brings God's blessings back to the people.[967] But Philip King argues that the personal relationship with God is established through confession

[961] Ehud Ben Zvi, *Hosea,* FOTL, Grand Rapids, Wm. B. Eerdmans Publishing Co, 2005, 288.

[962] Hubbard David Allan, *With Bands of Love* (Hosea), Grand Rapids, W.B. Eerdmans Publishing Co, 1968, 228-229.

[963] Stuart. D, *Hosea-Jonah,* Waco, Word, 1987, 212.

[964] Dearman, J.A, *The Book of Hosea,*" NICOT, Grand Rapids, Wm. B. Eerdmans Publishing Co, 2010, 337.

[965] Stuart. D, *Hosea-Jonah,* Waco, Word, 1987, 212.

[966] Allen R. Guenther, *Hosea-Amos,* Scottdale, Herald Press, 1938/1997, 205-206.

[967] J. Gordan McConville, *Exploring the Old Testament: A Guide to the Prophets,* vol. 4, Downers Grove, Inter Varsity Press, 2002, 144.

of sins and asking for forgiveness.[968] Brueggemann discusses how all these are based on God's compassionate love and Israel renewing their personal relationship with God.[969] God's love is explained through repentance to follow God's way (14:4; cf. Rom. 5:8). It impacts people in different ways. It invites people to repent of their sins (14:1) and whoever responds to God's call through his prophet call shall receive blessings from God (14:2).

In explaining that a call was given to people who had already stumbled, the purpose is not to save Israel from a frightening judgment, because the disaster has already taken place, but that the God of Israel, Yahweh, wants a new beginning.[970] It was not Yahweh who brought a collapse on Israel; rather it was Israel's guilt which brought its own collapse.

"Return, O Israel, to the Lord your God," talks about the return, though Hosea used several images in earlier chapters to articulate this thought. This is what this point to repentance would look like for people of Israel. From "silly dove" (7:11) to "save the nation" and that can be only by God alone. The people will finally fly like doves back to God (11:11). The people's faithfulness is compared with dew in this final chapter. The idea is that the dew will not vanish but brings newness and life that consists of God's care for nature and provision for the repentant people (14:5).

5.2.1.4. The Repetition of כשלת

The next word noted in the repetitive texture is כשלת which, in this context, means "looking back towards the sins of the people."[971] Macintosh notes that the meaning of the word *"stumble" is "the lack of strength."*[972] The Old Testament uses a metaphor of "being established on secure ground" as a sign of healthy life and newness in spiritual life, while the word "stumbling" (qal perfect) refers to a sign of sin (cf. 5:5b; Isa.3:8; 59:10, 14; Jer. 46:6).[973] In 14:2, the expression *"take words with you and return to the Lord"* (14:1 in MT), has four qal imperatives and one Piel cohortative.[974]

The meaning of this forceful expression is that God expects the people of Israel to respond in a proper way. Again the physician/patient concept is raised Israel has become weak with their wrongdoings and needs healing from this, so Yahweh reminds them to come back with true repentance and penitent prayer and then healing will be given.[975] These words must express repentance to God with true words and remains strong.

---

[968] Philip King, *Amos-Micah: An Archaeological Commentary,* Philadelphia, Westminster, 1988, 119.

[969] Brueggemann, *Theology of the Old Testament,* Minneapolis, Fortress Press, 1997, 415.

[970] J.L. Mays, *Hosea,* London, SCM Press, 1969, 162

[971] Beeby, H.D., *Grace Abounding: A Commentary on the book of Hosea,* Grand Rapids, Eerdmans, 1989, 178-179.

[972] Macintosh, A.A. *A Critical and Exegetical Commentary on Hosea,* Edinburgh, T and T Clark, 1997, 56.

[973] Mays, James Luther., *Hosea: A Commentary,* OTL, Philadelphia, Westminster, 1969, 186. Cf. Hubbard David Allan, *With Bands of Love* (Hosea), Grand Rapids, W.B. Eerdmans publishing co, 1968, 226.

[974] W.R. Harper, *A Critical and Exegetical Commentary on Amos and Hosea,* Edinburgh, T and T Clark, 1956, 411.

[975] Garrett. *Hosea, Joel,* NAC, 19A, Nashville, Broadman and Holman, 1997, 304.

The table illustrates the terms related to the words "return" and "stumble".

Table 20: the words "return" and "stumble" – Hosea 14:2-9

שוב	Return
ישראל	Israel
יהוה אלהי	Lord God
כשלת	Stumbled
לבנון	Lebanon
יפרח	Blossom
ילכו	Spread
יחיו	Flourish
רענן	Evergreen

Here, we see how the words are repeated, as well as their relation one to another. The word "stumbled" is used in connection with disloyalty in v. 4, and because of disloyalty, they will be struck down. People's upright walk is an expected positive response. Garrett brings to notice that the main aspect that is found in this unit is "return" and this is presented through the love of God which obliges Israel to return to their God in spite of their stumbling. The hope thus engendered is regarded as an open invitation to Israel to return (cf. 3:1-5): The Israelites must call their Physician to heal them. This healing will take place in the future. The call of Yahweh to Israel brings out the message that when they return with true penitence, God will forgive them and He will remain their God. The healing will be complete. The image here reveals the nature of God and His power over the people. Hosea forced them to repent for their sins and return to God with true words and repentance (cf. Psa. 51:16-17). The word spread or fragrance here means the roots of cedar in Lebanon (cf. Num. 24:6). The message of God will spread everywhere, the Jews will be renewed and other nations will be brought in and they will be like spreading branches and bring fruitfulness in abundant grace and good works. The assurance is that Israel would become productive and flourish like fragrance. Other nations would also flourish because they benefit from Israel's good work.

The word 'renown' is literally translated as 'remembrance.' Remembrance connotes the idea that Israel will be known worldwide and they will be admired because of God's promise that "I will make you as a great nation." The Lord will be admired through the people of Israel not idols. God will take care of Israel, because He provides them prosperity as a luxuriant cypress: from her the fruitfulness will come and they will be a blessing to many. The word 'return' occurs several times in Hosea to bring back the people and to be a blessing to others and the idea of hope continues in the future.

In chapter 14, the prophet invites Israel to repent in order to return to Yahweh. To convey this, the main metaphor used is healing. Here Hosea appealed to "Israel" using the honoured name for the nation. The repeated word in this section, שוב refers to Israel. Hosea wants the people to return to Yahweh and reminds them that everything will not be changed immediately. Hosea pronounces oracles of judgment but informs them that God does not want to punish them if they return. The main emphasis focused on the word שוב is due to the love of God which compels them to return. The people of Israel stumbled in their iniquities Hosea reminds them to return to their God. The healing will be complete when they return. The image here reveals the nature of God and His power over the people.

5.2.2. Progressive Texture

The progressive texture reveals the message that the people must truly repent and seek forgiveness. It includes people confessing their sins, leaving their apostasy, and following Yahweh.[976]

5.2.2.1. Model Prayer

The prophet instructs Israel to follow the model prayer and reminds them to implore God to take away their guilt and accept sincere prayers made by their lips.[977] Hosea reminds Israel, as in the Hebrew tradition, that God always looks with mercy on the orphan and those who are desperately in need of help.[978] The promise is that surely God will forgive his own children irrespective of their wayward activities (cf. 11:1-4, 8-11).[979]

כל-תשא עון	forgive us 14:2
בוט וחק	receive us 14:2
ונשלמה פרים שפתינו	we offer the fruit of our lips 14:2

The MT reads "we offer the fruit of our lips." According to Harper if Israel repents God will forgive their sins.[980] Keil proposes the meaning of the phrases that have to do with the prayers of penitential lips as thank offerings.[981] In a similar way, Laetsch says "these phrases are called as the gold figures of the characteristic of Hosea." The thank offering is to do with the true repentance of Israel that is the true offering spoken of by Hosea. Their lips overflow with gratitude and songs of praise and their hearts seek God's grace and forgiveness. The prayer to God to receive them means "receive us graciously."[982] The phrase is not about praise but about people's confession of their guilt. This shows that Israel is no longer proud, as they recognise that God is the source of everything. God is the one who provides life for Israel. The prayer of confession follows, with God's promise to forgive Israel's sins. God's reaction towards the healing of His people must be considered. The idea

[976] Macintosh, A.A, *A Critical and Exegetical Commentary on Hosea,* Edinburgh, T and T Clark, 1997, 561. Cf. Allen R. Guenther, *Hosea-Amos,* Scottdale, Herald Press, 1938/1997, 205-206.

[977] Mays, James Luther., *Hosea: A Commentary,* OTL, Philadelphia, Westminster, 1969, 186.

[978] Hubbard David Allan, *With Bands of Love* (Hosea), Grand Rapids, W.B. Eerdmans publishing co, 1968, 227.

[979] Gerald Morris, *Prophecy, Poetry and Hosea,* JSOT Supplement 219, Sheffield, Sheffield Press, 1996, 115-116.

[980] W.R. Harper, *A Critical and Exegetical Commentary on Amos and Hosea,* Edinburgh, T and T Clark, 1956, 412.

[981] Keil, *Minor Prophets,* Edinburgh, T and T Clark, 1871, 108.

[982] Wolff, *Hosea,* 231; cf. R. Gordia, The Text and Meaning of Hosea 14:3, *VT* 5, 1955, 87-91, these authors translates as good as word.

of relationship is presented that they will know that God is the healer. The literal meaning of this section is accepting Israel for their true confession and therefore doing them good. In medical terms, Israel is "taking its medicine" which will then bring healing. The prayer brings out God's pardon for their transgressions and then healing takes place. Healing in the Old Testament includes medical and surgical procedures and also treatment; this sometimes culminates in the functional repair of the damaged part of the body or mind. Here, healing refers directly to restoration of the general state of well-being and peaceful relationship with the covenant God.

5.2.2.2. Confession of Sins

The progressive texture explains people's confession in which they say that they will not depend upon military power, especially of the Assyrians.[983] This is shown in אשור אל נרואשו and אשור אל ונעישוי "Assyria cannot save us," "I shall respond to them and watch them." On the one hand, they are encouraged to leave their syncretistic faith, and on the other hand, they are persuaded to demonstrate their devotion toward Yahweh through their attitudes and actions.[984] Israel's repentance speech shows that they have become aware of their hope in Assyria and horses or idols cannot save them but it is only Yahweh as the physician / healer who can save them from political and military oppression, and false worship, when they confess to Him. Once Israel has "taken its medicine" by coming with true repentance, their covenant will be renewed. As they cry out -

אשור לא יושיענו	Assyria cannot save us 14:3
על־סוס לא נרכב	we will not ride on horses 14:3
ולא-נאמר עוד אלהינו	we will never call idols gods 14:3
אשר־בך ירחם יתום :	the Lord cares for the fatherless 14:3

Philip King points out that this shows that the people cannot be saved by political alliances.[985] Consequently Yahweh is eager to steer His covenant people away from their dependence on foreign military power because by depending on these they showed their lack of trust in Him. Convinced thus, the people realize that the covenant with God can save them from other nations. The procedure of healing continues. The people then renounce their relationship with other gods and confess to God that he, Yahweh, is their true God and they are His people. In addition, by restoring Israel's identity, Yahweh can show other nations how he "healed" his people. To establish this "healing" as witness in the eyes of other nations, a mutual relationship between God and His chosen people must be shown. The right offerings would be "words," prayers, the "fruit of the lips." But they must be genuine. God therefore wants His people to come with true confession and repentance and not with mere sacrifices and burnt offerings. Obliging thus His love and Israel's repentance are inseparable. Hosea portrays that Yahweh alone is the healer. The prophet clearly focuses on monotheism and the fact that it is God alone who can heal them and not the gods and kings from

[983] G.I. Davies, *Hosea-New Century Bible Commentary,* Grand Rapids, Wm. B. Eerdmans Publishing co, 1992, 303.

[984] Allen R. Guenther, *Hosea-Amos,* Scottdale, Herald Press, 1938/1997, 205-206.

[985] Philip King, *Amos-Micah: An Archaeological Commentary,* Philadelphia, Westminster, 1988, 125.

other nations. Assyria is presented here as subject, but in Hos. 5:13 the text indirectly refers to Yahweh alone, who is the healer of Judah and Ephraim. Though Assyria is a great king, he is not able to heal them; only Yahweh, the real and great King of Israel, is the healer. This fact is emphasised in 5:13 and 6:1. For this the prophet uses two different words, sickness and healing of the people. The prophet clearly brings out the message that Yahweh alone is the healer and the initiator of the covenant with Israel. When Israel turned away from Yahweh, the covenant was violated. In some places the prophet contrasts Yahweh with humans, because Yahweh is Israel's healer, a fact affirmed by Yahweh himself.

5.2.2.3. Apostasy

In 11:4 Hosea continues proclaiming the Lord's words to shows Israel how compassionate He is. The prophet urged the people to return to Him. The Hebrew word שוב is translated in verbal form, that God will heal their משובתם.[986] Macintosh notes that the term משובתם refers to more sickness (cf. Jer. 3:22; I will heal your "waywardness").[987] For Stuart, משובתם means the people turning back to worshipping false gods and this characterizes Israel in the past (cf. Hos. 5:4; 7:2; 11:5) and Yahweh's promise is to heal their apostasy.[988] This is a great hope for the people, since the prophet's message about doom is turned into hope for the future. The people's return is presented in the form of a physician who heals their sickness. God is not only a physician but also a healer.

Table 21: Summary of the progressive texture - Hosea 14:2-9

שוב	return (repentance) (v. 1)
עמכם דברים ושובו אל-יהוה	you and return to the Lord (v. 2)
אלהינו	our God (v. 3)
יהוה	Lord (v. 9)

The Lord reminds the people in v. 1 that they have stumbled because of their iniquity and their transgressions are before Him. In the middle of the section (vv. 4-7) God's nature is shown. The other aspect noted here is of two extremes first, the disloyalty of people of Israel and second, Yahweh's love: People's character is negative while Yahweh's character is positive.[989]

The progressive texture helps us to understand that Yahweh's love continues to be with Israel though they have gone astray by following other gods. The message to the people is that when they leave their waywardness and sin they will escape punishment. Verse 4 begins with the idea that God is going to answer their prayers. Yahweh's loving kindness presents a response in a figurative way and their future prosperity lies in the renewed covenant of love. Yahweh assures Israel that one day He will heal and reinstate His covenant with them. Israel committed sin, but because

[986] Mays, James Luther., *Hosea: A Commentary,* OTL, Philadelphia, Westminster, 1969, 187.

[987] Macintosh, A.A. *A Critical and Exegetical Commentary on Hosea,* Edinburgh, T and T Clark, 1997, 567-568.

[988] Stuart, D. *Hosea-Jonah.* Waco, Word, 1987, 213-214.

[989] Mays, James Luther., *Hosea: A Commentary,* OTL, Philadelphia, Westminster, 1969, 189.

of Yahweh's promise, the healing will take place but only in the future. The promise is related to God's generous love and the covenant term אהב.

The prophet clearly portrays Yahweh as healer in the present time, but also in the future. On the day of the Lord Yahweh will heal Israel's wounds and this will result in complete restoration for Israel and Judah. The prophet teaches hope in the future when the whole man will be healed. This is clearly established in the prophetic expectation of the kingdom of God. Not only righteousness and peace would prevail but sickness would also disappear. In addition the future healing and restoration will not only be for Israel but also for all other nations. Yahweh is the only real healer and He cannot be compared with other gods.

5.2.3. Narrative Texture

In the narrative texture, it is noted that Israel must leave their dealings with foreign alliances and deities and follow only Yahweh. Yahweh is the provider who reminds them to keep up their covenantal relationship with Him.

5.2.3.1. Metaphor of כטל

The emphatic כטל uses here as adverb to describe the pardon to call for one is entirely complete. God's love is described in rich and colourful metaphors, especially in the context of the words of judgment. Dempsey points out that in this context, Yahweh is presented as a lion, a leopard and an angry bear.[990] These animals are regarded as dangerous and destructive. In contrast, in the same verse, Yahweh is compared with dew which helps life grow. In the familiar threefold literary style of the book, the Lord uses three similes employing imagery of refreshment and revitalization (v. 5). The Lord first promises them that He will become "like the dew to Israel." Harper finds that the dew here notes a figure of beneficence and kindness.[991] James Limburg points out that the image of dew is already used in Hosea 6:4 and 13:3 as a negative concept that does not last long, but here the image is used in a positive sense to convey God's presence and influence.[992] The reversal of imagery is that the dew becomes symbolic here for a life-giving vitality that provides the source of renewed life and strength for Israel that is by God himself. The renewed strength brings water resources that are health, beauty, and fragrance to the land.

Noth says that in chapter 14, the dew brings new life and becomes a source of life for the people of Israel that is, by God Himself in the role of healer.[993] Thus the people of Israel will be nourished and healed by the love of Yahweh.

In the concluding verse of the last chapter here, Yahweh speaks of Israel's healing and His love for them. It is the sustaining presence of Yahweh as dew (טל) that heals the fickleness, dryness and unfruitfulness that are attributed to the people in

---

[990] Carol J. Dempsey, *The Prophets: A Liberation-Critical Reading,* Minneapolis, Fortress Press, 2000, 158.

[991] W.R. Harper, *A Critical and Exegetical Commentary on Amos and Hosea,* Edinburgh, T and T Clark, 1956, 413.

[992] James Limburg, *Hosea-Micah, Interpretation,* Westminster, John Knox Press, 2011, 51. Cf. Beeby, H.D., *Grace Abounding: A Commentary on the book of Hosea,* Grand Rapids, Eerdmans, 1989, 183.

[993] G.I. Davies, *Hosea-New Century Bible Commentary,* Grand Rapids, Wm. B. Eerdmans co, 1992, 305-306.

Hosea.[994] The prophet uses dew in a figurative and metaphorical way to communicate God's love for Israel.

5.2.3.2. Symbolism of Productivity in the Land

The symbolic reference of productivity talks about the crops and in the eschatological response refers to Hosea 2. The verb ענה is used in Hosea 2:23-25 and 14:6. Here Yahweh promises Israel that their land will be gifted back to them, which is symbolic of Israel receiving their covenant blessings. Because of their disobedience in following Baal, they lost all their belongings. Stuart says that when people leave their idols and follow Yahweh, the promise is that they will get their same land back.[995] The language that is used in this context is hyperbolic (e.g. milk and honey). Israel's future is explained through stability ("his shoots"), a visibility ("his splendour") and desirability ("his scent"). Here the theme of covenant blessing is symbolised through the agricultural gift of land, and is expressed by Hosea in covenant terms. (cf. Deut. 33:13-16; 30:9-10; Jer. 33:13; Amos. 9:13-14; Joel. 3:17).

A repentant and forgiven Israel would once again be fruitful, for she will receive and acknowledge that her fruit comes from the Lord.[996] The life of God's people will be lived out in true spiritual success that comes from their relationship to Yahweh. This new life is given out of his "love" towards his people. And this love needs to be understood as His personal reason. The good news about God's healing love, which represents the climax of this passage, is expressed here: *"I will heal their faithfulness; I will love them freely."* God's portrait of Israel's grand future concludes with scenes of living once again in the Promised Land. The people will find protection and rest under the shade of the new tree that is Israel.[997] The future of Israel will be like living once again in the Promised Land. The other nations will seek to find their blessings in connection with the renewed Israel. As Garrett mentions, if Israel is the metaphorical tree in whose shade other nations dwell, the conceptual unity and the relationship is maintained as an implied expectation.[998] The Gentiles also will be included in the eschaton and bring blessing in Israel. The prophecies of the future of the people will be fulfilled in the future. The healing has been completed; the patient is whole again. The shade tree here refers to the Lord: *they shall return and dwell beneath my shadow.*

The image of the protective shadow of Almighty God is an important one in the Scriptures (cf. Psa. 91:1). The following lines deal with details of future Israel and reference to the Israel, the people will come under the shadow of His wings.

The healer metaphor does not merely refer to the people alone but also to the land as it is in the text. The healing of the land and God's creation is emphasised in this context. In certain context it becomes difficult to distinguish between people and material, this is because of the materials used in understanding the concept of healing

---

[994] Dearman, J.A, *The Book of Hosea,*" NICOT, Grand Rapids, Wm. B. Eerdmans Publishing co, 2010, 341.

[995] Stuart, D. *Hosea-Jonah,* Word Biblical Commentary 31, Waco, Texas, Word Books, 1987, 215-216.

[996] J. E. Smith, *The Minor Prophets – Old Testament Survey Series,* Joplin, College Press, 1994.

[997] Allen R. Guenther, *Hosea-Amos,* Scottdale, Herald Press, 1938/1997, 206-207.

[998] Garrett, *Hosea, Joel, An Exegetical and Theological Exposition of Holy Scripture,* Nashville, Broadman and Holman, 1997, 275.

of people and land. This comprehensive healing includes the physical, the land, the city and the temple and offers abundance of prosperity and security and restoration of the fortunes of his elected people. This is evident in the life of the people of Israel when they were crossing of the Dead Sea. The prophet describes different dimensions of Yahweh's comprehensive healing in order to emphasise everything about God's healing of the land, and creation. Yahweh is presented here as the healer of the nation who will bring healing to the land and for his creation. The healing metaphor refers to the healing of a whole people not just individual. Yahweh's healing was not restricted only to his elected people alone, the healing is extended to other nations also (Egypt and Babylon).

5.2.3.3. The Call and Answer Motif

God's promise is reminiscent of the familiar call and answer motif that so often speaks of intimate communion between God and His people.[999] The call and answer motif underscores God's availability to come to the aid of His people for refuge and deliverance from various dangers (Psa. 20:6-9; 81:6-7; 102:1-2; 138:8). As here, the motif also has an eschatological setting (cf. Zec. 13:7-9).

Due to the restored relationship between Yahweh and His covenant people, their future will be bright and prosperous. Yahweh says in this regard, *"before they even call out, I will respond; while they are still speaking, I will hear"* (Isa. 65:24). The life of God's people will be lived out in true spiritual success that comes from their relationship to Him.

In the narrative texture, it is noted that Israel must leave their dealings with foreign alliances and deities and follow only Yahweh. Yahweh is the provider who reminds them to keep up their covenantal relationship with Him. Yahweh speaks of Israel's healing and His love for them. A repentant and forgiven Israel would once again be fruitful, for she will receive and acknowledge that her fruit comes from the Lord. The lesson here is that Israel must realise that their life is based on the Lord. The Lord predicts that Israel's future blessing would make it like an olive tree. The imagery is to show that the Israel will be like a luxuriant simile for Yahweh. Here the Lord who compares himself with the luxuriant tree, Israel's source of power and success is provided by the Lord. The assurance of blessing is attributed in the form of fruit vine. A repentant, forgiven Israel could be and they will once again be fruitful and people will be received and acknowledged because their fruit comes from the Lord. The life is given to them by God and success follows in relation to their surrender to the Lord, and He gives life to them.

5.2.4. Opening-Middle-Closing

Opening-Middle-Closing texture is about the beginning, body and conclusion of a selected pericope. The opening-middle-closing texture section explains Yahweh as the physician-healer. In this section, Hosea reminds Israel to abandon their cultic worship and return to Yahweh.

---

[999] Allen R. Guenther, *Hosea-Amos,* Scottdale, Herald Press, 1938/1997, 206-208.

5.2.4.1. Opening Texture

The opening texture discusses the prophetic exhortation and call for return. The prophet's reminder to Israel to return to their God is dealt with in this section.

The opening, middle and closing texture all discusses here the prophetic exhortation and call for return. Hosea reminds the people to return to Yahweh by a true confession. Hosea reminds them that there is hope for Israel through their repentance, and that they can escape going into exile. This unit is divided into two parts: first, a prophetic exhortation calling for return (vv. 1-2); and second, Yahweh's promise of salvation to Israel (vv. 4-8).[1000] In 14:2-8 (1-7), Hosea has coupled prophetic exhortation to Israel v. 2-4 (1-3) with God's promise of "restoration" vv. 5-9 (4-8). The patient's "medicine" is offered Israel is summoned, urged, and persuaded to return to Yahweh from their regretful situation. If the people will honestly return to God, He will in turn, respond to them and restore them in abundance and healing will take place.

The opening texture is about prophetic exhortation to Israel (14:2-4). This oracle has an historical element reminiscent of the final months of the Northern Kingdom's defeat by Shalmaneser V.[1001] It emphasises that the end of Ephraim with all its politics / policies and cult is imminent. Hosea here calls for a שׁוּב, a coming back to Yahweh. In Hosea's time, worship had become almost inarticulate, just "a dead routine of the legal sacrifices."[1002] The prophet urges a confession (a "medicine") which would come voluntarily from the heart.

5.2.4.2. Middle Texture

5.2.4.2.1. The Concept of Hope

Hosea 14:5-8 talks about Israel's future and their prosperity that lies with Yahweh. The metaphor of adoption used in this context is an accusation. The Israelites should know that it was God who adopted them. The adoption metaphor denotes of a new covenant, the people are invited to experience the love of God and turn to Him. In this context, it is noted that vv. 5-8 do not provide a date. The suggested wording of the prayer of penitence in v. 4 may presume a situation in which neither political nor military manoeuvring has validity any longer.[1003] They are invited, urged and pleaded to turn back to their God to escape from punishment. When people honestly confess their sins to God, then God will respond mercifully to them and He will renew His covenantal relationship with them. Again, the emphasis is on "taking the medicine" confesses and repents, turns again to Yahweh, who will forgive. In this way, the healing will be complete.

5.2.4.2.2. Prophetic Summons

The section 14:2-9 (1-8) is considered as a prophetic summons and which one should respond in penitence to the call of the prophet.[1004] Hosea 14:2-9 concludes the

---

[1000] Rudolph, W. *Hosea,* KAT, XIII/1, Gütersloh, Gütersloher Verlagshaus Gerd Mohn, 1966, 149-153.

[1001] Mays, James Luther., *Hosea: A Commentary,* OTL, Philadelphia, Westminster, 1969, 184-185.

[1002] Allen R. Guenther, *Hosea-Amos,* Scottdale, Herald Press, 1938/1997, 206.

[1003] Stuart. D, *Hosea-Jonah.* Waco, Word, 1987, 212.

[1004] A.A. Macintosh, "Hosea," *The International Critical Commentary,* edited by J.A. Emerton and G. N. Stanton Edinburg, T and T Clark, 1997, 558-559.

prophecies uttered by the prophet and reminds the people to pray for their forgiveness. The oracles of judgment over Israel turn into a message of hope. Hosea reminds Israel of their repentance and salvation and God's promise of restoration (vv. 5-9). The prophet reminds Israel to be a witness to being a covenant people. The prophecy points to a future in which the failures of the past will be overcome by Yahweh's redemption. Israel is reminded of their covenantal relationship of being His people through God's love song (14:4-8). Hosea concludes his prophetic summons with transformation, forgiveness and restoration.

5.2.4.3. Closing Texture

Hosea 14:2-9 concludes the prophecies of Hosea, and prayer is offered for Israel in Hosea's name.[1005] In chapters 1-3, the prophecies of anguish and wounding are clearly seen. The redactor presents Hosea's message containing doom, and particularly Samaria's terrible end (cf. 13:1-14:1). The idea is that Israel should realize the real situation and return to God with their true repentance and prayer Yahweh as the physician/healer has offered the appropriate medicine-now it is up to Israel to "take their medicine" and regain their previous health. Mays comments that this kind of prayer is understood as a means of access to God. The people of Israel should bring sacrifice and come with a broken heart for forgiveness.[1006] The future of Israel is envisioned here. Hosea presents an important message to the reader that God's promise of restoration is for the future of Israel. God shows His love to His people Israel, through which He reflects His Love towards all His people.

The opening, middle and closing texture discusses here the prophetic exhortation and call for return. The opening texture is about prophetic exhortation to Israel. Hosea reminds the people to return to Yahweh by a true confession. He reminds them that there is hope for Israel through their repentance, and that they can escape going into exile. Hosea 14:5-8 talks about Israel's future and their prosperity that lies with Yahweh. Hosea 14:2-9 concludes the prophecies uttered by the prophet and reminds the people to pray for their forgiveness. Hosea reminds Israel of their repentance and salvation and God's promise of restoration (vv. 5-9). The prophet reminds Israel to be a witness to being a covenant people.

5.2.5. Argumentative Texture

5.2.5.1. The Nature of Hosea's Plea

In Hosea 6:1 the prophet urges the people to return to their Lord which is seen as pre-requisite for Yahweh's healing. Hosea reminds Israel that repentance is not always seen as a pre-condition for healing. In Hosea 11 healing and forgiveness were offered despite the fact that Israel was continually sacrificing to other gods and burning incense to the idols. Hosea refers Israel as a child who continues to disrespect God's fatherly love (cf. Hos. 11:1-3). The divine announcement is seen as part of the healing in Hosea 14:5, the divine announcement does not bring result because the people continue in their backsliding. Yahweh's healing comes based on Israel's making true repentance and returning to Him. By confession and return,

[1005] Stuart. D. *Hosea-Jonah,* Waco, Word, 1987, 210.

[1006] Mays, James Luther., *Hosea: A Commentary,* OTL, Philadelphia, Westminster, 1969, 186.

the Lord will love them generously and spontaneously. The final chapter of Hosea begins with his last plea to the people of Israel to forsake their sinful and self-centred ways. His plea is a double layered one, which also contains some sound spiritual and practical advice.[1007] Sweeney proposes that "by appealing to Israel to "return" to Yahweh and to reject its alliance with Assyria, Hosea 14:2-9 recounts the primary theme of the book: rejection of Yahweh in favour of relations with Assyria, and seeks its reversal."[1008] Samuel J. Schulz points out that Hosea's first plea is a general call to the whole of Israel to acknowledge that their sin has brought them to the point of extinction. In the first instance, Hosea had challenged and condemned the priests who had misled the people with their syncretistic teachings (Hos. 4:4-5). In the following chapter (5:1-5), Hosea broadened the condemnation to include not only priests but also the upper class of the society, especially those from the tribe of Ephraim (vv. 4-5).[1009] Hosea's second plea is twofold, calling for both a return to the Lord and for repentance (v. 2). Hosea's use of two imperatives for "return" (vv. 1-2) and a third for "repent" is once again typical of his familiar threefold style.[1010] This second double plea return and repent is addressed to the whole of Israel. If the previously promised guarantees of divine acceptance, forgiveness, and restoration were to be realized (cf. 6:1-3; 11:10-11), it was imperative that Israel should act immediately. It does reveal God's patience to wait for Israel to return to Him.

Hosea 14 enforces the physician/patient healer/sufferer concept the healing will come from God's love. God is ready to heal the people of Israel when they come with true repentance, but this may not happen immediately.[1011] Like any physician-patient relationship, healing comes in the future, not immediately. In medical terms, when one obeys the instructions or prescription, healing will come eventually.

Here the prophet clearly explains that Yahweh's healing was more than medical or physical process; it was a spiritual healing of Israel and Judah. Here, Yahweh is presented as the healer of sins and broken relationships following judgment and punishment. Healing is presented in terms of forgiveness, followed by repentance; obedience is seen as pre-requisite for Yahweh's healing.

5.2.5.2. The Assurance of Salvation

In vv. 2-4 (1-3) Yahweh summons the people to return to Him, if they do not respond, they will experience severe consequences. It is a threat that later results in assurance.[1012] The first part of chapter 14 deals with the divine speech and the assurance of salvation.

[1007] Allen R. Guenther, *Hosea-Amos,* Scottdale, Herald Press, 1938/1997, 206.

[1008] Sweeney, Marvin A. *Twelve Prophets,* 2 vols. Collegeville: Liturgical Press, 2000, 136.

[1009] Samuel J. Schulz, *The Old Testament Speaks,* New York, Harper and Brothers Publishers, 1960, 388.

[1010] Andersen, F.I and Freedman, D.N., *Hosea: A New Translation with Introduction and Commentary,* New York, Doubleday, 1980, 645.

[1011] Grace I. Emmerson, *Hosea an Israelite prophet in Judean perspective,* JSOT press, Sheffield, 1984, 46.

[1012] H.D. Beeby, *Hosea, Grace Abounding*-ITC, Grand Rapids, Wm. B. Eerdmans publishing co, 1989, 178.

Table 22: Lord's Response

אהיה כטל	I will be like dew 14:5
אני עניתי	I will answer 14:8
אני ואשורנו	I will care 14:8
אני כברוש רענן	I am like a fruitful pine 14:8

Hosean metaphors of love continue to demonstrate salvation (vv. 5-8). The statement *I will be like the dew to Israel* has tenor of divine care and refreshment 14:5. The concept of dew is referred as important phenomenon for agricultural produce in the Syria-Palestine during the summer season in their life period.[1013] The renunciation in v. 4 and assurance of salvation in v. 9b are believed to be similar in structure.[1014] In the earlier section (Hos. 2-3), God is portrayed in the form of a fiancé and husband, and his love shows his own nature. This love is presented as spontaneous and unconditional (cf. 2:19-20). A similarity is seen here between 14:5-7 and the Song of Songs. In both cases, the hymn of love is presented in the form of imagery.[1015] The prophet adds delicacy and sarcasm to the rhetorical questions in relation to God and his relationship with other gods. Hosea affirms that Yahweh alone responds to Israel and cares for others (Ephraim). The wordplay brings out the poet's intention and the imagery continues. Hosea uses this language of love to persuade Israel to see reason and to come to their senses. Thus, Hosea uses a combination of a court like plea and persuasive wooing to get his message across.

5.2.5.3. Healing and Salvation

The Old Testament employs various metaphors for Yahweh as judge, king, and father. Here Yahweh is presented as healer. While this is not a major metaphor in the Old Testament, plays a significant role in the book of Hosea. The portrayal of Yahweh as healer is significant for the people of Israel. Sickness and death are seen in a negative way. Here, Yahweh is the healer and giver of life. Hosea refers to Yahweh in terms of divine restoration for the nation. Yahweh's healing comes after his judgment and punishing the people. The punishment is expressed in different forms and linked together with Yahweh as healer. James Ward in his article suggests that the concept of רפא is belonging to God. The richness of the metaphor and similes Hosea employed in referring to God's being and activity is unsurpassed in other biblical writings.[1016] Thus, the metaphor of God as רפא is expressed in the words of Hosea to a nation that is in need of restoration. Regarding Hosea 14 there are few research works done: Oestreich says that there are several interpretations based on Hosea 1-3, but Hosea 14 is neglected. For this reason, the research has chosen chapter 14 to indicate the metaphors and similes referring to Yahweh as healing, loving, dew and tree and

---

[1013] "Flora and Fauna Metaphors in Hosea," and "Similies and Metaphors for Political Actions in Hosea 4-14."

[1014] Dearman, J.A, *The Book of Hosea,*" NICOT, Grand Rapids, Wm. B. Eerdmans Publishing co, 2010, 333.

[1015] H.D. Beeby, *Hosea, Grace Abounding*-ITC, Grand Rapids, Wm. B. Eerdmans publishing co, 1989, 183.

[1016] J.M. Ward., "The Message of the Prophet Hosea," *Interpretation* 23, No. 4, 1969, 387-407.

these are the ones investigated in the book.[1017] The book deals with interpretation based on the background of their language conventions. The book brings out clearly that Hosea's metaphors and similes are deeply rooted in the Israelite language traditions. All the metaphors in Hosea 14 are traditionally connected with kingship. Recently, Seong-Hyuk Hong deals with the topic on illness and the healing metaphor in Hosea 14. The book focuses on social connotation of the metaphor in Hosea 5:8-6:3 and 7:1-7.[1018] This work incorporates a theoretical analysis of metaphor into a sociological discussion about the social reality of the eighth century Israel and Judah and comparative study of the concept of illness and healing in the ancient Near East and traditional East Asia (Korea) context.

In the Old Testament we find many metaphors for Yahweh, but there is no single metaphor which speaks about Yahweh as Israel's God. In the Bible, Yahweh as healer and the concept of healing play a significant role in the prophetic books.[1019] It is interesting to observe how the prophets present Yahweh as healer. According to the prophets, the books focus more on spiritual healing of Israel and Judah rather than on medical or physical healing of the individual (cf. Isa. 57:18-19; Jer. 3:22; 30:17; Hos. 14:5 [Eng. 4]). The healing metaphor conveys Yahweh as subject in prophetic literature. Repentance or return is seen as a pre-requisite for Yahweh's healing (Isa. 6:10; 19:22; Jer. 3:22; Hos. 6:1).[1020] In Hosea 11, healing and forgiveness are acknowledged despite Israel continuing to sacrifice and make offerings to Baal. The child, in Hosea 11 disrespected the love of God its father (cf. Hos. 11:1-3). In Hosea 14:5 [Eng. 4] noted the divine announcement of healing even though the people were backsliding and continued to do so.

Repentance and healing are not occasioned by Israel's repentance or her good intentions but because of Yahweh's generous and free grace. This can be seen נדבה (Hos. 14:5 [Eng. 4]) emphasises that Yahweh's love is spontaneous, generous and freely given.[1021] Hosea 14:2-4 (1-3) appears to be in prose form. Hosea uses terms like healing and salvation interchangeably for repentance in this context. The prophet calls the people to return to Yahweh with true penitence.[1022] In this passage, there are words like "healing" and "salvation, "which have great significance. This is evident in the following verses 5-9 (4-8).[1023] Synonymous parallelisms are dominant in this passage. It is important to note that the catch words in this passage, such as שוב, רפא, משובתה and ישב are used with a purpose.

[1017] Bernhard Oestreich: *Metaphors and Similes for Yahweh in Hosea 14:2-9 (1-8): A Study of Hoseanic Pictorial Language,* Friedensauer Schriftenreihe: Reihe A, Theologie, Frankfurt am Main, Peter Lang, 1998.

[1018] Seong-Hyuk Hong, *The Metaphor of Illness and Healing in Hosea and Its Significance in the Socio-Economic Context of Eighth-century Israel and Judah,* New York, Peter Lang, 2006.

[1019] Brueggemann, *Theology of the Old Testament: Testimony, dispute, Advocacy*, Minneapolis, Fortress Press, 1997, 230-261.

[1020] According to Mosis, 1989, 51, he believes that in Isaiah the term repentance or return depicts the physical return from exile. Mosis, R., Umkehr und Vergebung: eine Auslegung von Jer 3;21-4:2, Trierer Theologische Zeitschrift, 98: 39-60.

[1021] Carppenter and Grisanti, *NIDOTTE* 3, 1997, 31-33.

[1022] Dearman, J.A, *The Book of Hosea,*" NICOT, Grand Rapids, Wm. B. Eerdmans Publishing co, 2010, 333.

[1023] Dearman, J.A., *The Book of Hosea,*" NICOT, Grand Rapids, Wm. B. Eerdmans Publishing co, 2010, 333.

The themes of chapter 14 are much related to chapter 11. The narrator uses the same catch words in these two chapters (Hosea. 11, 14), like "to return," "to heal," and "to dwell." Stuart points out that Israel's hope is based on covenant promise. Hosea reminds Israel that God will not rebuke nor reject them completely. The concept of healing comes as a remedy for the entire nation, He will heal them at a 'time in the future' or 'at a time in the distant future,' God reminds them that, *"there is none beside Me"* and *"I am your God," "I will heal"* there is none beside Him and He is their God.[1024] Through Stuart's argument it can be accepted that the revival and restoration to life will be in the future. This looks like the fulfilment will take place in future generations. If Israel places hope in Yahweh, He promises a divine healing. Hosea talks about healing as both physical and spiritual in nature. According to Macintosh, the positive message comes from Yahweh alone and only He can reverse what has been done.[1025] But Wolff suggests "He will revive us, preserve life and restore to new life and He will make us whole."[1026] The assurance is that healing will bring salvation to the wounded people. He will heal their wounds and restore them to full life.

Israel acknowledges her guilt in her prayer; this was followed by Yahweh's promise to forgive Israel's guilt. It might have been difficult for Israelites to leave their apostasy. Yahweh declares that He is not only a physician who can help her external necessities, but that he can also heal her stubbornness. Yahweh adds that He has loved them freely and His promise of future readiness to continually love is in fact the expression of His love which is already at work. The verse portrays God not only as a physician who can heal them, but also as one who forgives their guilt spiritual healing as well as physical healing. Here, the nation is referred as sick and needs complete healing for this, Israel must repent and seek Yahweh's healing; this healing is not for the elected people Israel alone, but God also extends his healing to Egypt (Isa. 19:22) and Babylon (Jer. 51:8-9). This makes clear Yahweh's healing is not only limited to his chosen people but also to other nations. In the following references we see that they focus on the relationship between Yahweh as healer and other nations, the above texts referring to Egypt and Babylon. The prophet refers to Egypt looking for healing but becoming conceited. They are summoned to go to Gilead for healing medicine. This is followed by Yahweh's intention to heal Babylon but she could not be healed, because she is fallen. The above references portray that Yahweh's intention is to heal other nations, but the texts do not say if real healing was accomplished. The real meaning of the word refers to another nation and its healing. Yahweh's promise is to heal other nations such as Egypt when they repent. We see the dual role of Yahweh as one who both smites and heals (cf. Isa. 57:18-19).

5.2.6. Sensory and Aesthetic Texture

Sensory-aesthetic textures focus on the range of senses and discourses within the pericope. This suggests the senses and images that make things clear for the reader.

[1024] Stuart, D. *Hosea-Jonah,* Word Biblical Commentary 31, Waco, Texas, Word Books, 1987, 107-108.

[1025] H.W. Wolff, *Hosea* (G. Stansell, Trans.), Philadelphia, Fortress Press, 1974, 216.

[1026] Wolff, H.W., *A Commentary on the Book of the Prophet Hosea,* Philadelphia, Fortress, 1974, 117.

5.2.6.1. Zone of "Emotion-Fused Thinking"

This unit shows two things: first, God's promises of love; and second, withdrawal of His anger. In vv. 1-3, Israel's return is explained in detail. Israel is told how they can escape from judgment through repentance.[1027] But in vv. 4-8, a shift takes place through God's response in the form of a call to Israel. This is further strengthened through an indication by way of a love song of people's return.[1028] God's love forgives the remnant Israel and they respond to Him with a true return.

The next emotion in the passage is anger. The word שׁוּב "with anger" implies an object and Israel is collectively addressed in the singular. The covenant term אהב reminds them of Yahweh's love for their forefathers.[1029] The word is used as a technical term so that they may be loyal in their behaviour.

The Hebrew words: כי שב אפי ממנו can be translated as "because My anger turned back from him." Harper says that the pronoun is 3rd person singular that is collective. The Babylonian Codex has *from me,*[1030] it is qal perfect, which normally is in the past tense form.[1031] But Stuart translates it as *"for My anger will have turned from him,"* and he notes that there is a "prediction" that God's anger will turn into good in the future.[1032] The text refers to the incident that has taken place already; it is not talking about what is going to take place in the future. The statement is about Yahweh's anger turning away from Israel. It is not Assyria (idolatry) who is going to save them but God. This reveals that God is the one who remembers those who are forgotten.

5.2.6.2. Zone of "Self-Expressive Speech"

Wolff comments that vv. 5-7 is rich in colourful metaphors to bring about God's love persuasively.[1033] Hence God is expressed through a variety of images in zone of self-expressive speech. Yahweh is compared with a lion, a leopard and an angry bear, but now he compares himself with "dew" mainly because these animals endanger and destroy, but dew gives new life and productivity.[1034] כטל (verse 5) in Hosea is described as a sign of Israel's fickleness (6:4) that leads to complete evaporation (13:3), while v. 5 say that Yahweh will remain as dew that reverses fickleness, people's unfaithfulness, and their dryness. "Dew" here can be read as meaning "medicine," continuing the physician-patient concept of something offered to the patient to aid his recovery.

1027 Mays, James Luther., *Hosea: A Commentary,* OTL, Philadelphia, Westminster, 1969, 184-185.

1028 Hubbard David Allan, *With Bands of Love* (Hosea), Grand Rapids, W.B. Eerdmans Publishing co, 1968, 225.

1029 G.I. Davies, *Hosea-New Century Bible Commentary,* Grand Rapids, Wm. B. Eerdmans Publishing co, 1992, 305.

1030 W.R. Harper, *A Critical and Exegetical Commentary on Amos and Hosea,* Edinburgh, T and T Clark, 1956, 413.

1031 G.I. Davies, *Hosea-New Century Bible Commentary,* Grand Rapids, Wm. B. Eerdmans publishing co, 1992, 305.

1032 Stuart. D, *Hosea-Jonah,* Waco, Word, 1987, 215.

1033 Wolff, H.W., *A Commentary on the Book of the Prophet Hosea,* Philadelphia, Fortress, 1974, 235-236.

1034 G.I. Davies, *Hosea-New Century Bible Commentary,* Grand Rapids, Wm. B. Eerdmans, 1992, 305-306.

Here the prophet renders the flower's identification as "lily." The Hebrew term שושנה 'lily' is used of various flowers.[1035] Most English versions render the word as lily, but the Anchor Bible identifies it as the crocus.[1036] Walker identifies the flower in a question both as an iris that is of a delicate colour, orchid blue shade, and the flower known as Scarlet Martagon because of its magnificent red petals and sepals.[1037] As Macintosh puts it, "this unit has a series of similes that the prophet uses for Yahweh's love for Israel."[1038] The Hebrew word ינקותיו is used here as a sign of flourishing and growth.[1039] This is used as symbolic of what they will be like when they return to God. Hosea uses symbolism to picture how they will be a shady tree for others and they will become in the future shady trees.[1040] As a result, through God's love and mercy they shall flourish like olive tree and a cedar of Lebanon. The Israelites will become in the future beautiful like the olive tree. In ancient Israelite culture, the olive tree was an important asset.[1041] Thus, the Psalmist metaphorically likened himself to a flourishing olive tree through God's care and love for him (Psa. 52:8). The tree is associated with the covenant between the Lord and Israel. Israel is compared with a flourishing olive tree, that produces beautiful fruit and is destined to be burned (Jer. 11:16-17). They will become a source of beneficial products. Israel will take root strongly and grow like a cedar of Lebanon. The lily and the cedar of Lebanon both refer to Israel's prosperity in the future. Here we note God's assurance to Israel is a renewed relationship to Him; Israel's splendour shows that they will once again be "like an olive tree" (Hos. 14:6).[1042] The fulfilment of this promise will take place with Yahweh's help, and the assurance is given to them here through various similes.

5.2.6.3. The Zone of "Purposeful Action"

Another important aspect to be noted is that the prophet reveals not only the feelings but also the "actions" of God. Yahweh acts purposefully by promising restoration or healing to the people, while they need to make directed efforts to return to Him (another reference to "medicine)." Hosea compares restoration to healing which Assyria could not effect (5:13). However, Israel continues to look towards Assyria but not to Yahweh (6:1).[1043] We can see that there is some kind of continuation, because after the request for the restoration of their relationship with God, comes a pledge to modify their behaviour, so that restoration will not be necessary again for the people of Israel.

[1035] Garrett, *Hosea, Joel, An Exegetical and Theological Exposition of Holy Scripture,* Nashville, Broadman and Holman, 1997, 274.

[1036] Stuart. D, *Hosea-Jonah,* Waco, Word, 1987, 210.

[1037] W. Walker, *All the Plants of the Bible,* New York, Harper Publishers, 1957, 114.

[1038] Macintosh, A.A, *A Critical and Exegetical Commentary on Hosea,* Edinburgh, T and T Clark, 1997, 571.

[1039] Shank Harold, *Hosea-Micah,* Vol. 1, Joplin, Missouri, College Press Publishing Co, 2001, 139-140.

[1040] W.R. Harper, *A Critical and Exegetical Commentary on Amos and Hosea,* Edinburgh, T and T Clark, 1956, 408.

[1041] R.K. Harrison, "Olive Tree," *ISBE,* Rev. ed., Vol. 3:589-590.

[1042] W. Walker, *All the Plants of the Bible,* New York, Harper Publishers, 1957, 154.

[1043] David. F. Hinson, *Old Testament Introduction to the books of the Old Testament,* London, SPCK, 1974, 79-80. Hubbard David Allan, *With Bands of Love* (Hosea), Grand Rapids, W.B. Eerdmans Publishing co, 1968, 228.

If they follow God's instructions with immediate action, the positive message that comes to them is that their backsliding will be forgiven, they will be healed, and their relationship will be restored through the renewal of the covenantal relationship.

5.3. Inter-textuality

In inter-textuality we realise that Yahweh's anger and condemnation are explained as the background. The judgment that was pronounced earlier has been cancelled because of God's promise. The prophet announced doom on Israel, but on the other hand, God's passion is revealed through the power of love in the words "I will love them freely and generously (v. 5a)." Harper says that the phrase אהבם נדבה *"I will love them freely"* means *"I will love them with a free-will offering."*[1044] Wolff translates as "I will love them spontaneously."[1045] This means the noble love which accomplishes its task for whoever confesses their sin. Whereas Stuart, *"I will love them voluntarily"* and continues with that promise of generous love that employs the covenant term אהב.[1046]

In the Old Testament a key theme is that "*I, the Lord, am your healer*" (Exo. 15:26). The context of this verse is that the Lord of the covenant is "healer" one who prevents the diseases and afflicted Egyptians. This stands in sharp contrast to the priest physician in ancient Egypt, who functioned as healer in the literary and pictorial materials. The Egyptian priest physician performs magic and relied on superstition,[1047] whereas Hosea emphasises that the Lord is the healer and physician. God healed them from their broken heartedness and prayer of penitence bringing healing from the Lord. The Lord is not only the one who guided them in the wilderness journey but also the one with all power over sickness and authority. The covenant people are reminded that the healing comes from the Lord alone. In Hosea, the Lord promises his love graciously given to those who listen to the call to return to him for forgiveness. The themes of healing, forgiveness and salvation are intertwined in the Bible. Healing involves not merely physical restoration; it includes the deeper purpose of forgiveness and restoration into fellowship with God. In the Scripture healing is the experience or process which restores fallen and alienated human beings to intimate relationship, fellowship and communion with God.

In Deuteronomy 4:37 אהב את־אבתיך is translated as 'he loved your fathers,' this is used as a technical term to be found in the treaties meaning 'be loyal to,' or 'show faithfulness to;' it is understood as emotional closeness. This love cannot be earned by the people, but it is Yahweh's love. The love is a voluntary offering; God gives love as a blessing to His people. Expressed in a simple way, it is Yahweh's love for the wayward people, but, at the same time, the promise is conditional and needs to include penitent confession, and they need to return to Him. Dearman comments that

---

[1044] W.R. Harper, *A Critical and Exegetical Commentary on Amos and Hosea,* Edinburgh, T and T Clark, 1956, 413.

[1045] Wolff, H.W., *A Commentary on the Book of the Prophet Hosea,* Philadelphia, Fortress Press, 1974, 235.

[1046] Stuart, D. *Hosea-Jonah.* Waco, Word, 1987, 214-215.

[1047] R.K. Harrison, "Disease, Bible and Spade," *BA* 41, Dec, 1978: 185-186; K. Wilson, "Medicine in the Land Times of the Old Testament," in *Studies in the Period of David and Solomon and Other Essays,* ed. Tomoo Ishida, Winona Lake, Ind., 1982, 337-347.

it is Yahweh's healing of Israel אהב plays an important role in the book of Hosea; there is nothing like this in any other books in the Old Testament,[1048] although similar sentiments can be seen in the book of Isaiah 54:6-8. The prophet Isaiah condemns the hypocrisy of human religiosity by sacrificing to other gods God did not accept their sacrifices. The Lord expects genuine return to testify to the genuineness of their faith, including morality, justice, and compassion for the poor and needy people. Similarly, Micah condemns the sacrifices and worship practices that have compromised God's chosen people and do not reflect on the limitations or weakness of other gods. Instead they need to be involved in honest dealings and compassion for the people and the need of the hour. Yahweh can tear into pieces but at the same time He can also heal people. The word "hope" is referred to in 6:1 and the verb (heal) describes the activity of God.

Chapter 14 shows Yahweh's perseverance, a relentlessness that brings healing and hope through God's unconditional love. They might also be what they would have been if they had remained faithful and calls them to remain faithful to the covenantal relationship. The message emphatically comes out here as: return... and God will heal their apostasy. He is ready to restore their relationship by assuring them that He will love them (v. 5). This is a message of assurance."

Yahweh's anger and condemnation are explained as the background. The judgment that was pronounced earlier has been cancelled because of God's promise. The prophet announced doom on Israel, but on the other hand, God's passion is revealed through the power of love in the words *"I will love them freely and generously* (v. 5a)." In the Old Testament a key theme is that *"I, the Lord, am your healer"* (Exo. 15:26). In Deuteronomy 4:37 אהב את־אבתיך is translated as *'he loved your fathers,'* this is used as a technical term to be found in the treaties meaning 'be loyal to,' or 'show faithfulness to;' it is understood as emotional closeness.

5.4. Social Texture

Hosea's message is equally important in relation to true faith and worship that is reflected in practices and social concern. Israel's return is expected from her apostasy with true words of repentance; by doing this Yahweh will forgive their past sins and Israel will find pity.[1049] In return the Israel will say forgive our sins and we will offer praise and thanksgiving, because in you the orphans find mercy. A genuine faith should be reflected in Israel's spiritual journey with the Lord in whom the orphan and the fatherless find mercy. Some translations suggest that here by orphan is meant Israel. Garrett also suggests that the orphan here means the people of Israel, but God is compassionate to the fatherless and orphans so that the orphan seeks and finds compassion in God.[1050] The point to be noted here in Hosea's prayer is that the people of Israel have become orphans. In this context, the prophet urges the aliens

---

[1048] Dearman, J.A., *The Book of Hosea,*" NICOT, Grand Rapids, MI: Wm. B. Eerdmans Publishing Co., 2010, 340.

[1049] W.R. Harper, *A Critical and Exegetical Commentary on Amos and Hosea,* Edinburgh, T and T Clark, 1956, 408.

[1050] Garrett, *Hosea, Joel, An Exegetical and Theological Exposition of Holy Scripture,* Nashville, Broadman and Holman, 1997, 272.

and the orphans to return to the Lord with true repentance by confessing their sins and humbly requesting God's forgiveness.

In this context, the prophet's desire for Israel is that they would recognise the true situation. For Rudolph, there is no salvation without repentance. This shows the totality of the prophet's endeavour. Recent scholars have set apart this as prayer from a liturgical point of view. The requirement is to return to the Lord with sincere repentance and total submission. This passage is called a prophetic summons to repentance (cf. Jer. 3:22; 4:1). According to Stuart, the prophet explains about Israel's future achieved by true repentance.[1051] This shows God's promise of future restoration, by their returning to God to escape from punishment; it is only achieved by an honest expression of their penitence and truly seeking Him; and then God will respond mercifully to the people of Israel. By doing this, there is restoration and abundance of blessing for them. This is a striking expression of penitence on Ephraim's/Israel's part, if they speak these words with a true, honest, and willing intent. The assurance from Israel is that they will not enter into alliance with Assyria or Egypt nor they will worship their gods. This shows that they realise their dependence on political alliances and on idols was displeasing to God. The appeal comes from a nation who considers themselves an orphan without any power and alliances with other nations. Now they are calling on Yahweh who cares for the orphan and the fatherless. This shows that the people abandon their pride and self-sufficiency and totally depend upon their Yahweh and His compassion (cf. Lam. 5:3; Psa 10:14; 68:6; Deut. 10:18). Here Ephraim expresses their total inadequacy and confesses themselves as orphans. There are no legal rights and laws to be discussed, but they are completely depending on Yahweh's mercy and concern for the weak and powerless. This shows how the people humbled themselves in their confession.

The prayer that they offer to Yahweh is that they will return to their God with complete surrender.[1052] Dearman suggests that in this case, Israel has become orphaned by rejecting Yahweh's covenant and His instruction (8:1-3; 11:1-2).[1053] Macintosh remarks that the people are to pray to God for their sins and to submit them to Him. This was Hosea's prayer during his ministry to people of Israel.[1054] Though Israel stumbled but now they recognize their helplessness and turn back to Israel's God.

The image of an orphan is significant here. Parents who adopt an orphan are accepting someone from outside their family to be a part of their family. This carries the message that those not a part of the original family, or those gone astray, can come into the fold through the gateway of repentance.

God is compassionate to the fatherless and orphans so that the orphan seeks and finds compassion in God. The appeal comes from a nation who considers themselves an orphan without any power and alliances with other nations. Israel stumbled but, now they recognize their helplessness and turn back to Israel's God. The image of an orphan is significant here.

[1051] Stuart, D. *Hosea-Jonah.* Waco, Texas, Word, 1987, 211-212.

[1052] H.W. Wolff, *Hosea* (G. Stansell, Trans.), Philadelphia, Fortress Press, 1974, 235.

[1053] Dearman. J.A, *The Book of Hosea,*" NICOT, Grand Rapids, Wm. B. Eerdmans Publishing co, 2010, 339.

[1054] A. A. Macintosh, *A Critical and Exegetical Commentary on Hosea,* Edinburgh, T and T Clark, 1997, 565-566.

5.5. Cultural Texture

Hosea continues that people's confession should come with realisation that they will not depend upon other nations rather depend upon their God. The warning continues they should forget their idolatry, foreign alliances, and religious worship. They should worship only Yahweh and be true to their God and the Lord of the covenant. This section contains Yahweh's answer to the appeal that is found in Hosea 14:2 [MT 3]. Yahweh's promise is that He will do more than other nations, if Ephraim/ Israel truly repents.[1055] For Dearman, Yahweh is the speaker in this context and is ready to accept the penitence uttered by Israel.[1056] According to Wolff, the divine answer plays a central place in this chapter.[1057] In the Israelite tradition, an adulterer had to be stoned to death. However, in this book, we see how there is a deviation from this traditional law. Hosea had been told to seek his erring wife and to bring her back to the family (2:16-3:5). By that action, he would demonstrate God's own intention to "woo" His wayward wife Israel into a return to the covenantal relation with Himself (2:14-20).[1058] God had warned His people continually of their judgment and that He would withdraw Himself from them and leave them to their fate (5:15a). Irrespective of that, He never stopped loving His people (11:8-9). In another play upon the root word, שוב the Lord promises that, in the future, His justifiable wrath would be "turned away" from His people (v. 4).

The concept of return is followed with the verdict and announcement of abundant life that will be given by Yahweh as a result of His saving action. Hence, this penitential prayer is an acknowledgement of Israel's guilt, and God's love does not reject Israel's condition of apostasy. Rather, the promise is followed by their return to the Lord. This shows that God's desire is to heal Israel from their wickedness and disease of sin. Yahweh is the only redeemer and source of their healing (Hos. 11:1-4). In Hosea 14:4, the Lord again repeats that Israel's hope for future reviving and restoration is possible solely because of His desire and willingness to forgive the wayward, unrepentant, and unfaithful people. The prophet primarily uses the covenant term love to heal the people.

In another play upon the root word, שוב the Lord promises that, in the future, His justifiable wrath would be *"turned away" from His people* (v. 4).

5.6. Theological Texture

The theological texture discusses Hosea's urge for people to turn and seek the Lord with true and honest repentance, confession of sins, and prayer for God's forgiveness.[1059] The Lord reminds them to come with a genuine faith and commitment. Once they observe the Lord with true religious devotion, there will be a shift of

---

[1055] Stuart. D, *Hosea-Jonah.* Waco, TX: Word, 1987, 210-11.

[1056] Dearman, J.A., *The Book of Hosea,"* NICOT, Grand Rapids, Wm. B. Eerdmans Publishing Co., 2010, 338-339.

[1057] H.W. Wolff, *Hosea* (G. Stansell, Trans.,), Philadelphia, Fortress Press, 1974, 233.

[1058] Kidner, Derek. *Love to the Loveless: The Message of Hosea,* BST, Downers Grove, Inter Varsity, 1981, 121.

[1059] Dearman, J.A., *The Book of Hosea,"* NICOT, Grand Rapids, Wm. B. Eerdmans Publishing Co., 2010, 337.

identity from *"Not my People"* (1:9) to *"My people"* (2:23).[1060] Thus He restores them to their original status as God's covenant people. Hosea concludes with a message of reversal, "*Not my people*" to "*My people,*" and people's response is "*You are my God,*" the fulfilment of prophecy that they would know the Lord, and Yahweh would be their God.

Philip King notes that Hosea's children's names symbolise that the Lord promises a new name for the family members (Hos. 2:23). The changed names show the process of restoration and blessings that is involved with the naming of the children (v. 23).[1061] The first name יזרעאל means God's sowing זרע applies to earth as well as to seed.[1062] For John H. Walton, Jezreel has both negative and positive connotations. Its negative meaning is that God scatters but, in a positive sense, 'God sows,' which includes His blessings. Hosea uses the name Jezreel because this word in Hebrew (*yizreel*) is similar to *yisrael*, the word used for the nation of Israel (cf. 2:22).[1063] The word *Jezreel* is understood in three different ways: a) the Hebrew word sounds like a word for Israel and refers to it,[1064] b) The Hebrew word in this context refers to the concept that "God sows," and c) This is the name of Hosea's first son. The name refers to the bloodshed of Jehu in the valley of Jezreel.[1065] Here "Jezreel" is used in the negative sense as in 1:4-5. According to Mays, the elements of the natural process were personalized and defined. Here the cycle of seasons and the growth of crops are drawn into the covenant relation between Yahweh and Israel. Nature is de-mythologized in making an aspect of covenant history.[1066] The first name *Jezreel* (יזרעאל) symbolises judgment, but here the names have a meaning of grace and the act of renewing the covenant.[1067] The name Jezreel means calamity, but now God turns it into salvation and prosperity. God will provide for the people of Israel. What we see here is the transformation of His people that they would not be scattered on the judgment day, but they will be scattered as seed for God in their land as well as in other nations, and that they would enjoy a renewed covenantal relationship with God (Zech. 13:9; Rom. 9:25, 26). Given the meaning of the name Jezreel, it is clear why God says that he will plant them in her land. God is not only planting crops, but also planting a people. The point is that God will supply food and shelter and abundance blessing.

[1060] Hubbard David Allan, *With Bands of Love* (Hosea), Grand Rapids, Wm. B. Eerdmans Publishing Co., 1968, 228-229. Cf. Garrett, *Hosea, Joel An Exegetical and Theological Exposition of Holy Scripture,* B. and H. Publishing Group, 1997, 117.

[1061] Philip King, *Amos-Micah: An Archaeological Commentary,* Philadelphia, Westminster, 1988, 25-26.

[1062] Samuel J. Schulz, *The Old Testament Speaks,* New York, Harper and Brothers Publishers, 1960, 388.

[1063] John H. Walton, *Zondervan Illustrated Bible Backgrounds Commentary*, vol. 5, Grand Rapids, Zondervan Publisher, 1984, 13-14.

[1064] L. J. Wood, *Hosea, The Expositor's Bible Commentary*, ed., Frank E. Gaebelein, Grand Rapids, Zondervan Publishing, 1985, 180.

[1065] Dianne Bergant, "Symbolic Names in Hosea," *TBT* 20, 1982, 159-160.

[1066] Mays, Mays, James Luther., *Hosea: A Commentary,* OTL, Philadelphia, Westminster, 1969, 52-53.

[1067] Marvin Sweeney, *The Twelve Prophets: Hosea-Jonah,* Vol. I, Collegeville, The Liturgical Press, 2000, 36-37.

The second name *Not-pitied* becomes *Pitied*, and followed by that *Not-my people* changes to *My people*. The change takes place from unfaithfulness, which means punishment, to renewal of the relationship between Gomer-Israel and Hosea-Yahweh.[1068] This is portrayed in the form of a marriage to the fertility of the land and protection of the land. Macintosh remarks that Hosea's second and third children's names refer to the change of fortunes of the Israelites and renewal of the relationship with Yahweh. The climax that is noted is that the nation acknowledges that Yahweh alone is their God. The naming of the children shows restoration and sends a positive message to Israel that God will show mercy and Israel will be His people.

Hosea's plea is for people to turn, seek the Lord with true repentance, confession of sins, and prayer for forgiveness. He restores them to their original status as God's covenant people. Hosea concludes with a message of reversal, *"Not my people"* to *"My people,"* and people's response is *"You are my God,"* the fulfilment of prophecy that they would know the Lord, and Yahweh would be their God. Hosea's children's names symbolise that the Lord promises a new name for the family members (Hos. 2:23). The changed names show the process of restoration and blessings that is involved with the naming of the children יזרעאל mean God's sowing זרע applies to earth as well as to seed. *Not-pitied* becomes *Pitied*, and followed by *Not-my people* changes to *My people*. The change takes place from unfaithfulness, which means punishment, to renewal of the relationship between Gomer-Israel and Hosea -Yahweh.

The significant aspect of the theological texture is the metaphor of dew which brings out the idea of the Exodus wilderness experience of Yahweh and people of Israel. In Hosea 14, dew recalls Yahweh's manifestation and care for his creatures during their journey in the wilderness.

5.7. Prophetic Paradigm of Love

The concept of love can be seen in different ways through the lives of several of the prophets. This is especially so with Hosea, where it has become real, where God has used his marital life as a metaphor to make Israel understands that He still loves them. God makes use of Hosea for this purpose. Only then we can understand the word love and how much it means in the life of people, not just Israel in Hosea's time but at all times and in all places to the present day. Looking at the concept more broadly, 'love' is clearly linked in the mind of God; it is His love for all people that prompts His efforts to bring Israel back within the covenant, so that they can be a guiding light to all other people for all time. God is using Israel to carry His message to all nations; people must carry love of God to everyone.

Love within the prophetic writings visualizes that Israel should be a blessing among the nations, representing holiness and truth, and at the same time these qualities are to be followed by all of humanity.[1069] The essential and fundamental

[1068] Marvin Sweeney, *The Twelve Prophets: Hosea-Jonah,* Vol. I, Collegeville, The Liturgical Press, 2000, 36-37.

[1069] M. Daniel Carroll R., "Old Testament Prophets," *Evangelical Dictionary of World Missions,* edited by A. Scott Moreau, Grand Rapids, Baker Books, 2000, 705.

function of a prophet is to announce, to declare, and to proclaim the Word of God to man, whether of judgment, hope, assurance, trust or repentance. The prophetic office took on special significance in times of Israel's moral and spiritual decline. Sixteen of the Old Testament prophetic writings are part of the canon. The message of prophets was not only to bring other nations to the sovereignty of Yahweh but to exhort them to set their internal affairs right also. The two main criticisms by the prophets for which they condemned Israel were their practice of idolatry and social injustice. George W. Peters highlights a threefold significance of the message of Yahweh's prophets: It addresses immediate society or situations, so it is historical; it addresses the current society or situations, so it is existential; it addresses the Messianic society or situations, so it is prophetic.[1070] Throughout history, God has used prophets in His work in order to make the people of Israel understand how much He loves them. In Hosea's case, He has been even more explicit with the use of the three themes in human terms so that Israel has no excuse for misunderstanding Yahweh's message. At the same time, although Hosea does not speak to other nations directly, his actions and words have an embedded message for them. This message speaks of God's forgiving love towards all people, not just Israel. They are a witness of His love. In this chapter, Hosea throws light on Yahweh's commitment to Israel through the guidance, training, and care and the forbearance which He shows in the midst of Israel's infidelity (3:1), and in the forgiveness that turns aside anger and provides healing (14:4), a message full of meaning for other nations as well.

5.8. Summary of Hosea 14

The inner texture of Hosea 14 discusses important words in this section such as return, heal, apostasy and dwell. Chapter 14 talks about the eschatological hope for the people of Israel when they return with true repentance to seek the hope and promise of healing. For this, the prophet uses various synonymous parallelisms and chiasms which are dominant in order to bring out Yahweh's love towards Israel. The metaphor describes Yahweh's love towards his people in the form of dew, where people's return is expressed and Yahweh is addressed as the healer. The section ends with a note of hope for the future. The important words in this passage שוב, רפא, משובתה and ישב are used with a purpose.

Conclusion

Hosea 14 is about God's promise of blessing when Israel repents of their sins. The nation's repentance will open God's heart to mercy and forgiveness. The people of Israel will be restored as God's elected people and will obtain rich blessings because of Yahweh's covenant love. Israel as patient will be "cured" by returning to Yahweh. His mercy and forgiveness will bring healing in Israel's life and restore back their intimate relationship. This will also ease the other concerns of the nation as well. As shown in the exegesis, the word "love" has different shades of meanings. The real meaning of the word "love" in the life of the people has been examined in this chapter. The research has established that Yahweh's love is foundational for the redemption of the people of Israel, which gives them an identity. Further, this identity is protected

---

[1070] George W. Peters, *A Biblical Theology of Missions,* Chicago, Moody Bible Institute, 1972, 120.

by God for the sake of the other nations. It is important to bear in mind that the basis of the whole Book of Hosea is the restoration of the Yahweh-Israel covenantal relationship and the manner through which it is done.

Thus, this chapter has examined the meaning and importance of the three fundamental themes Apostasy, Healing and Forgiveness the themes around which the book revolves, and the importance of the imagery used. It has also gleaned their significance in the extension of the Yahweh-Israel relationship to other nations.

The next Chapter will examine the concept of the covenant and its consequences through the book of Hosea as well as its theological implications. It will examine how Yahweh has demonstrated His willingness to maintain the covenant in the face of Israel's turn to idolatry. It will also focus on the importance of the covenant, and its binding nature, demonstrated through the imagery of the human relationships described by Hosea.

Chapter 6

The Nature and Meaning of Covenantal Relationship in the Book of Hosea

Introduction

From the discussions in the previous chapters it is obvious that God's love is dominant in this book with the Sinatic covenant relationship between Yahweh and Israel as its base. In that sense, this chapter explores how the nature and meaning of covenantal relationship in Hosea can be better understood? The exegetical studies of the selected passages in the previous chapters emphasise the understanding of God's love and the importance of the covenant which are clearly embedded in the prophet's message. The use of images is a bold advance in prophetic language. Hosea uses the marital, parental and healing images examined in the previous chapters to depict God's covenant relationship with Israel. In this study, the possible origins for these images are proposed and parallels to these metaphors are considered. At the same time the covenant and its significance will be examine in detail. The thesis concludes that Hosea's unique contribution is the development of God's covenant with Israel in terms of love. The concept of the covenant and its importance in the Old Testament with specific reference to its use in Hosea will therefore be studied.

'Covenant' is the key concept in organizing event in the history of Israel. This research will discuss the nature and origins of Israel's covenantal ideas and its relatedness to Hosea. The theme of covenantal relationship runs through the entire book, but is seen particularly in the use of the three human love themes (as shown in the preceding chapters). Hosea perceives the covenant as a relationship of steadfast love, and his significant contribution to this concept is the stress on the centrality of God's love within the covenantal relationship using the three images. God's covenant with Israel is developed in terms of love not the stern judgmental love of the traditional Yahweh, but the soft gentler love between husband and wife, parent and child and physician and patient.

This chapter considers the covenant and how it conveys the message of love. While the imagery of love belongs to the realm of human experience, the imagery of "covenant" belongs to the realm of faith and religion. Hosea's use of figurative language in communicating the message of love does not downplay the solidity of that relationship. It is useful to consider how the metaphors of love are included and what the new insights are that they offer to Israel's understanding of covenant. This will help to further delineate and assess Hosea's special contribution to the understanding of Israel's unique relationship to Yahweh. Moreover, it will throw light on the intervention of divine love in the Old Testament. The concept of the covenant both in the Old Testament in general and specifically within the book of Hosea will be discussed. Additionally, the meaning of certain terms used in the covenantal language will also be considered. The use of love in its broader sense, with the various types of love displayed by Yahweh, will be studied. This chapter will also examine Hosea's understanding of the covenant and the idea of love found within the covenant.

6.1. Covenant in the Old Testament and in the Book of Hosea

The many images used by the prophet finds their source in the covenant. For this reason, it is important to reconstruct Hosea's understanding of covenant and its relation to his prophecy. Hosea's theology brings out the awareness of God's holiness and sovereignty through his appreciation of God's actions, which in Hosea's book are linked to the three themes and their inter connectedness with the people of Israel as discussed previously. Understanding Hosea's theology is not remotely theoretical but grows out of the grassroots of understanding of Israel as his people and his personal involvement. The book of Hosea starts with the situation where Israel has turned her back on Yahweh, broken the Sinatic covenant and gone to worship Baal. It is Hosea's task to bring her back, using the marital, parental and healing themes to do so. He also uses the Exodus event to remind Israel of the original covenantal relationship by electing and redeeming Israel out of Egypt (11:1).

6.1.1. Covenant in the Old Testament

The idea of the covenant has long been held by biblical scholars as the concept which directs the main theme of Scripture. Definitions include a legal relationship, a solemn promise or bindings by an oath, an obligation, or a voluntary agreement made between two parties, God and the people or between a king, leader and his people.[1071]

Through the covenant, God becomes the *"God of the people"* and the people become *"the people of God."*[1072] There is no boundary to this covenant community, it is open and invites all to be God's own people (Gen. 18:18-19; Isa. 11:4-5; Ps. 85: 10-13; 32:16-17).[1073] This alludes to the important connection between Deuteronomy 32:16-21 and Hosea, which talks about the inclusion of the gentiles in God's eschatological plan. The phrase "*not my people*" becomes "*My people*." Though Israel has rejected God, the covenant He made with Abraham remains in force. Thus Hosea 1-3 alludes to the inclusion of the Gentiles in God's salvation which begins in the Abrahamic covenant and culminates in the coming of the Davidic king throughout the books of the Minor Prophets. According to Mendenhall, "covenant in the Bible is considered as major metaphor used to describe the relation between God and the

[1071] R.A.F. MacKenzie, *Faith and History of the Old Testament,* Minneapolis, University of Minnesota Press, 1963, 37-38.

[1072] R.A.F. MacKenzie, *Faith and History of the Old Testament,* Minneapolis, University of Minnesota Press, 1963, 37-38.

[1073] Michael D. Guinan, *Covenant in the Old Testament,* Chicago, Franciscan Herald Press, 1975, 12f.

people of God."[1074] The idea of covenant becomes instrument in the rule when two parties make oath. A covenant is between two parties; it could be made by equals or between a vassal and lord. The covenant is based on the principles of consent, and all the people consent to Yahweh's covenant. Hosea uses his own marriage as symbolism for covenant, which provides legal form and the relationship with God. At the same time it provides God with an acceptable witness to their loyalty and love. The love of God is presented in the form of images of parental care as God's care for Israel, compassion to them, the idea of hope and restoration from God's judgment for the wayward people. Though the people broke the covenant by worshipping foreign gods, the prophet presents God as one who remembers his covenant with them which taught them about the knowledge of God. Hosea must carry the message to Israel that only by repentance and apology can the covenant be re-made, after which both physical and spiritual blessings and restoration will follow.

6.1.2. Special Form of Covenant

In Ancient West Asia (AWA), covenants controlled the interactions between two people, a group of people or even whole tribes or nations. There were two types of covenants in ancient times, and both were between human beings. But for Mendenhall, the Yahweh/Israelite covenants were of a different and unique type.[1075] Mendenhall asserts that the covenantal relationship with Yahweh between their deity and the people-was "the only unique feature of ancient Israelite society, culture, and religion."[1076] This is further affirmed by Milgrom comments in ancient Mesopotamia: "the idea of covenant between the deity and the people is absent."

Nicholson notes that in AWA, the human social order was validated by the cosmic order. But the covenant as theology stands outside this scheme. Yahweh stands over against the world. His purpose is not only to sustain it, but to transform it.[1077] This "God-Man" covenant relationship is designed to establish peace, a comprehensive wholesome well being. For McGrath, "the idea of covenant" is the basis for Israel and by extension, for the church that stands on God's faithfulness.[1078] But Walton argues that a theological covenant's main purpose is that it reveals God.[1079] The meaning and purpose of this type of covenant reminds us of God's deliverance and finds its culmination in revelation.

6.1.3. The Concept of Covenant in Hosea

The concept of covenant as it is explained in Hosea plays an important role in understanding the relationship between God and Israel, Israel has committed adultery by worshipping false gods; it is Yahweh's choice what He does with the

---

[1074] Mendenhall G.E, "Covenant," in Freedman, *ABD*, vol. 1, 1179.

[1075] Mendenhall, G. W, *Law and Covenant in Israel and in the Ancient Near East,* Pittsburg, Biblical Colloquium, 1955. 55.

[1076] Mendenhall, G. E., "Covenant Forms in Israelite Tradition," *The Biblical Archaeologist Reader,* Vol. III, ed. by Edward F. Campbell, Jr. and David Noel Freedman, New York, Doubleday and Company, Anchor Books, 1970, 89.

[1077] Ernest W. Nicholson, *God and His People: Covenant and Theology in the Old Testament,* Oxford, Clarendon Press, 1986, 208.

[1078] McGrath, 2003, 348.

[1079] Walton, *Survey of the Old Testament,* Winona, Eisenbrauns, 1994, 24.

covenant break it or keep it. E.C. Rust comments that, *"The Theology of Hosea"* crystallizes the foundation of Hosea's message as follows:

> It is ... not surprising that the covenant idea is the focal point of [Hosea's] message. For him, God is the covenant God and Israel is the covenant people so that the vicissitudes of Israel's history and its contemporary situation must be understood in terms of that covenant by which it is related to the living God.[1080]

This study offers some fresh insight into the covenant relationship of Israel and God because of Hosea's symbolic action. Hosea emphasises that the covenant is rooted in the love of God. No one in the Old Testament up to his time parallels Hosea's exhaustive treatment of this truth. So the argument comes full circle, as it is set out in the previous chapters Yahweh is a loving God, willing to hold out his arms to his sinning partner, and is using Hosea to describe that love and willingness in terms that Israel can understand human love. When Hosea talks about the covenant, it must be read in that way in human terms, not in the judgmental manner of Yahweh.

6.2. The Meaning of Covenant in Hosea

Hosea clearly brings out the prophetic message with the prophet raising charges against Israel. The prophet says *"Hear the word of the Lord you Israelites because the Lord has a charge to bring against you who live in the land: There is no faithfulness, no love, no acknowledgment of God in the land"* (Hos. 4:1). The nature of this call reflects the unique contribution to the tradition that Hosea makes: "religion is first and foremost a matter of relationship with God" and it is "personal."[1081] Hosea uses the word "covenant" rarely but uses the attributes of the covenant as the framework for his message to the people.

Through his own marriage to Gomer,[1082] Hosea saw the relationship between God and Israel as that of husband and wife with its attendant attributes of love, loyalty, compassion and grace.[1083] Adam Miller stresses that Hosea learned that at the core of the covenant is God's love for his people, expressed in the Exodus, and that God seeks a response of *"steadfast love"* and *"knowledge of God,"* one that Israel has failed to deliver.[1084] Hosea's marriage made visible the truth of their covenant failure; for they had failed to make meaningful connections between their theology and history on the one hand, and their real life problems on the other. In this accusation, Hosea identifies the aspects of covenant that for him constitutes its essence. They are אהב, חסד, ידע, דעת, אמת. Amos emphasised "righteousness" and "justice" as

[1080] Rust. E. C, "The Theology of Hosea" *Review and Expositor,* Vol. 54, 510-521, 1957, 510.

[1081] Norman D. Snaith, *Mercy and Sacrifice A Study of the Book of Hosea,* London, SCM Press, 1953, 39-40.

[1082] Daniel Patte, Jose Severino Croatto, Teresa Okure, *Global Bible Commentary,* Nashville, Abingdon Press, 2004, 265. Cf. Francis Landy, *Hosea,* Sheffield, Sheffield Academic Press, 1995, 41.

[1083] Norman D. Snaith, *Mercy and Sacrifice A Study of the Book of Hosea,* London, SCM Press, 1953, 40, 52.

[1084] Adam W. Miller, *Brief Introduction to the Old Testament,* Indiana, Warner Press, 1964, 104.

the central elements of covenant keeping.[1085] The meaning of keeping the covenant meant doing the stipulations and ordinances of God. According to Eichrodt, it was first and foremost a legal document.[1086] For Hosea it is to do with the motivation that lies behind obedience; for him, covenant is more than just behaviour. Looking closely at the concepts of covenant in Hosea will clarify his direction for us.

6.2.1. אהב in Hosea

The word אהב is used in verb form which implies God's election. The Hebrew root word for "love" אהב occurs 18 times in Hosea. The word is seen as central to the entire book and אהב is considered as central theme in Hosea's prophecy. This אהב is manifested in bringing out the people of Israel from Egypt.[1087] The use of the verb אהב plays an important role in his theology. The verb אהב 'to love' is derived from noun אהבת 'love' with God as subject and Israel as the object of God's love are seen several times in Hosea and Deuteronomy. The term אהב denoting God's love for his people is found in Hosea and Deuteronomy. The prophet and also Deuteronomy also employ the same root אהב in order to describe the human side of the relationship either the covenant obligation of love of God[1088] or Israel's apostasy in the shape of loving other gods.[1089] The verb in Hosea 11:1 is used to demonstrate Yahweh's love for Israel. Jacob says that the Hebrew word "אהב" is the most general word for love.[1090] According to Ralph, the book of Hosea clearly expresses Yahweh's election which plays a vital role in the acts of gracious love.[1091] For Dempsey this love is expressed in various forms in the book marriage metaphor (Hos. 2-3), parent-child (Hos. 11) and healer (Hos. 14).[1092] אהב signifies emotion and a strong desire.[1093] God loved them while they were in Egypt, while wandering in the wilderness and while he established them in the land (13:4-8). Beeby notes that this love starts with election and finds its culmination in the covenant (cf. 11:1-4.)[1094] In the Old Testament, the term אהב refers to kindred relationships. In the realm of love between humans, it is used in the positive sense for the attachment of one person to another in familial relationships such as a husband's love for his wife or a love of a mother or father for a child.[1095] For Smith, אהב means "the one doing the loving has some responsibility or

---

1085 Mays, James Luther., *Hosea: A Commentary,* OTL, Philadelphia, Westminster, 1969, 12.

1086 Eichrodt. Walter, *The Theology of the Old Testament,* vol. 1, London, SCM Press, 1961, 264.

1087 Rendtorff, *Theologie des Alten Testaments,* 57-58.

1088 Deut. 5:7; 6:5; 7:9; 10:12; 11:1, 13, 22; 13:4; 19:9; 30:6, 16, 20.

1089 Hos. 2:7, 9, 12, 14, 15; 3:1b; 4:18; 9:1, 10.

1090 Edmond Jacob, *Theology of the Old Testament,* New York, Harper and Row Publisher, 1958, 108.

1091 Ralph L. Smith, *Old Testament Theology, Its History, Method and Message*, Nashville, Broadman and Holman Publishers, 1993, 194-195.

1092 Carol J. Dempsey, *The Prophets: A Liberation-Critical Reading,* Minneapolis, Fortress Press, 2000, 154-155.

1093 W. Wilson, *New Wilson's Old Testament Word Studies,* Grand Rapids, Kregel Publications, 1987, 260.

1094 H. D. Beeby, *Grace Abounding, A Commentary on the book of Hosea,* Grand Rapids, Wm. Eerdmans, 1989, 141f

1095 Sakenfeld, Love, in *The Anchor Bible Dictionary,* vol. 4, David Noel Freedman, editor-in-Chief. New York, Doubleday, 1992, 376.

obligation towards the object of the love."[1096] In Hosea it is evident that a husband's love involves special care and treatment of the loved one. This term embeds the *kinship bond* which is reflected in the marriage relationship and which also applies to the relationship between Yahweh and Israel. The distinction between "אהב and חסד" is of an election love and a covenant love."[1097] Hosea used חסד six times, and the motif of the book is captured by the use of חסד in 6:6. Here Hosea contrasts covenant love,[1098] which represents the commitment of one's loyalty to God, with an external offering and sacrifice.[1099] The motif of love in the book of Hosea is not exhausted simply with a study of its vocabulary. The whole concept of marriage, parental and healing relationships in Hosea are bound up with love.[1100] Hosea's message is declared as a powerful metaphor in his calling as a prophet. His life indeed is transformed into a metaphor; his wife and children symbolise the people of Israel. Hosea himself seems analogous to God. His entire life can be viewed as a metaphorical message which depicts the relationship between God and Israel.

6.2.2. חסד in Hosea

The other important term that Hosea uses in his vocabulary for love is חסד. Jacob Edmond affirms that marriage is the realm *par excellence* for the exercise of חסד and it is not surprising that with the prophet Hosea, the term reaches its greatest significance, denoting the relationship of Yahweh to the people, the obligations of the people towards Yahweh and the obligations of the members of the nation to one another.[1101]

Without rendering חסד on both sides, the maintenance of a covenant was unthinkable. Eichrodt says that the possibility of the establishment and maintenance of a covenant rests on the presence of חסד. The divine exercise of חסד is based on God's covenantal relationship with his people. As Andersen points out, חסד is a matter of ultimate concern for Yahweh." The term is also understood as being an emotional word, rather than one that emphasises formal authority or power.[1102] Hosea stresses חסד for what Israel does for God. The term is closely associated with God's love for his people. Thus חסד constitutes the proper object of ברית and may almost be described as its content. Hence there was a strong conviction in Israel that Yahweh's kindness and readiness to help was something which could be expected of Him in view of His having established the covenant relationship.[1103]

[1096] Smith, R.L., Major Motifs of Hosea, *South Western Journal of Theology,* vol. 18, 22-32, 1975, 43.

[1097] N. H. Snaith., *The Distinctive ideas of the Old Testament,* London, Epworth Press, 1944, 94-142.

[1098] Jacob, Edmond, *Theology of the Old Testament,* Translated by Arthur W. Heathcote and Philip J. Allcock., London, Hodder and Stoughton, 1958,109.

[1099] J. Barton Payne., *The Theology of the Older Testament,* Grand Rapids, Zondervan Publishing House, 1962, 162.

[1100] Glueck, N.,חסד *in the Bible,* translated by A. Gottschalk, Cincinnati, Hebrew Union College Press, 1951, 37.

[1101] Jacob, Edmond, *Theology of the Old Testament,* Translated by Arthur W. Heathcote and Philip J. Allcock., London, Hodder and Stoughton, 1958,105.

[1102] Andersen and Freedman, *Hosea,* 430.

[1103] Eichrodt, *Theology of the Old Testament,* Tran, By J.A. Baker, vol. I, London, SCM Press, 1961b, 233.

6.2.3. ידע in Hosea

James D. Newsome notes Hosea's use of ידע as a central concept in the book to portray God's knowledge. Hosea reminds the people of Israel about their history and their relationship with God through the covenant and monotheistic commandments of the Decalogue that required "thou shall have no other gods before me." However, Israel was stubbornly unfaithful and a vital ingredient of the covenant relationship "conjugal fidelity" was lost.[1104] Now "although they offer sacrifices, though they eat flesh, the Lord does not accept them" (8:13).

In Hosea 6:1-3, the book contains a litany of repentance. Here the question is raised whether this litany represents genuine repentance on the part of the Israelites; a hypocritical offering or a sarcastic composition of Hosea himself. [1105] It must be considered that even if the community did sincerely wish to repent, their knowledge and understanding of God might not be sufficient to enable a true repentance. Hosea appears to seek a return to the relationship of the covenant, to the reality and experience of a holy God and His people in a relationship of loyalty, faithfulness and the knowledge of God.[1106] According to Lalmuankima, חסד is fully manifested in the form of complete loyalty to Yahweh and fulfilling the commands of the law.[1107]

6.2.4. דעת in Hosea

Hosea uses דעת as its verb form "know" refers to God's knowledge of Israel or Israel's knowledge of God. The knowledge of God is Israel's personal response to the salvation history of election and obedience to the requirements of the covenant. The term דעת אלהים implies a breach of relationship of allegiance or loyalty. The meaning is, knowing their God is acknowledging the way of the Lord and coming back to him personally and recognising his rule and giving allegiance to him. The prophet's use of the imagery of marriage implies that for him the relationship to the law was largely displaced by a living fellowship of love, which demanded the total allegiance of the human to the object of that love, and it could never be satisfied with the formal fulfilment of obligation. The knowledge is also a covenant concept that denotes owning another's claim upon oneself. To know God is to give him allegiance and obedience. For Hosea to know God is to fulfil all of his commitments to that individual. The word אמת contributes to distinct nuance of meaning of the essential idea of covenant relationship. דעת אלהים stresses the dimension of intimacy that characterises the relationship.

6.2.5. אמת in Hosea

The word אמת is close to the concept of truth. Hosea presents a deep and rich picture of God's love and grace, but he is also called "a watchman," and when the time is right

---

[1104] Van Gemeren, W. A. *Interpreting the Prophetic Word,* Grand Rapids, Acadamie Books, 1990, 111

[1105] Sakenfeld, Love, in *The Anchor Bible Dictionary,* vol. 4, David Noel Freedman, editor-in-Chief, New York, Doubleday, 1992, 105.

[1106] Limburg, James. *Interpretation: Hosea - Micah, A Bible Commentary for Preaching and Teaching,* Atlanta, John Knox Press, 1988, 129-130.

[1107] C. Lalmuankima, "Challenges from the Book of Hosea in Understanding the Kindness of God," *Bangalore Theological Forum,* Vol. XL, No. 1, June 2008, 154 (149-160).

the watchman must sound the alarm.[1108] The holiness of God was pictured for His people in the covenant, with its rewards and its judgments, and these very judgments reveal the seriousness with which God takes his covenant and his commitment to his people.[1109] Hosea not only reminds them in an unequivocal manner of the nature of Yahweh and calls them to return to and embrace their covenant relationship, but he also insists that only God can redeem and restore the relationship and its blessings. The word אמת is found twenty three times in conjunction with חסד which indicates the words belong to a similar context. The meaning of the word אמת is "firm." In the legal term the word אמת means the actual truth of a process or cause, this is found in Deuteronomy as "true charge" (Deut. 2:20). In the concept of overlap into the religious environment the term is used to designate God's word. The primary idea אמת of the word is used in the context of covenant. Mays writes the word אמת is understood in terms of firmness and reliability of a man whose word is good and is bound by his responsibility.[1110] The prophet uses this term אמת for reliability and trustworthiness on the occasion of the charge being levelled by Hosea against Israel. This is used in the context of expression and action, but rather denotes the quality of a relationship.

6.3. Love - Major Motif and Forms of Love shown by Yahweh

Among the many components in Hosea, Love is the major motif in the book. However, Hosea's message of Love takes on many forms. These forms of love are directly related to the covenantal idea as will be shown in the discussion that follows:

6.3.1. Love as the Basis of the Covenant

Love is the major motif in the book of Hosea. In the Old Testament, there are several motifs, but it is only Hosea who speaks most strongly about love, along with other themes such as sin, wrath, judgment and hope. The prophet uses four main Hebrew terms to speak about love: "אהב, חסד, נחם, רחם." The Hebrew word חסד, translated as "steadfast love," has the sense of "undeserved love." חסד is the most consistently expressed principle. It is a term used frequently in the Old Testament to refer to God's covenantal love, the enduring, and persistent commitment which Yahweh has for Israel which is exercised in good times and in bad. Lalmuankima comments that Hosea's continued reference to this term demonstrates his concern that Israel reciprocates this same loving loyalty to Yahweh.[1111] Hosea declares that God's people must be faithful to God as a wife to her husband or a child to its parent and not pursue other lovers: the baals and foreign nations (Hos. 2:2-13; 8; 11:1-11).[1112]

[1108] L. James., *Interpretation: Hosea - Micah, A Bible Commentary for Preaching and Teaching,* Atlanta, John Knox Press, 1988, 34.

[1109] L. James., *Interpretation: Hosea - Micah, A Bible Commentary for Preaching and Teaching,* Atlanta, John Knox Press, 1988, 34.

[1110] Mays, James Luther., *Hosea: A Commentary,* OTL, Philadelphia, Westminster, 1969, 62.

[1111] C. Lalmuankima, Challenges from the Book of Hosea in Understanding the Kindness of God, *Bangalore Theological Forum,* Vol. XL, No. 1, June 2008, 154 (149-160).

[1112] William Sanford, *Old Testament Survey: The Message Form, and Background of the Old Testament,* Grand Rapids, Wm. B. Eerdmans publishing company, 1982, 338.

R. B. Coote believes that the basic *leit motif* of the Exodus narratives was the bride rescue story. For him, the Jacob narrative in chapter twelve provides a parallel to the God-Israel relationship. As Jacob journeyed to a foreign country to take a wife, so also did Yahweh bring Israel from Egypt. He continues:

> It is important to note that the image of Yahweh as husband was an old one in Israel by the time of Hosea, and that it originated in the thematic framework of Israel's historical traditions.[1113]

For the prophets, love was generally used to refer to God's love for His people as a nation and only rarely to the people's love for God.[1114] Hosea shows love to be foundational for the covenant in explicit ways as well. Eichrodt says that Hosea is the first minor prophet to bring out the idea of love, because prior to Hosea, Israel knew only of Yahweh's goodness, justice and faithfulness. Here, Eichrodt does not refer to human love, which is the type of love that Hosea uses as his metaphor for the relationship between Yahweh and Israel. He speaks about God's love for Israel by using the term אהב as a powerful expression to convey love to others.[1115]

E.C. Rust's comment at the outset of his article, *"The Theology of Hosea"* makes the point that the covenant is at the base of his message. Everything revolves around the fact of the covenant.

> It is ... not surprising that the covenant idea is the focal point of [Hosea's] message. For him, God is the covenant-God and Israel is the covenant people.[1116]

N. Lohfink suggests that the only passage on love in Hosea that bears any resemblance to Moran's concept of love in Deuteronomy is Hosea 9:15. "Hosea 9:15 therefore shows that Hosea's conception of the love of God for Israel is also related to covenantal love, even though he gives this love in all other texts a new and different emphasis."[1117]

The *anabas* of God is founded on the action subsequently described toward his people (cf. Hos. 11:4). The ending of his אהבה is God's way of judging Israel (Hos. 9:15) which again assumes that אהבה is the essence of Israel's wellbeing.[1118] In fact, the strong word, "hate" (זנה) is used for God's response to Israel for their sin. It results in punishment which ravages the nation. God's love in the future will be dependent on Israel's obedience and love for Him. The divine love will bring blessing and they will be prospered in their works. In other words, for the one who follows God's precepts, God's anger changes from hate to love.

Although the word "love" is used generally across the whole book, Hosea emphasises this throughout the different forms of love which Yahweh exhibits at

---

1113 R. B. Coote, "Hosea XII," *Vetus Testamentum,* XXI, October, 1971, (389-402) 401.

1114 Purkiser, W. T., Richard S. Taylor and Willard H. Taylor, *God, Man and Salvation: A Biblical Theology,* Kansas City, Beacon Hill Press of Kansas City, 1977, 96.

1115 Eichrodt, Walther, "The Holy One in Your Midst: The Theology of Hosea," *Interpretation,* XV 259-273, July, 1961, 263.

1116 Rust. E. C, "The Theology of Hosea" *Review and Expositor,* Vol. 54, 510-521, 1957, 510.

1117 Lohfink. N, "Hate and Love in Hosea 9:15," *Catholic Biblical* Quarterly, vol. 25, 1963, 417.

1118 Limburg, *Hosea,* 9. Cf. Victor. H. Matthews, *Social World of the Hebrew Prophets,* Massachusetts, Hendrickson publishers, 2001, 75.

various times. Hosea names five forms of love which he argues Yahweh displays familial, covenantal, redemptive, compassionate and persuasive love.

6.3.2. Yahweh's love for Israel

6.3.2.1. Familial love

In this context, the attitude of God's love turns from judgment to restoration. The promise is that God still loves them and that will continue even in the future. This is because of undeserved love which calls for return. Hosea focuses on the aspect of familial love. According to Norman Snaith, "Hosea's contribution between God and His people is personal."[1119] For Wolff, Hosea's marriage is best known and used as an allegorised metaphor.[1120] This view is supported by Ibn Ezra that Hosea's marriage happened in a vision.[1121] Hosea constantly uses his own marriage to make a comparison between human matrimonial love and the covenantal Yahweh-Israel relationship. Familial love by which God revealed His purpose to bless humans is distinctive in the Hebrew Bible. John Sawyer calls it; Hosea clearly speaks about faith in God's love for his wayward people.[1122] God warns His people that while she has forgotten him, God has not forgotten her; the purpose of this statement is to win her back again. The prophet comes with the idea of restoring his wife, God makes promise of love. In the renewed relationship, future relationship is to do with Israel's loyalty with God and God alone. The family imagery is used to portray the situation in the present and future. The text brings out the rich language in defining reconciliation with God. The marital metaphor brings hope for the future based on obeying the Lord and Yahweh as Lord. The marital metaphor is both literal and metaphorical; the message is clear that the prophet calls for ministry.

6.3.2.2. Covenantal love

God elected Israel to enter into an important relationship, the relationship of father and son, Israel became son of God (11:1). There are numerous references in the book of Hosea to covenant and to covenant formulas leading us to understand this father and son relationship as a covenantal one, not a mythological one.[1123] The Lord will renew the covenant with Israel when they return to him and make relationship with him forever. According to John Taylor, the naming of the children and Hosea's message turns from warning to God's love.[1124] The nation rebelled and turned to foreign gods; now they will return to his covenant and restore the relationship. The promise is expressed through new marriage relationship between God and Israel.

[1119] Norman D. Snaith, *Mercy and Sacrifice A Study of the Book of Hosea,* London, SCM Press, 1953, 39-40.

[1120] H.W. Wolff, *Hosea: A Commentary on the book of the Prophet Hosea,* Philadelphia, Fortress Press, 1974, xxvi.

[1121] Ibn Ezra, *The Commentary of Rabbi: The Book of Hosea,* New York, Hermon Press, 1988, 19.

[1122] John Sawyer, *Prophecy and the Prophets of the Old Testament,* Oxford, Oxford University Press, 1987, 108.

[1123] Cf. W. Moran, "The Ancient Near Eastern Background of the Love of God in Deuteronomy," *CBQ* 25, 1963, 77-87; McCarthy, 'Notes on the Love of God in Deuteronomy and the Father-Son relationship between Yahweh and Israel,' *CBQ* 27, 1965, 144-147; Ackerman, 'The Personal is Political: Covenant and Affectionate Love in the Hebrew Bible,' *VT* 52, 2002, 437-458.

[1124] John Taylor, *The Minor Prophets,* Grand Rapids, Wm. B. Eerdmans, 1970, 4.

Ben Zvi says that covenant is precisely the relationship between God and his people, followed by the element of hope - hope against the hopelessness that book clearly brings out to its readers. In the covenantal love there is glimpse of hope of restoration and the fulfilment of covenant with the Lord. Through the covenant, Hosea's message includes fulfilment in the latter days. The promise of God to the patriarchs will become fulfilled in the future. The prophet encourages the people to return to the Lord and establish her covenant relationship with him. For Hosea, the essential fact was that Israel was bound to Yahweh by חסד, *"covenant love."* As the wife of Yahweh, (metaphor for the covenantal relationship) Israel was expected to follow God's leadership and laws commanded or given to them. But Israel failed to follow and failed to observe the covenant situations.[1125] The Lord attached himself to Israel and bound Israel to him in a relationship of love with God and it becomes subject to means of election.

6.3.2.3. Redemptive love

The element of love in Hosea's 'divine love' theme is that God loved Israel from the beginning of its history. This love was considered as an active relationship and establishing love which is seen from the beginning in Egypt (11:1).[1126] This love is seen as visible and rendered in the salvation history in the form of exodus and redemption from the bondage (cf. 13:4), as divine election. God's love is important element in his election of Israel and in the exodus experience. Love redeems. God is filled with pain and grief because of Israel's betrayal, but He still desires to redeem her. Stuart notes, the personal details given by Hosea are to a certain few, but the message is linked with Yahweh. The book's message serves as the interest of the divine message of wrath and redemption. For H.C. Philip, "divine love understands, redeems and is creative."[1127] Though the people went away, God still went after them to find them and bring them back to Himself. The book proclaims the truth from destruction, and the redemption and restoration come by God's action. The relationship between two entities demands a new commitment. This serves as a climax by restoring the relationship between God and Israel. God's loving presence; his patience and plan for his redemption of his people are laid out. Israel had extensive knowledge about her history and origin. The metaphors used in the book about marital relationships has message very much relevant to the world. The promise of restoration of the people in a future day lets Hosea depict vividly the visions of destruction and restoration of the elected people.

6.3.2.4. Compassionate love

This love has strong emotional and effective feelings and it uses several strong metaphors stressing the tenderness in God's relationship to Israel and His loving care. The metaphor presents God as father who takes care of his son and helps him to grow in maturity. The metaphor brings out God's loving and caring love towards Israel. The shift from rebuke and condemnation to a loving appeal is to be noted

---

[1125] Őstborn. G, *Yahweh and Baal: Studies in the book of Hosea and related documents,* Lund, Gleerup, 1956, 80.

[1126] Els, 'אהב', 279.

[1127] H. C. Philip, "The Book of Hosea," *The Interpreter's Bible,* Vol. 6, ed., by G. A. Buttrick, New York, Abingdon Press, 1956, 557.

here. Israel brought destruction upon herself and in no way could she obtain mercy from Yahweh. But here, it is Yahweh who is presented as merciful to those who do not deserve mercy. The divine love is presented here as unmerited mercy and forgiveness. The goal of God's love is the perfect fellowship with the redeemed Israel. This is expressed through the metaphors of marital and parental relationships and healing. The broken relations will be replaced by a new covenant relationship. God's compassion and grace cannot be measured against an occasion of repentance, pain and suffering. They know through their covenant commitments that God's compassion for his people extends into the distant future. God's inclusion of other nations in his concern and compassion for all humanity is also clearly seen in the prophet's dealings. The promise is that the Lord will restore and fulfil his present work and be pleased with the success of his love.

6.3.2.5. Persuasive love

The crucial element of theme here is that God loves a wayward and rebellious people. God's love is patient and forbearing in spite of Israel's continuous apostasy. The ultimate feature of God's love seen in the book of Hosea is its persuasion. In chapters 6, 10, 12 and 14 Yahweh warns Israel to repent and return to Him. Israel's apostasy was the cause of the whole trouble; her return is the first step to be taken toward reconciliation.[1128] It also reminds the people of Israel of the covenant that God made with them: *"I will be your God and you will be my people."*[1129] When the people disobey God's love, they will be sent to exile and dispersal. The climax pictures God's love and reconciliation with Israel. Here, God announce his plan to bring his disobedient people into his fold and gives assurance of forgiveness. Hosea concludes the story with his own experience of God's love for his wayward wife and the divine effort in bringing her back into reconciliation. If people respond to God, God will respond to them. The message here is to show love to your God and continue with legal relationship. Hosea asked them to return to Yahweh and love Him and remain faithful with their commitment.

6.4. Concept of Love in the Covenant and Hosea's Understanding

Hosea's understanding of "covenant" and how he relates this to his prophecy requires consideration. The word "covenant" (ברית) rarely occurs in literature prior to the seventh century.[1130] Except for חסד, all the other terms can be somehow connected to the terminology in ancient West Asian treaties.[1131] Of all the prophets prior to that time, only Hosea uses the word in its theological sense.[1132]

6.4.1. Hosea's Understanding of Covenant

A survey of the book produces sufficient evidence that its author was knowledgeable about the covenant tradition and infused it into his message.[1133] Reference to the

[1128] Harper, *A Critical and Exegetical Commentary on Amos and Hosea,* New York, 1915, 411.

[1129] Mays, James Luther., *Hosea: A Commentary,* OTL, Philadelphia, Westminster, 1969, 186.

[1130] R.A.F. MacKenzie, *Faith and History of the Old Testament,* Minneapolis, University of Minnesota Press, 1963, 36.

[1131] F. C. Fensham, *"Covenant Alliance,"* New Bible Dictionary, Leicester, Inter Varsity Press, 1982, 240-242.

[1132] J. Bright, *A History of Israel,* Philadelphia, Westminster Press, 1959, 152-153.

[1133] James Muilenburg, *"The 'Office' of the Prophet in Ancient Israel,"* in The Bible in Modern

sojourn tradition is found in 2:17, 5:1-2, 9:10, and 13:5. In chapter eleven, the Exodus motif is followed by the Wilderness motif.[1134] The concept of covenant is deeply embedded in these motifs.

The hypothesis also has been maintained that Hosea, standing in the stream of the covenant tradition, discovered antecedents which occasioned the use of the Yahweh-Israel marriage. Therefore, the pertinent question here is the relationship of the covenant tradition to Hosea. Brueggemann says that the eighth century prophets can be understood only in terms of the covenant, with its accompanying historical and legal traditions.[1135] The Decalogue had probably already been understood to be a "fixed quantum" by the time of Hosea.[1136]

With the covenant between Yahweh and Israel at the heart of his theology, Hosea's focus is on his own people rather than on any other peoples. Hosea stands in the Mosaic tradition of the conditional covenant.[1137] For Hosea, violation of the terms of the covenant results in annulment of the covenant: *"You are not my people and I am not your God"* (Hos. 1:9). Therefore Hosea could not speak of a general God but only of Yahweh, who revealed Himself and acted within the bounds of history in the context of the covenant.

This study demonstrates that Hosea offers some fresh insights into the covenant relationship between Israel and God. He stressed that the covenant was personal communion, rooted in the love of God. This perspective of the covenant shaped Hosea's major themes. It also examines Hosea's understanding of covenant based upon the language of love, אהב, חסד, רחם, נחם, אמת, and דעת אלהים concluding that Hosea perceived the covenant as a relationship of steadfast love. This relationship originates from the incomprehensible love of God and is central to Hosea's whole message. The covenant thus established a community with characteristics of a great family with common life and will.[1138]

6.4.2. Love - The Foundation of the Covenant

Unlike other eighth century prophets, Hosea does not use the terms "justice" and "righteousness." Instead, he focuses on חסד, steadfast love, faithfulness and the knowledge of God. Most interpreters have seen the imagery primarily in covenantal terms. Hosea shares with Deuteronomy the vocabulary of love (אהב) as a motivation for Yahweh's choice of Israel. The form of the covenant tradition known to Hosea included legal material, probably covering both cultic and moral actions (6:7, 8:1). Relationships play an important role in the lives of the people of Israel,[1139] because

---

Scholarship, ed. by J. Philip Hyatt, London, Carey Kingsgate Press, 1965, 93ff.

[1134] Stanley Jones, *"Exodus Motif in the Book of Hosea and its relevance to the Socio-religious Context of India,"* Faith Theological Review, Vol. 16, No. 1, March 2015, 36.

[1135] Brueggemann, *Tradition for Crisis: A Study in Hosea,* Richmond, John Knox press, 1968, 13, 17, and 21.

[1136] Muilenburg, *"'Office' of the Prophet* in Ancient Israel,' in Bible in Modern Scholarship, ed. J. Philip J. Hyatt, Nashville, Abingdon, 1965, 93, 64.

[1137] R.A.F. MacKenzie, *Faith and History of the Old Testament,* Minneapolis, University of Minnesota Press, 1963, 38-39.

[1138] Scott, R. B. Y., *The Relevance of the Prophets,* New York, Macmillan Company, 1953, 24.

[1139] Greathouse, William M. *Wholeness in Christ*, Kansas City Beacon Hill Press, 1998, 22.

God made a covenant with them at Mount Sinai, but the people of Israel had forgotten their promises and the relationship that they had with Him in the early days.

Hosea's understanding of Israel was rooted in the traditions concerning the patriarchs, the Exodus, wilderness wanderings, the conquest of the land and the covenant at Sinai.[1140] Israel had broken the covenant (6:7; 8:1). In 4:1-3 Hosea brings a law-suit against Israel, and the indictment lists violations which mirror the covenant stipulations found in the Decalogue: no improper oaths, no false witness, no stealing, no murder and no adultery. Lalmuankima says that in addition, the people lack the covenant qualities of faithfulness, covenant loyalty and knowledge of God.[1141] The Mosaic covenant, with its promises of material blessings to Israel for her obedience, is no longer in force.[1142] From the religious side, the people of Israel have deserted God (Yahweh), their Covenant God, and followed the god called Baal.[1143] According to Kevin J. Vanhoozer,[1144] Hosea understands God, Israel, and the world as founded on the concept of the covenant, specifically the covenant between God and Israel. The message of the Mosaic covenant turns from disobedience to blessings under the covenant and God will place them in the state in which He elected them.

6.5. Rhetorical

Phrases such as "*my people*"[1145] (1:9; 2:3), "*not my people*"[1146] (1:8-9), "*not pitied*"[1147] (1:6), and "*you shall be my people*"[1148] (2:25) are based upon the covenant with Israel (cf. Ex. 6:7). Honeycutt states the phrase "*I am*" not for you, the "*your God*" is absent in the text.[1149] The "*I am*," reminiscent of אהיה אשר אהיה (Ex.3:14), is an avowal of renunciation strongly contrasted with the former covenant promise of His presence.[1150] God as a deity of covenant and relationship is ubiquitous in the book. "Yahweh" is used forty five times compared to twenty six for "God," but the usages of "God" usually have a suffix personalizing it.[1151]

In Hosea 1-3 the Lord commands Hosea to marry Gomer. Following their marriage, Gomer chooses to be unfaithful to Hosea and commits adultery. The Lord uses the symbol of this marriage to describe His relationship with Israel.

[1140] Mays, J. L., *Hosea: A Commentary,* OTL, Philadelphia, Westminster, 1969, 7-14.

[1141] C. Lalmuankima, "Challenges from the Book of Hosea in Understanding the Kindness of God," *Bangalore Theological Forum,* Vol. XL, No. 1, June 2008, 154 (149-160).

[1142] John F. Walvoord and Roy B. Zuck, *The Bible Knowledge Commentary: An Exposition of the Scriptures,* Wheaton, Victor Books, 1983, 1584-1585.

[1143] D. A. Hubbard., *With Bands of Love,* Grand Rapids, Wm. B. Eerdmans co, 1968, 10.

[1144] Kevin J. Vanhoozer, *Dictionary for Theological Interpretation of the Bible,* Grand Rapids, Baker Academic, 2005, 308-311.

[1145] Mays, James Luther. *Hosea: A Commentary,* OTL, Philadelphia, Westminster, 1969, 29.

[1146] Honeycutt, Roy L. "Hosea" *The Broadman Bible Commentary,* ed. by Clifton J. Allen. Vol. VII. Nashville, Broadman Press, 1972, 11.

[1147] Ibid.,

[1148] Muilenberg, J., *"The 'Office' of the Prophet in Ancient Israel,"* J.P. Hyatt (ed.), *The Bible on the Modern Scholarship,* Nashville, Abingdon, 1965, 93-94.

[1149] The MT does omit "your God" which is included in the footnote as a possibility.

[1150] Honeycutt, *"Hosea,"* 11 - 12. See the fine discussion of Wolff who stated that the "I am not" is a predicate noun standing for the name of Yahweh; Wolff, *Hosea,* 21.

[1151] Ibid., xxv.

Israel - the wife is unfaithful to the Lord the husband and has sought after other lovers, which unfaithfulness is symbolic of Israel's worship of false gods. After detailing the judgments that would come upon the Israelites for breaking their covenants, the Lord mercifully invites them to repent and enter into the covenant again. In the cycle of repentance, redemption, and restoration evident in Hosea's prophecy and even his marriage (Hosea 1:2-3:3) Hosea powerfully presents the image of the nation as the bride of the Lord.

God used the covenant lawsuit, also called the trial speech or lawsuit oracle,[1152] to charge or indict Israel for their idolatrous breach of the stipulations of the Mosaic Covenant.[1153] In the covenant lawsuit God is portrayed figuratively "as the plaintiff, prosecuting attorney, judge, and bailiff in a cosmic court case against the defendant, Israel."[1154] The form is most often related to ancient Near Eastern juridical trial procedures or international suzerain vassal treaties.[1155] God used the pre-exilic writings of prophets to serve as His messengers, or covenant enforcement agents, in accusing the people of Israel and Judah of breach of covenant, and to warn them of impending judgment as an inevitable consequence.[1156]

Anyone who reads Hosea will be impressed by the prophet's conception of the deity. For Amos, as well as for most of his predecessors, Yahweh is conceived primarily as a god of justice. He gave laws for his people to obey, and disobedience of these laws must inevitably bring punishment sufficient to atone for the wrongdoing. But for Hosea, Yahweh is a god of love and mercy. Our best understanding of Yahweh's nature can be grasped by means of analogies drawn from family relationships. The love of a husband for his wife and the love of a father for his children are appropriate

---

[1152] AageBentzen, *Introduction to the Old Testament,* 2nd ed., Copenhagen: Gad, 1952, 1:199 - 200. See also Hans Walter Wolff, *Hosea: A Commentary on the Book of the Prophet Hosea,* trans. Gary Stansell, Hermeneia (Philadelphia: Fortress, 1974), 31 - 33, 65 - 69; and Claus Westermann, *Basic Forms of Prophetic Speech,* trans. Hugh Clayton White, Philadelphia: Westminster, 1967; reprint, Louisville: Westminster/John Knox, 1991), 169 - 180, 199 - 204.

[1153] The literature on the covenant lawsuit or rìp - pattern employed in the pre-exilic writing prophets is quite extensive, including among others, the following works: B. Gemser, The *Ríb* - οτ Controversy - Pattern in Hebrew Mentality"; Julien Harvey, "Le 'Rîb - Pattern / réquisitoireprophétiquesur la rupture de l'alliance," *Biblica* 43 (1962): 172-96; Delbert R. Hillers, *Treaty - Curses and the Old Testament Prophets,* Biblica et orientalia (Rome: Pontifical Biblical Institute, 1964); Herbert B. Huffmon, "The Covenant Lawsuit in the Prophets," *Journal of Biblical Literature* 78, December 1959, 285-95; Kirsten Neilsen, *Yahweh as Prosecutor and Judge: An Investigation of the Prophetic Lawsuit (Rib - Pattern),* trans. Frederick Cryer, Journal for the Study of the Old Testament Supplement Series (Sheffield: JSOT, 1978); James Limburg, "The Root TT and the Prophetic Lawsuit Speeches," *Journal of Biblical Literature* 88 (1969): 291 - 304; idem, "The Lawsuit of God in the Eighth - Century Prophets" (Th.D. diss., Union Theological Seminary, 1969); Westermann, *Basic Forms of Prophetic Speech',* and G. E. Wright, "The Lawsuit of God," in *Israel's Prophetic Heritage,* 26 – 67.

[1154] Fee and Stuart, *How to Read the Bible for All Its Worth,* 177. The clearest example of this "cosmic lawsuit" form is found in the 3Π oracle delivered against sinful Israel in Micah 6:1 - 7:10.

[1155] Kohler's informative study of the riò - pattern employed in Isaiah 40 - 55 suggests that the literary form originated in the legal proceedings associated with lawsuits conducted in ancient Israel ("Deuterojesaja [Jesaja 40 - 55] stilkritisch untersucht," 110 - 20). Wolff supported and further developed Kohler's views, stating that the 3H literary form "most probably has its setting in the announcements of judgment given by the court assembled at the city gate" (Wolff, *Hosea*, 66).

[1156] Charles H Silva, Literary Features in the Book of Hosea 4-8, *Bibliotheca Sacra* 164, July - September 2007, 291-306.

symbols for indicating the character of the deity. Speaking for Yahweh, Hosea declares, "When Israel was a child, I loved him, and out of Egypt I called my son." And again, "How can I give you up, Ephraim? How can I hand you over, Israel? I will not carry out my fierce anger, nor will I turn and devastate Ephraim."

Hosea explicitly mentions the covenant; we can also assume that the traditional covenant language with the term אהב influenced his marriage metaphor. There are two important new developments in the imagery of Hosea. The first is the very personal and intimate aspect of the relationship expressed by the marriage motif. The prophet demonstrated metaphor of marriage and adoption. In Hosea 14 Yahweh heals Israel's apostasy and love relationship reaches the goal God had in His mind since calling them out of Egypt.

6.6. Inter-textuality

An intertextual approach reveals a direct and indirect covenantal element in the book. The covenant between Yahweh and Israel are at the heart of his theology. Hosea's message begins with *"return, O Israel"*; the verb "return" is central word in Hosea's strong vocabulary throughout his message.[1157] The significance from an intertextual analysis is its connection to Israel as the subject to return to the Lord.[1158] Hosea elucidates his phraseology in a covenantal context. The prophet echoes covenant terminology of returning to the Lord. The covenant between God and his people is the background of the statements made by Hosea. The compassionate nature of God is presented in the form of covenant partner. Though Israel is unfaithful and ungrateful the response of the covenant partner is to show love to the wayward behaviour. The theological affirmation is to do with "forgive transgression of his people and to love them freely." The characteristic of divine love is lovingly presented and dynamic acts are recorded within the created order. Hosea traces the basis of Yahweh's love in holy nature. Yahweh's loving character brings out theological hope of restoration.

The theme of covenant in Hosea is considered as one of the major themes in the book. The prophet uses the idea of covenant in his prophetic literature. Hosea 14 summarises the entire message of the whole book. The covenant element is seen in the message beginning with return *O Israel, to the Lord your God....* (14:2). The verb שוב is seen as central word in Hosea's vocabulary and throughout his message.[1159] The importance of intertextual analysis is that the connection between Israel and return to the Lord their God is based on the idea that the people have followed and worshipped Baal.[1160] The people of Israel sinned against the Lord and have gone astray.[1161]The prophet brings out the message very clearly to Israelites that the return is the only option and it is clearly explained and echoes in his messages. The return to the Lord is part of the recommitting to the terms of the covenant after they have fallen

---

[1157] D. Stuart, *Hosea-Jonah,* WBC, 31, Waco, Word Publishers, 1987, 213.

[1158] Cf. Hos. 2:9, 11; 3:5; 6:1.

[1159] Douglas Stuart, *Hosea-Jonah. Word Biblical Commentary* 31 Waco: Thomas Nelson, 1987, 213.

[1160] The following passage clearly explains about it, the following passages: Hosea 2:9, 11; 3:5; 6:1; 7:10, 16 and 12:7.

[1161] The references clearly shows that how the people of Israel have forgotten their Lord and went after worshipping other god, Baal. Hosea 4:5; 5:5 and 14:10.

and committed adultery and their apostasy (Deut. 4:30-31). The message is that the return to the Lord should be made when they are in distress and have failed to keep their covenant with God. The Lord will not forget the covenant which He made with their ancestors (Deut. 30:1-10).

As in Deuteronomy 4:30, Hosea says that you must obey the commandments and follows the Lord when you return. The term שוב is a verb related to the covenant between God and Israel. The prophet clearly echoes and insists that Israel should return to their God, Hos. 14:2.[1162] The same idea and elements of returning to their God after having broken their covenantal terms are also is seen in the Davidic covenant when King Solomon dedicated the newly build temple. King Solomon speaks about these elements in a way that also helps elucidate Hosea's phraseology in a covenantal context. Similarly, Hosea also echoes the covenant terminology of returning to their God (cf. 1Kings. 8:33-35), the question is should the people of Israel be routed by an enemy because they have sinned against the Lord. The idea of returning is clearly expressed with the object being the Lord. The terminology and elements in the book of Hosea and Kings is to show that the same direction, the covenant between God and Israel is the background of the statements made by both Hosea and King Solomon.

The reason is explained by the prophet why Israel needs this message of returning is *for you have fallen because of your sin* (14:2). This is directly connected with the covenant elements found in Leviticus 26:37-40, where the idea is clearly expressed using the same words in the same order *they shall confess their iniquity and their fathers.* The introduction of the book shows that the book is deeply rooted in covenantal elements. Through the terminology used in this section it is shown that the prophet wanted Israel to understand that they should return to the covenant between them and their God. According to Stuart the term שוב is a covenant verb, because they stumbled and their iniquities are part of the vocabulary of the covenant elements that is seen in the final chapter of Hosea. They are introduced so that the hearer may know in which context the message is prophesied and what the response of the people should be.

In Hosea 14:3 we see a description of the actions that Israel is expected to perform during this return to the covenantal relationship. Stuart notes that it is expected that the people of Israel should *return to the Lord* and plead to God to *forgive all their sins.*[1163] Similar aspect appears in the Bible in the context of the covenant between God and Israel (cf. Exo. 34:7; Num. 14:18; Isa. 33:24 and Mic. 7:18). The prophet says to the people *to accept the Lord and do good what the Lord has told* in Hosea (8:3 and 3:5). The word טוב is to connected with blessings mentioned to Israel as one of the covenant elements directly linked to God's act of being faithful as the Lord opens his wellbeing (Deut. 28:12) so that they can spread blessings to them. The same word טוב appears when Israel would שוב to the Lord after having broken the relationship.

The text emphasises the faithfulness of the Lord towards Israel and it uses the language of the Lord being compassionate to the people of Israel. The Lord's speech

---

[1162] Cf. Hosea 4:8; 5:5; 7:1; 8:13; 9:7, 9; 13:12; 14:2a; Deut. 4:30; 30:2 and 10.

[1163] Douglas Stuart, *Hosea-Jonah. Word Biblical Commentary* 31, Waco: Thomas Nelson, 1987, 215.

follows with the covenant logic, the promise of restoration and assurances that if Israel heals the breach of the covenant Yahweh will love them freely and generously. The people of Israel know only God can forgive their covenant curses and heal their apostasy (Deut. 28:27, 35). The covenant word "love" is rooted primarily in the covenant term (cf. Deut. 4:37; 5:10; 7:7-9, 13; 23:5; Hos. 11:1). The promise of blessings and restoration to prosperity is a concept found in the covenant as well.

6.7. Social Texture

Hosea uses the word 'covenant' rarely, but rather uses the attributes of the covenant as the framework for his message to the people. Hosea calls people to return to the covenant and to holiness of life, making it clear that this return is relational and that ritual and rules, in and of themselves, are insufficient. The nature of this call reflects the unique contribution to the tradition that Hosea makes: 'religion is first and foremost a matter of relationship with God' and it is 'personal.'[1164] On God's side, it consists primarily of love and compassion and gracious condescension; on man's side it consists of dutiful love and humble trust.[1165]

Because of the parallelism of verse six and since a burnt offering was a type of sacrifice, it would appear that the comparative is also to be understood in the first line (6:6a). It was not that sacrifice per se was condemned but that "marriage love" was desired more (cf. 1Sam. 15:22f.). Truly, proper sacrifice and burnt offerings would result from a faithful relationship, but the propriety of the former was impossible without the marriage. Hosea lists two further reasons for summoning the people to listen: (1) God has a charge involving Israel's violation of its basic covenant with the Lord, which (2) is demonstrated in Israel's threefold conduct before the Lord. Israel is charged with infidelity, disloyalty, and a virtual failure to know God in their lives. They who were custodians of vital religion and the basic covenant with God had themselves failed to acknowledge God's primacy in their lives. Moreover, they had twisted the law of God to their own benefit. Because the people willingly followed the priests in their apostasy and degraded lifestyle, God will punish Israelite society in general, priests, prophets, and people alike. Indeed, all Israel stood guilty of not only deserting God in their feigned faith in him and in the desecration of his standards, but they have entered into the idolatrous worship of other so-called gods and practiced the debased religious rites associated with them. This was especially true of their worship of Baal. Rather than receiving the expected benefits of worshiping him, while going through the motions of Yahweh in their unfelt observance of the sacrificial system and supposed obedience to the law, they will find that their syncretism had failed. For the religious practices that they had chosen could not achieve what they promised. Only the Lord can bestow true blessings to his people, including the life giving rain they expected Baal to provide.

Many times the people of Israel have disobeyed the word of the Lord, and broken the covenant. There are many symbolic actions and metaphors in the book

[1164] Norman D. Snaith, *Mercy and Sacrifice A Study of the Book of Hosea,* London, SCM Press, 1953, 39-40.

[1165] N. D. Snaith, *Mercy and Sacrifice A Study of the Book of Hosea,* London, SCM Press, 1953, 39-40.

that express this to show how much Yahweh loves them, and which are designed to encourage them to return to follow Him and not to follow after any other gods.

Through his own marriage to Gomer-bath-Diblaim, Hosea saw the relationship between God and Israel as that of husband and father[1166] with its attendant attributes of love, loyalty, compassion and grace. Through this enacted prophecy, Hosea learned that at the core of the covenant is God's love for his people, expressed in the exodus, and that God seeks a response of *'steadfast love'* and *'knowledge of God,'* one that Israel has failed to deliver. Hosea's marriage made visible the truth of their covenant failure, for they had failed to make meaningful connections between their theology and history in one hand, and their real life problems....they acted as if faith in Yahweh alone were an impracticable policy for life. As a result they dishonoured him even as they thought they continued to honour him.[1167]

The prophecy of Hosea draws attention to the God of the covenant as a God of love and grace who seeks relationship with his people with all its attendant joys and pain. What is new is the depth of Yahweh's love for a sinful people, as Eichrodt wrote: "for the first time in the history of Israel, the message of the love of God is heard in Hosea's proclamation as the center of God's action with his people... Hosea breaks through this sober reticence and dares to speak of Yahweh's affection for Israel using the chief expression of the powerful passion which joins a man and wife."[1168]

Hosea's understanding of "covenant" and how he relates to his prophecy requires consideration. The kind of images he uses, the sin he condemns, the judgment, the prophecies, and the hope finds source in the covenant. The word ברית occurs rarely in literatures prior to the seventh century. Of the prophets prior to that time only Hosea uses the word in its theological sense, three times.[1169] Except for חסד, all the other terms can be somehow connected to the terminology in ancient west Asian treaties.[1170] Along with ברית various other terms are used in a covenantal context. The most important are אהב 'to love,' חסד 'covenantal love' or 'covenant solidarity,' טוב 'goodness' or 'friendship,' שלום 'covenantal peace or covenantal prosperity' and ידע 'to serve faithfully in accordance with the covenant.'

6.8. Cultural Texture

Often the prophet's background, the moral and spiritual condition of the nation or nations, as well as God's covenantal agreement with the nation of Israel is essential to understand the historical setting. In the prophetic books, the challenge is to adapt theological beliefs or systems, which express a consistent understanding of the covenants, the plan of redemption, the progression of revelation and God's plan and purpose for unfolding history in the life of both Israel and Gentile nations, to other cultures. James Chukwuma says that election is intimately connected with love because Israel being the elected people of God is the covenant community that is

---

[1166] Ibid., 40, 52. Hosea also uses the father – child imagery.

[1167] Raymond C. Ortlund. *Whoredom: God's Unfaithful Wife in Biblical Theology,* Leicester Appollos, 1996, 48.

[1168] Van Gemeren, W. A. *Interpreting the Prophetic Word,* Grand Rapids, Acadamie Books, 1990, 119.

[1169] J. Bright, *A History of Israel,* Philadelphia, Westminster press, 1959, 152-153.

[1170] F. C. Fensham, *"Covenant Alliance,"* 240.

meant to manifest the nature of Yahweh and the benefits of life under Yahweh.[1171] God works through his faithful people to reconcile and restore broken relationships. God never limited His message to the boundaries of Israel; He wanted Israel to proclaim the message of salvation and to reach out to other nations (Isaiah 49:6). This is a call for Israel to move away from her centre that is the temple in Zion and reach out to the world.

The Mosaic covenant, with its promises of material blessings to Israel for her obedience, is no longer in force.[1172] From the religious side, the people of Israel have deserted Yahweh, their Covenant God, and have gone after the god called Baal.[1173] In order to have a deeper understanding of the term covenant in this book, it ought to be looked at from the perspective of divine marriage, just as Hosea did. According to Őstborn, "Marriage is by Hosea only utilized as a metaphor illustrating the intimate relationship that ought to exit between Yahweh and Israel, that is in other words, the covenant."[1174]

David Allan Hubbard describes "no faithfulness" as "lack of truth telling and truth doing which result in instability, infidelity and unreliability" and "no kindness" as "lack of concern for needy neighbours, which the covenant insists on as the appropriate response to the steadfast love Yahweh has shown His people."[1175] According to Kevin J. Vanhoozer,[1176] Hosea's understanding of God, Israel, and the world is founded on the concept of covenant, specifically the covenant between God and Israel. Israel's very existence was bound up with their identity as those in a covenant relationship with God, whose calling was to represent God before the world. They were Yahweh's people, and he was their God.[1177]

Prophetic books tell us how the nation came under judgement of God when the people completely ignored the Mosaic covenant. In such situations the prophets strongly condemned the priests, kings and people for their disobedience to the Mosaic covenant, especially under the rule of Davidic reign.[1178] Therefore the prophets insisted that the priests did not know the law (Hos. 4:6, Jer. 2:8). The prophets warned against Israel and their breach of the covenant.[1179] During the monarchical period the prophets kept alive the idea of covenant and their warnings. Their preaching's were essentially a reminder to Israel of its failure to keep the covenant. The Deuteronomic reform returned to the ancient Mosaic concept of the covenanted people. This was a

---

[1171] James Chukwuma Okoye, *Israel and the Nations: A Mission Theology of the Old Testament,* New York, Orbis Books, 2006, 4.

[1172] John F. Walvoord and Roy B. Zuck, *The Bible Knowledge Commentary: An Exposition of the Scriptures,* Wheaton, Victor Books, 1983, 1584-1585.

[1173] David Allan Hubbard, *With Bands of Love,* Grand Rapids, Wm. B. Eerdmans co, 1968, 10.

[1174] Gunnar Ostborn, *Yahweh and Baal: Studies in the book of Hosea and related documents,* Stockholm, Lund's University, 1956, 80.

[1175] Hubbard, David Allan., *Hosea,* Leicester, Intervarsity Press, 1989, 97.

[1176] Kevin J. Vanhoozer, *Dictionary for Theological Interpretation of the Bible,* 308-311.

[1177] Gordon J. Thomas. '*A holy God among a holy people in a holy place: the enduring eschatological hope.*' In 'The Reader Must Understand: *Eschatology in Bible and Theology*.' ed. K. E. Brower and M. W. Elliott, Leicester: Intervarsity Press, 1997.

[1178] Mendenhall, G.E., *Law and Covenant in Israel and the Ancient Near East,* Pittsburg, Biblical Colloquim, 1955, 46.

[1179] Ibid., 19.

true reformation in which Israel turned aside from the deviation of the monarchy and returned to the true word of the covenant, which had been given by Moses.[1180]

Hosea reflected on Israel's ancient traditions and mentioned several historical events that reflected God's covenant faithfulness to His aberrant people, and Israel's history of idolatrous unfaithfulness.[1181] Gemser suggests that Hosea's condemnation of Israel's sins was based on God's "justice," that is, "God maintained moral order in the world national and individual affairs. It is not a mechanical, automatic order of nature and natural 'laws,' but of theistic, genuine God given laws and regulations.[1182]

There is also a consensus among biblical scholars that Hosea was the first to employ the metaphor of husband for the deity, portraying Israel in a negative way with the female imagery as God's adulterous wife.[1183] Weinfeld in his book on *Deuteronomy and the Deuteronomic School* says that the marital metaphor must be later addition in the covenant traditions of the Pentateuch, and he continues that the prophets were responsible for the development of the idea of marital love between God and Israel.[1184] In the same line Abma argues that Hosea is the first to employ the term ברית as a theological term to define Israel's calling.[1185] The idea of marital metaphor is previously used with respect to Israel's relationship with forbidden deities in the Sinai covenant. Dearman says that there is a possibility that Hosea was the first written prophet in Israel to present to the people the monotheism service of Yahweh.[1186]

There are no historical evidences of the idea of marriage and covenant being used elsewhere in the ancient Near East to define exclusively the relationship between deity and people. In that case the marital metaphor is unique in the OT and examples through few biblical references would be appropriate for further explanation:

1. Jer. 7:23: "I will be your God and you shall be my people."[1187]
2. Ex. 6:7: "I will take you for my people and I will be your God."
3. Eze. 14:11: "They will be my people and I will be their God."

[1180] McCarthy. D.J., *Old Testament Covenant: A Survey of Current Opinions,* Oxford, Basil Blackwell, 1972, McCarthy, *Covenant in the Old Testament...,* 220.

[1181] Charles H Silva, Literary Features in the Book of Hosea 4–8, *Bibliotheca Sacra* 164, July–September 2007, 291-306.

[1182] B. Gemser, "The *Rîb - or* Controversy - Pattern in Hebrew Mentality," in *Wisdom in Israel and in the Ancient Near East,* ed. M. Noth and D. Winton Thomas, Supplements to *Vetus Testamentum,* Leiden: Brill, 1960, 120-37

[1183] Quoted in J.A. Dearman's book on *Hosea,* by G. Yee, *"Hosea," in Women's Bible Commentary, ed. C. Newsom and S. Ringe,* Louisville, Westminster John Knox, 1998, 207.

[1184] M. Weinfeld, *Deuteronomy and the Deuteronomic School,* repr. (1972; Winona Lake,) 1992, 81-82.

[1185] R. Abma, *Bonds of Love: Methodic Studies of Prophetic Texts with Marriage Imagery (Isaiah 50:1-3 and 54:1-10, Hosea 1-3, Jeremiah 2-3*), Assen, Van Gorcum, 1999

[1186] Dearman, J.A., *The Book of Hosea,*" NICOT, Grand Rapids, Wm. B. Eerdmans Publishing co, 2010, 55.

[1187] The idea is that the prophetic formula of declaration is different: for example in 2Sam. 7:14: "I will be a father for him (father) and he will be a son for me (my son)," this statement is similar to with numerous parallels in ancient Near Eastern adoption contracts. This reference comes out clearly that God's promise to build a house of David (7:11). In other places God's binding promise to David and his house is called a "covenant" (2Sam. 23:5).

There are different words used to express the idea of marriage: the verb "to be" *(hayat)* is used two times in Jer. 7:23. Whereas in Ex. 6:7 the word *haya* is the second verb, but in the first usage it is God "takes" *(laqah)* Israel, a term commonly used in marriage. In each of these references we find that Yahweh is Israel's God and Israel is Yahweh's people.[1188]

The prophet incorporated love and gracious covenants into his messages. Though Hosea has oracles, judgments and punishments they are placed in a positive way to bring out the message of hope. The understanding of covenant as restoration is an important aspect noted here. Hosea's major contribution to the study of the Old Testament is covenant, where it is said that covenant is restoration. In the prophecy of Hosea the main aspect that has been found is the basis for covenantal relationship in the love of God. But the Old Testament record relentlessly makes the point that covenant unfaithfulness has the most severe consequences. Oaths with sanctions and curses are built into the covenant structure.

6.9. Historical Texture

Scholars have recognized the idea of covenant in the book of Hosea, with two verses in Hosea 6:7 and 8:1; references talk about covenant between God and Israel.[1189] The idea of covenant was common before the eighth century, but it became understandable only thereafter. In reference to Hosea 6:7 and 8:1, there has often been questions about whether it is a covenant between God and Israel that had been broken, or one between humans. The Hebrew translation of the verse reads like this: *"like Adam they transgressed covenant, there they broke faith with me."* There are different opinions on whether this name Adam refers to a land or name in the book. But the prophet may have been the first biblical writer to use the marital image for Yahweh's relationship to Israel.[1190]

Steven McKenzie quotes that covenant image is one among the many in the book, but covenant image is not central to his message.[1191] In Hosea the term "ברית" is used five times. Out of those five times three of them refer to something other than the covenant between God and Israel.[1192] Dearman brings out the concept of covenant in Deuteronomy in an innovative way to understand the idea through the metaphor of marital and son ship relationship; metaphors that are part of the prophet Hosea's usage.[1193] He continues that the references 6:7 and 8:1 may refer to analogy with treaties and political relationships (cf. 12:1 [MT 2] or association with oaths

---

1188 Dearman, J.A., *The Book of Hosea,*" NICOT, Grand Rapids, Wm. B. Eerdmans Publishing co, 2010, 56.

1189 There is an argument with the scholars that whether the idea of covenant was prevalent or was it later additions. Especially the book of Isaiah chapters 4-55 and 56-66 are considered to be later works from the six and fifth century BCE. These sub divisions are called as second or Deutero Isaiah and third sections is called as Trito-Isaiah respectively.

1190 Steven L. McKenzie, *Covenant Biblical Themes Series*, Missouri, Chalice Press, 2000, 24.

1191 Steven L. McKenzie, *Covenant Biblical Themes Series*, Missouri, Chalice Press, 2000, 25.

1192 In Hosea we find covenant is with the "beasts of the field, the birds of the air, and the creeping things of the grounds" (2:18 (MT. 20)). This expresses the fertility and harmony of the land, this shows the reestablishment of the covenant between Yahweh and Israel is characterized in terms of marriage. J.L. Mays, *Hosea*, OTL, Philadelphia, Westminster Press, 1969, 138-141.

1193 Dearman, J.A., *The Book of Hosea,*" NICOT, Grand Rapids, Wm. B. Eerdmans Publishing co, 2010, 53ff.

(cf. 10:4)).[1194] Dearman says that the term fits contextually and theologically of household metaphors of marriage and children. The idea of covenant relationship in the book brings into light that the idea was from where Yahweh redeemed Israel from slavery and the people were guided by a prophet, Moses, to the Promised Land.[1195]

G. von Rad explains that Israel's history as related in the Old Testament represents the way in which Israel retold its history. G. von Rad was a staunch supporter of traditional German Old Testament scholarship; tradition history therefore plays a decisive role in his theology. The history of Israel in the Old Testament is not one history. G. von Rad's organizing principle is the theme of saving history or Salvation history *Heilsgeschichte.* According to him, both the distinctive and characteristic feature of the literature of the Old Testament and of the religious beliefs of ancient Israel is a conviction that God directed the history of the people.

Before broaching this subject, it should be pointed out that the covenant as an integral part of Israel's history stemming from the Mosaic period has been proved sufficiently by G. E. Mendenhall.[1196] Therefore, the pertinent question here is the relationship of the covenant tradition to Hosea. The eighth century prophets can be understood only in terms of the covenant with its accompanying historical and legal traditions. It was by this that they determined the present status of Israel, judged and pronounced judgment,[1197] and promulgated the message of hope for the future.[1198] The Decalogue had probably already been understood to be a "fixed quantum" by the time of Hosea.[1199] Brueggemann has isolated successfully these apodictic laws in the Hosean text.[1200] In addition, the prophet castigated and condemned Israel specifically according to covenant stipulations.[1201]

In this situation God uses Hosea as His messenger to alert the people of Israel. It was because they had forgotten their covenant with Yahweh; Yahweh reminds them of the covenant that He had made with them. The people of Israel have broken the covenant and followed Baal. Here God urges them to come back with true repentance.

The people of Israel had sinned against God's love. They had experienced Yahweh's election, His provisions, His protection, and more of His blessings than

---

[1194] Quoted in J.A. Dearman book entitled *Hosea,* covenant is may be a theological use that is taken from the book of Deuteronomy. But covenant idea that is symbolized between Yahweh and Israel must have come later. But in the study of Barr points out that the term ברית is opaque, but it has no significant.

[1195] Dearman, J.A., *The Book of Hosea,*" NICOT, Grand Rapids, Wm. B. Eerdmans Publishing co, 2010, 53ff.

[1196] George E. Mendenhall, "*Covenant Forms in Israelite Tradition,*" in The Biblical Archaeologist Reader, ed. by Edward F. Campbell, Jr. and David Noel Freedman (3 vols.; Garden City, Doubleday & Company, Anchor Books, 1970), III, 25 - 49. There can no longer be any doubt that the election of Israel was given expression in terms of a legal compact in the wilderness days; G. Ernest Wright, The *Old Testament Against Its Environment* (London: SCM Press, Ltd., 1950), 62. See also John Bright, *A History of Israel*, 2nd ed.; Philadelphia, Westminster Press, 1972, 144-66; and Eichrodt, *Theology of the Old Testament,* I, 36.

[1197] Brueggemann, *Tradition for Crisis: a Study in Hosea,* Richmond, John Knox, 1968, 13, 17, and 21, See also R. E. Clements, *Prophecy and Covenant*, London: SCM Press, 1965, 69.

[1198] Scott., *The Message of Hosea,* London, SPCK, 1921, 111.

[1199] There appears to be universal agreement on the fact that Hosea was acquainted with the Elohist narratives; Muilenburg, *"'Office' of the Prophet,"* 93, 64.

[1200] Brueggemann, *Tradition for Crisis: a Study in Hosea,* Richmond, John Knox, 1968, 37-43.

[1201] Cf. 4:6; 6:7; 7:13; 8:1; 8:12; 8:14; etc. Cf. 12:9b where the threat follows and is based upon the reference to the past in 12:9a; ibid, 37, 28.

any other people on the earth, but they had walked away from Him and spent His gifts to them to satisfy their lewd desires. They had not only committed spiritual adultery, but they had become spiritual prostitutes. They had sinned against His love as well as against His light.

6.10. Theological Texture

Through marital, parental and healing metaphor Hosea delineates the relationship between Yahweh and Israel as familial and personal. Yahweh is depicted as husband, father and physician who persistently love his people, despite of their rebellious and ungrateful attitude. Hosea clearly brings out the message that God's love is important for Israel's survival. Hosea presents Yahweh as a loving husband, father and healer who suffers internally due to their disorientation. Hosea speaks of Yahweh's divine nature which is love. Love is the reason why God entered into relationship with humanity in general and Israel in particular. For the prophet covenantal relationship is very important theme which was why he delivered his prophetic message to the people of Israel. Also During eighth century BCE there was absence of justice and morality in the society, to draw his people's attention to their behaviour. Hosea felt the need and pleaded with his people for repentance and restoration.

The prophet was aware of his traditions, customs and religion of his time, he grieved over people who were guilty and he called people to return to the Lord try to avoid the judgment that is going to come upon them and society. For this, the prophet fought to deliver the message of God's love which would redeem and restore Israel. Hosea was well experienced in family conflict with Gomer and that made him to reflect on the relationship between God and Israel. Hosea communicated clearly the love of God for the people of Israel and called on them to deliver themselves from the bondage of idolatry.

The prophets insisted that the priests did not know the law (Hos. 4:6, Jer. 2:8). The prophets warned against Israel and their breach of the covenant. They were indeed concerned with the covenant, even though they avoided the use of the word.

Most interpreters have seen the imagery primarily in covenantal terms. Hosea shares the vocabulary of love (אהב) as a motivation for Yahweh's choice of Israel. Gemser suggests that Hosea's condemnation of Israel's sins was based on God's "justice," that is, "God maintained moral order in the world national and individual affairs. It is theistic, genuine God given laws and regulations."[1202] Hosea reminds of people of Israel how God maintained the relationship with His creatures.

This overview of Hosea's controlling genre, prophetic function, and theological and covenantal perspective, reveals that Hosea's rhetorical purpose was to serve as God's covenant enforcement mediator.[1203] Most of the oracles God spoke through Hosea were of judgment and not blessing.[1204] In this role, he enforces God's covenant

[1202] B. Gemser, "The *rip or* Controversy - Pattern in Hebrew Mentality," in *Wisdom in Israel and in the Ancient Near East,* ed. M. Noth and D. Winton Thomas, Supplements to *Vetus Testamentum,* Leiden: Brill, 120-37, 1960.

[1203] R.A.F. MacKenzie, *Faith and History of the Old Testament,* Minneapolis, University of Minnesota Press, 1963, 39-40.

[1204] Stuart, Douglas., *Hosea – Jonah, Word Biblical Commentary,* vol. 31, Waco, Texas, Word, 1987, 7.

mandates by accusing the people of sin, announcing the imminent judgment for continued covenant violation, and announcing the nation's future restoration and salvation. Hosea reminds Israel that his complete thrust was to do with *"What God is to Israel and what Israel is to God."*[1205] Hosea notices common injustices in his period due to the irresponsibility of rulers, their corrupt attitudes and their negligence of their faith, and believed these to be the reason for breaking the covenantal relationship with Yahweh.[1206] Hosea reminds Israel that Yahweh expects an exclusive relationship from Israel.

Hosea attains "the richest and most profoundly developed understanding of the idea of love in the whole Old Testament" and he "brought out overwhelmingly the quite irrational power of love as the ultimate basis of the covenant relationship."[1207] Eichrodt skilfully reformulates the triple aspect of God's covenant, with His people, with the world, and with a man, as a unifying biblical theme. He goes on to argue that "the whole course of Israelite history, in which the religious sense of solidarity is bound up with the Sinai tradition, affords further evidence that the covenant union between God and Israel was an original element in all sources, despite their being in part in very fragmentary form." Further, the covenant at Sinai that started with Moses relies on one important element within 'Israel's experience of God,' namely," *the factual nature of the divine revelation.*"[1208]

According to Weems the marriage metaphor itself did not originate with the prophet, but this idea was developed and derived from the Ancient Near Eastern context.[1209] In this regard, the marital metaphor is unique in the Old Testament.

However, unlike other eighth century prophets Hosea does not use terms like justice and righteousness. Instead Hosea focuses on חסד steadfast love, faithfulness and knowledge of God. Whether the relationship with Gomer is taken literally or allegorically, the theme of the book of Hosea is the love of God as expressed in covenant. Andrew Dearman[1210] uses God as head of his household. Most interpreters have seen the imagery primarily in covenantal terms. Hosea shares in Deuteronomy the vocabulary of אהב as a motivation for Yahweh's choice of Israel. The form of covenant tradition known to Hosea included legal material, probably covering both cultic and moral actions (6:7, 8:1). J. L. Mays on the significance of the covenant in Hosea notes that it is a formal structure of the relationship instituted by Yahweh's election of Israel.[1211]

[1205] Smart, *Hosea - Man and Book,* IDB, Vol. 2, eds. C.A. Buttrick, New York, Abington Press, 1962, 652.

[1206] Smart, *Hosea - Man and Book,* IDB, Vol. 2, eds. C.A. Buttrick, New York, Abington Press, 1962, 652-653.

[1207] Eichrodt, Walter, *The Theology of the Old Testament,* vol. 1, London, SCM Press, 1961, 251.

[1208] Eichrodt, W., *Theology of the Old Testament,* trans. J. A. Baker., Philadelphia, Westminster Press, 1961. (First German edition 1933, subsequently revised), 37.

[1209] Renita J. Weems, *Battered Love: Marriage, Sex, and Violence in the Hebrew Prophets,* Minneapolis, Fortress Press, 1995, 27-28.

[1210] Dearman, J.A., *The Book of Hosea,*" NICOT, Grand Rapids, Wm. B. Eerdmans Publishing co, 2010, 6.

[1211] Mays, James Luther. *Hosea: A Commentary,* OTL, Philadelphia, Westminster, 1969, 116.

Hosea's contribution to Israel's covenant thought is an exploration of a unique contribution that Hosea made to the development of Israel's covenant understanding. The study begins with the meaning and development of covenant thought in the Old Testament. It also examines Hosea's understanding of covenant based upon the language of love אהב, חסד, רחם, נחם, אמת, and דעת אלהים, concluding that Hosea perceived covenant as a relationship of steadfast love. This relationship originates from the incomprehensible love of God and is central to Hosea's whole message.

The prophet uses four main Hebrew terms to speak about love: אהב, חסד, רחם, נחם.' According to Wolff an onomatopoeic word which means "to breathe after," "to pant."[1212] The word signifies emotion and strong desire. According to Norman Snaith, "the distinction between 'אהב and חסד' is that of election love and covenant love."[1213] The term אהב used by Hosea indicates the all encompassing love of God. This Hebrew word is predominantly used in the Old Testament to denote love for God, love for fellow man, love for inanimate things.

Love is signified and proclaimed in the book through his life in a dramatic and passionate way. It talks about Yahweh's love for the people of Israel, with pathos and the power of divine love depicted to the readers.[1214] In Hosea we can find dynamic characteristics of divine love. Though the Old Testament has these characteristics of love, Hosea is something special and it is presented with much force. While reading carefully, these characteristics enable the reader to understand the depth and mystery of God's love portrayed in the book. It brings out the "unfailing love of God for God's people" in the Scriptures; חסד is not normally used to describe human behaviour.

Hosea clearly symbolises the state of the covenantal divine-human relationship. Hosea's marriage is a symbol of God's relationship with the nation of Israel.[1215] God describes the relationship not as that of a master and slave, but as husband and wife in 2:16.[1216] In chapter 11 God describes Israel as his child whom he loved and cared for. Like Gomer, however, Israel was a wife engaged in prostitution; God knew that his chosen people would betray Him. Yet He chose them and loved them anyway with unconditional love.

The covenantal relationship plays an important role in the lives of the people of Israel,[1217] because God made a covenant with them at Mount Sinai, whereas the people of Israel had forgotten their promises and the relationship that they had with Him in the early days when He brought them out of the land of Egypt. Many times

---

[1212] Wolff, H.W. *A Commentary on the Book of the Prophet Hosea,* Philadelphia, Fortress Press, 1974, 35.

[1213] N. H. Snaith, *The Distinctive ideas of the Old Testament,* London, Epworth Press, 1944, 94-142.

[1214] Eichrodt, Walter., *The Theology of the Old Testament,* vol 1, London, SMC Press, 1961, 281.

[1215] See for example comments and discussion in Van Gemeren, Prophetic Word, 108, Interpretation 9, Ortlund, 50. H. D. Beeby, *Grace Abounding: A Commentary on the Book of Hosea,* Grand Rapids, Eerdmans, 1989, 14. Derek Kidner. *The Message of Hosea: Love to the Loveless,* Leicester, Intervarsity Press, 1981, 19. Even those who see as a real relationship dispute whether when God told Hosea to go marry a harlot it meant one who was a harlot, one who would become a harlot or one who was a temple - prostitute.

[1216] Ibid., 16ff.

[1217] Greathouse, William M. *Wholeness in Christ, Toward a Biblical Theology of Holiness.* Kansas City Beacon Hill Press of Kansas City, 1998, 22.

the people of Israel disobeyed the word of the Lord and broke the covenant. There are many symbolic actions and metaphors in the book that show how much Yahweh loves the Israelites. The hope is that the people of Israel don't follow after any other god and that they follow their God Yahweh who made a covenant with them. In this situation God uses Hosea as His messenger to alert the people of Israel, because they have forgotten their covenant with Yahweh. The people of Israel had broken the covenant and followed Baal. Here God urges them to come back with true repentance.

Conclusion

The major contribution of Hosea to the study of the Old Testament is the understanding of covenant as restoration. The basis for covenantal relationship is the love of God. The prophet Hosea incorporated "love and covenant" in his prophetic message. The prophet uses the love of God as the foundation. To this, he adds important themes in the book such as משפט, חסד, צדק and אמונה to build up his covenant theory. An examination of the prophet's ideas helps us to understand that God's love is Hosea's unique contribution to Israel's covenantal thought.

This chapter has shown how Hosea understands God, Israel, and the world as being founded on the concept of the covenant, more specifically the covenant between God and Israel. Hosea offers some fresh insight into the meaning and importance of the covenant in the Old Testament, its place in the context of Israel's history, and the covenantal relationship between Yahweh and Israel. It is clear that Hosea's rhetorical purpose was to serve as God's covenant enforcement mediator. Through his message, Hosea reminds Israel that Yahweh expects an exclusive relationship. For Hosea God's covenantal relationship was paramount. This covenantal relationship, formed as a result of the Sinaitic covenant, emphasises the reality and experience of God with His people in a sacred bond. Hosea constantly reminds Israel of Yahweh's love for her. However, Israel had failed to respond to God's yearning for steadfast love. But in the final chapters of the book the concept of hope enters when the physician-patient medical relationship is pursued.

If Israel would take the remedial medicine and return to Yahweh by seeking forgiveness, the covenant can be repaired and Israel will be in a right relationship with Yahweh again. All the terms אהב, חסד, אמת, דעת אלהים, that denote faithfulness, loyalty and allegiance form the center of covenant. Each of these terms underlines the centrality of a steadfast personal relationship to the covenant. This shows that the importance of the covenant is paramount, for Hosea. In the following chapter, the importance of the book and its relevance to the 21st century Indian context is examined. It also considers whether the message of Hosea is relevant or not today.

Chapter 7

Relevance of the Research in the Contemporary Indian Context

Introduction

The research in the previous chapters has examined Hosea's use of metaphor and image to carry Yahweh's message to Israel. Through the three images of marriage, parenthood and healing Hosea has conveyed to Israel Yahweh's love for them. His "steadfast love" which has not changed despite Israel turning to idols and the raisin cakes of Baal worship. The research has examined the concept of covenantal love, the love forged at Sinai and broken by Israel when she turned to foreign gods and images of golden calves. Now it is necessary to propose some relevant significance for the 21st century Indian context by applying the findings from the study of these passages and the concept of covenant to the Indian context and the church's role in it, the key areas being the church as model and the idea of restoration and reconciliation.

The concept of covenant works as a powerful message which touched the religious, political, cultural and social environment conditions of Israel. Hosea saw complete denial of the covenant between Yahweh and people of Israel. The prophet's usage of the term ברית is not a simple word to denote a treaty, or a simple relationship with Yahweh and Israel. Hosea clearly symbolises the state of the covenantal divine-human relationship as one of love the love of God for His wayward children, which is not, extinguished even when those children turned their backs on Him to worship other gods. Now it is important to consider how relevant Hosea's message to Israel is for 21st century India and whether it has any application for today's India. The important thing to remember is that Hosea's message to Israel still does have relevance today. God's love for Israel can be interpreted as extending to us, and that His forgiveness for us who have turned away from Him to worship other idols of wealth, materialism, greed and ecological destruction is still valid. More importantly this forgiveness includes restoration and reconciliation which are graciously offered by the loving God. There is a strong argument that Yahweh's message through Hosea is still relevant today by juxtaposing the contemporary world with Israel during Hosea's time. It is interesting to note that four issues which are important today could easily find their counterparts in Hosea's Israel mistreatment of the ordinary people, discriminating against various classes of people, narrow minded religious beliefs and abject poverty.

7.1. The Concept of Love in the Book of Hosea

The key to the interpretation of Hosea's message is the metaphors marital, parental and healing. This interpersonal relationship can be defined as love because it is precisely the relationship between two partners.[1218] The relationship between partners assume a more sensitive and personal role. With the prophet a bold new language is involved to express an experience of intimacy not permitted yet for covenantal languages, in terms of faithful, generous and loving. It is noted God's character is described as loving as he initiates the relationship with his elected people Israel. Here we see the quality of love is not measured by justice but by mercy, because mercy embraces Israel whose self-destructive affairs with other gods (Baal) were near disastrous. Hosea's skill shows that the marital, parental and healing metaphors and similes describe the loving nature of Yahweh and Israel's relationship that provides special insight into divine-human relations. The marital metaphor symbolises the story of Yahweh's relation to Israel. The theme becomes central to its readers' attention. The wilderness journey makes sense of the renewal of the covenant. The previous chapters show how God was taking care of Israel in the wilderness, and how the people of Israel responded in trust and gratitude at the time of their exodus journey. Then how Israel changed and turned her back on Yahweh, breaking the husband-wife bond. Then it was Hosea's place to try to bring the people back to the bonds of the covenant. Israel's lack of faith was confronted by Yahweh's deep and steadfast faith seeking a renewal of the covenant relationship.

The term love which the prophet employs to describe the relationship between God and Israel is important aspect noted here. The word אהב is as old as the Hebrew language, whereas the prophet gives new meaning in its fullness and presents as the rich and deep emotional relationship, which becomes meaningful to its readers; Yahweh's love both for Israel and himself become important. During the wedding ceremony, both the partners make covenant with each other that they will love and cherish one another. In the Bible we see that Yahweh had everything to give and Israel to receive. On the other hand, Israel's love was regarded as loyalty to the covenant, loyalty that could be expressed by complete obedience to God's spoken word at Mount Sinai, and devotion to its cult. Thus, the word אהב brings different idea and meanings when it is used for the relationship between God and Israel.

According to Hosea Israel's "marriage" to Yahweh through the covenant had never been a true marriage. Hosea employs the term "love" to distinguish the relationship between the divine husband and Israel's loyalty to other gods. The assurance comes from the Lord that *'she is my wife, and am I her husband'* (Hos. 2:2). The prophet employs important terms apart from love. Hosea speaks

[1218] Anderson, B.W., *Understanding the Old Testament,* New Jersey, Prentice Publisher, 1957, 304-305.

of God's righteousness, which Hosea combines with God's judgment and justice (Hos. 2:19). The word righteousness represents description of Holiness of God, when it enters into the sphere of human life. Hosea 2:19 speaks of the covenant love relationship and God's love through which He linked himself to the people of Israel in history. Righteousness is revealed to Israel not purely in ethical terms rather in terms of fellowship with him. God's fellowship is presented in the redemptive history, where God's righteousness comes to save them and brings them to the Promised Land.

This idea is further exemplified in Hosea's usage when the statement there is no '*knowledge of God*' is repeated again and again to bring to notice to the people and when he speaks of Israel's knowing God. Israel did not recognise that the Lord brought them out of the Land of Egypt and it is because of the lack of knowledge and the intimate awareness that caused people to turn away from Yahweh. This shows how much God suffered himself until Israel was redeemed from her apostasy. The knowledge of God is emphasised because of its being the climax of Hosea's metaphors.

The relevance of the idea of love in Hosea is found in the present day context. The concept of love is Hosea's greatest contribution to the history of the Old Testament. The prophet mentions the relationship of God to man as that of his love to his wife Gomer. Hosea is the first one to recognize that the great commandment is that of "*Shema*," and you shall love your God with all your soul and might. In this case the prophet was the first one to distinguish this fundamental religious principle. The prophet was ignored in his time, but his principles for which the prophet was firm are triumphant and still prevalent in today's context. The message of Hosea became one of the principles and messages to help form the basis of Christianity. Hosea's expressive style reflects firmly in today's context, and his prophetic message is still very relevant today. The message warns Christians that they can also become the object of wrath and condemnation if they persist in the way of pride and arrogance.

Hosea warns his readers and us through his message urgently to seek the Lord and to establish relationship with God's righteousness and His kingdom. In that way we can enjoy love and peace in every area of our lives and can expect to live to enjoy the benefits and to live with others in harmony with vision of renewal of Zion and of God's everlasting presence as it was in past history and is today.

But today a change seems to have taken place. Morality is lost; selfishness and materialism have paved the way for disaster. The relationship between people has undergone various changes, there is no love and affection, and rather there is lot of hatred and enmity between people. In today's context marriage which was regarded as holy and pure has experienced a radical change; it has become convenience and the relationship between husband and wife is only trivial, in the relationship there is no committed love and affection. As a result there is large number of divorces takes place, in the courts, the relationship between parents and children have also undergone severe radical changes. There is no place for ethical values and principles any more. Because of these reasons the society has also undergone many changes, and people have lost their faith in religion and its institutions.

During the prophet's time emphasis was placed on the theoretic union between God and man. This union was based on the moral relation between two parties, which leads to communion of love with an element of holiness without any action; they spoke against the corruptions of their day in their society. They raised their voices against the injustices of their day; they were spokesperson of their time. They tried their best to help the society by rectifying whatever was necessary to bring changes whenever there was need. They were not only speakers but they were also shown in action to bring changes in their society. The prophets raised their voice against the corruption and injustice and fought to create a society in which the act of God was dwelling among them and brought social changes in their lives. The prophets wanted to bring a new society and they were called the pioneers of a new society. In today's context when we look at the prophets they are different, but the message and actions of the prophets are still very relevant to the present context. They bring changes in the modern society, in terms of injustice; violence and lawlessness were the issues of their time and still are.

It is argued by many people that technology and scientific systems are today's values and norms and are a sort of religion. This is because there is always an underlying logic of human dignity and the meaning of human life. When we look at the above statement, in our present context our present societies have lost this common image of humanity. When it comes to the society that was formed according to God's will and purpose, the Old Testament offers many more details in particular to understand the idea in a better way.

The understanding of human existence did not begin as a single unit but it has started as community, which is the fundamental basis for peace. The importance of institutions of communities like society, tribe, nation and family are all focus on the concept of action in righteousness. These institutions aim at God's control of history in the Bible. God's action brings people under one umbrella of salvation. It is God's righteousness which looks at primarily purpose of community and it is not for individual.

This view brings out the important idea that everybody looks upon everyone else as their brothers and sisters in the community. This brotherhood creates partners for the covenant not in materialistic terms but in accordance with life. This extends to all the economic, political conditions and liberty. For God's creation is not only for humanity but also for the earth and everything in it. Whoever respects the creator becomes responsible to improve the spiritual as well as material conditions in which humanity has to live in harmony and peace. The service to humanity is service to God that is the relationship God expects from humanity and so He commands us to love one another. The greatest commandment of the Bible is that to love others as yourself. The commandment is known by everyone, is to love in accordance with an unbroken love to God with all your heart, soul, mind and strength. This aspect is evident in the history of Christianity that this kind of love has been encountered between individual to individual. The idea of commandment to love goes back a long way and it is seen clearly in the Old Testament. The righteous are oriented towards common welfare of the community. In every aspect we are in our times challenged by God to fill up this love with righteousness, to fulfil this task it is important to love our neighbours and take care of them in the society. The love includes changing unjust and inhuman conditions in which the miseries of individuals are obviously based. God's endeavour to establish a just and honest society shows some similarities with the Old Testament ideas. The prophets raised their voices for their rights when they were denied them in their struggles and today they are also included in the struggle that reminds us of the struggles of the prophets for the people of their time. The message and struggle of the prophets are still very much relevant and appropriate to our context today in our lives and also in our societies. The challenge that comes to us is that the Christian task is to take it seriously and adopt the message of the prophetic literature in our contemporary context and its situations. What are needed are reasonable plans to carry out the goals for a better and more just society which is based on a convincing anthropology and reciprocal love.

This brings to our notice that the prophet's message is very relevant today in a deeper and real sense. The prophet's messages become warning and hope for the present generations and generations to come. The message of prophet has the timeless quality and driving force of authentic spiritual communication. The Word of God brings power and authentic spiritual utterances. The Bible enriches us to read more and that enriches and teaches us to be selfless and fearless and helps to enrich the souls spiritually and gives authority. This helps us today in terms of discovering what were the conditions of the prophetic movements that inspire us to promote spiritual vitality in the society. The prophets of their time were tremendously concerned with the social conditions and public issues making spiritual crisis in their day. The prophets address the issues not in a simple way or in general terms of sin and repentance, rather they uttered the message of God that they had religious obligations, the awareness of the present situation and people's activity and their social life: this reminds the people of their time as well as us that God is living God, He is at work in the souls of the individuals presently and also lives among the struggles and confusion that is taking place in our society and in social life today. In today's context we find ruthless forces and struggle that crush the spirits of humankind, there God is present in power and enriches men and women to take courage. Power brings change in their life and grants self sufficiency according to His words and demands. This reminds and warns us that even today His judgments are in the earth.

In this context, the prophet Hosea particularly brings out the idea of redeeming love into his message effectively and forcefully to convey the prophetic message as directed by God. This teaches us that we must love people for themselves, remembering how much God loves them and continues to do so. Other prophets like Amos and Isaiah demands attention and they raised their voices on behalf of the poor who were deprived justice and the loving kindness of which they have been denied their rights. The words of prophets are timeless, even their words and utterances have much relevance in our context. This is evident in every aspect of our time and the message begins with the call to repentance and to love their God. The lesson from the prophets is that we learn there must be collective repentance for social sin and the deprivation of morality and also personal repentance. This reminds and warns us that we should go back to moral action for the environment which needs attention at the present time. The reason is that we need responsibility to the principles of society and to bring to end selfish and internecine struggles of possessions and satisfactions, for the sake of position and power which needs attention in the practical life of those who do not believe in the existence of God. This is the attitude which is prevailing so much in our modern life.

The important aspect to note is that every individual possesses individual freedom which is responsible for him promoting moral consciousness. This was evident and can be seen through the experience of men like Hosea. There came into our tradition and to our knowledge the inner freedom of spirit which creates the demand for common and religious liberties. This brings to notice of everyone the struggle for freedom of conscience and of worship as being important aspect of our life which should be inbuilt in our daily life.

Therefore, we learn lesson and gain knowledge from the life of the prophet Hosea, the depth of moral earnestness which can gird the democratic idea with the conviction of eternal righteousness. God is at work in the past history to create for Himself a chosen generation and people whose hearts will honour His laws and follow the commandments which is given to us teach justice and right and sustain personal dignity and foster community among humanity. This reminds us to build just society with equal rights for everyone and to live in harmony. God is present in every situations and lives and is present in the democratic struggle but He lives within us and encourages us to face life situations. This leads us to live and to confront struggles of our times. Democracy can fulfil its promise and abide its ways, only as it reaches to embody ever more fully the ways in which the kingdom of God will be established on the earth.

7.1.1. The Prophetic Paradigm of Love: Implications

The prophetic paradigm in the book of Hosea is depicted through the imagery of love. Hosea used simple imagery to convey Yahweh's message. We will consider how this message could be translated into the current Indian context.

7.1.2. The Task of the Church and its Response

The Church is empowered to be an agent of God. The role of the Church is to raise its prophetic voice against the evils in the society, where there is lack of God's love and to ensure that His love is communicated to all people. The task of the Church is to take the issues of its members seriously, address these issues and be an instrument to bring awareness among its people and society.

7.1.3. The Church's Love towards People

This research brings out the understanding of God's love through the three-fold concepts of love in the marital, parental and medical forms. Through the relationships of husband and wife, parent and child and doctor and patient Yahweh, through Hosea, demonstrates His love in ways that Israel can understand. In the 21st century the church stands in the place of the Old Testament prophets and must carry God's message to the world in ways that 21st people will understand. The church represents God's acts and shows how He suffers for them and becomes responsible in times of social violence. The church plays an important role in creating awareness towards the issues faced in today's world. Hosea adopted the method of showing love to characterize Yahweh as the deliverer who is compassionate, universal and powerful.

7.1.4. The Church as Model

This research has demonstrated that "God's love" in Hosea is presented as gifting new life. In Hosea 2-3, Yahweh promises Israel blessings and restoring her into her former condition. In the present Indian context of family and community, there are conflicts, tensions, misunderstanding, and divorce; this is where the church must take on its role as a church; it must become a church that goes beyond its routine boundaries into the wider world, to bring God's message to all people. It must see its role as representing the acts of God with scope for restorative love and reconciliation, educating its members and bringing development in their lives. This means the church must be sensitive to current issues and responsive to take actions that bring changes. The church must understand it plays an important role in monitoring and introducing changes in the society, family and individuals by liberative, educative and restorative direction. It must accept that it is not there just to preach God's love, but to show God's love and how it can bring restitution and reconciliation. It must demonstrate how 'fullness of life' can be achieved by the individual and by the wider society. This is the form of love that the Indian church must practice; unless the church can practice "love" in its wider sense, it cannot understand the meaning of God's love. This is the task of the Indian church in contemporary India, and it is essential it realises this and acts on it.

The message, in the words of Peter Gomes, is this:

> God's immediate and ultimate relationship to the world is one not of power or indifference but of affection: For God so loved the world. God's power is subordinate to His love. The world is subordinate to His love. The world is a place that is beloved of God. Like creation it is good, although terrible things happen in it, for it is not perfect, it is not without pain, and the price of our freedom is to learn to cope with a world of ambiguity and danger, pain, joy and opportunity. Through all of that, God relates to us out of his love for us…

The Church must exist for the very important reason that it must proclaim God's promise of restoration and provision of liberation and to usher in a just, peaceful and harmonious society. The question is: How do we apply it? "Love" makes the Church's solidarity with the poor, oppressed and marginalized not just a preferential option, but an obligation. The weaker sections of our society are the worst affected groups. The Church's solidarity with the poor should thus become a real and living Christian experience. A profit oriented, accumulative, consumerist and competitive economic system that pushes aside the powerless and the weak is to be challenged by *words* of love, as well as by works of love.

Fr. Immanuel Claps writes

> In his infinitive love for the world God continuously pursues His redemptive purposes. The Church is in the world as an instrument of renewal and restoration. The Church is called to share the healing and restoration with the world. In every age and place the Church addresses the world's ills and problems by declaring and affirming God's plan for the universe. That is, its ultimate transfiguration and glorification already disclosed in the resurrection of Christ and manifested in the Scriptures and in the sacraments celebrated in faith.

Love in *action*, in its essence, is love: This involves a number of activities. It seeks to proclaim the good news of liberation and invites the world to interact with God's truths and the values of the Gospel. Moreover, *Love in action* relates to "the human life and activates the mystery of Christ and his Church, elucidating for the faithful and for the world how the Church lives her life of faith by fostering generous services to the world." To do this, people must make serious efforts to reciprocate God's love by mirroring it to the specific issues that bring misery and bondage.

In present day India, here are several issues that can be described as "bringing misery and bondage," just as they did in Hosea's time. They include exploitation, discrimination, religious fundamentalism and poverty.

7.1.5. In the Context of Exploitation

Yahweh's mercy and compassion is indicated by the prophet to be exercised by taking care of the orphan. During the period of Hosea the social identity came from the extended family with the patriarchal head in the society. The fatherless are without the support and guidance of a parent and thus they are exploited and they are entered into slavery. Similarly, the orphans and widows were often at the mercy of the greedy and unsavory elements in the society. Their recognition is often exploited according to the law. But the Lord's compassion towards the orphan is affected through the rejection of covenant and instruction. The people of Israel found itself in the position of an orphan. The root word רצץ 'to crush' is employed in the context of social exploitation of the weak. Hosea spoke against the allusions of the rich people. The two conceptual terms in the context of social exploitation and economic justice are חסד and משפט means the social exploitation of various kinds. This includes various kinds of oppression and exploitation of the underprivileged people.

Similarly, in India, the Dalits and tribals are exploited and oppressed even today. They have collectively remained at the bottom of the hierarchical and stratified Indian society for more than 3000 years. The religio-cultural social ideology and the economic structures of the caste system have perpetuated this division in Indian society. The exploitation of dalits includes *victimization* through caste-atrocities and *obstructions* to their social progress, *violations* of their human and cultural rights, *suppression* of their protests for full social membership, and *social* and *political patronage and co-option* to be subservient to the power interests of the ruling castes/class. *A Dalit woman faces multiple exploitations* due to social, economic, gender and patriarchal domination. These are the areas where the church must be seen to be active. The church must fight against injustice and promote Dalits and tribals to higher levels in society and support the on-going dalit struggle for liberation.

7.1.6. In the Context of Discrimination

In the book of Hosea throughout the text the prophet portrays Israel's God. The Lord is sovereign over peoples and other gods and whose sense of ethics will not allow for injustice and the inordinate assertion of power of one people over another. The prophet clearly explains this; God makes no discrimination between the guilty humankind and the non-humankind: all creation will experience the God's love for them. God's actions are not destructive but constructive; these images of an anthropomorphic, androcentric God reflect both the culture of the day. Finally the text makes clear that the Israel's God is not only sovereign over all nations, peoples and gods but also is one who is more powerful than the most powerful of nations and peoples on the face of the earth. Israel's God is Lord of all creation and Lord of history.

In India, half of the population are women. They are considered as weak and not accepted as equal to men in society. As Ambedkar said "the position of women in Indian society is a position devoid of all rights." Even today, many women have no power or position either in the home or in society. They are encouraged to be self-denying and self-sacrificing. Despite laws preventing such acts, serious and criminal discrimination against women is still common, in the form of wife beating, female infanticide, domestic violence, dowry deaths, forced widowhood, bride burning and sati. The low value of female life has reduced the chance for girls to be born. The depiction of women as sex objects in the media still continues. These beliefs are so deep rooted that any changes are difficult to bring about in the attitudes of the society. This is another area where the church can intervene, fighting to ensure women receive equality wherever possible.

7.1.7. In the Context of Religious Fundamentalism

In Hosea's time it is noted that fundamentalism is deciding whether what is at work is a political ideology that is built within religious movement. Fundamentalism merely denotes strong belief in core doctrine of faith. During Hosea's time there was some kind of religious and moral pollution in their relationship to Yahweh. It is because of the wrong teachings that lead them to charged moral infidelity. This is expressed through his own wife who was as religious himself in a different way. The religious practices of the time were the last word in religion and she practiced them with complete devotion. Hosea clearly pictures that Yahweh is a God of love and mercy. Yahweh's nature is grasped through the imageries drawn from family relationships.

The "politicizing of religion" and the "religionization of politics" has given rise to religious fundamentalism. The growing religious fundamentalism has led to persecution of Christians in several parts of India. Religious hatred has caused social divisions that need to be healed. While Christians are a miniscule religious minority, it is necessary for the Church to stand up for the entire society and not just for its members, to either defend them from attack or to show itself as a resilient community.

7.1.8. In the Context of Poverty

Hosea clearly explains the parallels through his own tragic marriage to his unfaithful wife to that of the covenant between Yahweh and Israel. Israel have broken the covenant and become unfaithful to their God through idolatry and oppression of the poor. The enemies came sweeping through the land, the oppression of the people by their rulers and excessive taxes and persecution. The orphans and widows by reason of their desolate condition were in a special sense a subject of poverty. God commanded His people to care of the poor. The poor to be treated with kindness and they are to be treated as equal before God. The people are to be devoted to the poor and help them in their need or distress and show hospitality to them. Christopher Wright in his book on the Old Testament texts: the causes of poverty are because of natural disasters and oppression. How this reflects on the experience of the poor people in the contemporary present context.

The benefits of India's development over the last 50 years have been concentrated in the top 10% of India's population. Goods and Services have become inaccessible to more than 40 % of India's population. In fact, it estimated that there are 360 million below the poverty line. According to United Nations report about 30 crore people still live in extreme poverty in India and they face deprivation in terms of access to basic services like education, health, water, electricity and sanitation. India has population about 125 crore.[1219] The poor struggle to sustain themselves and their families with scarce resources. The rich-poor divide is ever increasing and conditions of poverty are getting worse each year. The church should be speaking with a loud voice, to ensure that the poor and hungry are fed. It should fight for meaningful employment, fair wages, better conditions, and economic justice for the poor.

Hosea used human metaphors of marital, parental and physician-healing love to convey the message of God's love for His people. The Church must remind people that love is the greatest attribute of all, and they must exercise it. God is also a loving God, who fights for His people. The Church must do justice, love kindness, and walk humbly before God,[1220] fighting the social evils if there is to be any hope for the world. This research shows how these images are still relevant today for the Indian church to be a messenger of God's love.

7.2. Prophetic Paradigm: and its Implications

7.2.1. Marital Love - Hosea 2-3

God's love is portrayed through the use the metaphor of marital relationship which represents intimacy and personal relationship. Hosea's marriage to an unfaithful Gomer, God's relationship to an unfaithful Israel and the message of love that their relationship portrays still holds good in modern times. Through his life Hosea brings out the message of God's love, and emphasises the value of marriage in our context, how marital relationship is important. Often, the pursuit of happiness outweighs marriage vows and marriages lose their significance. This is where the church needs

[1219] The Times of India, February 4, 2015.

[1220] Micah 6:8

to ensure the message of love in the book of Hosea will shine through to make people or help them understand the sanctity of marriage in the Christian context. Wedding ceremonies today have become ritualistic in nature and have therefore lost their meaning. It is the role of the church and the pastor to be practical and counsel the couple seeking marriage about God's plan and purpose in their lives and in their union. Hosea's action in taking Gomer back is an example to be borne in mind. This reminds us to preserve the traditional values practiced in our society. Hosea's portrayal of God's love as promising love that brings blessing and restoration in the life of Israel in spite of people's rebellious acts and worshipping idols highlights the value of marriage in our context.

7.2.2. Parental Love: Parenthood - Hosea 11

Hosea pictures the parent-son relationship as Yahweh as a parent grieving over Israel, the rebellious child who has turned away from Him. The metaphor of parental love conceptualizes God as Father - an image that is rare in the Old Testament. This illustrates God's continuing love for his children. The story illustrates how Hosea reveals the grieving heart of God through anger. Yet Yahweh as a parent exhibits not only pain, but also patience in His relationship with this rebellious child. Hosea 11 emphasises the role of God in dealing with Israel and the faithfulness and obedience, or lack of it, of Israel as a son.

Hosea 11 speaks of God's continuous love for His children. Today, we still experience the same love of God in our lives, even though we may have rebelled and rejected Him as our Father. The people of Israel turned away from God to worship the idols of Baal. Today, we may not worship graven images, but we place more importance on money, material wealth and instant gratification through social media. Since these take precedence in our lives, we tend to ignore the call of God. In Hosea, we see that God continues to love His children despite their disobedience. This is a reassurance for us today that no matter how much we have gone astray, God still loves us as a Father loves His children, and is waiting for us with open arms, for us to repent and come back to Him.

In the Bible, we notice that God punishes His people for disobedience. The punishment comes after instruction and warning, not before. This vividly depicts parental discipline. Hosea 11:2 shows us that before punishment, the wayward children should be assured of love and desire for reconciliation, just as the Israelites were given messages and promises of restoration. In today's context, we can put Hosea 11 into action by disciplining our children when they do something wrong but showing them that our love for them never fades no matter what they have done.

7.2.3. Physician - Healer Love - Hosea 14

The metaphor of healing in Hosea 14 (v. 4) highlights the proclamation of salvation which portrays the unconditional love of God towards Israel. The healing metaphor begins with devastation and denunciation and finally ends with healing of the nation. While this refers specifically to the Yahweh-Israel relationship, it has obvious implications for today. Broken relationships in the family, society and community need to be restored. To achieve this, both physical and spiritual healing are needed.[1221] In Hosea, we see the broad concept of healing: the concept of restoration and building up a family relationship as community. In a world filled with pain, we still have hope when we turn to God, keeping in mind that His promise of restoration and healing still holds good even today.

The role of the Church is to be a mediator of healing in the world, and this flows from its task of proclaiming the reign of God. This rule of God's love, inaugurated by the ministry, death, and resurrection of Jesus, enables people to discover the fullness of salvation. Because the Christian community experiences the presence and the power of the risen Christ in its midst, it is called to continue the work of Jesus that brings wholeness to broken people. Christians believe that their faith and identity are intimately connected with human wholeness.[1222] But these concepts are more than a way of showing us a God-Me relationship. They are reminders of our obligations towards each other, so that by reaching out to those around us, we are carrying God's love further. Healing people in all spheres of life is part of the church. The church is a place where the community of believers are united by their common faith. The church must help and heal fractured communities and individuals through worship, liturgy, spiritual nurture, encouragement, and supportive participation in the community. The challenge before us is to identify the problems and present the need so as to bring therapeutic healing in the life of an individuals, family, society and Church. God's love is genuine and extends forgiveness, redemption and deliverance to all so that individuals within the society and society as a whole can experience life in all its fullness. The prophet's message of God's healing is extremely relevant in today's context.

Hosea's prophecy was a powerful and life changing message of Yahweh, which led Israel to repentance. God loved the people of Israel and showed them compassion and love. For this the prophet used imagery as a paradigm for covenantal relationship. Hosea characterizes Yahweh in a different light as compassionate, deliverer, merciful and, above all, loving. In today's context, the message of Hosea has reached out to God's people with the message of hope. He is the same God who loves the people even today and His heart is filled with compassion and love towards the people. God's love is offered to every human being. The book of Hosea demonstrates God's love and concern for us, and in today's world it is the role of the church to convey that message, just as Hosea did to Israel. When the book of Hosea is carefully studied the immediate response we get is that Yahweh has a concern for humanity, a fact the church must pursue. The fact that Yahweh asked and commanded Hosea indicates His urgency for His task.

[1221] In Greek; *therapeuo* is 'to heal or cure, *'iaomai,* 'to restore,' *hygiaino*, 'to make well again' or 'to heal the whole person,' and *sozo*, 'to rescue or deliver in order to heal the whole being.' All these indicate the thoroughness and comprehensiveness of Christ's healing work. Healing may be described in terms of the curing or restoring to health of a sick person, but it can also refer to the process of reconciling broken human relationships and to the development of a just social and political order among races and nations. Therefore, healing refers to wholeness.

[1222] Robin Ryan, C.P, "Healing and the Church," *The Collegeville Pastoral Dictionary of Biblical Theology,* edited by Carroll Stuhlmuller C.P, Bangalore: Theological Publications in India, 2005, 420.

Christian witness has a complex relationship with Indian cultural trends. People live in a pluralistic religious setting where numerous ideologies are propagated. Many organizations and societies exist in India for social welfare and rehabilitation, which show that people are concerned about harmony in society. But it can be difficult for individuals to live out God's message, because it must be cultivated in a society that is filled with mass poverty, crime, violence, strikes, corruption at the highest levels, and economic disparity. These are serious questions that confront each individual. Perhaps the answer is for each one to take the concept of "love" to his or her heart, and to live it out in his/her own lives in their own individual corners of the world. If each one is guided by the concept of love in its broadest sense, then even in fragmented India, there may be some forward movement to be seen.

Conclusion

The church in India today needs to demonstrate God's love and include this vital component in her task. The message of Hosea therefor is to take the message of God's "steadfast love" to heart, and to apply it to our own lives and circumstances. If we can be kind to neighbours and to those we do not know by name, then we are spreading God's love in our own small corners of the world. This is the identity the church must adopt in its role, walking in the footsteps of Hosea as a 21st century prophet and messenger. Hosea's prophecy was a powerful and life-changing message of Yahweh, which led Israel to repentance. In today's world it is essential that the church conveys the same message. Hosea characterizes Yahweh in different roles, each designed to indicate His overwhelming love for His people and above all His love in action. In today's context the church must carry the message of Hosea to demonstrate God's message of hope and love.

The characterization of Yahweh in the book of Hosea as a loving God becomes an important concept. Yahweh is the same God who loves the people even today and His heart is filled with compassion and love towards all of them, and this is the message today's Indian church must carry. The church must not forget that God's love is for all people, not just Indian Christians, and it must keep its role of modern-day in mind. If it does, then the Church may have a chance to spread its message beyond its national boundaries, to touch the lives of people living in the neighbouring countries, where hunger, poverty and injustice also exist.

To conclude family and society need to demonstrate God's love and what God intended in the life of humankind. In today's context, it is noticed that life is entangled with corruption, infidelity, irresponsible living and immorality in the society. In this context, the message of Hosea warns to maintain strict discipline, living as an example to others within the family and in the society. This helps to draw moral standards of life and helps us to be vibrant.

Conclusion

The analysis of the book of Hosea using a socio-rhetorical approach has enabled us to develop a clearer understanding of the metaphor of love. It allows this research to explore the function of the imagery of love within the covenantal relationship. The book of Hosea focuses on the personal aspect of God's love for His people (2-3), and emphasises the call 'to share the love of God and be truthful to that love' (11:1). It also offers the forgiveness of sin, reconciliation, and return to God. This is reflecting and executing love in action (6:1, 11 and 14:1). Love plays an important role in bringing back Israel to God. A Socio-rhetorical approach enables one to discern the function of the imagery of love within the covenantal relationship. God's efforts to make Israel understand the significance of the covenant relationship linking them lays an emphasis on the very basis of human relationships. Such understanding helps human to envisage parent-child relationship profoundly. The marital, parental and healing metaphors have been strongly advocated in this study. Further, the inter-textual relationship and the use of rhetorical imagery are employed to bring out the several meanings implicit in the text.

The manner, in which the theme "God's steadfast love" is presented in the book of Hosea, using the three images of marriage, loving parent and physician, has been considered. Hosea presents a loving God who would go to any extent to win over his people's love, through reconciliation, healing, and compassion. These metaphors Yahweh as husband, parent and physician are ones that the Israelites could easily relate to since they describe love in human terms. Hosea uses these three specific human relationships to highlight God's love for the people of Israel. These are the most important and powerful symbols which can be used to demonstrate the depth of Yahweh's love. These images remind Israel that she has broken the Sinaitic covenant, gravely impairing the relationship. The broken covenant hurt Yahweh and yet he is willing to repair it on account of his "steadfast love." Yahweh's love is nuanced. The theological aspect of bringing out Israel is explained through the marriage metaphor. This אהב is manifested in bringing out the people of Israel from slavery. Hosea concludes the story with his own experience of God's love for his wayward wife and the divine effort in bringing her back through reconciliation. The phrase "I bent down to them and fed them" is that Yahweh who took care of them during their journey and fed them in the wilderness journey. Here Yahweh's love was depicted as parent's love for his child. Hosea asked them to return to Yahweh and love him and remain faithful with their commitment. The acts of God have scope for restorative love and reconciliation. Yahweh was not presented as a harsh God in contrast to the general depiction of him in the Old Testament. In Hosea Yahweh is a loving God, who is willing to forgive and forget Israel's offence and even welcome her back into His arms. This image of Yahweh gives a new dimension to the relationship established through the Sinaitic covenant between Yahweh and His people. In fact, it opens up the potentiality of God's love relationship beyond Israel to other nations as well.

In chapter two, this research uses socio-rhetorical methodology as an interpretive device that provides the means to see the importance of Yahweh's message emphasised through social, political, economic and religious relationships. Both sociological and rhetorical textures are helpful for studying Hosea, as has been demonstrated in the following chapters. Sociological analysis helps to show how the Scripture is part of an intricate social matrix that must be taken into consideration for a holistic interpretation. Rhetorical analysis helps us to show how the book of Hosea crafted Yahweh's arguments logically by using imagery understandable to Israel in human terms.

Several studies have been undertaken by biblical scholars past few decades employing marriage imagery with various kinds of metaphors in the study of Hosea 1-3. Many of these works concentrate on Hosea 1-3 within the context of prophetic marriage metaphor. Though Hosea has used several images in the book, he went further and specifically adopted imageries such as marriage, parenthood and the act of healing as metaphorical devices in chapters 2-3, 11 and 14. These images are best interpreted through the use of socio-rhetorical methodology.

In this endeavour, we discovered the use of love metaphors and its theological importance. The steadfast love of Yahweh remains as a crucial point in Hosea which creates space for forgiveness. God's loving attitude is emphasised and that enables him to portray him as a loving God. Yahweh's command to Hosea indicates his urgency to bring Israel back. Hosea pleads with Israel to "turn back and seek forgiveness and you will be forgiven and rewarded." It is important to consider at this point, why Yahweh was eager to restore the Sinatic covenant with Israel as a nation whom He had brought out of the land of Egypt. God's passionate love for Israel is vivid here because they had greater role to play in God's plan of salvation. Thus, this research suggests that through bringing her back, God also wanted to bring other nations to himself.

It is worth considering the importance of both geography and history in this context. Israel's past and present is inextricably linked to other nations, both large and small, surrounding her. She does not exist in isolation. Therefore it could be argued that Yahweh, who wishes to spread his love to other countries as well as to Israel, has chosen to do so by placing emphasis on Israel. In this way knowledge of Yahweh will spread by sheer social contact to the other nations surrounding her, given that it was how the knowledge of Baal and other Eastern gods reached Israel. God first reached out to Israel in loving relationships through the images of husband, father and healer to bring her back to him and restore her to the original status as God's chosen people. So while the explicit focus has been on God's love to Israel, there is also an implied aspect of God's love to other nations. Thus a parallel can be seen between Yahweh's use of images to describe His love for Israel and for others.

This research has explored the metaphorical images of love and their interaction between them. This reflects on God's love for the children of Israel as a loving father. God intends Israel to reflect his character (that is, love) to other nations. It is through Israel's restoration that God intends to reach out to the other nations. Hence, Israel needs to serve as 'light to the nations' depends largely on her willingness to be restored. If Israel will be restored to Yahweh, then his love for Israel can be extended to other nations. This theme runs throughout the Old Testament which is explicitly expressed in Hosea. Geographically, Israel is in a strategic place which would serve to spread the new ideas and concepts into various nation states.

In chapter three, this research has analysed and found out that Hosea's marriage is a symbol of God's relationship with the nation Israel (see Hosea 2-3). The prophet linked his message closely with his personal life. As God's direction, Hosea married Gomer and bore three children. The names of Hosea's children communicated a specific message of judgment to the Israelites. The prophet's word flowed out of his own familial experience. Hosea 2-3 is about the cycle of repentance, redemption and restoration evident in Hosea's own marriage as well as in his prophecy. To emphasise this, God describes his relationship not in the capacity of a master and slave but rather in the form of a husband and wife. Hosea 2 and 3 illustrates God's truthful and at the same time unconditional love. The command in Hosea 2-3 "to once again, love a woman who is loved by a friend," and the response "I bought for myself" is a demonstration of "love in action." *Words* of love need to be translated into *works of love.* Hosea's response (v. 2) shows how costly love can be. Hosea pictures Yahweh as the devoted husband and Israel as an unfaithful wife. Hosea gives a new meaning to sanctity-that is the sanctification in a relationship which is motivated by grace. Yahweh redeems Israel, his wife, from the penalty of death by paying the price and loving her. Yahweh selects the most abominable method to express his love for his people. Hosea is interpreting and giving a new and revolutionary meaning to the covenantal relationship. In Hosea 3:5, King David talks about the restoration of Davidic kingship over Israel and Judah (cf. Jer. 17:25; 22:2) and that the Messiah will fulfil the Davidic covenant and thereby fulfil the blessings included in the Davidic covenant. Here the Messiah is pictured as the "New David" because he will ultimately fulfil the ideals of the Davidic covenant that will be passed on to Davidic descendants. The idea presented is that the children of Israel would repent and return and seek the Lord. God often uses the deprivation to bring back the lost children to the Lord and the hope of the new King is promised to them.

Hosea's message has cycles of judgment and restoration. It repetitively brings out the following aspects: God will bring punishment for their sin, but He will then bring His people back to Himself, because of His love for Israel. Though the people turned away from the Lord and going after other gods, they can return to him from the darkness of idolatry. As discussed above, the names of the prophet's children God addresses to Israel changes from "not my people" to "my people." God reminded them that He would ultimately restore their relationship with Him, using the love imagery and personal languages for His wayward people.

In chapter four, this research attempts to see how Hosea 11 describes Israel as his child whom God loved and cared for and chosen them with an unconditional love. This becomes real, especially in the life of the prophet, where God used Hosea's marriage as a metaphor. In Hosea 11, the Lord is presented in the form of illustrative analogies: He loves people as a father, and as a shepherd, even though they have betrayed him and gone after the Canaanite god Baal. God is presented through relational imageries. The greatness of God's love is portrayed in the form of a father's love for His children. God is heartbroken when people desert Him. The brokenness of God's heart is reflective of the pain of a parent. The prophet reiterates that God loves everyone as His children. The destiny of the stubborn children is defined as being stoned to death. But Yahweh redeems his son Israel with his self-giving love (11:1). The imagery used by Hosea is, to a great extent, similar to Israel's imagery. Through this imagery, Hosea wants to convey the new deeper meaning of the covenantal relationship (Sinaitic covenant). Hosea gives a more precise meaning to this steadfast love by way of actualizing his relationship with the people who reject Yahweh.

In chapter five, this research analyses the usage of the healing metaphor. Hosea used several images in earlier chapters to discuss about return, but finally Hosea 14 envisages what repentance would look like for the people of Israel. Hosea 14 talks about the restoration to healing which is openly promised (v. 4). The restoration is deeply personal "*I will love them*" (v. 5) and is through a renewed relationship. Hosea says Yahweh will heal the faithlessness of Israel (14:4). The people in those days did not know how to get healed. Ephraim went to Assyria for healing but this plan was failed (Hos. 5:13). Yahweh reminds the people they cannot cure themselves or be cured by any other; only He will heal them and love them freely. Even the history provides evidence that when the people at the foot of Mount Sinai made an image of a calf and worshipped it, and although they were severely judged, Yahweh healed their faithlessness, forgiven them and loved them (Ex. 34:6-7).

Further, the people's faithfulness is also compared with dew in Hosea 14. The idea is that the dew will not vanish but will bring newness of life that consists of God's care for the nation and provision for its repentant people. Two distinct theological perspectives of repentance emerge from this: First, there is a theology on Yahweh's gracious unmerited initiative in being willing to restore the nation of Israel. Secondly, Israel's repentance is a prerequisite for the restoration to become a reality. Both are based on the covenant. Yahweh is profoundly gracious in paving the way for Israel's restoration and Israel's responsibility is to stand firm in her relationship with Yahweh and be ruled by Him. This reflects God's tender affection and love demonstrated by His compassion. The prophet's message ends positively with a hope of restoration. Thus, it is an image of happiness, harmony, and the healing of the people of Israel. The theme of forgiveness, restoration and renewal runs throughout the book. The presentation of the quality of God's love, which is inclusive of faithfulness and mercy, is vividly demonstrated within the book.

It is interesting to observe that Yahweh's steadfast determination is seen throughout the book. Yahweh upholds the covenant, irrespective of what Israel did on her part. This is where the Old Testament's image of Yahweh changes from familiar stern Lord to loving God, willing to forgive and forget and to welcome his people back. This depiction of loving Yahweh is often overlooked. The idea of God's steadfast love is powerful which the Indian church must recognise, recover and reclaim. The church must be ready and willing to reflect God's attitude and offer hope for reconciliation.

The exegesis of Hosea 2-3, 11 and 14 illustrates the concept of love clearly through an examination of metaphors and symbolism that illustrate the depth of God's love for the people of Israel. The metaphors play an important role in the life of the prophet. Yahweh uses the symbols of the three human relationships to describe the relationship between God and Israel. Yahweh is the one who waits both for the return of the people and for them to seek His forgiveness.

The Bible richly depicts the love of God through the covenantal relationship. Hosea's own family experience taught him what אהב, חסד, and ברית mean to Yahweh. It is through his own attitudes towards his wife that he came to know what the love of God meant. Hosea's love for his wife Gomer was so strong that even her acts of adultery could not kill it. Hosea realized that Yahweh's love for His people was as strong as his own love for his wife.

In chapter six, out of these three images (marital, parental and healing), it is demonstrated that the marriage metaphor originated with Hosea, and that no other prophets had used it previously. It is observed that the marriage metaphor has its origin in the covenant between Yahweh and Israel. In the marriage metaphor Yahweh is described as the husband of Israel, not of the land of Israel. Although the use of the marriage metaphor was known in other religions, it was always associated with fertility rites and the fruitfulness of the earth. However, its use in Hosea is quite different. All three metaphors are intimately connected to Yahweh and Israel covenant. The metaphors developed from the argument of Hosea. It brings out the idea of covenantal bond and the relationship between Yahweh and Israel. The reason for its use is that the message could be easily understood by the people. As above discussed, these aspects have been traced through some unique parallels discovered between family relationships and the Yahweh/Israelite Sinaitic covenant. In depicting these features, this research argues that this study has added a valuable dimension to the literature on the book of Hosea.

In addition, covenantal relationship is emphasised throughout the book of Hosea. The prophet's prophecy was a powerful and life-changing message from Yahweh, which was designed to lead Israel to repentance. Although, they did not loved God but He continued to love and remained faithful in covenantal obligations. The book of Hosea presents above all the image of the loving God. Hosea characterizes Yahweh as demonstrating different characteristics, such as God as compassionate, merciful, loving and liberating. In today's context the message of Hosea is that God reaches out to His people with the message of hope. The God who loved Israel is the same God who loves the people today and his heart is filled with compassion and love towards the people. The emotional bond of the covenantal relationship relates specifically to the God and Israel relationship but it also extends to other nations. The covenant in the book of Hosea states God as committed to His nations and creation. The prophet reveals clearly how God accomplishes and declares the renewal of the covenant. The central theme in this section is God's covenant which attempts to restore and discipline them. This gives hope for future generations.

In chapter seven, the message of Hosea certainly has its relevance to the contemporary Indian context. While it deals with broken commitments and shattered relationships it also points the way to redemption and reconciliation. Among the Minor Prophets, the book of Hosea emphasises the concept of God's steadfast love in strongest terms. He speaks about the loving kindness of the Lord to a wayward and adulterous people. The church needs to be in Hosea's shoes. The church must strive to carry Hosea's message of steadfast love, and to entreat people to turn back to Him and seek His forgiveness. However, the church's realisation of her role and importance, in seeking redemption and reconciliation, is in question. It is the task of the church to admonish those who go astray; it is equally the task of the church to remind people to return to God, seeking forgiveness and bearing in mind He may still support the covenant, as He did in Hosea's time. The church must bear this message, not just to India but to all the countries.

The book portrays the character of God as a lover who initiates the relationship with his beloved Israel. This is clearly seen as the quality of love is not measured as justice, but rather purely on the basis of mercy. It clearly presents the nature of God and Israel's relationship and provides special insight into divine and human relations. The unique conceptualization of love in Hosea is a greatest contribution to the history of thought. It admonishes Christians not to become objects of condemnation in the pursuit of pride in their personal and private lives. This study suggests that in His wider vision God's love is for all people, not just for Israel. This would logically lead us to questions regarding Israel's election. There is a question about the reason for God choosing Israel to be a light to the nations if all other countries were also to be included in the concept of God's love. It also opens up God's loving relationship not only to the Israelites but also potentially to other nations.

It is clear that the Prophetic Paradigm in Hosea is love. The various facets of God's love, namely (a) Love in action, (b) Parenthood and (c) Promise of healing, add an important dimension for the present context. God desires all people, regardless of their attitudes to God, to be brought into the relationship they have been created to possess. חסד and אהב combine to give a clear passion that originates in the very heart of God. The message of Hosea is that God reaches out to His people with the message of hope. The God who loved Israel is the same God who loves all people and who acts with compassion and love towards them, and this is made clear in Hosea.

The focus of this research is to bring out this imagery of love through applying the socio-rhetorical method. There are different terms for love in the book and there are reasons for it. The comprehensive analysis of love in the book lies within the scope of the dissertation. This research is limited to the basic theme of the book of Hosea, which is "steadfast love." This love plays an important role in the life of Hosea and in his message to the people of Israel. The texts selected for this study best represent this theme: (1) Hosea 2:16-3:5, (God has suffered because of the unfaithfulness of Israel); (2) Hosea 11:1-11 (unconditional love of God in the face of people's rejection); (3) Hosea 14:2-9 (God will continue to love Israel despite her behaviour towards Him). Thus, the predominant concept that revolves around the book is 'love.' Hosea's mission is to bring Israel back so that they will be a model to other nations.

This work has contributed to the on-going research in the study of the book of Hosea especially in understanding the metaphors. It has explored in detail the imagery of love in terms of marital, parental and healing metaphors and brought out implications. The focus is on the inter-locking relationship between the metaphors of the three relationships. In addition to this, the focus of the study has been on God's love to Israel, and in addition also an implied aspect of God's love to other nations. God is willing to restore Israel to her original status, and at the same time wants her to be 'a light to the nations.'

For, further research in this book, the missional aspect would yield much fruits. Thus, this research leaves space for future researchers to work on the concept of mission in the book of Hosea. The contribution from this study is exploring God's love in terms of metaphors, leaving implications that these are aspects for other researchers to follow. The book of Hosea is concerned with God's love in all its aspects; at the time it was written it would have carried a powerful message to Israel. A message of great love and assurance that brings forgiveness was at hand if it was genuinely asked for, as this research has shown.

BIBLIOGRAPHY

Primary Sources

Books / Books Section

Abma, R. Bonds of Love: Methodic Studies of Prophetic Texts with Marriage Imagery (Isaiah 50:1-3 and 54:1-10, Hosea 1-3, Jeremiah 2-3), SSN 31, 1999.

Albertz, R. A History of Israelite Religion in the Old Testament Period: From the Beginnings to the End of the Monarchy, Louisville, John Knox, 1994.

Andersen, F.I and Freedman, D.N. Hosea: A New Translation with Introduction and Commentary, New York, Doubleday, 1980.

Andersen, Francis I and David Noel Freedman. Hosea: The Anchor Bible, New York, Doubleday, 1998.

Anderson, B W. Understanding the Old Testament, N.J, Prentice Hall, 1958.

Ao Atula. Towards a Renewed Understanding of Health and Healing: A Prophetic Response, Christian World Imprints, New Delhi, 2017.

Bakthtin, M. Rabela is and His World, H. Iswolsky, trans. Bloomington, Indian University, 1968.

Bailey. Kenneth E. Through Peasant Eyes, Grand Rapids, Eerdmans, 1980.

Barth, Karl. On Marriage, Social Ethics Series, ed. By Franklin Sherman, Philadelphia, Facet Books, 1968.

Barr, J. The Semantics of Biblical Language, Tottenham, London, SCM Press, 1983.

Bauman, G. Love and Violence: Marriage as Metaphor for the Relationship between YHWH and Israel in the Prophetic Books, Translated by Linda M.M, Collegeville, Liturgical Press, 2003

Beeby, H.D. Grace Abounding: A Commentary on the book of Hosea, Grand Rapids, Eerdmans, 1989.

Birch, Bruce C. Hosea, Joel, and Amos, Louisville, Westminster, John Knox Press, 1997.

Black. M, The Labyrinth of Language, New York, Praeger, 1968.

Blenkinsopp, J. A History of Prophecy in Israel: From the Settlement in the land to the Hellenistic Period, Philadelphia, Westminster, 1983.

Botterweck, G.J. ידע, Band III, Leiferung, 4/5, 1980.

Botterweck, G.J. and Ringgren, H., Theologisches Worterbuch zum Alten Testament, 6 Bande, Stuttgart, Kohlhammer, 1999.

Bright, J. A History of Israel, Philadelphia, Westminster Press, 1959.

Bright, J. A History of Israel, 3rd ed. London, SCM Press, 1981.

Brown, Francis and Driver, S.R. and Briggs, Charles A. A Hebrew and English Lexicon of the Old Testament, Based on the Lexicon of William Gesenius, As Tra., by Edward Robinson. Oxford: Clarendon Press.

Brueggemann, W. Tradition for Crisis: a Study in Hosea. Richmond, John Knox, 1968.

Buss. Martin J, The Prophetic Word of Hosea: A Morphological Study, Berlin, Verlag Alfred Topelmann, 1969.

Bullinger, E W. Figures of Speech used in the Bible, Grand Rapids, Baker Book House, 1968.

G, B Caird. The Language and Imagery of the Bible, Philadelphia: Westminster, 1980.

Calvin, John. Commentaries on the Twelve Minor Prophets, Grand Rapids, Eerdmans, 1950.

Catherine (ed). Paperback Oxford English Dictionary, New Delhi, Oxford University Press, 2006.

Chaney, Marvin L. "Bitter Bounty: The Dynamics of Political Economy Critiqued by Eight Century Prophets," 15-30 in Reformed Faith and Economics, ed. Robert L. Stivers. Lanham, MD, University Press of America, 1987.

Childs, B.S. The Book of Exodus, Philadelphia, Westminster Press, 1974.

Childs, B.S. Introduction to the Old Testament as Scripture, Philadelphia, Fortress Press, 1979.

Clements, Ronald E. Prophecy and Covenant, London, SCM Press, 1965.

Cohen. T, "Figurative Speech and Figurative Acts," in Philosophical Perspectives on Metaphor [ed. M. Johnson] Minneapolis, University of Minnesota Press, 1981.

Cole, W G. Sex and Love in the Bible, New York, Association Press, 1954/1959.

Cranfield. "Love," in A Theological Word Book of the Bible, ed. by Alan Richardson, New York, Macmillan Company, 1950.

Daniels, Dwight R. Hosea and Salvation History, BZAW 191, Berlin, de Gruyter, 1990.

Davies, G.I. Hosea. Grand Rapids, Eerdmans, 1992.

Davies, G.I. Hosea, Sheffield, OTG, 1993.

Dearman, J.A. The Book of Hosea," NICOT, Grand Rapids, Wm. B. Eerdmans Publishing co, 2010.

Dempsey, Carol J. The Prophets: A Liberation-Critical Reading, Minneapolis, Fortress Press, 2000.

Denham, J Smith. Gospel in Hosea, London, Paternoster Row, 1883.

Dentan Robert C., The Knowledge of God in Ancient Israel, New York, Seabury Press, 1968.

Devaux, R. Ancient Israel: Its Life and Institutions, 2nd ed. London, Darton, Longman, 1988.

Dillard, Raymond B. and Tremper Longman III. Introduction to the Old Testament, Grand Rapids, Zondervan Publishing House, 1994.

Doorley, W J. Prophet of Love: Understanding the Book of Hosea, New York, Paulist Press, 1991.

Dozeman, Thomas B. "Old Testament Rhetoric Criticism," in The Anchor Bible Dictionary, ed. David Noel Freedman et al., vol. 5, New York, Doubleday, 1992.

Driver, G R. The Babylonian Laws, Oxford, Clarendon, 1952.

Driver, S R, An Introduction to the Literature of the Old Testament, New York, Meridian Books, 1960.

Dumbrell, William J. The Faith of Israel. Its Expression in the Books of the Old Testament, Leicester, Appollos, 1988.

Eichrodt, W. Theology of the Old Testament, Vol. 1, Translated by J.A. Baker, London, SCM Press, 1961b.

Elmslie. How Came Our Faith? A Study of the Religion of Israel and Its Significance for the Modern World, Cambridge, Cambridge Press, 1948.

Farr, George. "The Concept of Grace in the Book of Hosea," Zeitschrift fur die Alt Testamentliche Wissenschaft, LXX, 1958.

Fensham, F Charles, "Father and Son as Terminology for Treaty and Covenant," in Near Eastern Studies in Honour of William Foxwell Albright, ed. by Hans Goedicke, Baltimore: Johns Hopkins Press, 1971.

Fishbane, Michael. Biblical Interpretation in Ancient Israel, Oxford, Clarendon, 1985.

Fohrer, Georg and Ernst Sellin. Introduction to the Old Testament, trans. by David E. Green, Nashville, Abingdon Press, 1965.

Fohrer, G. Theologische Grundstrukturen des Alten Testaments, Berlin, New York, 1972.

Foss, Sonja K. Rhetorical Criticism: Exploration and Practice, Illinois, Waveland Press, 2008.

Gary, A Herion. "Covenant," Eerdmans Dictionary of the Bible, David Noel Freedman, Grand Rapids, Eerdmans, 2000.

Garrett, D.A. The New American Commentary: Hosea, Joel, Vol. 19a, London, Broadman and Holman Publishers, 1997.

Gibson, J C L. Canaanite Myths and Legends. Edinburgh, T and T Clark, 1978.

Gibson, J C L. Language and Imagery in the Old Testament, Peabody, Hendrickson Publishers, 1998.

Given, John James. Hosea, Kegan Paul, Trench and Company, 1888.

Gluck, J J. "Some Semantic Complexities in the Book of Hosea," Studies on the Books of Hosea and Amos, Pretoria, Potchefstroom, Herald, 1966.

Glueck, N. חסד in the Bible, Translated by A. Gottschalk, Cincinnati, Hebrew Union College Press, 1951.

Goldingay, John. Models for Interpretation of Scripture, Grand Rapids, Eerdmans, 1995.

Gottwald, Norman K. A Light to the Nations, New York, Harper and Row Publishers, 1959.

Gottwald, Norman K. The Tribes of Yahweh: A Sociology of the Religion of Liberated Israel, 1250-1050 BCE, Maryknoll, New York, Orbis, 1979.

Gottwald, Norman K. The Hebrew Bible - A Socio-Literary Introduction, Sheffield, Sheffield Academic Press, 1985.

Gottwald, Norman K. (ed) The Hebrew Bible in its Social World and in Ours, Atlanta, Scholars Press, 1993.

Gottwald, Norman K. "Sociological Method in the Study of Ancient Israel," in The Bible and Liberation: Political and Social Hermeneutic, Mary Knoll, Orbis Books, 1993.

Guinan, Michael D. Covenant in the Old Testament, Chicago, Franciscan Herald Press, 1975.

Hahn, Herbert F. Old Testament in Modern Research, Philadelphia, Muhlenberg Press, 1954.

Harper, William Rainey. A Critical and Exegetical Commentary on Amos and Hosea, Edinburgh, T and T Clark, 1915.

Harper, William Rainey. A Critical and Exegetical Commentary on Amos and Hosea, Edinburgh, T and T Clark, 1956,

Harrison, R.K., Old Testament Times, Michigan, Eerdmans, 1974.

Harrison, R K. "Hosea" in The Zondervan Pictorial Encyclopedia of the Bible, edited by Merrill C. Tenney, vol. 3, Michigan, Zondervan Publishing House, 1975.

Hayes, John H. Amos Eighth century prophet, Nashville, Abingdon, 1988.

Hays, J H. ed. Old Testament Form Criticism, Trinity University monograph series in religion, Vol.2, San Antonio, 1974.

Hermann, Schultz. Old Testament Theology, II, Trans. by J.A. Paterson, Edinburgh, T and T Clark, 1895.

Heschel, Abraham J. The Prophets, I, 2 vols, New York, Harper and Row Publishers, 1962.

Hillers, Delbert R. Treaty - Curses and the Old Testament Prophets, Biblica et orientalia Rome: Pontifical Biblical Institute, 1964.

Hill, Andrew E. A Survey of the Old Testament, Grand Rapids, Zondervan Publishing House, 1991.

Hobart, Freeman E. An Introduction to the Old Testament, Prophets, Chicago, Moody Press, 1968.

Honeycutt, Roy L. Hosea and his Message, Nashville, Broadman, 1975.

Honeycutt, Roy L. "Hosea" The Broadman Bible Commentary: edited by Clifton J. Allen. Vol. VII. Nashville, Broadman Press, 1972.

Hong, Seong-Hyuk. The Metaphor of Illness and Healing in Hosea and its Significance in the Socio-Economic Context of Eight-Century Israel and Judah, New York, Peter Lang. 2006.

Horn, Siegried H. "The divided monarch" Ancient Israel: A History from Abraham to the Roman Destruction of the Temple, edited by Hershel Shanks, Washington, Biblical Archaeology Society, 1989.

Hubbard, David Allan. With Bands of Love (Hosea), Grand Rapids, W.B. Eerdmans publishing co, 1968.

Hubbard, D A. Hosea: An Introduction and Commentary, Tyndale OT Commentaries, Leicester, Inter Varsity Press, 1989.

Jack, B Scott. The Book of Hosea: A Study Manual, Shield Bible Study Series, Grand Rapids, Baker Book House, 1971.

Jacob, Edmond. Theology of the Old Testament, trans. by Arthur W. Heathcote and Philip J. Allcock, London, Hodder and Stoughton, 1958.

Jeanrond, Werner G. A Theology of Love, New York, T and T Clark, 2010.

Jepsen, Alfred. "אמת" Theological Dictionary of the Old Testament, ed. by G. J. Botterweck and Helmer Ringgren, Translated by John T. Willis, Vol. I.

Jobling, D. "A Deconstructive Reading of Hosea 1-3," in T.J. Sandoval and C. Mandolfo, eds. Relating to the Text. Interdisciplinary and Form Critical Insights on the Bible. JSOTSupp, 384; London, Clark International, 2003: 206-215.

Johnson, M. "We are in the midst of Metaphormania" Philosophical Perspectives on Metaphor, Minneapolis, University of Minnesota Press, 1981.

Kaiser, Walter. Toward an Old Testament Theology, Grand Rapids, Zondervan Publishing House, 1978.

Kaiser, Walter C. Back Toward the Future, Grand Rapids, Baker, 1989.

Kakkanattu, J P. God's Enduring Love in the Book of Hosea. A Synchronic and Diachronic Analysis of Hosea 11:1-11, Tubington, Mohr Siebeck, 2006.

Keefe, A.A. "The Female Body, the Body politic and the Land: A Socio-political reading of Hosea 1-2," in Brenner (ed.) A Feminist Companion to the Latter Prophets, Sheffield, Sheffield Academic Press, 1995.

Keil, F. The Twelve Minor Prophets, Bible Commentary on the Old Testament, trans. by James Martin, 2 vols. Grand Rapids, Wm. B. Eerdmans Publishing Company, 1949.

Kelle, Brad E. Hosea 2: Metaphor and Rhetoric in Historical Perspective, SBL Academia, Atlanta, SBL, Leiden, Brill, 2005.

Kennedy, G A. New Testament Interpretation through Rhetorical Criticism, Chapel Hill, University of North Carolina Press, 1984.

Kidner, Derek. Love to the Loveless: The Message of Hosea, BST, Downers Grove, Inter Varsity, 1982.

King, Philip J. Amos, Hosea, Micah: An Archaeological Commentary, Philadelphia, Westminster Press, 1988.

Knight, George A. F, Hosea: Introduction and Commentary, London, SCM Press, 1960.

Knight, G. A. F. Hosea; God's Love, London, SCM Press, 1969.

Laetsch, T. Bible Commentary, The Minor Prophets, Missouri, St. Louis, 1956.

Labuschagne, C. J. "The Similes in the Book of Hosea," Studies on the Books of Hosea and Amos, 1964-65.

Lalfazuala. Human Rights in Deuteronomy: A Sociological Approach, Delhi: ISPCK, 2004.

Landy, Francis. Hosea, Sheffield, Sheffield, 1995.

Lehman, Chester K. Biblical Theology, vol. 2, Scottdale, Herald Press, 1946.

Lewis, Jack P. New International Version Study Bible, Grand Rapids, Zondervan Bible Publishers, 1985.

Limburg James, Interpretation: Hosea - Micah, A Bible Commentary for Preaching and Teaching, Atlanta, John Knox Press, 1988.

Limburg. James. Psalms, Louisville, Westminster John Knox Press, 2000.

Lindblom, Johannes. Prophecy in Ancient Israel, Oxford, Basil Blackwell, 1962.

Louw, J.P. Semantics of New Testament Greek, Philadelphia, Fortress Press, 1982.

Malina, B.J. The New Testament World: Insights from Cultural Anthropology, Revised edition Atlanta, John Knox Press, 1993.

Martin, Buber. The Prophetic Faith, trans. by Carlyle Witton-Davies, New York, Macmillan Company, 1949.

Martin, J.D. "Israel as a Tribal Society," in R.E. Clements (ed.), The World of Ancient Israel: Sociological, Anthropological and Political Perspectives, Cambridge, Cambridge University Press, 1989.

Matthews, I. G. The Religious Pilgrimage of Israel, New York, Harper and Brothers Publishers, 1947.

Matthews, Victor H. Social World of the Hebrew Prophets, Massachusetts, Hendrickson Publishers, 2001.

Matthews, Victor H. The Hebrew Prophets and Their Social World, Grand Rapids, Baker Academic, 2012.

Maurice, Wright J. God's Covenant Plan, New York, Xulon Press, 2012.

Macintosh, A.A. A Critical and Exegetical Commentary on Hosea, Edinburgh, T and T Clark, 1997.

McKeating, Henry. Books of Amos, Hosea and Micah, CBC, Cambridge, Cambridge University Press, 1971.

McCarthy, D.J. Treaty and Covenant: A Study in form in the Ancient Oriental documents and in the Old Testament, Rome, Biblical Institute Press, 1978.

McCarthy, Dennis J. Old Testament Covenant: A Survey of Current Opinions, Oxford, Basil Blackwell, 1972.

McComisky, T.E. The Covenants of Promise, Nottingham, Inter Varsity Press, 1987.

McComisky, T.E. "Hosea." In The Minor Prophets: An Exegetical and Expositional Commentary, 1:1-237, 3 vols. ed. by T.E. McComisky. Grand Rapids, Baker, 1992.

McKenzie, S.L. Dictionary of the Bible, New York, MacMillan, 1965.

Mays, James Luther. Hosea: A Commentary, OTL, Philadelphia, Westminster, John Knox Press, 1969.

Mays, James Luther. Hosea: A Commentary, London, SCM Press, 1969.

Mendenhall, G. W. Law and Covenant in Israel and in the Ancient Near East, Pittsburg, Biblical Colloquim, 1955.

Mendenhall, G.E. "Covenant," The Interpreters' Dictionary of the Bible Vol.1, edited by George Arthur Buttrick, Nashville, Abingdon Press, 1962.

-------------------- "Covenant Forms in Israelite Tradition," The Biblical Archaeologist Reader. Vol. III. Edited by Edward F. Campbell, Jr. and David Noel Freedman, New York, Doubleday Company, Anchor Books, 1970.

Menezes, Rui de. The Cultural Context of the Old Testament, Bangalore, Theological Publications in India, 2005.

Meynet, R. Rhetorical Analysis: An Introduction to Biblical rhetoric, Sheffield, Sheffield Press, 1998.

Miller, Adam W. Brief Introduction to the Old Testament, Indiana, Warner Press, 1964.

Miller, J.M. and Hayes, J.H. A History of Ancient Israel and Judah, Philadelphia, Westminster, 1986.

Morris, G. Prophecy, Poetry and Hosea, Journal of Study of the Old Testament Supplement Series 219, England, Sheffield Academical Press, 1994.

Morris, L. Testaments of Love in the Bible, Grand Rapids, Eerdmans, 1981.

Muilenburg, James. "The History of the Religion of Israel," The Interpreter's Bible, ed. George Arthur Buttrick. 12 vols. New York, Abingdon Press, 1952.

Muilenberg, J. "The 'Office' of the Prophet in Ancient Israel," in The Bible in Modern Scholarship, ed. by J. Philip Hyatt, Nashville, Abingdon Press, 1967.

Myers, Jacob M. Book of Hosea, the Book of Joel, the Book of Amos, the Book of Obadiah, the Book of Jonah, Richmond, John Knox Press, 1959.

Neher, Andre. Prophetic Existence, trans. by William Wolf, South England, A. S. Barnes and Co, 1969.

Kirsten, Neilsen. Yahweh as Prosecutor and Judge: An Investigation of the Prophetic Lawsuit (Rib - Pattern), trans. Frederick Cryer, Journal for the Study of the Old Testament Supplement Series, Sheffield: JSOT, 1978.

Neufeld, E. Ancient Hebrew Marriage Laws with special reference to general Semitic laws and Customs, London, Longmans, 1944.

Nicholson, Ernest W. God and His People: Covenant and Theology in the Old Testament, Oxford, Clarendon Press, 1986.

NIV Archaeological Study Bible, An Illustrated walk through Biblical history and culture, Grand Rapids, Zondervan, 2005.

Nwaoru, E.O. "Imagery in the Prophecy of Hosea," AAT 41, Wiesbaden, 1999.

Nyberg, H.S. Studiesn zu Hoseabuche: Zugleich ein Beitrag zur Klarung des Problems der Alttestamentlichen Texkritik, Uppsala, 1935.

Oestreich, Bernhard. Metaphors and Similes for Yahweh in Hosea 14:2-9 (1-8): A Study of Hoseanic Pictorial Language, Friedensauer Schriftenreihe, Reihe A, Theologie, 1, Peter Lang, 1998.

Ortlund, Whoredom: God's unfaithful wife in Biblical Theology, Grand Rapids, Wm. B. Eerdmans, 1996.

Ostborn. G, Yahweh and Baal, Studies in the book of Hosea and related documents, Lund, Gleerup, 1956.

Park, Kyung Hee. Divine Love in Hosea 11, Southern Baptist Theological Seminary, 2004.

Patte Daniel, Jose Severino Croatto, Teresa Okure, Global Bible Commentary, Nashville, Abingdon Press, 2004.

Paul, Praveen. Ideation of Power in the Book of Hosea with Particular Reference to "אהב:" A Postcolonial Reading, Delhi, Living Light Media Center, 2015.

Payne, J. Barton. The Theology of the Old Testament, Grand Rapids, Zondervan Publishing House, 1962.

Pentiuc, E.J. Long-Suffering Love: A Commentary on Hosea with Patristic Annotations, Brookline Holy Cross Orthodox Press, 2002.

Phillips, J. B. Four Prophets: Amos, Hosea, First Isaiah, Micah, New York, Macmillan Publishing Co., 1963.

Premnath, D.N. "Amos and Hosea: Socio-historical Background and Prophetic Critique, Word and World 28/2, Spring 2008.

Ringgren, H. Israelite Religion, Stuttgart, Kohlhammer Verlag, 1966.

Robbins, V.K. Exploring the texture of texts: A guide to socio-rhetorical interpretation, Pennsylvania, Trinity Press International, 1996.

-----------------, The Tapestry of Early Christian discourse: Rhetoric, society and ideology, London, Routledge, 1996.

Robinson, H Wheeler. Two Hebrew Prophets: Studies in Hosea and Ezekiel, London, Lutterworth Press, 1948.

Ryken, Wilboit and Longman. The Dictionary of Biblical Imagery, Vol.4, Downers Grove, Inter Varsity Press, 2010.

Sailhamer, J.H. Introduction to Old Testament Theology: A Canonical Approach, Grand Rapids, Zondervan, 1995.

Sakenfeld, K.D. Faithfulness in Action: Loyalty in Biblical Perspective, Philadelphia, Fortress Press, 1985.

Sakenfeld, Katharine Drob. Love, in The Anchor Bible Dictionary, vol. 4, David Noel Freedman, editor-in-Chief, New York, Doubleday, 1992.

Sanford, William. Old Testament Survey: The Message Form, and Background of the Old Testament, Grand Rapids, Wm. B. Eerdmans Publishing Company, 1982.

Sargent, James E. Hosea, Joel, Amos, Obadiah and Jonah, Nashville, Abingdon Press, 1994.

Schillebeechx, E. Marriage: Human Reality and Saving Mystery, New York, Sheed and Ward, 1965.

Schmidt, W.H. Introduction to the Old Testament, London, SCM Press, 1984.

Schulz, Samuel J. The Old Testament Speaks, New York, Harper and Brothers Publishers, 1960.

Scott, Jack B. The Book of Hosea: A Study Manual. Shield Bible Study Series, Grand Rapids, Baker Book House, 1971.

Scott, Melville. The Message of Hosea, London: Society for Promoting Christian Knowledge, 1921.

Scott, R. B. Y. The Relevance of the Prophets, New York, Macmillan Company, 1953.

Senior, Donald and Caroll Stuhlmueller. The Biblical Foundations for Missions, New York, Orbis Books, 1983.

Sherwood, Yovanne. The Prostitute and the Prophet: Hosea's Marriage in Literary-theoretical Perspective, Sheffield, Sheffield, 1996.

Smart, Hosea - Man and Book, IDB, Vol. 2, eds. C.A. Buttrick, New York, Abingdon Press, 1962.

Snaith, Norman H. The Distinctive ideas of the Old Testament, London, Epworth Press, 1944.

Snaith, Norman. Mercy and Sacrifice: A Study of the Book of Hosea, London, SCM Press, 1953.

Stuart, Douglas. Hosea-Jonah, Word Biblical Commentary 31, Waco, Texas, Word Books, 1987.

Sweeney, Marvin A. Twelve Prophets, 2 vols. Collegeville: Liturgical Press, 2000.

Terrien, S. Till the Heart Sings, A Biblical Theology of Manhood and Womanhood, Philadelphia, Fortress Press, 1985.

Tidball, D. An Introduction to the Sociology of the New Testament, Exerter, The Paternoster Press, 1983.

VanGemeran, Willem A. New International Dictionary of Old Testament Theology and Exegesis, Vol. 1-2, UK, Paternoster Press, 1996.

Vanhoozer, Kevin. Theological Interpretation of the Old Testament, Grand Rapids, Baker Academic, 2008.

Vasholz, Robert I. English Standard Version Study Bible, Wheaton, Crossway Bibles, 2008.

Von Rad, Gerhard. Genesis, Philadelphia, Westminster, 1972.

Von Rad, Gerhard. Old Testament Theology, Volume One, London, SCM Press, 1975.

Young, E.J. An Introduction to the Old Testament, London, The Tyndale Press, 1949.

Walvoord, John F. and Roy B. Zuck. The Bible Knowledge Commentary: An Exposition of the Scriptures, Wheaton, Victor Books, 1983.

Wallis, Gerhard. "אהב" Theological Dictionary of the Old Testament (TDOT) eds. Johannes Botterweck and Helmer Ringgren, Translated by John T. Willis, Vol-1, Grand Rapids, 1974.

Watson, Duane F. "Why we need Socio Rhetorical commentary and what it might look like?," Rhetorical Criticism and the Bible, Stanley E. Porter and Dennis L. Stamps, JSNT Supplement Series 195, Sheffield, Academic press, 2002.

Ward, James M. Hosea: A Theological Commentary, New York, Harper and Row Publishers, 1966.

Westermann, Claus. Basic forms of Prophetic speech, translated by H.C. White, Philadelphia, 1967.

William, Greathouse M. Wholeness in Christ, Toward a Biblical Theology of Holiness. Kansas City, Beacon Hill Press, 1998.

Wright, G. Ernest. The Old Testament Against Its Environment, London, SCM Press, Ltd., 1950.

Wright, G. Ernest. "The Faith of Israel," The Interpreter's Bible, ed. by George Arthur Buttrick, 12 vols, New York, Abingdon Press, 1952.

Wright, G. Ernest. "The Lawsuit of God: A Form-Critical Study of Deuteronomy 32," in B.W. Anderson and Walter Harrelson, eds., Israel's Prophetic Heritage: Essays in Honour of James Muilenburg, New York, Harper and Brothers, 1962.

Wolff, Hans Walter. A Commentary on the Book of the Prophet Hosea, Philadelphia, Fortress, 1974.

Yee, G.A. Composition and Tradition in the Book of Hosea: A Redactional Critical Investigation. SBLDS, 102; Atlanta: Scholars Press, 1987.

Yee, G.A. "Hosea," in Women's Bible Commentary, ed. C. Newsom and S. Ringe, Louisville, Westminster John Knox, 1998.

Yee, G.A. "She is not my wife and I am not her husband:"A Materilastic Analysis of Hosea 1-2 Leiden, Koninklijke, Brill, 2001.

Zvi, Ehud Ben. Hosea, Grand Rapids, Wm. B. Eerdmans Publishing Company, 2005.

Unpublished

Ao, Chubamongba. 'In all the Work of Your Hands' in Deuteronomy: An Inquiry on Rhetoric of Work, D. Th Dissertation, SATHIRI/UBS, 2017.

Buck, F. "Die Liebe Gottesbe im Propheten Osee" (unpublished doctoral dissertation at the Pontifical Biblical Institute, Rome, 1953.

Paul, Praveen. Ideation of Power in the Book of Hosea with Particular Reference to "אהב:" A Postcolonial Reading, Serampore: Senate of Serampore College, SATHRI/UTC, 2012.

Poplin, Wayne W. Hosea's Use of Nuptial Imagery, New Orleans, Baptist Theological Seminary, D.Th Thesis, 1975.

Prabhakarrao, Bandari P. Political Thinking of the Eight Century Prophets with Special Reference to Hosea and Isaiah [THESIS], Serampore, 1969.

Robertson, N. J. Study of the Analogies Used for the Love of God in the Book of Hosea [THESIS]. Serampore: Senate of Serampore College, 1991.

Swamidas, K E. Relevance of the Message of Amos and Hosea to the Christian Preachers' Task in India Today [THESIS], Serampore, 1956.

Thomas, N.P. "The Concept of דעת אלהים in the Book of Hosea," Unpublished Th.D. Dissertation, New Orleans Baptist Theological Seminary, 1969.

Walker, T. W. "The Metaphor of Healing and the Theology of the book of Hosea," Princeton Theological Seminary, (Ph. d Dissertation), 1997.

Journal Articles

Ackerman, Susan. "The Personal is Political: Covenantal and Affectionate Love (אהבה, אהב) in the Hebrew Bible," VT 52, 437-458, 2002.

Alt, A. Hosea 5:8-6:6, Ein Krieg und seine Folgen in prophetischer Beleuchtung, Kleine Schriften II, 163-187, 1919.

Bechtel, L.M. "The Metaphors of Canaanite and Baal in Hosea," in J. Kaltner and L. Stulman, eds. Inspired Speech. JSOTSupp. 378; London: T and T Clark, 203-15, 2004.

Boshoff, W. "The Female Imagery in the Book of Hosea: Considering the Marriage Metaphor in Hosea 1-2 by Listening to Female Voices," OTE 15 23-41, 2002.

Bosman, H. "Adultery, Prophetic Tradition and the Decalogue," in K.D. Schnuck ed., Wunschet Jerusalem Frieden: Collected Communications to the XIIth Congress of the International Org. for the Study of the O.T. Frankfurt am Main: Lang, 21-30, 1988.

Botha, P.J. "The Communicative Function of Comparison in Hosea," OTE 6, 57- 71, 1993.

Bowman, C.D. "Prophetic Grief, Divine Grace: The Marriage of Hosea," ResQ 43 229-42, 2001.

Braaten, L.J. "Earth Community in Hosea 2," in N. Habel, ed., The Earth Story in the Psalms and the Prophets, London: Sheffield Academic Press, 185-203, 2001.

Braaten, L.J. "God Sows the Land: Hosea's Place in the Book of the Twelve," SBL Seminar Papers (2000), 218-42, and in P.L. Redditt and A. Schart, eds. Thematic Threads in the Book of the Twelve. BZAW 325; Berlin: de Gruyter, 104-32, 2003.

Bussche, H. "La ballade de l'amourmeconnu, Commentary on Hosea," BVC 41, 286-303, 1961.

Buss, M. "Hosea as a Canonical Problem: With Attention to the Song of Songs," in S.B. Reid, ed. Prophets and Paradigms, JSOTSupp 229, Sheffield, Sheffield, 79-93, 1996.

Clines, D.J. "Hosea 2: Structure and Interpretation," in E.A. Livingstone, ed., Papers on Old Testament and Related Themes (Studia Biblica 1978) JSOTSupp. 11. Sheffield: JSOT, 1979.

Coote, R. B. "Hosea XII," Vetus Testamentum, XXI, October, 389-402, 1971.

Crotty, R. Hosea and the knowledge of God, AusBR10, 1-16, 1971.

Davidson, A.B. "The Prophet Hosea," The Expositor IX, 241-164, 1879.

Dozeman, T.B. "Hosea and the Wilderness Wandering Tradition," in T. Romer and S. McKenzie, eds. Rethinking the Foundations: Historiography in the Ancient World and in the Bible. Berlin: Walter de Gruyter, 55-70, 2000.

Eichrodt, Walther. "The Holy One in Your Midst: The Theology of Hosea," Interpretation, XV, July, 259–273, 1961.

Eidevall, G. "Grapes in the desert Metaphors, Models, and Themes in Hosea 4-14," ConBOT 43, Stockholm, 20-36, 1996.

Ellison, H. L. "The Message of Hosea in the Light of His Marriage," The Evangelical Quarterly, XLI, January-March, 3-9, 1969.

Emmerson, G.I. Hosea: An Israelite Prophet in Judean Perspective, JSOTSup 28, Sheffield, JSOT Press, 183-194, 1984.

Evan, Dijk-Hemmes F. "The Imagination of Power and the Power of Imagination: an Intertextual Analysis of Two Biblical Love Songs; the Song of Songs and Hosea 2," JSOT 44, 75-88, 1989.

Fensham, F.C. "The Marriage Metaphor in Hosea for the Covenant Relationship between the Lord and his People," JNSL 12, 71-78, 1984.

Fideles, P.S. "The Cross of Hosea Revisited: The Meaning of Suffering in the Book of Hosea." Review and Expositor 90: 175-190, (1993).

Friedman, M.A. "Israel's Response in Hosea 2:17b: 'You are my Husband,'" JBL 99, 199-204, 1980.

Gemser, B. The Ríb - or Controversy - Pattern in Hebrew Mentality"; Julien Harvey, "Le 'Rîb - Pattern / réquisitoire prophétiquesur la rupture de l'alliance," SVT 3, 120-137, 1962.

Gordis, R. "Hosea's Marriage and Message," HUCA 25, 9-40, 1954.

Hall, G. "Origin of the Marriage Metaphor," HebStud 23, 169-171, 1982.

Hempel, J. "Prophet and Poet," The Journal of Theological Studies, XL, April, 113-132, 1939.

Howard, Jr D. M. "Rhetorical Criticism in Old Testament Studies" Bulletin for Biblical Research 4, 87-104, 1994.

Huffmon, Herbert B. "The Covenant Lawsuit in the Prophets," Journal of Biblical Literature 78, December, 285-295, 1959.

Huffmon, H. B. 'The Treaty Background of Hebrew ', BASOR 181, 1966.

Janzen, J.G. “Metaphor and Reality in Hosea 11,” Semeia 24, 7-44, 1982.

Jenni, E. “Das Wort olam im AT,” ZAW 65, 1-35, 1953.

Jeremias, J. Gott und Geschichteim Alten Testament, EvTh 40, 381-396, 1980.

--------------, Der Prophet Hosea, Gottingham, Vandenhoek, ATD 24/1, 18-20, 1983.

Jones, Stanley. “Exodus Motif in the Book of Hosea and its relevance to the Socio-religious Context of India,” FTR, Vol. 16, No. 1, March, 32-40, 2015.

Josiah, Ucheawaji G. “Hosea’s Perspective on the Knowledge of God and its Relevance to Rivers State, Nigeria,” Vol. 11, No. 1, March, 5-15, 2014.

Kelley, P.E. “The Holy One in the Midst of Israel: Redeeming Love (Hosea 11-14)” Review and Expositor 72 No. 4, 175-190, 1975.

Kruger, P. A. “Prophetic Imagery: On Metaphors and Similes in the Book of Hosea,” Journal of Northwest Semitic Languages 14, 143-151, 1988.

Kruger, P.A. “The Marriage Metaphor in Hosea 2:4-17 against Its Ancient Near Eastern Background,” OTE 5, 7-25, 1992.

Kuzhuvelil, V. Mathew. “No Pooja but Prema, No Yajna but Iswara Jnana: An Indian Hermeneutics on the Book of Hosea,” Jeevadhara 12, 105-110, 1982.

Lalmuankima, C. Challenges from the Book of Hosea in Understanding the Kindness of God, Bangalore Theological Forum, Vol. XL, No. 1, June, 149-160, 2008.

Light, Gary W. The New Covenant in the book of Hosea, Review Expositor, 90:2, Spring, 1-15, 1993.

Limburg, James. “The root ריב and the Prophetic Lawsuit Speeches,” Journal of Biblical Literature 88.3, 91-304, 1969.

Lohfink, N. “Hate and Love in Hosea 9:15,” Catholic Biblical Quarterly 25, 417-430, 1963.

Lundbom, J.R. “Contentious Priests and Contentious People in Hosea IV 1-10,” VT 36, 52-70, 1986.

McDonald, J.R.B. “The Marriage of Hosea,” Theology 67, 149-156, 1964.

Machinist, P. “Hosea and the Ambiguity of Kingship in Ancient Israel,” in J.T. Strong and S.S. Tuell, eds. Constituting the Community. Winona Lake, Eisenbrauns, 153-81, 2005.

McKenzie, S.L. “The Jacob Tradition in Hosea XII 4-5,” VT 36, 311-322, 1986.

-------------------- Knowledge of God in Hosea, JBL 74, 22-27, 1955.

Mays, James Luther. Metaphor and Reality in Hosea 11, Semeia 24, 45-51, 1982.

Mendenhall, G.E. “The Hebrew Conquest of Palestine,” BA 25, 66-87, 1962.

Moran, W.L. The Ancient Near Eastern Background of the Love of God in Deuteronomy,” Catholic Biblical Quarterly, Vol. 25, 72-87, 1963.

Muthunayangam, Daniel Jones. “Contemporary Approaches to the Old Testament Interpretation”, Interweaving Methodology and Praxis Exploring Disciplinary Option in Today’s World. Edited by Indukuri John Mohan Razu (Bangalore: BTESSC/SATARI, 169-204, 2007.

Nasuti, H.P. “Long-suffering love: a commentary on Hosea with Patristic Annotations,” CBQ, 66/2, 298-299, 2004.

Neef, H.D. Die Heilstraditionen Israels in der Verkundigung des Propheten Hosea, Berlin, BZAW 169, 15-59, 231-235, 1987.

North, F.S. "Solution of Hosea's Marital Problems by Critical Analysis," JNES 16, 128-130, 1957.

Nwaoru, E.O. "The Role of Images in the Literary Structure of Hosea vii 9-viii 14," VT 54, 216-222, 2004.

Odell, M.S. "Who Were the Prophets in Hosea?" BibTh 18, 78-95, 1996.

O'Kennedy, D.F. "Healing as/or Forgiveness? The Use of the Term rp in the Book of Hosea," Old Testament Exegesis 14, 458-474, 2001.

Owens J.J, Exegetical Study of Hosea', Review Expositor 54, 522-543, 1957.

Patterson, R.D. "Parental love as metaphor for divine-human love," JETS 46/2, 205-216, 2003.

Peckham, B. "The Composition of Hosea," HAR 11, 331-353, 1987.

Polan, G.J. "Hosea's Interpretation of Israel's Traditions," TBT 39, 329-34, 2001.

Rowley, H.H. "The Marriage of Hosea," BJRL 39, 200-233, 1956.

Rudolph, W. Praparierte Jungfrauen? (Zu Hosea 1), ZAW 75, 65-73, 1963.

Rudolph, W. Hosea, KAT, XIII/1. Gütersloh, Gütersloher Verlagshaus Gerd Mohn, 108-135. 1966.

Rust, E. C. "The Theology of Hosea" Review and Expositor, Vol. 54, 510-521, 1957.

Sakenfeld, Katherine Dropp. "How Hosea Transformed the Lord of the Realm into a Tempermental Spouse," BRev 20/1, 28-33, 52, 2004.

Sandhya, Shency. A Call to Return to the Lord (Hos. 6:1-6), Vol. XXXX, No. 3, Bible Bhashyam, September, 146-156, 2014.

Schaeffer, Christa. EVT 55, 114–140, 1995.

Schmidt, J.J. "Yahweh's Divorce in Hosea 2 - Who is that Woman?" SJOT 9, 119-132, 1995.

Seow, C.L. "Hosea 14:10 and the Foolish People Motif," CBQ 44, 212-24, 1982.

Silva, Charles H. Literary Features in the Book of Hosea 4–8, Bibliotheca Sacra 164, January, 34-44, 2007.

Smith, R.L. Major Motifs of Hosea, South Western Journal of Theology, vol. 18, 22-32, 1975.

Snyman, G. Social Reality and Religious Language in Hosea 1-3, Old Testament Essays, 8 (2), 90-112, 1993.

Soggin, J.A. Shubzuruckkehren, THAT Band II, 63-80, 1976.

Stager, L.E. The Archaeology of the family in Ancient Israel, BASOR 260, 1-35, 1985.

Thompson, J.A. "Israel's Lovers," VT 27, 475-81, 1977.

Tushingham, A.D. "A Reconsideration of Hosea Chapters 1-3," JNES 12, 150-59, 1953.

Vall, G. "Hosea and Knowledge of God," TBT 39, 335-41, 2001.

Van, Leeuwen C. Hosea, PredOT, Nijkerk, 1968.

Van, Leeuwen C. Hosea, 3e, aangevulde druk, Nijkerk, Callenbach, 91-96, 1984.

Van, Leeuwen C. "Meaning and Structure of Hosea X 1-8," VT 53, 367-378, 2003.

Vogels, W. "Hosea's Gift to Gomer," Biblica 69, 412-21, 1988.

Wagenaar, J.A. "I Will Testify Against Them and Challenge Them: Text and Interpretation of Hosea 14:9," JNSL 26, 2, 127-34, 2000.

Waterman, L. "Hosea, Chapters. 1-3 in Retrospect and Prospect," JNES 14,100-109, 1955.

Watson, W.G.E. "Reflexes of Akkadian Incantations in Hosea," VT 34, 242-47, 1984.

Weems, R.J. "Gomer: Victim of Violence or Victim of Metaphor," Semeia 47, 87-104, 1989.

West, G. "The Effects and Power of Discourse: a Case Study of a Metaphor in Hosea," Scriptura 57, 201-212, 1996.

Westbrook, R. "Adultery in Ancient Near Eastern Law," RB 97, 542-580, 1990.

Whitt, W.D. "The Jacob Traditions in Hosea and their Relation to Genesis," ZAW 103, 18-43, 1991.

Williamson, H.G.M. "Jezreel in the Biblical Texts," TA 18, 72-92, 1991.

Yee, G.A. "Gomer: Victim of Violence or Victim of Metaphor?" Semeia 47, 87-104, 1989.

Zvi, Ehud Ben. "Observations on the marital metaphor of Yahweh and Israel in its ancient Israelite context: general considerations and particular images in Hosea 1.2, "JSOT, 28/3 363-384, 2004.